"Most particularly in an age of illiberal populism, 'liberalism' urgently needs redefinition, away from its bizarre US definition as yet another collectivism. Chartier's brilliant and wide-ranging book defends a new, and old, liberalism in detail. It is, as he says, 'a confident reassertion of liberalism,' but willing to listen to the other side, and to consider. His 'radical' liberalism is in fact a modest and reasonable program for a flourishing world of natural law equals."

DEIRDRE N. MCCLOSKEY, *University of Illinois at Chicago*

"I can't name a higher intellectual priority than reframing and reviving liberalism. Chartier does just this in his humane, learned, and erudite manifesto. His liberalism seeks appealingly to foster the good life and universal ennoblement through voluntary means—in a way consistent with human rights and social harmonies. Read it. Believe it."

JEFFREY A. TUCKER, *American Institute for Economic Research*

"This book is a rich exploration of two strands of natural law theory and how they contribute to flourishing for us all. Linking his preferred natural law view with the broad liberal tradition, Gary Chartier shows how 'natural law liberalism' might shed new light on a wide range of issues."

JOHN HAGEL, author, *The Power of Pull*

"This is a masterful work. Drawing on a version of Aristotelian natural law theory and Scottish Enlightenment insights into spontaneous order, Gary Chartier elaborates a natural law position that supports liberal social and political views. But Chartier takes his arguments in unexpected directions, and in so doing illuminates issues of genuine theoretical and practical significance. In each case, Chartier's analysis helps to elaborate and defend his theoretical framework. *Flourishing Lives* is philosophy at its best—advancing our understanding of natural law and drawing on this understanding to support timely and provocative conclusions."

JAMES STACEY TAYLOR, *College of New Jersey*

FLOURISHING LIVES

This book elaborates, illuminates, and illustrates a confident and attractive account of social and political liberalism in light of a rich understanding of flourishing and fulfillment rooted in a version of natural law theory. Examining issues in ethics, law, and politics—including consumer responsibility, the assignment of grades by teachers, deception by lawyers, war and empire, and the use of victim-impact statements in parole decisions—Gary Chartier shows how natural law theory can effectively support pluralism, diversity, social equality, integrity, peace, and freedom.

Gary Chartier is Distinguished Professor of Law and Business Ethics and Associate Dean of the Tom and Vi Zapara School of Business at La Sierra University.

Flourishing Lives

EXPLORING NATURAL LAW LIBERALISM

GARY CHARTIER

Tom and Vi Zapara School of Business
La Sierra University, California

CAMBRIDGE
UNIVERSITY PRESS

CAMBRIDGE
UNIVERSITY PRESS

University Printing House, Cambridge CB2 8BS, United Kingdom

One Liberty Plaza, 20th Floor, New York, NY 10006, USA

477 Williamstown Road, Port Melbourne, VIC 3207, Australia

314–321, 3rd Floor, Plot 3, Splendor Forum, Jasola District Centre, New Delhi – 110025, India

79 Anson Road, #06–04/06, Singapore 079906

Cambridge University Press is part of the University of Cambridge.

It furthers the University's mission by disseminating knowledge in the pursuit of education, learning, and research at the highest international levels of excellence.

www.cambridge.org
Information on this title: www.cambridge.org/9781108493048
DOI: 10.1017/9781108675253

First published 2019

Printed and bound in Great Britain by Clays Ltd, Elcograf S.p.A.

A catalogue record for this publication is available from the British Library.

Library of Congress Cataloging-in-Publication Data
NAMES: Chartier, Gary, author.
TITLE: Flourishing lives : exploring natural law liberalism / Gary Chartier.
DESCRIPTION: Cambridge [UK] ; New York, NY : Cambridge University Press, 2019. | Includes bibliographical references and index.
IDENTIFIERS: LCCN 2019008052 | ISBN 9781108493048 (hardback)
SUBJECTS: LCSH: Liberalism. | Law – Philosophy. | Natural law.
CLASSIFICATION: LCC K487.L5 C43 2019 | DDC 340/.112–dc23
LC record available at https://lccn.loc.gov/2019008052

ISBN 978-1-108-49304-8 Hardback

For
Elenor Louise Andromeda Persephone
Levitias Babette Barbara Webb
and
Nicole Regina

Contents

Acknowledgments

I welcome the occasion the publication of this book affords to say "thank you" to many people.

Thanks are due, of course, to the usual suspects—A. Ligia Radoias, Aena Prakash, Annette Bryson, Alexander Lian, Andrew Howe, Carole Pateman, Charles Teel, Jr., Christopher C. Reeves, Coco Owen, Craig R. Kinzer, David B. Hoppe, David Gordon, David R. Larson, Deborah K. Dunn, Donna L. Carlson, Elaine Claire von Keudell, Elenor L. Webb, Eva Pascal, Fritz Guy, Gen Mensale, Jeffrey D. Cassidy, Jesse Leamon, John Thomas, Kenneth A. Dickey, Kirsten Rasmussen, Lalé Welsh, Lawrence T. Geraty, Maria Zlateva, Michael Orlando, Nabil Abu-Assal, Nicole Regina, Patricia M. Cabrera, Roger E. Rustad, Jr., Ronel S. Harvey, Sheldon Richman, Stephanie Burns, Trisha Famisaran, Varsha Pravinsih, W. Kent Rogers, Wonil Kim, and Xavier Alasdhair Kenneth Doran—for the usual reasons.

I am glad to have been able to engage with Elenor Webb, Alexander Lian, Chris Tollefsen, Craig R. Kinzer, David Gordon, Elias Rizkallah, Eugene Volokh, Fritz Guy, Jeffrey D. Cassidy, John W. Webster, Lee H. Reynolds, Mark C. Murphy, Nathan C. Nobis, Robert D. Goldstein, Robert L. Beshara, Sheldon Richman, Stephen R. L. Clark, Stephen R. Munzer, Vernon Howe, and Zachary Woodman regarding materials included or projected for inclusion in the book. David, in particular, commented on the entire manuscript in draft and offered many helpful observations. It will be clear—no doubt to him, but also, I suspect, to other readers—that much more needs to be said in response to a number of his pointed queries. I am grateful for opportunities for dialogue and exchange with Nicole Regina, Brian Hebblethwaite, John Hick, Seana Shiffrin, Annette Bryson, Steve Munzer, Fritz Guy, Richard Rice, Ken Dickey, David Gordon, Sheldon Richman, Stephen Clark, and David Larson, all of whom have helped me to develop as a philosopher; none of them is, of course, liable for any errors in this book. I am happy to acknowledge the roles that philosophers including John Finnis and Charles Fried have played in inspiring my work in legal philosophy, in particular, even if none would likely embrace many of the things I've said here. Germain Grisez died early in 2018; while he would have disagreed vigorously with many of my conclusions, I learned a tremendous amount from him and I deeply respect his integrity and intellectual rigor. More broadly, the New Classical Natural Law theorists—Grisez and Finnis, but also, notably, Robert P. George, Joseph M. Boyle, and Chris Tollefsen—deserve immense credit for their rigorous development of the natural law tradition and the stimuli their work has provided for mine. In different ways, Alexander Lian, Arthur Isak Applbaum, Deborah K. Dunn, Elissa Kido, Fritz Guy, Mark C. Murphy, Peter Beinart, and the late Richard Rorty spurred me to write earlier versions of several of this book's chapters, and I'm grateful. My comrades at the Center for a Stateless Society—including Sheldon Richman, Roderick T. Long, Charles W. Johnson, Kevin Carson, Joseph R. Stromberg, William Gillis, and James Tuttle—can hardly be held responsible for my idiosyncratic views, but dialogue with them has certainly helped to shape my thinking about a number of topics in moral, legal, and political philosophy. And of course I'm thankful for the stimulation and challenge offered by a number of academic compatriots—among them David Schmidtz, R. Kevin Hill, Neera Badhwar, Aeon J. Skoble, Matt Zwolinski, Fernando R. Tesón, James Stacey Taylor, Edward P. Stringham, Tony Gill, Chris Coyne, Peter T. Leeson, Kevin Vallier, Douglas R. Rasmussen, Douglas Den Uyl, Jason Brennan, and Guido Pincione.

La Sierra University served as the context for my research and writing. I thus want to thank John Thomas, Randal Wisbey, Joy Fehr, and Elias Rizkallah, among others, for enabling me to work on this book during my time at La Sierra. Libraries, of course, contribute indispensably to almost all varieties of research, and mine has been no exception. So I am happy as always to thank multiple members of the La Sierra University Library's faculty and staff—including Jeff de Vries, Hilda Smith, Jill Start, Sandra Hartson, and David Ramos—for their assistance. I finished writing this book in Riverside's Back to the Grind; I am more than pleased to express my appreciation to Darren Conkerite for maintaining this welcoming—thoroughly liberal—space.

I owe an obvious debt of gratitude to John Berger and Finòla O'Sullivan at Cambridge University Press for supporting the publication of this book, and to Emma Collison, Silvia Glick, Karthik Orukaimani, Beth Hamer, Danielle Menz, and the typesetting team at Integra for help at various stages of its production. (Silvia and Emma deserve particular praise for their eagle-eyed attention to detail.) I also acknowledge my appreciation for the approvals that I received for my reuse in this book of material that first appeared elsewhere,[1] and for the willingness of Deirdre

[1] The relevant publications (I'm the sole author of each): [*Consumers, Boycotts, and Non-Human Animals*,] 12 BUFF. ENVTL. L.J. 123 (2005) (University at Buffalo); *Contested Practices: Arthur Isak Applbaum's* Ethics for Adversaries, 10 JAHRBUCH FÜR RECHT UND ETHIK 254 (2002) (Duncker & Humblot); *In Defence of the Anarchist*, 29 OXFORD J. LEGAL STUD. 115 (2009) (Oxford University Press); *Libertarianism and the Varieties of Virtue*, BLEEDING HEART LIBERTARIANS, June 10, 2016, http://bleedingheartlibertarians.com/2016/06/libertarianism-and-the-varieties-of-virtue/ (Bleeding Heart Libertarians); *Niebuhr's Ghost?*, 5 CONVERSATIONS IN RELIGION & THEOLOGY 91 (2007)

McCloskey, James Stacey Taylor, Jeffrey A. Tucker, and John Hagel to endorse the book. (Professor McCloskey's rapidity and graciousness, in particular, led me unequivocally to support her beatification.)

As usual, I will donate the author royalties I receive for this book to AntiWar.com. I am grateful to this exceptional source of news and inspirer of activism for its role in fostering peace and freedom. I encourage all of my readers to consider supporting it.

And, to Nicole: je t'aime et je t'adore.

(Wiley-Blackwell); *Norms that Encourage Diversity*, CATO UNBOUND, July 20, 2016, http://www.cato-unbound.org/2016/07/20/gary-chartier/norms-encourage-diversity (Cato Institute); *On the Threshold Argument against Consumer Meat Purchases*, 37 J. SOC. PHIL. 235 (2006) (Wiley-Blackwell); *Richard Rorty's American Faith*, 85 ANGLICAN THEOLOGICAL REV. 255 (2003) (Seabury); *Self-Integration as a Basic Good: A Response to Chris Tollefsen*, 52 AM. J. JURIS. 293 (2007) (Oxford University Press); *The Naked Truth about Libertarianism*, CATO UNBOUND, July 11, 2016, http://www. cato-unbound.org/2016/07/11/gary-chartier/naked-truth-about-libertarianism (Cato Institute); *Toward a Consistent Natural Law Ethics of False Assertion*, 51 AM. J. JURIS. 43 (2006) (Oxford University Press); *Truth-Telling, Incommensurability, and the Ethics of Grading*, 3 B.Y.U. EDUC. & L.J. 37 (2003) (Brigham Young University); *Two Faces of the Right to Privacy in Litigators' Ethics*, LITIGATION ETHICS, Spring 2006, at 1 (American Bar Association); *Victims and Parole Decisions*, 11 JAHRBUCH FÜR RECHT UND ETHIK 405 (2003) (Duncker & Humblot).

Introduction

Liberals

I. NATURAL LAW AND LIBERALISM

In this book, I explore, illustrate, and seek to illuminate a radical version of liberalism articulated and defended using natural law theory.

A natural law theory in the broadest sense is one that sees moral requirements as rooted in the way things are. It need not straightforwardly *identify* moral facts with natural facts; it might, alternatively, treat the moral as supervenient on the natural. But it will maintain, at minimum, that there could not be two worlds comprising identical sets of natural facts but different sets of moral facts. More narrowly, however, we can think of natural law theories of morality, law, and politics as rooted in *particular aspects* of how things are—especially, aspects of how *human persons* are.[1] I will be concerned here with two strands of natural law thinking.

(*i*) A natural law view in the first sense is one, typically Aristotelian, that treats flourishing, fulfillment, well-being, welfare as the basic moral category. Because flourishing is basic to ethics conceived in this sense, choosing correctly means choosing appropriately in relation to flourishing. Of course, choices with respect to flourishing can go wrong in various ways, some of which may be characterized using highly general principles.[2] The requirements of natural law in this sense are both universal and natural because they apply in virtue of our

[1] *See, e.g.*, Mark C. Murphy, *The Natural Law Tradition in Ethics*, Stanford Encyclopedia of Philosophy, Sep. 27, 2011, https://plato.stanford.edu/entries/natural-law-ethics/; 1 Terence E. Irwin, The Development of Ethics: A Historical and Critical Study—From Socrates to the Reformation 545–70 (2007); 2 Terence E. Irwin, The Development of Ethics: A Historical and Critical Study—From Suarez to Rousseau 70–87 (2008). *Cf.* John Finnis, *Natural Law Theories*, Stanford Encyclopedia of Philosophy, Nov. 4, 2015, https://plato.stanford.edu/entries/natural-law-theories/ (focusing especially on theories of *law*).

[2] The salience of these generic norms, rather than any thought that the authoritativeness or content of natural law depends on anything like an act of legislation, explains the relevance of talk about "law" in this connection. The idea of natural law does not involve the notion of any sort of legislative enactment, human or divine.

generic characteristics (so that, on the most plausible reading, they bind any creatures relevantly similar to us who are capable of moral agency).[3] I focus here especially on one variety of Aristotelian natural law theory, the New Classical Natural Law theory.[4] For simplicity's sake, I will frequently refer to "NATURAL LAW theory" when discussing orthodox and unorthodox versions of this distinctive variety of natural law theory, and to "NATURAL LAW theorists" when alluding to its orthodox and unorthodox proponents.

(*ii*) The latter variety of natural law thinking, grounded in the ideas of the Scottish Enlightenment, and so notably of Adam Smith, and continued most notably in the contemporary era by Friedrich Hayek, is concerned with "the superiority of spontaneous over man-made order."[5] On this sort of view, social order emerges naturally in the course of ongoing human interaction. It is "the result of human action, but not the execution of any human design."[6] Natural law theorists identified with the spontaneous order tradition have seen social order as emerging on a bottom-up rather than a top-down basis. The spontaneous order approach complements the Aristotelian in at least two ways. (*a*) It undermines support for models of social interaction to which top-down control is central, and thus helps to create space for the exercise of practical reason that is itself an element of flourishing. As a result, (*b*) it helps to encourage the development of social institutions that promote prosperity in ways that allow for the expression of diverse styles of life, and so of diverse ways of flourishing.

3 I have drawn here on Murphy's analysis, even as I have modified it; *cf.* Murphy, *Tradition, supra* note 1, at §1.4. Murphy takes divine origin and epistemic accessibility to features of a paradigmatic natural law theory. Natural law theorists can, of course, be theists; but they will not suppose that the divine will or any divine command does or could determine the *content* of natural law (apart from determining or, alternatively, helping to determine the relevant natural facts with which morality necessarily covaries).

4 *See generally* JOHN FINNIS, NATURAL LAW AND NATURAL RIGHTS (1980); JOHN FINNIS, FUNDAMENTALS OF ETHICS (1983); 1 GERMAIN GRISEZ, THE WAY OF THE LORD JESUS: CHRISTIAN MORAL PRINCIPLES (1983); GERMAIN GRISEZ & RUSSELL SHAW, BEYOND THE NEW MORALITY: THE RESPONSIBILITIES OF FREEDOM (3d. ed. 1988); JOHN M. FINNIS ET AL., NUCLEAR DETERRENCE, MORALITY, AND REALISM (1987); GERMAIN GRISEZ & JOSEPH M. BOYLE, JR., LIFE AND DEATH WITH LIBERTY AND JUSTICE: A CONTRIBUTION TO THE EUTHANASIA DEBATE (1979); JOHN FINNIS, MORAL ABSOLUTES: TRADITION, REVISION, AND TRUTH (1991); 2 GERMAIN G. GRISEZ, THE WAY OF THE LORD JESUS: LIVING A CHRISTIAN LIFE (1994); JOHN FINNIS, AQUINAS: MORAL, POLITICAL, AND LEGAL THEORY (1998); ROBERT P. GEORGE, IN DEFENSE OF NATURAL LAW (2001); 3 GERMAIN GRISEZ, THE WAY OF THE LORD JESUS: DIFFICULT MORAL QUESTIONS (1997); Germain Grisez, Joseph M. Boyle, and John Finnis, *Practical Principles, Moral Truth, and Ultimate Ends*, 32 AM. J. JURIS 99 (1987); John M. Finnis, Germain G. Grisez, and Joseph M. Boyle, *"Direct" and "Indirect": A Reply to Critics of Our Action Theory*, 65 THOMIST 1 (2001); MARK C. MURPHY, NATURAL LAW AND PRACTICAL RATIONALITY (1999); MARK C. MURPHY, NATURAL LAW IN JURISPRUDENCE AND POLITICS (2006); ALFONSO GÓMEZ-LOBO, MORALITY AND THE HUMAN GOODS: AN INTRODUCTION TO NATURAL LAW ETHICS (2002); TIMOTHY CHAPPELL, UNDERSTANDING HUMAN GOODS: A THEORY OF ETHICS (1995). Obviously, the theorists I cite embrace a variety of views, not always agreeing with me or with each other.

5 ERIK ANGNER, HAYEK AND NATURAL LAW 6 (2007).

6 ADAM FERGUSON, ESSAY ON THE HISTORY OF CIVIL SOCIETY 205 (5th ed., 1782).

In Part II, I outline a NATURAL LAW account understanding of what makes for a good life before turning, in Part III, to the requirements of practical reasonableness, themselves elements of flourishing, which specify and constrain our choices with respect to flourishing.[7] I note in Part IV why the kind of NATURAL LAW approach I prefer doesn't become bogged down in the disputes regarding egoism and altruism that have preoccupied many modern moral theories. Since I'm attempting to advance a *liberal* theory, I explain in Part V how I understand liberalism; then, in Part IV, I indicate how the variety of NATURAL LAW thinking I defend might support liberal moral and political views. I conclude with an overview of what follows in the remainder of the book in Part VII.

II. ASPECTS OF LIVING WELL

While in this book I draw on both the Aristotelian and spontaneous order traditions of natural law thinking, in the introduction, I seek particularly to clarify NATURAL LAW theory, not only because I will draw on it explicitly throughout but also because it is somewhat less familiar than a number of other approaches to moral, legal, and political philosophy. (As should be clear, I'm largely *describing* and *expounding* rather than *warranting* my preferred theoretical approach here. While I do note some considerations that count in its favor, I have no illusions that what I offer here amounts to a defense of all of its controversial elements.)

According to a number of distinctively contemporary approaches to moral theory, the point of ethics is to enable detached, atomistic individuals to pursue their preferences in a manner that leaves space for others to do the same.[8] These approaches typically treat people's preferences as relatively arbitrary givens. As long as one takes interpersonal morality seriously, then, on these views, one may reasonably pursue any sort of life one likes. One's welfare or well-being will *consist in* the satisfaction of one's preferences. By contrast, Aristotelian ethics, and so NATURAL LAW theory, can be understood as asking: *How should one live well?* Thus, NATURAL LAW theory begins with an understanding of *flourishing*.

Like others in the Aristotelian tradition, NATURAL LAW theorists note that we rarely find it difficult to answer the question whether a plant or a nonhuman animal is flourishing. We understand from careful reflection on their characteristics and environments what makes things go well for these organisms. "Whether or not a given individual . . . is or is not flourishing *qua* member . . . of whatever plant or animal species it is to which it . . . belong[s] is in itself a question of fact . . ."[9] And

7 I happily acknowledge the NATURAL LAW theorists as the source of inspiration for these proposals, while absolving them of any responsibility for clumsiness or what may ultimately prove to be errors on my part.

8 *Cf.* DAVID GAUTHIER, MORALS BY AGREEMENT (1986).

9 ALASDAIR MACINTYRE, DEPENDENT RATIONAL ANIMALS: WHY HUMAN BEINGS NEED THE VIRTUES 64 (1999); *cf. id.* at 79. *Cf.* OWEN FLANAGAN, THE PROBLEM OF THE SOUL: TWO VISIONS OF MIND AND HOW TO RECONCILE THEM 265–86 (2002); PHILIPPA FOOT, NATURAL GOODNESS 25–51 (2001).

natural law theorists suggest that we can be as confident about judgments regarding the flourishing of human beings as we are about the flourishing of other creatures.

Various aspects of activity and experience can all be seen as instances of flourishing. In many, perhaps most, cases, it will be obvious to us whether something is or isn't a way in which a given life might go well. But we can also reflect *critically* on our judgments about flourishing. We can ask whether they cohere with (or require the revision of) our existing considered judgments about our own and others' well-being. We can ask where our inquiry stops when we try to make sense of paradigm cases of reasonable action—at what point explaining an action seems to refer to an objective, a perceived good, beyond which no further appeal is needed in order for the action to count as reasonable. We can ask what element of someone's being or capacities or activity has been adversely affected by what we clearly take to be an injury. We can ask whether anything like a cross-cultural or cross-historical consensus supports treating something as a dimension of well-being. We can ask whether *denying* that something is an aspect of well-being—and so affirming, in effect, that one can treat it as important or unimportant at one's whim—entangles us in self-contradiction. And perhaps we can ask whether a given aspect of an organism's being, experience, and activity represents the development of one of its *capacities*—capacities that can often be straightforwardly identified through naturalistic inquiry.[10]

There is likely to be some disagreement around the edges. But most people will be inclined to agree that among the aspects of any human person's well-being are aesthetic experience, friendship, imaginative immersion,[11] knowledge, life and bodily well-being, peace of mind, play, practical reasonableness, self-integration, sensory pleasure, and skillful performance.[12] We can refer to these as basic *aspects of well-being or welfare*, basic *dimensions of flourishing or fulfillment*, basic *goods*. Because what makes a choice reasonable is its relationship to well-being or welfare, because only sentients have welfare, and because morality is a matter of choosing reasonably, the only moral questions concern our choices with respect to the flourishing of sentients—others or ourselves—and so with respect to these goods.

10 *Cf.* MacIntyre, *supra* note 9, at 64–65; Grisez & Shaw, *supra* note 4, at 43–53, 89–97.

11 I have in mind the kind of absorption in an imaginary world in virtue of which one allows oneself to treat it at least part of the time as if it were possibly or actually real and in which one cares about, and so responds emotionally to, the fate of the world and the fates of its residents—the kind of absorption that gives rise to and is expressed in enthusiastic fan subcultures. The person who opts to enter such a world and who welcomes emotional engagement with the lives of those who inhabit it is not willfully deceiving herself, but participating in the good of imaginative immersion, which has drawn people to attend to stories from time immemorial. Someone might argue that imaginative immersion is more simply understood not as a separate good but as an aspect of aesthetic experience. But aesthetic experience seems to me to be more concerned with the formal properties of a state of affairs and their relationships with each other rather than with our identification with the inhabitants of a fictive world. A recent exploration of imaginative immersion: The Aesthetic Illusion in Literature and the Arts (Tomáš Koblížek ed., 2017).

12 *See, e.g.*, Chappell, *supra* note 4, at 37–45 (1995); Murphy, Rationality, *supra* note 4, at 96–138; Gómez-Lobo, *supra* note 4, at 6–25; Grisez & Shaw, *supra* note 4, at 77–88; Grisez, Principles, *supra* note 4, at 121–25; Finnis, Law, *supra* note 4, at 59–99.

Basic goods are not abstractions or Platonic objects:[13] they are ways in which lives can go well, can flourish, ways in which welfare or fulfillment can be realized.[14] And they are equally *basic*. They're *basic* because reasonable actions can be explained with reference to them, and other goods people reasonably seek to realize or promote can be understood as instances of these goods (or of combinations of these goods). Any of them may reasonably be regarded as a proper terminus for the explanation or justification of an action. A chain of nested reasons for action can rightly be seen to end in one or more of these basic goods.

No basic good is best seen as an instance of or a means to any of the others. Nor are they instances of or means to some yet more fundamental value—happiness, say, or preference satisfaction. Happiness is satisfaction in the realization of objectives independently regarded as worthwhile. Satisfactions are differentiated by their objects and occasions—there is no single thing, *satisfaction*, in which the various goods participate in any interesting sense. Preference satisfaction matters primarily because *the things preferred* matter (both objectively and from the standpoint of the agent). And so forth.

Various lists of basic goods are on offer, and not much turns on the broad categories we employ. One thing that *does* matter, however, is my inclusion of *sensory pleasure* on the list. On a typical NATURAL LAW view, sensory pleasure is at best a concomitant of participation in some aspect of fulfillment; it's a pointer to the value of what one is doing or experiencing. It has no independent value. On this view, which I reject, seeking sensory pleasure for its own sake isn't reasonable. I think it's perfectly sensible to say something like this about *emotions*, which do, of course, include sensory components. We can describe some emotional reactions as reactions typically involving *pleasure*, to be sure. But these emotions wouldn't *be* emotions if they weren't—or, at any rate, didn't involve as integral—cognitively meaningful *judgments*: an emotion is ordinarily the pairing of a sensation and a cognition.

When our psyches are functioning well, our emotions point us to the value or meaning of what we are doing or experiencing or contemplating. And they can serve

13 Natural law theory is not committed to Platonism here or elsewhere. And credible accounts of moral objectivity and truth not allied to any sort of robust moral ontology are available: *see, e.g.*, Annette Bryson, *Non-Inflationary Realism about Morality: Language, Metaphysics, and Truth* (2017) (unpublished Ph.D. dissertation, University of Michigan).

14 The deep character of these goods is an interesting and, I think, open issue. One might understand them as expressions of our inherent potential, *cf.* GRISEZ & SHAW, *supra* note 4, at 43–53, 89–97, of developed natural capacities, *see, e.g.*, MARTHA C. NUSSBAUM, CREATING CAPABILITIES: THE HUMAN DEVELOPMENT APPROACH (2013). One might see them as constituted by a range of natural desires, *see* LARRY ARNHART, DARWINIAN NATURAL RIGHT: THE BIOLOGICAL ETHICS OF HUMAN NATURE (1998), or as constructed by a process of reasoning about ends, *see* MARK LEBAR, THE VALUE OF LIVING WELL (2013). One might understand them to matter as the products of a certain kind of extended evolutionary history; *see* WILLIAM D. CASEBEER, NATURAL ETHICAL FACTS: EVOLUTION, CONNECTIONISM, AND MORAL COGNITION (2005). I do not believe we need to settle on one of these accounts, or any alternative, at this point, provided we can agree that the basic goods are, indeed, instances of flourishing.

both to prompt and to solidify our projects. But an emotion isn't *itself* the value or meaning of a particular good, which might be present even if the sensory signals that might otherwise be provided by the emotion were absent. That's why it makes no sense to seek happiness, understood as satisfaction or elation, as one's ultimate goal, or to treat it as the underlying point of any good. For it will always be reasonable (in a deliberate echo of G. E. Moore) to ask whether any instance of happiness is occasioned by something *worth* being happy about.[15] And the same will be true, in general, of seeking any emotion as a goal.

The point of skiing is the challenge and risk associated with the activity, and the development of the skill needed to meet the challenge and risk. It's not the anxiety and exhilaration that accompany (and prefigure) one's time on the slopes. One could get the anxiety and exhilaration in a simulator or a laboratory; but one couldn't realize the actual goods involved in skiing.[16]

By contrast, we *do* seek straightforwardly sensory pleasures—take, as obvious examples, the pleasures of orgasm or chocolate consumption—for their own sake. (Of course, orgasm and chocolate consumption may both, in different ways, foster friendship as well.) And I believe that we do so quite reasonably.[17]

The various aspects of well-being are *incommensurable*.[18] That is, there is no way to compare friendship, say, and knowledge quantitatively. That's true of the broad categories, and it's true of all the individual instances of those categories. Those individual instances are also *non-fungible*: none can be given up without loss, so none is a perfect substitute for any other.

In addition, none is in itself qualitatively superior, none merits qualitative priority, to any of the others. That no basic aspect of well-being, and no instance of any such aspect, is quantitatively superior to any other follows from their incommensurability. But of course this leaves open the possibility that one might be *qualitatively* superior

[15] And note that this is true even if sensory pleasure is a basic aspect of well-being. Happiness and sensory pleasure are not identical.

[16] *See* Robert C. Solomon, About Love: Reinventing Romance for Our Times 80 (1994). *Cf.* Martha C. Nussbaum, Upheavals of Thought: The Intelligence of Emotions 64 (2001). The Aristotelian views embraced—quite reasonably, as it seems to me—by Solomon and Nussbaum are in stark to contrast to those of, for instance, Richard Rorty. While there is, as far as I can see, no inherent conflict between Rorty's pragmatism and critical reflection on the objects of desire (critical reflection, that is, extending beyond reflection on the compossibility of one's own desires and the possibility of their joint realization with those of others), Rorty seems to think critical reflection on our ends is impractical or possible or pointless. "For Mill, James, Dewey, Habermas, and the other philosophers of social democracy, the answer to the question 'Are some human desires bad?' is: No, but some desires do get in the way of our [whose?] project of maximizing the overall satisfaction of desire." Richard Rorty, *An Ethics for Today*, *in* An Ethics for Today: Finding Common Ground between Philosophy and Religion 7, 15 (2011).

[17] *See* Gary Chartier, Public Practice, Private Law: An Essay on Love, Marriage, and the State 115–19 (2016).

[18] *See, e.g.*, Finnis, Law, *supra* note 4 at 92–95; Finnis, Ethics, *supra* note 4, at 86–90; Grisez & Shaw, *supra* note 4, at 132; Murphy, Rationality, *supra* note 4, at 182–87. *Cf.* Isaiah Berlin, Four Essays on Liberty (1969).

to another. There might be, say, some kind of lexical ordering in virtue of which one was required to pay attention to friendship before aesthetic experience. And of course, this might be thought to be clearly true in one case: one cannot *not* exhibit either incidental or deliberate regard for the basic good of practical reasonableness in the course of any appropriate choice. Even here, however, the *point* of one's action need not be to act reasonably; one is not, at least much of the time, choosing to act reasonably *under that description* even when one does act reasonably, and it is deliberate prioritization that seems to me to be in view when one envisions lexical priority here. More broadly, the various basic goods don't seem to present themselves phenomenologically as qualitatively ranked; and, absent some persuasive argument that they are, I think we are free to assume that they are not.[19]

John Rawls used the label "primary goods" for a range of *instrumental* goods valuable in the course of pursuing any goal someone might have—"liberty and opportunity, income and wealth, and the social bases of self-respect."[20] But these goods are precisely *not* primary. They do not provide basic reasons for action. They are not constitutive of flourishing. None can reasonably serve as a final end of action. (Actions that promote or realize various basic aspects of welfare may, of course, be acts that also promote Rawlsian primary goods. Protecting the capacity for practical reasonableness, for instance, may sometimes simultaneously protect liberty.) Rather, they are thoroughly useful *means* to the realization of the basic aspects of well-being in our lives and the lives of others.

III. CHOOSING WELL AS INTEGRAL TO LIVING WELL

Morality is concerned with acts in which one constitutes oneself. A morally *appropriate* act is one that is open to, marked by appropriate regard for, all real goods, as realized in our own lives or those of others (though none of us can or should, of course, pursue all goods simultaneously, or perhaps ever). By contrast, a morally *inappropriate* act is one in which one identifies with injuries, with attacks on basic goods, of one sort or another.[21]

One way of flourishing, as I noted earlier, is *reasoning and choosing well with respect to flourishing*—practical reasonableness. Practical reasoning is reasoning about what to do, and this will frequently be a quite mundane matter. But even the simplest exercise in instrumental reasoning finally makes sense as a way of living well, and of ensuring that one lives well. Practical reasonableness as an aspect of

19 Thanks to David Gordon for insights related to this point.

20 John Rawls, A Theory of Justice 54 (2d ed., 1999).

21 *Cf.* Finnis, Ethics, *supra* note 4, at 139 (maintaining that "[w]hat choices create is not merely some new wants, preferences, habits . . . , but also a new (not wholly new) identity or character. All free choices last in the sense that they change the person.").

flourishing can be *specified* in a variety of ways. These ways include at least the following:[22]

(*i*) *The Principle of Recognition*. Choose genuine, rather than illusory, goods for oneself and others.[23] Don't act except in order to realize or promote or facilitate participation in authentic aspects of welfare (directly or indirectly).

(*ii*) *The Principle of Fairness*. Judge and choose *in a rationally consistent manner* with respect to those whom one's actions affect. Treat them in the same way unless there's a justification for treating them differently. (*a*) One justification for treating them differently might the realization of a particular good. For instance, if I am to be your friend, if we are to participate in the good of friendship, I can't give my time and loyalty equally to everyone. Similarly, if I'm to pick you as a member of a team that will participate in an athletic contest, if you and your teammates are to participate in the good of play, I may reasonably pick you in light of your athletic ability. (*b*) Another justification might be that a given distinction is permissible in light of a rule I am willing consistently to endorse as applied to myself and my loved ones along with the others involved.[24] I might agree, for instance, that one good turn be met with another, and thus be willing to endorse a rule permitting the acknowledgment of merit.[25]

(*iii*) *The Principle of Respect*. Don't *injure* any moral sentient by purposefully or instrumentally attacking any basic aspect of her well-being. The irreducible heterogeneity of the basic goods—their incommensurability, non-fungibility, and lack of inherent priority—means that the various general ways of flourishing are incommensurable and non-fungible, as are all the particular *instances* of flourishing. And this means, in turn, that any sort of consequentialist calculus is a nonstarter, since there will be no rationally necessary way of aggregating various goods and effecting quantitative comparisons of the aggregates. It also means that there will be no rational justification for choices to injure one instance of flourishing—whether for its own sake (out of revenge,

22 *See, e.g.*, GRISEZ & SHAW, *supra* note 4, at 117–53; GRISEZ, PRINCIPLES, *supra* note 4, at 205–28; FINNIS, LAW, *supra* note 4, at 100–33, 304; FINNIS, ETHICS, *supra* note 4, at 75–76; MURPHY, RATIONALITY, *supra* note 4, at 198–212; GÓMEZ-LOBO, *supra* note 4, at 42–44. I bear any blame for problems associated with the labels and formulations of these principles offered here.

23 Reasonably chosen ends must be real goods; if something isn't actually valuable, what would it mean to choose it reasonably? However, among the real goods people reasonably pursue is the good I've called *imaginative immersion*.

24 This is a matter of what one is willing to accept and what one can consistently accept. It is thus similar to the constraint on moral judgment embraced by R. M. HARE, FREEDOM AND REASON (1963). There will not necessarily be a fact of the matter about what just anyone could be willing or unwilling rationally to universalize in particular circumstances. What's important is what a given agent is *willing to accept* for herself and for others similarly situated.

25 *See* FINNIS, AQUINAS, *supra* note 4, at 197. It doesn't follow, of course, that one *bad* turn deserves another, as I'm quite sure it doesn't.

say, which in effect denies the value of the goods attacked) or in the interest of another good (since one good can neither outweigh nor trump another).

(*iv*) *The Principle of Commitment.* Adhere resolutely, though not fanatically, to personal *commitments* that establish priorities and that allow one to participate deeply and richly in particular goods.[26]

(*v*) *The Principle of Efficiency.* Seek to realize goods—and, in particular, act in fulfillment of one's commitments—*efficiently*. Opt for the least costly ways of achieving one's goals (within the terms set by one's priorities and by the other requirements of practical reasonableness).

IV. SELF AND OTHER

This book represents a self-consciously liberal political and social project. And liberalism is sometimes criticized as naively atomistic, as beginning with the assumption that people are and should be separate from and unconcerned about each other, disconnected, coming together only to pursue their own goals before separating again. This atomistic conception is perhaps not worthy of quite as much ridicule as it often receives, in particular because it can help to foster norms, rules, and institutions that keep dominant players in political and social settings from abusing the weak and marginalizing dissenters. But it doesn't accurately characterize liberalism as an historical tradition. And NATURAL LAW theory, the basis for the kind of liberalism I elaborate here, is certainly focused not on adjudicating the conflicting claims of detached individuals but, rather, on providing insight that can inform the flourishing of agents who are essentially social—who are *molecular* rather than atomic individuals.[27] It rejects the opposition between self and other, between egoism and altruism, that is at the heart of the modern ethical picture. On the NATURAL LAW view, the reasonable moral agent is unapologetically concerned with her own flourishing. But this does not put her at odds with others. Instead, the reasonable agent understands her flourishing in a way that integrally connects it with the flourishing of others.[28]

(*i*) Some goods are essentially *common*, essentially *shared*. These include (*a*) goods that essentially, not just instrumentally, involve common endeavor (many instances of *play*, for instance). But they also include (*b*) the well-being of particular others (our friends, lovers, children, etc.) which we experience and treat as our own as well as (*c*) the shared *identities* of friends and lovers.

26 *See* GARY CHARTIER, THE LOGIC OF COMMITMENT (2017).

27 *See* Sheldon Richman, *Molecular Individualism*, THE FREEMAN: IDEAS ON LIBERTY, March 1, 1998, http://www.thefreemanonline.org/columns/perspective/perspective-molecular-individualism/.

28 Thanks to Roderick Long and Sheldon Richman for multiple insights related to this important topic. *Cf.* TALBOT BREWER, THE RETRIEVAL OF ETHICS 192–235 (2009) (contrasting, unfavorably, "modern dualism about the good"—including the dualism of self and other—with ancient views).

While a respectful parent recognizes that her child is *other*, so that the child's *good* is the parent's own good even as the child's *identity* is clearly separate from hers, to some extent two friends and to a much greater extent two lovers form a *we*.[29]

(*ii*) The requirements of practical reasonableness are concerned with the flourishing both of the agent and of those other than the agent. Choosing well and reasoning well about choice are themselves aspects of flourishing: They are instances of the good of practical reasonableness. And staying true to what one believes is part of the good of self-integration. The reasonable agent seeks to flourish in part precisely by instantiating in her choices the excellences of practical reasonableness and of self-integration, and so, where appropriate, by choosing rightly in relation to others. And notice that neither the others nor the right choices are understood here as *instrumental* to flourishing. Rather, the agent flourishes—choosing well, participating in the good of practical reasonableness—precisely by acknowledging the value and showing regard for the well-being of the other. And the agent flourishes—maintaining her self-integration—precisely by adhering to requirements she reasonably embraces, requirements in virtue of which, again, she acknowledges the value and shows regard for the well-being of the other.

(*iii*) While one flourishes precisely *by* acting reasonably, choosing well, in relation to the other in accordance with the requirements of practical reasonableness, this kind of choice to flourish *also* yields various reinforcing benefits. (*a*) It can exhibit an aesthetic excellence that is not only valuable on its own but is also a source of appreciation by others. (*b*) It can reinforce one's self-confidence and self-respect—especially, but not only, when choosing well is emotionally, physically, or logistically difficult but one does it anyway. (*c*) It can prompt the respect and admiration of others, valuable as a reinforcement for one's own self-concept and as an occasion for positive interpersonal relationships and as a source of support for one's reputation. (*d*) Participating in aptly structured institutional roles and rules yields multiple benefits for the participants and for others, often simultaneously. Appropriately fulfilling the role of a physician, for instance, means realizing a range of basic goods in one's own life—notably the various excellences associated with skillful fulfillment of one's role—while also helping others to realize the good of health and bodily well-being *and* generating the instrumental good of compensation which in turn facilitates one's own participation in other basic goods and one's ability to contribute to the well-being of others in various ways. Similarly, the norms and rules that make possible the operation of markets promote widely shared instrumental and intrinsic benefits. These benefits include not only the *instrumentally* valuable

[29] *See, e.g.*, Robert Nozick, *Love's Bond*, *in* THE EXAMINED LIFE: PHILOSOPHICAL MEDITATIONS 68, 70–74 (1989); GARY CHARTIER, THE ANALOGY OF LOVE 142–43 (2d ed., 2017); SOLOMON, *supra* note 16, at 194–217; FINNIS, LAW, *supra* note 4, at 134–160.

money which market participants gain but also the *intrinsically* valuable relationships they develop in the marketplace, the intrinsically valuable skills they nourish there, the basic goods in which their products enable *others* to participate, and so on. Markets are widely beneficial, and the benefits they yield are simultaneously realized in multiple lives.[30]

Aristotelian NATURAL LAW theory recognizes and affirms the first set of ways of integrating the welfare of self and other. The second set of ways is inherent in the theory itself. And the theory provides good reason to support the kinds of norms and institutions that make possible the third set of ways, itself a central element of the other sort of natural law theory in view here, spontaneous-order natural law theory.

V. THE SHAPE OF LIBERALISM

Affirmed and facilitated by natural law theory, the realization of shared benefits for self and others as a feature of reasonable action and of appropriately designed social institutions is among the grounds of liberalism as an approach to politics, law, society, culture, and personal life. Liberalism embraces political and social norms, rules, and institutions that foster individuality, creativity, experimentation, rational criticism, and diversity.[31]

A. *Varieties of Liberalism*

Political liberalism, as I understand it, rules out the imposition of a comprehensive understanding of the good life by force and thus precludes forcible interference with nonviolent conduct of all sorts. *Social* liberalism embraces the conviction that (*i*) lives of many different kinds are good lives, lives worth living, (*ii*) we should be agnostic about the merits of many other varieties rather than rejecting them outright, and (*iii*) even when nonviolent ways of life and patterns of interaction are unequivocally unreasonable, social pressure shouldn't be used to discourage them except in extreme cases. Political and social liberalism both encourage the emergence, development, and display of diverse styles of life and patterns of social organization. And each sort of liberalism features an ongoing drive toward greater moral, legal, and political inclusiveness—toward cosmopolitanism, toward regard for the legitimacy of diverse ways of being, toward enlargement of the moral community in various ways.[32]

30 *See, e.g.*, ROBERT SUGDEN, THE COMMUNITY OF ADVANTAGE: A BEHAVIOURAL ECONOMIST'S DEFENCE OF THE MARKET (2018); ARNOLD KLING, SPECIALIZATION AND TRADE (2016).

31 *See* ANTHONY DE JASAY, CHOICE, CONTRACT, CONSENT: A RESTATEMENT OF LIBERALISM (1991); LUDWIG VON MISES, LIBERALISM: THE CLASSICAL TRADITION (Ralph Raico trans., 2005). *Cf.* Deirdre Nansen McCloskey, *Why You Are Not a Conservative*, REASON, Nov. 2018, *available at* http://reason.com/archives/2018/10/25/why-you-are-not-a-conservative.

32 *Cf.* JOHN STUART MILL, ON LIBERTY 103–39 (1859).

B. *The Liberal Spirit*

Liberalism—political and social—celebrates individuality, variety, pluralism, creativity, freedom. As a social, cultural, and moral doctrine, liberalism incorporates enthusiasm for the *liberal spirit*. This spirit is marked, as I've said, by enthusiasm for individuality, variety, pluralism, creativity, freedom. And of course it also acknowledges a range of moral requirements that are not distinctively liberal. Certainly, the liberal should not suppose that just any action that is inconsistent with political liberalism, any action that does not involve the misuse of force, is morally reasonable. Conduct that doesn't involve the use of force can, and frequently does, amount to the mistreatment of others or of oneself. Someone energized by the liberal spirit will challenge such mistreatment even while granting that it may not reasonably be met with the use of force.

Liberalism is individualistic in its social, cultural, and political manifestations. It is concerned with the individual as both the bearer of rights and the subject of flourishing *and* as the underlying, genuinely existing source of all social realities. Only individuals experience and act. While individual actions shape the contexts in which other individuals act, while individuals influence each other in various ways, so that new dynamics emerge when people interact in groups, individuals remain normatively and explanatorily foundational. Individuals are the loci of moral concern: concern with groups matters, when it does, because of their significance for individuals. The flourishing that matters morally is the flourishing of individuals. Individuals flourish in relationships, including both dyadic and group relationships. But the flourishing of the relationships doesn't occur apart from the flourishing of the individuals who participate in them. And the purported needs of groups can't license authority figures or majorities from suppressing minorities or dissenters.

A further defining characteristic: Liberalism is *optimistic*. It is "the party of hope."[33] It recognizes, of course, the reality of human finitude; it is not utopian. Nonetheless, it sees social problems as soluble, the persistence of tribal paranoias and ancient hatreds as anything but inevitable, and growth as liberating and invigorating.

C. *A Liberal Social Order*

Liberalism is committed to valuing and nurturing a social order marked by *peaceful, voluntary cooperation*. This means that it embraces a norm of respect for the capacities of agents to shape their own lives. And it emphasizes, therefore, that we can and should use, not force, but, rather, intellectual or emotional or imaginative persuasion or the instrumental inducement of exchange to encourage others to engage with us. But liberalism stresses not only the peaceful, voluntary character

[33] Richard Rorty, Achieving Our Country: Leftist Thought in Twentieth-Century America 14 (1997).

of social interaction but also its *cooperative* character. We all flourish when we cooperate; extended social cooperation offers us all opportunities for flourishing that would be entirely absent were we isolated.

In a liberal order, people seek to flourish together in diverse ways while respecting everyone's right to be free from manipulation through the use of force or fraud. Thus, markets both are instances of and means of facilitating flourishing. Liberal enthusiasm for markets grows from multiple sources, but it notably embodies an awareness that shared prosperity is self-reinforcing, yielding a "general community of advantage"[34] that creates multiple opportunities for people to realize the various basic goods. But the liberal appreciation for the value of immediate and extended social cooperation is hardly limited to a celebration of the genuinely transformative, emancipatory potential of markets. It extends to the whole range of consensual engagements possible for us as social creatures, both instrumentally valuable and inherently fulfilling.

D. *Embracing Diversity*

Liberalism has consistently embraced human diversity. It has rarely if ever been a movement or tradition animated *solely* by a concern with political freedom—freedom from the forcible imposition of others' wills. Rather, it has also importantly been a movement that has reflected a deep desire for social, cultural, and psychic liberation from dominance by others and for the resultant freedom to explore and experiment.

There are, of course, important differences between social, cultural, and psychic freedom on the one hand and political freedom on the other. The use of force is a particularly intrusive and objectionable way of constraining people's options,[35] one that forecloses possibilities more strikingly than perhaps any other. But while they're certainly different, the analogy between freedom from the aggressive use of force and freedom from social pressure, including social pressure internalized as psychic constraint, is not a superficial or trivial one. In each case, other people subject, or seek to subject, us to their wills, to make us do what they want for reasons that are not our own. They manipulate, or attempt to manipulate, our actions by imposing, or threatening to impose, serious costs if we don't comply with their wishes. And, just as we have reason to want to avoid being subjected to the wills of others by means of force, we surely have reason to want to avoid being subjected to their wills by means of social pressure. It is important to recognize that, as John Stuart Mill observed, "[t]here is a limit to the legitimate interference of collective opinion with individual independence: and to find that limit, and maintain it against encroachment, is as

34 John Stuart Mill, Principles of Political Economy with Some of Their Applications to Social Philosophy 678 (W. J. Ashley ed., 1920).

35 *See* Gary Chartier, An Ecological Theory of Free Expression 24–27 (2018).

indispensable to a good condition of human affairs, as protection against political despotism."[36]

So it is hardly surprising that people who value political freedom should also be people who value social, cultural, and psychic freedom. There is no *logical contradiction* between valuing the one kind of freedom while being indifferent or even opposed to the other. Nonetheless, "envisioning . . . or even championing [non-violently maintained authoritarianism and hierarchicalism in a liberal society] . . . would certainly be weird."[37] There is, in short, a natural fit between the desire for freedom from violence, from legal constraint, and the desire for other kinds of freedom.[38] Similarly, there is a natural fit between the desire for social, cultural, and psychic freedom and the distinguishable but related appreciation for human variety, even eccentricity.

E. Diversity and Flourishing

No doubt any life we could recognize as a human one would exhibit certain characteristics in virtue of which there might be limits on just how the person whose life it was could be expected to flourish. But these limits are rather general ones. Humans differ from each other, often quite dramatically. If so, it seems to me, then, because how someone can flourish will be a function of how she or he is, as it were, *put together*, the ways in which people will flourish can be expected to differ, perhaps quite dramatically, as well. One of the great beauties of human existence is the immense variation humans, left to their own devices, can put on display in their attempts to discover and embody congenial approaches to flourishing. Innumerable geeky subcultures—from Trekkers to polyamorists—that are often either ignored or mocked by the self-proclaimed mavens of the mainstream can reflect a genuine awareness of the richness of human possibility. The other people in our lives may flourish in ways quite different from the ways in which we ourselves live well. Political and social liberalism can and should offer people a more-than-tolerant—indeed (in many, if not all, cases) a positively enthusiastic—celebration of the reality and value of human diversity.

F. Diversity and Social Ecology

The ecology of a flourishing society is substantially enriched by this kind of diversity. Social improvement happens when people put alternative patterns of life on display

36 MILL, LIBERTY, *supra* note 32, at 14.

37 Charles W. Johnson, *Libertarianism through Thick and Thin, in* MARKETS NOT CAPITALISM: INDIVIDUALIST ANARCHISM AGAINST BOSSES, INEQUALITY, CORPORATE POWER, AND STRUCTURAL POVERTY 131, 137 (Gary Chartier & Charles W. Johnson eds., 2011), *available at* http://radgeek.com/gt/2011/10/Markets-Not-Capitalism-2011-Chartier-and-Johnson.pdf.

38 *Cf.* DAVID SCHMIDTZ & JASON BRENNAN, A BRIEF HISTORY OF LIBERTY (2010).

and when others observe those patterns with sufficient accuracy and empathy that they can tell whether those they observe are flourishing in recognizable ways. Observers can then either reject, modify, or embrace the styles of life they have witnessed others practicing.

Argument matters, no doubt. But persuasion by example is likely to be far more effective in at least many cases. "Experiments in living," in Mill's felicitous phrase,[39] can thus play a crucial role in social progress. This means that our communities and societies need to welcome such experiments.

> In this age, the mere example of nonconformity, the mere refusal to bend the knee to custom, is itself a service. Precisely because the tyranny of opinion is such as to make eccentricity a reproach, it is desirable, in order to break through that tyranny, that people should be eccentric. Eccentricity has always abounded when and where strength of character was abounded; and the amount of eccentricity in a society has generally been proportional to the amount of genius, mental vigour, and moral courage which it contained. That so few now dare to be eccentric, marks the chief danger of the time.[40]

Liberals instinctively value not just political freedom but also social, cultural, and psychic freedom. One of liberalism's tasks is to make clear what it might mean actively to value the richness of human diversity, to discipline our tendencies to censoriousness and conformity in light of our own ignorance, and to welcome experiments in living as essential preconditions of social innovation. To do these things is to express liberalism's commitment to human community at its best.

G. *Space for Social Conservatives?*

Liberalism can and must include support for freedom of expression, freedom of association, and property rights, and therefore for the freedom of socially conservative people not to engage in behaviors and relationships to which they object. I don't favor using social pressure to turn principled conservatives into liberals any more than I favor using such pressure to suppress the kind of nonviolent conduct to which social conservatives may themselves object. Liberals should seek to influence by example, argument, artistic expression—not by shunning or shaming, much less using force.[41] People should be free to identify with socially conservative ideals (as long as these ideals are not imposed using actual or threatened force) whether or not liberals believe those ideals are injurious or have been embraced for inadequate reasons. And I would not for an instant want to see a commitment to social liberalism

39 Mill, *supra* note 32, at 103–39.

40 *Id.* at 120–21.

41 Thus, I find the idea of a ban on the *burqa* preposterous and thoroughly illiberal.

cashed out in terms of the use of force to interfere with even quite unreasonable nonviolent behavior.[42]

Voluntary communities ought to be free to embrace a variety of norms. And, indeed, it's clear that communities need norms to flourish: normless communities fall apart. The question, I think, is largely one of which norms communities ought to embrace. As I've noted, there can be value in seeing different patterns of life put on display in different communities with different norms. My own preference would be for norms that encourage people to welcome individual diversity, ones that do not threaten dissenters with shame or exclusion and that leave them free nondisruptively to challenge repressive patterns of behavior using neither force nor shaming and rejection but rather reasoned debate and the evocative display of appealingly liberal, appealingly liberating, alternatives.

H. Classical, Modern, and Radical Liberalism

The characteristics I have identified are plausibly seen as common to multiple varieties of liberalism. But, despite these commonalities, the diverse kinds of liberalism differ in important ways. Liberalism originally emerged as, among other things, (*i*) a deepening of the Western religious emphasis on the distinct and irreplaceable value of the particular person; (*ii*) an outgrowth of the Reformation's rejection of institutional authority and increasing, if hesitant, recognition of the value and inescapability of private judgment; (*iii*) a response to the recognition, in light especially of the Wars of Religion, that using force, and especially state power, to impose a vision of the good could not but prove a source of destructive and interminable conflict; (*iv*) an acknowledgment of the potential of market freedom to create and disseminate vast wealth; (*v*) an increasing awareness of the indefensibility of royal power, linked, arguably, with an attempted reassertion of the integrity and independence of institutions monarchs had sought to supplant; and (*vi*) a generalization of the attitude embodied in the increasingly successful project of modern science, an attitude rooted in appreciation for open-ended inquiry and for the rational criticism of existing assumptions.[43]

Liberalism sought to provide a bulwark against arbitrary power—as exercised initially by kings and later by their parliamentary successors *and* as delegated to governments' aristocratic and corporate cronies. It sought to protect diversity and to

42 *Cf.* Brian Barry, Culture and Equality (1999) (seemingly defending some state interventions into illiberal but voluntary subcultures).

43 For a provocative analysis of the development of liberalism, *see* the "bourgeois trilogy": Deirdre N. McCloskey, The Bourgeois Virtues: Ethics for an Age of Commerce (2006); Deirdre N. McCloskey, Bourgeois Dignity: Why Economics Can't Explain the Modern World (2010); Deirdre N. McCloskey, Bourgeois Equality : How Ideas, Not Capital Or Institutions, Enriched the World (2016). John Milton, perhaps best seen as a proto-liberal, anticipated (*v*) even as his own approach embodied and was rooted in the religious attitudes summarized in (*i*) and (*ii*). *See, e.g.*, John Milton, Areopagitica (1644).

allow decisions to be made at the lowest possible level. It was egalitarian, not in the sense that it sought to erase individual differences or to equalize resources but in the sense that it presupposed and defended people's equality of moral worth, social status, and political authority. It thus embraced freedom of religion, freedom of speech, freedom of trade, and, accordingly, limited government. Increasingly, therefore, it also embraced the cause of peace. Early liberalism did not, of course, commit to these values consistently, but it highlighted their importance and gave them pride of place in politics.[44]

The liberal tradition began to divide toward the latter part of the nineteenth century. Some liberals, whom today we tend to label *classical liberals*, saw the core commitments that had characterized the liberal tradition for the preceding two centuries as best served through opposition to state power. They understood the growing technocratic state as a tool of exploitative elites and a barrier to progress. Other liberals, whom today we tend to label *modern liberals*, maintained that the best way to further core liberal values of freedom, equality, and diversity was not to limit state power but to expand it.[45]

This book is an exercise in moral, legal, and political theory rather than intellectual history, and I do not propose here to tease out all the relevant distinctions and the diverse and sometimes opposing elements of the various strands of the liberal tradition. I do, however, want to suggest, as a matter more of gesture than of argument, that at least a partial reconciliation between classical and modern liberalism might be effected by what I'd like to label *radical liberalism*.

Radical liberalism holds that the two primary divisions of the liberal tradition might be able to reunite were both to acknowledge that modern liberal ends could be achieved using classical liberal means.[46] Put less tersely: radical liberals agree with classical and modern liberals about the importance of autonomy and social and cultural diversity. But they suggest that the social and economic ills that led modern liberals to cheer for state power are frequently, at any rate, *products* of state power;[47] and that the remedy for these ills is thus not more top-down management but rather more bottom-up self-organization, more freedom. Indeed, while I will not argue the point here (except, indirectly, in Chapter 9), radical liberals argue that the proper solution is *anarchy*.

44 On the American context, *see, e.g.*, RUDOLF ROCKER, PIONEERS OF AMERICAN FREEDOM (1949).

45 Modern liberalism frequently celebrated managerial and social-scientific expertise. The "new class" that emerged near the end of the nineteenth century arguably played into the hands of economic and political elites that sought to use the skills of the budding technocrats and their capacity to shape public opinion in the service of maintaining the power of the wealthy and well connected in a new era. *See, e.g.*, MURRAY N. ROTHBARD, THE PROGRESSIVE (2017).

46 *See* Benjamin R. Tucker, *State Socialism and Anarchism: How Far They Agree, and Wherein They Differ*, *in* MARKETS NOT CAPITALISM, *supra* note 37, at 21.

47 *See, e.g.*, MARKETS NOT CAPITALISM, *supra* note 37; SOCIAL CLASS AND STATE POWER: EXPLORING AN ALTERNATIVE RADICAL TRADITION (David M. Hart *et al.* eds., 2018).

Noam Chomsky rightly links anarchism with the liberal tradition;[48] liberalism can, indeed, be radical. The late Karl Hess once observed that, despite all the changes he had undergone, he had never been a liberal.[49] Hess's politics were in many ways precisely and resolutely liberal, in the sense in which I use the term here. But he meant to stress that he was not a meliorist but a radical, not a member but a passionate critic of the bipartisan American establishment. By "liberalism," he clearly had in mind a kind of accommodationist centrism. It should be clear that this is not the kind of liberalism I mean to defend here. The sort of liberalism I embrace is deeply skeptical about violent revolution; but it is also entirely uninvested in the maintenance of established religions and social hierarchies, or of the status quo more generally. It is a genuinely radical liberalism.

VI. HOW AN UNORTHODOX VERSION OF NATURAL LAW THEORY SUPPORTS RADICAL LIBERALISM

I believe that NATURAL LAW theory can be understood as providing a robust basis for radical liberal norms, rules, and institutions. Thus, I elect here to spell out my own, preferred, radical version of liberalism using this theoretical approach. At the same time, I trust that those who are not inclined to embrace radical liberalism will still find both the account of the relationship between NATURAL LAW theory and liberalism more broadly *and* my development of particular liberal perspectives throughout the book of interest.

Natural law theory is appealing for multiple reasons: in particular, because it focuses on what makes actual lives go well, on what makes them flourish, in this way arguably avoiding the alienating qualities of consequentialist and Kantian approaches. It treats questions about what makes for personal well-being as calls for serious, substantive reflection. And it promises to transcend familiar dichotomies between fact and value and between egoism and altruism. However, despite—or perhaps, on the view of some commentators, precisely because of—these appealing features, traditional understandings of natural law theory have characteristically been socially conservative, communitarian, or both: in short, illiberal. And they are often thought to be illiberal precisely because they involve substantive commitments regarding the shape of the good life. Kantian and classical utilitarian theories have frequently been seen as especially friendly to liberalism because they treat

48 *Cf.* Anthony Arnove, *Forward*, *in* NOAM CHOMSKY, THE ESSENTIAL CHOMSKY at vii (Anthony Arnove ed., 2008); Matthew Robare, *American Anarchist*, THE AMERICAN CONSERVATIVE, Nov. 22, 2013, *available at* http://www.theamericanconservative.com/articles/american-anarchist.

49 *See* KARL HESS: TOWARD LIBERTY (Boston University College of Communications, School of Broadcasting and Film, Graduate Film Program, 1980), *available at* https://www.youtube.com/watch?v=gmKI7psLnd4. This film, produced and directed by Roland Hallé and Peter Ladue, won the 1981 Academy Award for Best Documentary Short Subject. For more developed accounts of Hess's views, *see* KARL HESS, DEAR AMERICA (1975); KARL HESS, MOSTLY ON THE EDGE: AN AUTOBIOGRAPHY (Karl Hess, Jr., ed., 1999).

people's preferences as equivalent in merit, as entering into moral deliberation just as preferences. By contrast, Aristotelian views are frequently understood as ruling out a wide swath of possible lives as morally appropriate, and so as confining and puritanical. But it is entirely possible for a natural law theory to be genuinely liberal.

To be sure, NATURAL LAW theory has often been advanced by moral, legal, and political theorists inclined to embrace heteronormativity, to reject sexual liberation, and to endorse communitarian politics, though its most visible representatives have also been willing to accept relatively strong protections for freedom of speech and some version of Mill's Harm Principle.[50] My contention, however, is that NATURAL LAW theory can provide an appealing grounding for liberal politics and social norms.

A. *Liberal Politics and* NATURAL LAW

There are several ways in which the version of NATURAL LAW theory I defend can be seen as helping to support a radical liberal political vision.[51]

(*i*) Orthodox NATURAL LAW theory can welcome as appropriate in its own terms a diverse array of good lives. There are many different goods people can embody in their lives, and many ways in which the commitments that (to one degree or another) organize people's lives can be structured. The requirements of practical reasonableness leave open many different options for her to pursue. There are innumerable goods, and innumerable ways in which lives in which those goods are realized can be configured. Thus, our "[b]asic commitments shape our response to, our participation in, basic values—in the form of choices of career, of marriage, of forms of education, of preference for wealth as against leisure or liturgy . . . ."[52] While only some ends are worth realizing or pursuing, as aspects of one's own well-being or others, the range of such ends is very broad indeed. Not all preferences are equally valuable, but many different preferences are, indeed, preferences for genuinely valuable goods. (Indeed, recognizing, as NATURAL LAW theory does, that the various goods we seek to realize are incommensurable actually increases the range of reasonable choices, since it undermines both utilitarian and other sorts of rational-choice constraints on reasonable action at the political and personal levels.)

50 *See* ROBERT P. GEORGE, MAKING MEN MORAL: CIVIL LIBERTIES AND PUBLIC MORALITY (1993); FINNIS, AQUINAS, *supra* note 4, at 228 (noting that Aquinas's "position is not readily distinguishable from the 'good simple principle' . . . of John Stuart Mill's *On Liberty*").

51 I don't claim here to speak for other proponents of radical versions of liberalism: I'm talking throughout about my own preferred versions of liberalism and of NATURAL LAW theory. Apropos of the latter: though I don't quote it, this Section is effectively an extended dialogue with John Finnis, *Limited Government*, *in* 3 COLLECTED PAPERS: HUMAN RIGHTS AND COMMON GOOD 83 (2011). I would hardly expect my programmatic outline of a complex and controversial position to change Finnis's mind; I thank him, though, for the stimulus his discussion has offered.

52 FINNIS, ETHICS, *supra* note 4, at 91.

(*ii*) The range of good lives is broader, I think, than orthodox NATURAL LAW theorists might be inclined to suppose. In part, this is because we have good reason to recognize a broader range of goods than those acknowledged by most NATURAL LAW theorists. If sensory pleasure is a genuine good, for instance, then it can be reasonable to engage in nonprocreative sex precisely in order to experience pleasure. And this means, in turn, that a key objection to varieties of lives featuring pleasure-oriented nonprocreative sex is off the table.[53]

(*iii*) In turn, the range of practical requirements is somewhat narrower than the ones typically preferred by orthodox NATURAL LAW theorists. My approach affirms a pared-down set of practical principles, thus reducing the normative constraints on personal creativity. Thus, for instance, there is reason to make commitments, and, having made them, to keep them, but one need not seek to plan one's life in any comprehensive way, as some NATURAL LAW theorists may suppose.

(*iv*) If practical reasonableness is important, so, therefore, is the capacity to choose. Freedom is prerequisite to virtue.[54] Forcible interference with people's attempts to shape their own lives as such will certainly be inconsistent with the recognition that practical reasonableness is a genuine good. (As I'll note subsequently, nonviolent social pressure undertaken precisely to constrain others' exercise of practical reasonableness with respect to the shapes of their own lives will often be ruled out as well.)

(*v*) By acknowledging a broad range of factors that constrain reasonable property rules,[55] and by (as I note below) challenging the legitimacy of states, and so of state definition of these rules, liberal NATURAL LAW theory offers solid grounding for robust property rights that are, in important respects, pre-political. Such rights serve as, among other things, limits on interference with lifestyle choices on paternalistic or other sorts of moralistic grounds. Thus, at the political level, in particular, the approach I seek to expound helps to secure the space needed for individual experiments in living.

(*vi*) The version of NATURAL LAW theory I advance limits what may reasonably *count* as a legally cognizable injury, and thus what may justify forcible interference with someone's free disposition of her own life.[56] On this view, *physical force* is special—risky and potentially objectionable for a wide range of reasons, and thus in need of very robust justification. A reasonable bright-line rule limits the legitimate use of force against someone's body or justly acquired possessions to those cases in which force is required to end or remedy the target's

53 Thanks to David Gordon for insights on this point.

54 *See* Albert Jay Nock, *On Doing the Right Thing, in* ON DOING THE RIGHT THING AND OTHER ESSAYS 161, 173–74 (1928). Thanks to Sheldon Richman for calling this essay and its implications to my attention.

55 *See* GARY CHARTIER, ANARCHY AND LEGAL ORDER: LAW AND POLITICS FOR A STATELESS SOCIETY 49–153 (2013); CHARTIER, EXPRESSION, *supra* note 35, at 14–20.

56 *See* CHARTIER, EXPRESSION, *supra* note 35, at 23–27.

unjust use, precisely, of physical force (or to respond to her implicit or explicit threat to make imminent unjust use of such force). This bright-line rule substantially constrains what the law may justly do, and thus leaves considerable space for self-creative personal activity. To be clear: My view is *not* that the only immoral conduct is conduct involving the (mis)use of physical force. It is, rather, that force may only be used to deal with *this particular kind* of immoral conduct. By contrast, if retribution were appropriate, a broader range of (actual or putative) wrongs might reasonably be met with force.[57]

(*vii*) On the radical liberal NATURAL LAW view, *compensation* for injuries caused by an unjust use of force will qualify as a just response to such a use. Retribution and deterrence will not. If there is reason to reject retributive punishment in particular, another justification for forcible interference with putatively immoral conduct disappears.

(*viii*) Radical liberalism continues the liberal project of increasing inclusion by treating at least some nonhuman animals as morally considerable.[58]

(*ix*) Radical liberalism denies that the state enjoys legitimate authority. It thus eliminates an institutional platform for illiberal interference with personal exploration.[59] The state is illegitimate, dangerous, and unnecessary. (*a*) It is illegitimate because there is a strong presumption in favor of the following requirement: except when used to defend against, restrain, or provide restitution for the prior unjust use of physical force, physical force may not be used against someone's body or possessions without her consent and because; and, more broadly, authority may not be exercised over someone without her consent. Most use of force by states—and force is nothing if not the state's métier—is nonconsensual and thus presumptively wrong; the same is true of state action generally. Ruling out its use of force effectively rules out the state's existence and operation. (And this is so even if the presumption against nonconsensual force is not only defeasible but on some occasions rightly defeated.[60]) (*b*) The state is dangerous because it is violent, it makes

57 Of course, someone who accepts retributive punishment might think that it should be confined to responses to wrong use of force. Retributivism need not be wedded to an expansive view of state power. But denying legitimacy to retribution does rule out one important justification for the exercise of such power. Thanks to David Gordon for insights on this point.

58 *See* CHARTIER, ANARCHY, *supra* note 55, at 93–108.

59 *See id.* at 157–241.

60 It is never reasonable to violate the Principle of Respect. So, for instance, it's never reasonable to torture (given that torture is, by definition, purposeful or instrumental attack on bodily well-being, mental well-being, and, if this is taken to be a separate good, peace of mind). Nonconsensual purposeful or instrumental attacks on people's bodies are always wrong (as are many consensual ones, though these should not be precluded by law). But in many cases the requirement of consent will flow from the Principle of Fairness. And the Principle of Fairness does not require us to make suicide pacts. The presumption against violating consent is defeasible. Given, however, that it is unreasonable to create and maintain state institutions, there will not normally be in place any institution capable of violating the consent requirement if people have acted reasonably in the first place. *Cf.* CHARTIER, ANARCHY, *supra* note 55, at 160–65.

war, and it consistently restricts freedom while serving the interests of the wealthy and well connected. While the traditional state was obviously oppressive and exploitative, a vehicle for the exercise of monarchical power, the modern state is often legitimated as a benign product of collective choice. But collective choice is a rhetorical fiction, masking the oppressive activities of state actors. (*c*) The state is unnecessary because social order can be achieved in its absence. The notion that the state is unnecessary receives substantial support from the other strand of natural law thinking that underlies my work, the spontaneous order tradition. The capacity of societies to organize themselves from the bottom up, from the grass roots, is a key reason to doubt the necessity of the state.[61] But even if one judges that the state is finally inescapable, the spontaneous order tradition emphasizes the limited value of state regimentation of society and, indeed, of the inherent limits on the state's ability to impose on society an order superior to that created through voluntary cooperation.[62]

(*x*) A related point: The need to ensure that *retribution* is carried out in accordance with public standards and clearly defined procedures in light of properly obtained and interpreted evidence has been advanced as a justification for the existence and operation of the state.[63] It's not clear that this is correct: non-state institutions could carry out retribution in the specified way. But the denial that retribution could be legitimate in the first place removes another putative justification for the state from the table.

(*xi*) Radical liberalism offers an account of the common good that differs significantly from the one advanced by orthodox NATURAL LAW theory.[64] Alive to the reality of diverse human characteristics and commitments, it *affirms* that there are multiple, overlapping communities to which people belong, each of which may embrace goods common to its members. It also affirms that most or all of us need support in our various efforts to pursue and realize various goods for ourselves and the people in our lives. Radical liberalism *denies*, by contrast, that there is or needs to be any single, all-inclusive community to which all people, or all people in a given geographic area, belong. It thus denies that any group to which people belong for the purpose of resolving disputes or protecting people against violence needs to be comprehensive, to concern itself with anything other than these particular tasks. It denies that

61 *See, e.g.*, PETER T. LEESON, ANARCHY UNBOUND: WHY SELF-GOVERNANCE WORKS BETTER THAN YOU THINK (2014); ANARCHY, STATE, AND PUBLIC CHOICE (Edward P. Stringham ed., 2005); EDWARD P. STRINGHAM, PRIVATE GOVERNANCE: CREATING ORDER IN ECONOMIC AND SOCIAL LIFE (2015); MICHAEL TAYLOR, COMMUNITY, ANARCHY, AND LIBERTY (1984).

62 *See* Friedrich A. Hayek, *The Use of Knowledge in Society*, 35 AM. ECON. REV. 519 (1945); Ludwig von Mises, *Economic Calculation in the Socialist Commonwealth*, *in* COLLECTIVIST ECONOMIC PLANNING 87 (F. A. Hayek ed., 1935).

63 *Cf.* FINNIS, AQUINAS, *supra* note 4, at 239–52.

64 *See* FINNIS, *Government*, *supra* note 51, at 83–94; *cf.* FINNIS, AQUINAS, *supra* note 4, at 234–45.

such an association needs to be the primary facilitator or encourager, or a facilitator or encourager at all, of institutions promoting virtue. And it rejects the idea that any protective or dispute resolution association needs to be a *community* at all rather than an arm's-length association, or that such an association should be a territorial monopolist like the modern state. The members of a protective association do, of course, share a common good: the good that is the framework of rights protected by the association, rights that provide the space within which diversity can thrive and individuality be expressed. But there is no need for them to share any *other* sort of common good (though of course in a particular case they might, if, for instance, the protective association is coextensive with an institution with a broader goal—say, a religious community). The point is not that people don't need communities that embrace and support important aspects of their lives; it is simply that such communities need not be comprehensive and that no community need be coextensive with any association charged with keeping the peace.

(*xii*) My preferred account of NATURAL LAW theory supports cosmopolitanism. The Principle of Fairness points to a basic equality among persons—equality in social status, moral worth, and political authority. Acknowledging this equality, while discerning the fundamentally arbitrary character of national boundaries and recognizing the mischievous uses to which they are consistently put, gives us good reason to be doubtful about anything like national loyalty. We can reasonably acknowledge ties with those with whom we enjoy actual, meaningfully interactional relationships of various kinds, ties that can plausibly be regarded as aspects of the basic good of *friendship*. Our ties to small-scale communities in which we actually engage and interact in meaningful ways, communities both geographic and virtual, may well qualify some relationships within these communities, while less than intimate, as *friendships*, broadly speaking, and thus as worthy of special moral standing. But relationships based on nothing more than distantly shared ancestry or subjection to the same political authorities are hardly instances of friendship even in a very attenuated sense.[65] Once we see that states' claims to authority are indefensible, these relationships will seem largely arbitrary, lacking any deep claim on us. There is thus little or no reason, without some further justification, to treat nurturing or preserving *these* relationships, or furthering the interests of those with whom they unite us, as justifying any sort of special status in our moral deliberation for fellow nationals. There will be various sorts of reasons for taking them specially into account, no doubt, but they don't enjoy any special moral claim on us simply because of birth or political status.

65 *Cf.* CHARTIER, ANARCHY, *supra* note 55, at 28–29 n. 43 (responding to an observation on this point by Sandy Thatcher).

Radical liberalism certainly might be defended on other grounds, but the version I advance here is self-consciously rooted in NATURAL LAW theory. It seeks to limit the degree to which force can be used to impose any vision of the good on anyone. But it does not seek to do so on purportedly neutral grounds. Rather, precisely on the basis of an attractive understanding of flourishing, it seeks to constrain the use of force (and, secondarily, certain kinds of social pressure) to promote flourishing. It gives pride of place to individual diversity and creativity and institutional pluralism because these are aspects of or means to or preconditions of acknowledged, substantive goods. And the restraints it places on the use of force against people's bodies and justly acquired property also flow from its understanding of flourishing.

B. Grounding Social Liberalism

There really are people who think, or talk as if they think, that, as long as conduct should be *legal*, it must also be *moral*. The view that this is so is silly on its face. Any plausible account of what should be legal will make sense in light of a rich understanding of the good life quite outside the sphere of law and politics, so there will always be more to say about what's good apart from what makes for good law. I have sought to articulate a conception of liberalism in light of such a rich understanding. So I completely reject any sort of minimalism about ethics.

But I also want to reject an illiberal moralism. The liberal position I've sought to articulate is first of all political, concerned with limits on the use of force. But it is also social: it values a rich diversity of individual lives, relationships, associations, ways of being, and it is committed not only to limits on forceful interference with human diversity but also to constraints on the use of social pressure to do so.

We can often see that people are capable of flourishing, of finding genuine fulfillment, even when their lives are quite different from our own. In this case, we can embrace their differences from us as genuinely good. But sometimes, of course, we aren't sure. Sometimes, we may wonder if their choices are foolish or self-destructive or injurious to others. And sometimes, obviously, their choices may be all three. Affirming the value of freedom and diversity is a far cry from embracing relativism or subjectivism. Objectively speaking, there are many ways in which people's lives can go well, and many in which they can't. Not every option is a good option. But the reality of human fallibility and ignorance is such that we can rarely be confident regarding our own judgments about how other individuals ought to live their lives. That's true even if we assume, arguendo, that we are right about the various aspects of well-being and so the contours of practical reasonableness (as of course we may not be). For, among other things, we won't necessarily know about the various relevant features of other people's lives or their circumstances, and we will therefore be prone to making mistakes about how to apply the relevant requirements.

Our difficulty in doing so will be a function of a broad range of intellectual and moral limits. Our penchant for self-deception will be especially significant. So, too, will be the insecurity that prompts us to seek confirmation for our own life choices in the choices of others. We want to believe we have chosen well, and so we want to believe that others will acknowledge the merits of the putative goods we have selected, and thus validate our choices. We are thus tempted to ignore or dismiss choices different from our own, even when they seem to lead to or to constitute flourishing lives, and even, often enough, to conceal alternate choices from ourselves, perhaps by eradicating from our social worlds those who make them. Given this sort of temptation, it seems especially crucial that we actively practice the discipline of being open to human diversity.

The rejection of illiberal moralism should lead us to be concerned on several fronts with the use of social pressure to push people to alter nonviolent behavior we regard as unreasonable.[66] The deployment of this kind of pressure seems hard to square with the Principle of Recognition, the Principle of Fairness, and the Principle of Respect. Deploying it is often unreasonable because moralistic or punitive. To the extent that we would be unwilling to accept a rule or norm allowing us to be pushed around ourselves, we act unreasonably when we push others around. We too readily suppose that we know what others' flourishing is likely to involve. We have reason to value the development of people's ability to reason practically, which is undermined by inhibiting social pressure. We act unreasonably when we deprive others of access to the information provided by the public display of alternate ways of being. And the use of rejecting social pressure can be deeply wounding.

(*i*) Defensive shunning—avoiding interactions with those likely to hurt one—makes perfect sense (though the Principle of Fairness and the Principle of Commitment might preclude some instances even of defensive shunning). The same is true of defensive boycotting—declining to engage in transactions with dishonest vendors in order to avoid being cheated, for instance. By contrast, it is unreasonable to shun or boycott as an expression of the conviction that somehow associating or transacting with bad people is itself intrinsically bad, a source of impurity. *Impurity, defilement, isn't real.* We can

66 As I have observed the use of shaming and shunning as devices for behavioral control in the years since I last discussed the topic in print, I have come to the conclusion that the enthusiasm for these means of nonviolent social pressure I expressed in *Anarchy and Legal Order* was excessive. For those earlier remarks, *see* CHARTIER, ANARCHY, *supra* note 55, at 325–27. It makes sense to limit the use of force to cases in which it's needed to defend against others' unjust use of force. And it makes sense to apply a similar principle in the case of nonviolent action. We reasonably avoid others who might want to engage with us *not* to punish or manipulate them but, instead, when we need to do so to avoid something bad, whether being bored or being verbally abused. Others are not *unclean*, inherently worth shunning, whatever they've done. We should assail others verbally, not to punish or upset them but, instead, to stop them from effecting nonviolent injuries or to prompt them to remedy such injuries when they've caused them. A conversation with Zachary Woodman helped me to think through this issue more fully.

become physically dirty, but we don't become metaphysically dirty. Nothing renders us in need of metaphysical purification. So acting on the basis of concern with purity is unreasonable as a general matter—arguably inconsistent with the Principle of Recognition, since it involves the pursuit of unreal goods. We aren't rendered impure by contact with other people, and this means that shunning, in particular, on the basis of concern with purity is unreasonable.

Similarly, associating with other people doesn't mean that we endorse anything they've done or said unless we *say* it does using words or unambiguous symbols. Of course there are gray areas: I might signal support for someone's behavior in an ambiguous way that allows me subsequently to deny that I was seeking to convey approval of her actions. But simply interacting with someone, even interacting supportively as a romantic partner, friend, or business associate, does not inherently constitute endorsement of any of her choices apart from the choice to interact. There's no need to shun anyone as a way of not endorsing her behavior. (People do sometimes read association as endorsement. But reading association as endorsement is generally quite unwarranted, and the practice of doing so deserves no encouragement. There should be no "misinterpreter's veto" on personal or professional interactions.)

(*ii*) Punitive shunning designed to injure some basic aspect of another's well-being (friendship, say) is always inconsistent with the Principle of Respect. And punitive shunning designed to injure some aspect of well-being (financial well-being, say) that's only instrumentally valuable *for the purpose* of indirectly injuring some aspect of well-being is also problematic. Punitive shunning designed to injure some instrumentally valuable good is problematic as an expression of hostility—an attitude we have good reason not to nurture.

(*iii*) We typically don't like to be pushed around. We don't like to be subjected to social pressure. When, as will often be the case, we would be unwilling to endorse a norm or rule that permitted us to be pushed around or subjected to social pressure, we act unreasonably, per the Principle of Fairness, when we seek to push others around by subjecting *them* to social pressure through shunning, shaming, or censure. (To be clear, expressing disagreement is a valuable source of insight. Disagreement and censure aren't identical, and one can quite reasonably—and, indeed, helpfully—disagree without rejecting or shaming.)

(*iv*) This is certainly true when we attempt to make others conform to our own preferences as an expression of dominance—or as a way of avoiding the experience of being unsettled by being confronted with challenges to our preferred ways of doing things. But it is also true when we apply pressure paternalistically. The paternalistic exertion of social pressure through shaming, shunning, or censure, designed to push other people to act in what we take to be their own best interests, is indefensible for multiple reasons quite apart from the unfairness that obtains in the case of pushing people around generally. In particular, it seems likely in many cases to be unreasonable because the person exerting the pressure unreasonably takes her- or himself to know more than she or he does. The person exerting the pressure may well not know enough about the relevant social or moral realities and may not be sufficiently aware of the circumstances of the person to whose behavior she or he objects.

(*v*) Suppressing particular nonviolent patterns of behavior using social pressure—rather than intellectual or emotional persuasion or arm's-length commercial inducement—can inhibit people's development of the capacity to exhibit practical reasonableness.

(*vi*) The use of social pressure to encourage conformity may sometimes stifle the behavioral exploration of alternate ways of flourishing. Human beings have different histories, different physical constitutions, different psyches, different capacities, different commitments. Because they do, there are many different ways in which their lives can go well. Attempting to standardize people's ways of being, to eliminate this diversity, would be to disregard, perhaps even to seek to suppress, the reality that flourishing and fulfillment take many forms. The suppression of diversity is problematic not only because it may keep people from making choices suitably reflective of their own circumstances, preferences, and commitments but also because putting alternative ways of being on display can be beneficial to others. Displays of various behavioral options can help observers assess the merits of those options and decide whether to emulate them, thus facilitating their participation in the goods of knowledge and practical reasonableness. They can also offer observers other goods, including aesthetic experience.

(*vii*) Even where we can be confident that people are making bad choices, shunning or otherwise rejecting them as individuals is likely to be extraordinarily unhelpful—to be deeply wounding and alienating and inconsistent with the demands of loyalty and compassion (which flow from the requirements of practical reasonableness).

Thaddeus Russell's superb *A Renegade History of the United States* tells a story of cultural and institutional change to which ongoing tension between the censorious and the free-spirited—including the frivolous, the drunkards, the sexually experimental—is essential.[67] Russell does not suggest that everyone should be a renegade. But he does maintain—plausibly, on my view—that human freedom and well-being are persistently expanded when those who reject established norms and sober virtues (and not only the cultural avant-garde) press their claims against what they experience as the stultifying demands of the majority. Russell points, effectively, to an ecology of positive social change in which the task of pushing the envelope plays an inescapably important role. There's certainly a role in Russell's ecology for actively

67 *See* Thaddeus Russell, A Renegade History of the United States (2010).

fostering the well-being of others, including the kind of well-being involved in the embrace of good character traits. But the use of shaming and shunning to do so might undermine the ability of that ecology effectively to yield ongoing social innovation.

No doubt we should encourage people to avoid purposefully or instrumentally attacking their own well-being or that of others, neglecting their responsibilities to others, or disregarding their commitments. But this is frequently *not* what people are doing when we instinctively disapprove of their choices; they are often simply acting out priorities that we happen not to share. And that they are not gives us no reason to regard their choices as unreasonable and so to press them to make alternative choices. This is not because all options are equally good, but because the range of good options is very broad, and certainly might include possibilities that some of us might be too quick to view as frivolous or harmful.

C. *Liberalism and the Left*

If the defining commitments of the political left are to the rejection of *exclusion*, *subordination*, *deprivation*, *militarism*, and *imperialism*,[68] then natural law liberalism qualifies as a position on the left.[69]

(*i*) The Principle of Fairness grounds a rejection of arbitrary exclusion and subordination in personal relations and voluntary institutions as also in the legal and political realm.

(*ii*) Robust protections for individual rights—rooted in the Principle of Fairness and the Principle of Respect—rule out the forcible imposition of exclusionary and subordinative norms, as also of rules that sustain cartels and make and keep people poor.[70]

(*iii*) Market order imposes persistent costs on those who engage in arbitrary exclusion.[71]

(*iv*) The Principle of Fairness grounds property rules and rules of market interaction that rule out the privileges responsible for structural poverty while reducing the likelihood of accidental deprivation by increasing overall prosperity

68 *Cf.* CHARTIER, ANARCHY, *supra* note 55, at 378–86. I don't discuss imperialism explicitly in this context, though what I say about war is obviously relevant to empire building. I say a bit more about the demerits of empire in Chapter 8, *infra*.

69 Whether they do or not is, of course, an interesting and open question. One justification for the putative induction from leftist rhetoric and practice offered here might be that these were the defining commitments of the most vibrant leftist movement of recent decades, the New Left of the 1960s and early 1970s. For a compelling depiction of this movement by an early president of the preeminent New Left organization, Students for a Democratic Society, *see* CARL OGLESBY, RAVENS IN THE STORM: A PERSONAL HISTORY OF THE 1960S ANTIWAR MOVEMENT (2008).

70 *See, e.g.*, MARKETS NOT CAPITALISM, *supra* note 37.

71 *Cf.* GARY BECKER, THE ECONOMICS OF DISCRIMINATION (2d ed., 1957).

and making available resources that enable effective responses to deprivation when it occurs.

(*v*) The Principle of Respect and the Principle of Fairness can be understood as weighing strongly against the legitimacy of the state, and so against state-made wars and tax-funded armies and military-industrial complexes (the military-industrial complex is, of course, a creature of tax funding). In any case, they underlie a variety of norms that protect noncombatant immunity, count against the legitimacy of the national security state and of aggressive and pre-emptive war, and ground resistance to colonialism and neocolonial interventions.[72]

VII. THE PLAN OF THE BOOK

In this book, I seek to explore a range of issues through the lens of NATURAL LAW liberalism. In so doing, I hope simultaneously to offer insight into these issues and to illuminate the features of what I take to be an appealing approach to ethics, law, and politics. I begin by illustrating NATURAL LAW theory's implications for questions in personal ethics, before turning to the legal system and then to the political order. The themes of liberalism, radicalism, flourishing, and natural law play out in various ways throughout the book.

One distinctively liberal—but perhaps from many people's perspectives still radical—feature of my approach to NATURAL LAW theory is its support for care and respect for nonhuman animals. In Chapter 1, I apply NATURAL LAW theory's careful and precise understanding of boycotts to an issue directly related to the moral status of animals: I seek to understand what kinds of choices are appropriate with respect to the boycott of the meat industry proposed by vegetarians, vegans, and others.

Liberals rightly value truth and truthfulness. But natural law theories frequently treat *any* choice to lies as an attack on flourishing, and this seemingly extreme position might seem to make natural law theory a poor fit with liberalism. While agreeing that there are good reasons to object to lying, I suggest in Chapter 2 that an attractive reading of NATURAL LAW theory might allow for the moral acceptability of a limited range of lies.

Natural law theory's opposition to lying and its conception of the various goods that are the objects of our choices as incommensurable have implications for our thinking about the undertheorized practice of assigning grades to students. This practice is one to which liberals, concerned with fairness and merit, should perhaps pay more attention. In light of concerns related to truth and incommensurability, there is, I suggest, good reason to reject a number of conventional grading techniques and approaches, putatively warranted by what I call "academic

[72] *See* Chapter 8, *infra*.

consequentialism" and "academic retributivism." I explore my liberal understanding of grading in Chapter 3.

A lack of regard for truth is a feature not only of problematic grading practices but also of aggressive advocacy as some people understand it. Liberals favor adversarial advocacy, in the courtroom and elsewhere. And a NATURAL LAW concern with fairness prompts us to see adversarial practices as frequently valuable. But while the practice of aggressive advocacy by attorneys might yield positive results, attorneys themselves might still sometimes act unreasonably in engaging adversarially. The same may be true of professional adversaries of other sorts. In Chapter 4, evaluating one positive proposal regarding adversaries' ethics, I seek to show how NATURAL LAW theory might help to clarify the moral status of some adversarial practices.

Issues related to truthful communication arise in more than one context related to legal practice. The liberal NATURAL LAW approach entails *both* regard for a lawyer's own protected, private sphere *and* regard for a client's informational privacy. In Chapter 5, I consider the tension between these two kinds of privacy.

Radical liberalism and NATURAL LAW theory ground a vigorous critique of the carceral state and of imprisonment in anything like its current form. But a NATURAL LAW analysis can also serve as the basis of a negative assessment of current practices that does not depend on embracing this critique. In Chapter 6, I seek to show why plausible theories of statist criminal justice, even if taken to justify not only imprisonment but also the use of victim testimony to help determine prisoners' initial terms of confinement, likely do not warrant the use of this kind of testimony in assessing parole requests.

While it provides support not only for prison abolitionism but also for anarchism, the liberal and cosmopolitan version of NATURAL LAW theory I defend need not deny that people will sometimes in fact opt to welcome ties with each other rooted in history and heritage. And of course it can offer insights not only in relation to an envisioned stateless society but also in the context of contemporary statist politics. But liberalism and NATURAL LAW theory rightly prompt skepticism regarding affirmations of national identity. I suggest in Chapter 7 that the putative liberal Richard Rorty's attempt to articulate a liberal American patriotism provides a useful case study—and proves ultimately unsuccessful.

While it opposes states and state action, radical liberal NATURAL LAW theory also provides vigorous support for any existing state's adoption of an anti-militarist, anti-imperialist foreign policy. Anti-interventionism and anti-imperialism have been persistently, if not universally, valued in the liberal tradition. In Chapter 8, I bring a NATURAL LAW perspective critically to bear on an alternative liberal view, an attempt to defend a chastened militarism as a liberal option.

Radical liberalism is anarchistic. And there are positive reasons to embrace anarchism from a NATURAL LAW perspective. But the radical liberal must also grapple with criticisms of anarchism, including ones from within the natural law tradition itself. In Chapter 9, I explain why I believe several related criticisms of anarchism are unsuccessful.

In the Conclusion, I seek to clarify some of the ways in which the treatments of multiple issues in this book might illustrate my own version of radical liberalism, grounded in NATURAL LAW theory. I note the significance throughout of liberalism, radicalism, and flourishing. And I underscore some insights offered by the individual case studies I've considered.

While the book's chapters are clustered—with the first three concerned especially with personal ethics, the second three with legal practice and the legal system, and the final three with politics—the issues and approaches I examine are relevant to each other in multiple ways. Lying disrupts personal relationships and manipulates individuals, but it is also a kind of presumptive wrongdoing in which state actors, in particular, persistently engage, especially when promoting, overseeing, and defending wars and engaging in empire building. Nationalism exemplifies the dubious us-versus-them mentality that treats members of the out-group as of lesser value, but a similar kind of collectivism is evident in the denial of moral standing to nonhuman animals in relation to human ones. And so forth.

Radical NATURAL LAW liberalism represents an appealing development of the liberal tradition, with the capacity to integrate concerns evident in both classical and modern strands of that tradition. I hope this book will helpfully highlight ways in which this kind of liberalism—expressed in moral, legal, and political contexts—can effectively encourage the emergence of genuinely flourishing lives.

1

Boycotts

I. THINKING LIBERALLY ABOUT THE MEAT INDUSTRY

Liberals value markets.[1] Markets offer us unique opportunities to flourish in unparalleled ways. The values and institutions that make efficient market interactions possible have yielded unbelievable benefits for people throughout the contemporary world, especially when compared with people who lived before the beginning of "the Great Enrichment,"[2] beginning in around 1800.

Markets offer us effective means of realizing particular aspects of well-being *we* seek. But some market participants act, or threaten that they will act, wrongly in producing the goods and services they offer us. And, when they do, we may sometimes have reason to *boycott* them. Consumers might choose to boycott particular firms or industries for multiple reasons: to protest bad behavior, to avoid responsibility for bad behavior, or to avoid consistent bad treatment.

Natural law theory offers a supple, flexible approach to thinking about the morality of boycotts. I want to illustrate this approach by considering some issues related to proposed boycotts of industries that offer meat and nonhuman animal by-products for human consumption.[3] (I'll refer collectively to these industries in what follows as the "meat industry.") The considerations I adduce here are relevant to proposed boycotts of other *animal* industries (say, those that engage in the harmful testing of potential medicines and other products on animals)[4] and to proposed boycotts of other industries unrelated to animals. But I'll explore the issue of boycotts by focusing in some detail on the merits of particular aspects of a potential boycott of

[1] *Cf.* Robert Sugden, A Community of Advantage: A Behavioural Economist's Defence of the Market (2018); Arnold Kling, Specialization and Trade (2016).

[2] *See, e.g.*, Deirdre N. McCloskey, *The Great Enrichment Was Built on Ideas, Not Capital*, FEE, Nov. 22, 2017, https://fee.org/articles/the-great-enrichment-was-built-on-ideas-not-capital/.

[3] Unless context indicates otherwise, when I refer to "meat" I have in mind flesh taken from previously living, conscious creatures (including flying creatures, land creatures, and sea creatures) killed so that their tissues can be eaten. I will not ordinarily use "meat" without qualification to refer to lab-grown meat, the consumption of which doesn't pose the same sorts of issues as the consumption of flesh taken from once-living sentients.

[4] Here and throughout, by "animals" I will mean *nonhuman animals*, unless the context suggests otherwise.

a specific industry. I hope that doing so will help to clarify the kind of reasoning that might be appropriately involved in comparable cases—in particular, ones involving the choices facing participants in large, impersonal markets.

The version of NATURAL LAW theory I defend here, which places well-being, welfare, flourishing, fulfillment on center stage, isn't moralistic or rigoristic: it doesn't treat interpersonal morality as an end in itself, but rather as an aspect of fulfillment, of flourishing. The same, I have emphasized, is true of liberalism: it's about living well. And it values and seeks to nourish and protect autonomy and ordinary life.[5]

The fact that a position seems moralistic does not, of course, show that it's false. The rejection of slavery, for instance, might have been dismissed by some people in earlier generations as a challenge to a practice that had been widely accepted for millennia and that appeared to be an unquestioned part of ordinary life. Slavery's currency obviously didn't make it right. But liberalism does, as I say, prize ordinary life and personal autonomy. Liberals will rightly acknowledge that ordinary life may sometimes need to change, that personal autonomy can be exercised unreasonably. Nonetheless, liberalism will find the fact that a position seeks to upend ordinary life or constrain autonomy a reason, not to argue that it must be false, but rather to ask whether there might be defensible alternatives.

Of course, liberalism has also stressed the importance of being open to *extending* moral consideration when argument and insight require doing so, and this may sometimes mean the recognition of new responsibilities—including responsibilities that do constrain autonomy or alter ordinary patterns of living. These might—I would say, should—include responsibilities to nonhuman animals, which raise important questions about food.

Choices related to food implicate a variety of aspects of flourishing. For the individual consumer, of course, eating is a source of sensory pleasure, aesthetic experience (as she perceives the ways in which different flavors and textures are woven together),[6] and bodily well-being. Perhaps in some cases it will also involve opportunities for play, as when food is integrated into social or erotic games, and for the development of knowledge and practical reasonableness. Shared meals can also serve as occasions for the solidification of friendship and for religious rituals. And particular dietary choices can in various ways help to constitute our identities. The production and distribution of food can be an exercise in skillful performance, and it can foster knowledge by making various sorts of discoveries possible. The resources provided directly and indirectly to producers and distributors of food by its purchasers can enable them to flourish in a variety of ways. But these positive *contributions* to fulfillment made by the consumption, distribution, and production of food are matched in some cases by serious *injuries* to well-being. At the same time, some

5 On the valuation of ordinary life, *see* CHARLES TAYLOR, SOURCES OF THE SELF: THE MAKING OF THE MODERN IDENTITY (1989).

6 *Cf.* MARK C. MURPHY, NATURAL LAW AND PRACTICAL RATIONALITY 109–11 (1999).

foods are produced in ways that are deeply injurious to the flourishing of nonhuman animals—attacking, in their cases, the goods of life and bodily well-being, friendship, and play, among others. And this means that choices related to the use of animal flesh – in particular, for food—matter morally for multiple reasons.

I believe the following proposition (AVOID) is correct: *People have decisive reasons,*[7] *at least under ordinary circumstances,*[8] *to avoid killing nonhuman animals (or, at minimum, some large subset of this class) for the purpose of eating their flesh,*[9] *and to avoid torturing or otherwise purposefully injuring them under any circumstances.*[10]

Reasonable people may certainly reject AVOID, but my concern here is not with their arguments. My interest, rather, is in what AVOID might entail. Consider a related claim, DECLINE: *One should ordinarily decline to purchase meat.*[11] While

7 In essence, I think the case for AVOID is that the animals we most often kill for food are similar enough to humans in their capacity to feel, act, and form bonds of affection that plausible reasons for not harming humans will generally be reasons for not harming them, either, and that all positive arguments against AVOID with which I am familiar fail. *See, e.g.*, GARY CHARTIER, ANARCHY AND LEGAL ORDER: LAW AND POLITICS FOR A STATELESS SOCIETY 93–108 (2013); Gary Chartier, *Aligning Natural and Positive Law: The Case of Non-Human Sentients, in* ANIMALS: NEW ESSAYS 355 (Andreas Blank ed., 2016); STEPHEN R. L. CLARK, THE MORAL STATUS OF ANIMALS (1977; 2d ed. 1984); PETER SINGER, ANIMAL LIBERATION: A NEW ETHICS FOR OUR TREATMENT OF ANIMALS (2d ed., 2002); PETER SINGER, PRACTICAL ETHICS 55–65 (2d ed., 1993); TOM REGAN, THE CASE FOR ANIMAL RIGHTS (1983); MARK ROWLANDS, ANIMALS LIKE US (2003); DANIEL A. DOMBROWSKI, HARTSHORNE AND THE METAPHYSICS OF ANIMAL RIGHTS (1988); JOHN L. HILL, THE CASE FOR VEGETARIANISM: PHILOSOPHY FOR A SMALL PLANET (1996); STEVE F. SAPONTZIS, MORALS, REASONS, AND ANIMALS (1987); STEPHEN R. L. CLARK, ANIMALS AND THEIR MORAL STANDING (1998); EVELYN PLUHAR, BEYOND PREJUDICE: THE MORAL SIGNIFICANCE OF HUMAN AND NONHUMAN ANIMALS (1995); Cora Diamond, *Eating Meat and Eating People*, 53 PHIL 465 (198). *But cf.* R. M. Hare, *Why I Am Only a Demi-Vegetarian, in* ESSAYS ON BIOETHICS 219–35 (1993); Gary Varner, *A Harean Perspective on Humane Sustainable Agriculture, in* PERSONHOOD, ETHICS, AND ANIMAL COGNITION 235 (2012); KATHRYN PAXTON GEORGE, ANIMAL, VEGETABLE, OR WOMAN? A FEMINIST CRITIQUE OF ETHICAL VEGETARIANISM (2000).

I suggest elsewhere that AVOID may reasonably be understood as grounding legal protection for nonhuman animals' interests. *See* CHARTIER, ANARCHY, *supra* note 7, at 315–18. On the basis of regard for animals' well-being, other legal scholars, including Cass Sunstein, Steven Wise, and Gary Francione, have argued for substantial legal protections for nonhumans. *See, e.g.*, Cass R. Sunstein, *The Rights of Animals*, 70 CHI. L. REV. 387 (2003); STEVEN M. WISE, RATTLING THE CAGE: TOWARD LEGAL RIGHTS FOR ANIMALS (2000); GARY L. FRANCIONE, INTRODUCTION TO ANIMAL RIGHTS: YOUR CHILD OR THE DOG (2000); ANIMAL RIGHTS: CURRENT DEBATES AND NEW DIRECTIONS (Cass R. Sunstein & Martha C. Nussbaum eds., 2004). *Cf.* Martha C. Nussbaum, Book Review, *Animal Rights: The Need for a Theoretical Basis*, 114 HARV. L. REV. 1506 (2001). Whether nonhuman animals should enjoy legal rights is not, however, my concern here.

8 That is, those that obtain for most likely readers of this book.

9 Or for the purpose of wearing parts of their dead bodies or in the course of using them to test medical and other consumer products, but this is not my immediate concern.

10 Even if one believes that it is morally appropriate to kill animals painlessly after they have enjoyed happy lives, it is clear that the treatment of animals on factory farms, which remain responsible for the vast majority of our animal products, is exceptionally hurtful. Thus, even if AVOID is understood only to preclude substantial mistreatment, the fact that most animal products come from factory farms means that the same questions about diet addressed here are likely to be relevant.

11 As Barry L. Casey, *A Radical Case for Vegetarianism*, 11 SPECTRUM 7 (1981), may first have helped me to see a long time ago, there are diverse, interconnected reasons for being a vegetarian: financial, aesthetic, economic, and environmental concerns also help to make vegetarianism attractive.

the two are regularly linked, DECLINE does not follow by implication from AVOID.[12] Very rarely, after all, does the consumer kill an animal before eating it; rather, she purchases animal products in a market or a restaurant, or is offered them in someone's home or at a public function. There's a difference between (*i*) directly injuring or killing and (*ii*) participating in a social web in which one's actions connect one with others who injure or kill.[13] It is at least logically possible that one might have good reason not to kill or torture animals *without also* having good reason not to purchase or consume meat from unjustly killed animals.[14] And in principle, one could purchase or consume meat without any unjust harms having been caused to

[12] This is a fact to which discussions of these matters do not always attend. For instance, James Rachels, *The Basic Argument for Vegetarianism*, *in* FOOD FOR THOUGHT: THE DEBATE OVER EATING MEAT 70, 71 (Steve F. Sapontzis ed., 2004) maintains that because "our enjoyment of the way meat tastes is [not] a good enough reason to justify the amount of suffering that the animals [killed to give us meat] are made to endure," it follows that "we should stop eating the products of this business." But it is not clear why the undesirability of a social practice should, without further ado, entail our renunciation of its products. *Cf.*, *e.g.*, COLIN MCGINN, MORAL LITERACY: OR, HOW TO DO THE RIGHT THING (1992). McGinn explains very carefully and persuasively that "our treatment of other species . . . immorally benefit[s] . . . [us] at the expense of other animals," *id.* at 18–26, before asking what should be done in light of the fact that this is the case. He urges us to minimize our dependence on animals and treat their well-being as parallel with that of human animals—from which it certainly follows that we ought not to kill them for food. But he does not lay out the steps required for the move from this premise to the judgment that "[t]his will mean, just for starters, stopping eating meat if you live in one of the societies in which it is perfectly possible to find other sources of food, i.e., almost everywhere on earth." *Id.* at 26. SAPONTZIS, ANIMALS, *supra* note 7, at 200–1, recognizes that the entailment from a general premise about the well-being of animals to a conclusion about dietary choices is not straightforward, but he nonetheless does not focus in great detail on the distinction between the actions of those who mistreat and kill animals in order to render them edible and the actions of those who actually eat the animals. Similarly, in his *Editor's Introduction*, *in* FOOD, *supra*, at 9, 13, Sapontzis acknowledges that "although when we think about meat eating versus vegetarianism, what we focus on is what we put in our mouths, that's not what the ethical debate is about. . . . When the ethics of eating meat is debated, however, the focus is on what animals and people have to go through to produce meat . . . and so forth. The act of consuming meat is not the ethical issue." But we need more clarity about the relationship between "what animals and people have to go through" and "what we put in our mouths." HILL, *supra* note 7, at 40–67 argues plausibly against the social practice of killing animals for food, but says little in this context about the choices of the individual consumer. RAYMOND G. FREY, RIGHTS, KILLING, AND SUFFERING: MORAL VEGETARIANISM AND APPLIED ETHICS 28–29 (1983) does make this point clearly. My disagreement with Frey is a function of my belief, which he does not share, that animals have morally cognizable interests, and my doubts about consequentialism as a criterion of moral rightness or obligation. (One implication of Frey's use of consequentialist argument is that he is able to weigh the benefits to animals that might accrue from the elimination of the meat industry against the harms to those who work for, invest in, or consume the products of this industry. But if the treatment of animals is often—as I think it is—unjust, then it will be reasonable to think of ending this injustice as enjoying lexical priority over preventing harms that might result if unjust practices were eliminated. Further, of course, if the various goods involved are, as I think can plausibly be argued, incommensurable, the relevant consequentialist calculation will prove to be impossible.)

[13] All, or almost all, of us participate in such a web; *cf.* MICHAEL ALLEN FOX, DEEP VEGETARIANISM 169–70 (1999).

[14] *Cf.* CHRISTOPH VON FÜRER-HAIMENDORF, MORALS AND MERIT: A STUDY OF VALUES AND SOCIAL CONTROLS IN SOUTH ASIAN SOCIETIES 187 (1967) (noting the view that the butcher, but not the consumer of meat, is morally culpable). I owe this reference to Stephen Clark.

any animal as a means of making one's purchase or consumption possible.[15] So the proponent of DECLINE who believes that it follows from AVOID must construct an argumentative bridge that links the two claims. A NATURAL LAW analysis of boycotts might help to illuminate the potential for the construction of this kind of bridge.

In Part II, I suggest an approach to thinking about boycotts in light of NATURAL LAW theory. For this purpose, I'll draw on a NATURAL LAW understanding of *cooperation with others in the unwarranted infliction of injury* (COOPERATION). I'll use the proposal for a consumer boycott of the products of the meat industry to illustrate the use of NATURAL LAW thinking about COOPERATION as a way of examining moral questions about boycotts. Given that the NATURAL LAW approach to boycotts requires us to understand the likely consequences of our choices, I focus in Part III on what we have reason to believe about the market impact of meat industry boycotts. In Part IV, I consider a range of specific questions regarding participation in meat industry boycotts. I conclude in Part V.

II. WHEN MUST WE BOYCOTT?

Others sometimes unwarrantedly cause injuries. Sometimes, we interact with them in ways related to their effectuation of these injuries. In virtue of our interactions, we may sometimes reasonably be regarded as engaged in COOPERATION with them.[16] In this case, our COOPERATION may be *purposeful* or *causal*.[17] One engages in purposeful COOPERATION when one accepts the purpose of bringing about the injury as one's own. One engages in causal COOPERATION when in one way or another one's action increases the probability that the injury will occur.[18]

Purposeful COOPERATION is *always* wrong because inconsistent with the Principle of Respect.[19] *Causal* COOPERATION may or may not be reasonable. This kind of COOPERATION, "if not wrong for some other reason, is wrong if, and only if, . . . [the person cooperating] should not accept the bad side effects of contributing to" the occurrence of the injury.[20] Whether this is so will ordinarily be a function of the choice's consistency with the Principle of Fairness (though of course the other requirements of practical reasonableness may sometimes be relevant).

15 If the meat came from an animal whose death resulted from natural causes, for instance.

16 *Cf.* 1 GERMAIN GRISEZ, THE WAY OF THE LORD JESUS: CHRISTIAN MORAL PRINCIPLES 300 (1983) (elaborating ways in which one might injure).

17 *See* 3 GERMAIN GRISEZ, THE WAY OF THE LORD JESUS: DIFFICULT MORAL QUESTIONS 871–97 (1997). Grisez refers to "formal" and "material" cooperation. For alternative analyses related to the potential for cooperative responsibility, focusing on the doctrine of *novus actus interveniens*, *see* H. L. A. HART & A. M. HONORÉ, CAUSATION IN THE LAW 129 (1959) (*cited in* ALAN DONAGAN, THE THEORY OF MORALITY 44 (1977)); Michael S. Moore, *The Metaphysics of Causal Intervention*, 88 CALIF. L. REV. 827, 832–50 (2000). Roderick T. Long offers yet another instructive approach: *see* Roderick T. Long, *On Making Small Contributions to Evil*, PRAXEOLOGY.NET, praxeology.net/SmallContributions-REVISED.doc.

18 GRISEZ, PRINCIPLES, *supra* note 16, at 301.

19 *Id.* at 302.

20 GRISEZ, QUESTIONS, *supra* note 17, at 873.

The reasonableness of a given instance of COOPERATION can be addressed with respect to the following factors:[21]

1. *Acceptability*. A cooperating act ought to be morally acceptable apart from its potential status as an instance of COOPERATION,[22] so that, among other things, the act must be undertaken, per the Principle of Recognition, to realize or promote a real good; must not be undertaken, per the Principle of Respect, to injure instrumentally or purposefully; and must be consistent, bracketing the issue of COOPERATION, with the Principle of Fairness.[23]
2. *Magnitude*. "[T]he magnitude of the various bad side effects"[24] of cooperation needs to be taken into account.
3. *Likelihood*. The likelihood that bad side effects will occur,[25] *or* that avoiding cooperation can reasonably be expected to *prevent* the relevant injury,[26] should be taken into account, along with "the . . . number of those who" can reasonably be predicted to be injured.[27]
4. *Alternatives*. The availability of "a feasible and morally acceptable alternative way to" seek one's goal,[28] or a substitute satisfactory to you, is relevant as well.

Participating in a boycott might, in different cases, be admirable but not required; morally permissible but neither admirable nor required; required; worthy of disapprobation but not impermissible; or unequivocally unreasonable and impermissible.[29] Whether not participating in the boycott is wrong will depend on whether, by declining to join the boycott, one is engaged in purposeful COOPERATION

21 *See id.* at 876–84. On other ways in which responsibility for (potentially) foreseen but unintended consequences might figure in non-consequentialist theories, *see, e.g.*, CHARLES FRIED, RIGHT AND WRONG 15, 28, 42, 156 (1978); John Finnis, *Commensuration and Practical Reason*, *in* INCOMMENSURABILITY, INCOMPARABILITY, AND PRACTICAL REASON 215, 227–32 (Ruth Chang ed., 1997); DONAGAN, *supra* note 17, at 46–52.

22 *See id.* at 876. Grisez refers to "its constituting cooperation."

23 *See id.*

24 *See id.* at 878.

25 *See id.*

26 *See id.* at 882–83.

27 *Id.* at 883.

28 *Id.*

29 There will also be various possible relationships between (*i*) a boycott's moral status and (*ii*) the legal status of the firm or industry activities occasioning the boycott. (It might, for instance, be morally admirable to boycott an industry in virtue of activities that not only are but ought to be legally permissible, just as it might be morally wrong to boycott an industry in virtue of activities that are currently legally prohibited.) These relationships, while interesting and important, aren't directly relevant here.

To say that a given boycott is unreasonable is not, of course, to say that one ordinarily has any *positive* responsibility to purchase particular goods or services, but only that avoiding the purchase of these goods or services *for particular reasons* is wrong; not doing so for other reasons may be perfectly sensible. On an unreasonable boycott, *see* BENJAMIN F. POWELL, OUT OF POVERTY: SWEATSHOPS IN THE GLOBAL ECONOMY (2014).

or in unreasonable causal COOPERATION.[30] To put the matter positively, and in terms of the analysis of COOPERATION I've just summarized, it will be reasonable to purchase the good or service someone is proposing that one boycott in the following circumstances:

1. *Acceptability*. One is purchasing the good or service in order to realize or promote a genuine good; one is not doing so to injure purposefully or instrumentally; and, the issue of COOPERATION aside, making the purchase is fair and otherwise consistent with the other requirements of practical reasonableness.
2. *Magnitude*. Accepting the magnitude of the bad side effects of the purchase is consistent with the Principle of Fairness.
3. *Likelihood*. It is consistent with the Principle of Fairness to make the purchase given the likelihood that the bad side effects will occur and the likelihood that not doing so will prevent the relevant injury, given, in particular, the number of those likely to be injured.
4. *Alternatives*. One's purpose in making the purchase cannot be achieved without making the purchase; *or* it is consistent with the Principle of Fairness (and any other applicable requirements) to treat alternatives as unsatisfactory substitutes and so to make the purchase despite their availability.

III. MARKET IMPACT

Whether participation in a meat industry boycott is required in a particular case depends on whether causal COOPERATION with the industry is reasonable in that case. And whether this is so depends on the likely causal impact on the meat market of the potential boycotter's envisioned choice in the given case.

A. *The Consumer in Today's Meat Market*

To ask whether someone's choice will *cause* the killing, and perhaps torture, of an animal is to ask whether the choice will be, roughly, a *but-for* cause of the wrongful injury: someone causes an outcome in the relevant sense only if the outcome would not have occurred *but for* her action.[31] Each action is particular. A consumer buys

30 Similar issues arise when the activity in question doesn't, or needn't, involve any wrongdoing, but simply elevates risk in some way. Driving on the highway is an obvious example.

31 This has been a standard act-consequentialist way of understanding causation. *Cf.* J. J. C. Smart, *An Outline of a System of Utilitarian Ethics*, *in* J. J. C. SMART & BERNARD WILLIAMS, UTILITARIANISM: FOR AND AGAINST 1, 9, 30 (1973) ("the rightness or wrongness of an action is to be judged by the consequences, good or bad, of the action itself"; "the only reason for performing an action A rather than an alternative action B is that doing A will make mankind (or, perhaps, all sentient beings) happier than will doing B"). Non-consequentialist theories will have reason to employ it as well.

It is important to distinguish the relevant *causal* claim from claims about *moral* responsibility. The NATURAL LAW approach I discuss here is only one of many ways in which one might think about the relevant moral issue. A view in accordance with which, say, members of a relevant group share

this *item* this *time* and declines to buy that one. The circumstances in which generically similar choices are made vary, as do their consequences. So someone interested in whether she must boycott the meat industry in a particular case must seek to judge whether her choice *in that case* to purchase meat will likely cause the killing, and perhaps the torture, of animals.[32] She may of course adopt a general policy. But the appropriateness of the policy is a function of the appropriateness of its application *in each particular case*, even if she need not consciously reflect on that appropriateness in each case.

The causal consequences of a given choice by an individual consumer to avoid purchasing a particular meat industry product depend on how the process of meat production and distribution actually works. Does KILL IT YOURSELF model this process accurately? On this scenario, the consumer is also the producer. She kills a chicken and eats it. Here, her choice leads directly to the death of the chicken. What about RUDIMENTARY MARKET? Here, the consumer communicates directly with a farmer, asking the farmer to sell her fresh chicken meat, knowing that her request will trigger the farmer's killing of the chicken.

At least in developed societies, people aren't participants in markets accurately modeled by KILL IT YOURSELF or RUDIMENTARY MARKET. Ordinary consumers in a complex market economy don't kill the animals they eat, nor do they issue instructions to others which result directly in the killing of specific animals. Some boycott proponents, however, while they recognize the difference between the real world of meat consumption and the worlds envisioned in KILL IT YOURSELF and RUDIMENTARY MARKET, seem to think that the actual world mimics these imaginary worlds.[33]

The intuition that it does is nicely captured in SIMPLE MARKET: the consumer purchases a product from a retailer; the retailer orders a replacement from

moral liability for a given outcome is an alternative way of thinking about the moral issue; it is not an alternative account of the causal connection between an individual's action and the outcome.

This kind of causal analysis might be insufficient if there were a meaningful sense in which the consumer and the meat industry participated in a meaningful cooperative scheme. The existence of a scheme of this kind might in some cases significantly enhance the causal links between meat production levels and the choices of individual consumers, and so consumers' causal responsibilities for those levels. But there fairly clearly is no such scheme, consistently linking consumers and producers by means of consciously shared purposes and meaningful deliberate coordination. The argument I discuss below, THRESHOLD, is intended to get to essentially the same result as an argument attributing shared responsibility for a cooperative scheme—namely, proportionate responsibility for the harms resulting from the actions of multiple agents—but without the unsustainable notion that there really *is* a cooperative scheme involving meat purchasers, suppliers, and producers. However, THRESHOLD is unpersuasive.

32 As Peter Singer puts it, "Our custom is all the support that factory farmers need." SINGER, ETHICS, *supra* note 7, at 63. I think the choices of those moral vegetarians whose driving concerns have to do with economics and politics rather than animal flourishing are best understood along similar lines, too, but I don't need to argue the point here; *cf.* FREY, RIGHTS, *supra* note 12, at 17–23 (discussing types of moral vegetarianism not motivated primarily by a concern with animal well-being).

33 This is, at any rate, a natural way to read Peter Singer, *Animal Liberation: Vegetarianism as Protest, in* FOOD, *supra* note 12, at 108, 115 (speaking of the carnivore as "prepared to take the life of another").

a supplier; the supplier orders a replacement from a producer. If the real-world market for meat in which most of us in developed societies participate worked like this, for each dead chicken purchased by a consumer from a grocery store or restaurant, the retailer would purchase a replacement dead chicken. The consumer obviously does no injury to a chicken that has already been killed before she purchases its dead body when she eats the dead body. But, on SIMPLE MARKET, her purchase instructs the grocery store to buy a new one, with the result that the store's supplier will order another dead chicken from a farmer, so that another chicken will be killed for later consumption. The number of animals killed is thus a straightforward rectilinear function of a single variable, the number of purchases.[34]

But SIMPLE MARKET doesn't accurately model the real-world market for animal flesh. It's now a commonplace in moral debates about vegetarianism that the impact on the meat market of uncoordinated individual purchasing decisions by consumers is minimal or nonexistent.[35] A key reason for this conviction, though not the only one, is the enormous size of the market (especially in relation to the number of people who decline to buy its products).[36] In the United States, for instance, according to a projection reported at the beginning of 2018,

> For all the buzz about pea protein and lab-grown burgers, Americans are set to eat more meat in 2018 than ever before.
>
> . . . [T]he average consumer will eat 222.2 pounds of red meat and poultry this year, . . . surpassing a record set in 2004. Meanwhile, domestic production will surpass 100 billion pounds for the first time, as livestock owners expand their herds on the back of cheap feed grain.[37]

34 This model is obviously oversimplified insofar as it assumes that individual animals are purchased. In most cases a consumer will purchase a portion of a dead animal, rather than the whole animal, and of course what she purchases may include tissue from more than one dead animal.

35 As in standard parlance, *vegetarian* here means *lacto-ovo vegetarian*. I reserve the term *vegan* for a proponent of the view that one should avoid not only meat but also animal products that can in principle be obtained without killing.

36 *See* Raymond G. Frey, *Utilitarianism and Moral Vegetarianism Again: Protest or Effectiveness, in* FOOD, *supra* note 12, at 120; FREY, RIGHTS, *supra* note 12, at 208–10. Vegetarians (and, I assume given the context, vegans) seem to make up about 5 percent of the global population (India, with around 30 percent, is a striking exception), while vegetarians and vegans evidently constitute around 5 percent of the US population; *see* Marcelo Gleiser, *Is A No-Meat World Really Better?*, NPR, June 28, 2017, https://www.npr.org/sections/13.7/2017/06/28/532880755/is-a-no-meat-world-really-better.
The customer queues at my local Good Burger provide welcome evidence that the US numbers may be increasing. On the global market, *see, e.g.*, Hanna Ritchie & Max Roser, *Meat and Seafood Production & Consumption*, OUR WORLD IN DATA, 2018 [Aug. 2017], https://ourworldindata.org/meat-and-seafood-production-consumption.

37 Megan Durisin & Shruti Date Singh, *Americans' Meat Consumption Set to Hit a Record in 2018*, SEATTLE TIMES, Jan. 2, 2018, https://www.seattletimes.com/business/americans-meat-consumption-set-to-hit-a-record-in-2018. *Cf.* UNITED STATES DEPARTMENT OF AGRICULTURE, LIVESTOCK, DAIRY, AND POULTRY OUTLOOK, Aug. 16, 2018, http://usda.mannlib.cornell.edu/usda/current/LDP-M/LDP-M-08-16-2018.pdf. Beef production this year is projected to be roughly 27.1 billion pounds. *See* Russell Knight & Lekhnath Chalise, *Cattle/Beef, in* OUTLOOK, *supra*, at 3, 3. "Total commercial pork

The size of the market means that many or most market signals will simply be *lost*.

Thus, Raymond Frey maintains: "If I give up eating apples, I am most unlikely to reduce by even one apple the number grown . . . , and I can see no reason to think there is a difference in market forces here between chickens and apples."[38] Frey is a critic of moral vegetarianism, but numerous philosophers supportive of vegetarianism have also made the point clearly. Peter Singer agrees that "[t]he loss of one consumer from the millions who buy animal flesh makes so small a difference that it is impossible to say that it affects the number of animals reared and killed."[39] Hud Hudson concedes that "the [meat] industry is not fine-tuned enough to be affected at all by [his] becoming a vegetarian."[40] James Rachels notes "that no animals will actually be helped simply by one person['s] ceasing to eat meat."[41] Similarly, Gaverick Matheny characterizes as "plausible," the "assumption that most meat purchases are causally inefficacious," explaining that "a single meat purchase is too insignificant, relative to the vast number of other meat purchases, to be noticed by the manager of a factory farm."[42]

Similarly, Russell Shafer-Landau essentially endorses the view that "[t]he ordinary consumer of meat is so remote in the causal nexus of animal suffering, that one cannot properly attribute to any such consumer any causal, hence moral, responsibility for the admittedly wretched fates suffered by farm animals."[43] Tzachi Zamir apparently shares the belief that "personally refraining from eating animal flesh will not save a single animal" and that "one's own actions cannot modify outcome[s] for future animals."[44] Nathan Nobis acknowledges the reasonableness of what he labels

production for 2018 is forecast to be 26.7 billion pounds." Mildred Haley, *Pork/Hogs*, *in* OUTLOOK, *supra*, at 13, 13. Broiler production for 2018 is estimated at 42.6 billion pounds. *See U.S. Red Meat and Poultry Forecasts*, *in* OUTLOOK, *supra*, at 25, 25. *Global* meat production in 2017 reached 323,000,000 (presumably metric) tons; *see* ORGANIZATION FOR ECONOMIC COOPERATION AND DEVELOPMENT & UNITED NATIONS FOOD AND AGRICULTURAL ORGANIZATION, OECD-FAO AGRICULTURAL OUTLOOK 2018–2027 at 149 (2018), *available at* http://www.fao.org/docrep/i9166e/i9166e_Chapter6_Meat.pdf.

38 FREY, RIGHTS, *supra* note 12, at 211. *Cf.* Peter Wenz, *Act-Utilitarianism and Animal Liberation*, 60 PERSONALIST 423 (1979) (thanks for Frey for this reference).

39 Peter Singer, *Utilitarianism and Vegetarianism* ", 9 PHIL. & PUB. AFF. 325, 335 (1980).

40 Hud Hudson, *Collective Responsibility and Moral Vegetarianism*, 24 J. SOC. PHIL 89, 94 (1993). Thanks to Nathan Nobis for this reference and a number of the others; *see*, *e.g.*, Nathan Nobis, *Vegetarianism and Virtue: Does Consequentialism Demand Too Little?*, 28 SOC. THEORY & PRACTICE 135, 142–43 n. 20 (2002).

41 James Rachels, *The Moral Argument for Vegetarianism*, *in* CAN ETHICS PROVIDE ANSWERS? AND OTHER ESSAYS IN MORAL PHILOSOPHY 99, 106 (1997).

42 Gaverick Matheny, *Expected Utility, Contributory Causation, and Vegetarianism*, 19 J. APP. PHIL 293, 293 (2002).

43 Russ Shafer-Landau, *Vegetarianism, Causation and Ethical Theory*, 8 PUB. AFF. Q. 85, 86 (1994).

44 TZACHI ZAMIR, *Killing for Pleasure*, *in* ETHICS AND THE BEAST: A SPECIESIST ARGUMENT FOR ANIMAL LIBERATION 46 (2009), *available at* https://digitalcommons.calpoly.edu/cgi/viewcontent.cgi?article=1049&context=bts. Zamir seems to think that this fact can't reasonably figure in the arguments of critics of vegetarianism: "Tax paying, cooperating with a draft, personal charitable aid to large-scale goals that one endorses, will all become irrational." *Id.* I suspect I'm not alone in finding the implications as regards taxation and conscription welcome. The issue of "charitable aid to large-

the "'impotence of the individual' objection."[45] And Stephen Clark observes: "it is (I fear) unlikely that I have relieved any animal, or diminished the gross total of animal suffering (if such a total has any real existence), by not eating flesh-foods."[46] Similarly, in the course of an exchange with his utilitarian friend Frey, he says:

> I may as well admit that in my judgment Frey has the technical victory [over Singer] here: even if some other farming practices than the present ones were, all told, a better option, there is precious little reason to think that any single act of mine would lead to the amelioration of those present practices. So I can have no utilitarianly-grounded obligation to give up eating flesh, to campaign against what ideally would be reckoned an inferior result, or to castigate those who make a different calculation.[47]

Proponents and opponents of moral vegetarianism thus agree regarding the causal relationship between individual actions and meat market outcomes.

B. *Recovering the Vanishing Consequences*

It is very likely, then, that, in most cases, uncoordinated individual consumer meat purchases won't cause animal death or torture.[48] However, employing the argument I'll call THRESHOLD, some philosophers have maintained that such purchases are still morally impermissible.

Proponents of THRESHOLD acknowledge that most individual abstainers will have no influence at all on the number of animals bred on factory farms—that, often enough, as Singer notes, "one more person['s] becoming a vegetarian will make no

scale goals" is more complicated, and I won't address it here except to say that much charitable giving need not be giving to "large-scale causes" (indeed, there is probably good reason for it not to be, *see, e.g.*, Frank Jackson, *Decision-Theoretic Consequentialism and the Nearest and Dearest Objection*, 101 ETHICS 461 (1991)) and that there is, in any case, a difference between whether giving to such causes is reasonable and whether *not* giving to them is wrong (which seems to be the issue more directly relevant to the question whether we're required to join the meat industry boycott).

45 *See* Nobis, *supra* note 40, at 142–44.

46 CLARK, STATUS, *supra* note 7, at xi. He goes on: "My point here is not merely that vegetarians are unwise to base their project on utilitarian calculation, but that no-one can really base any project (except that of mere convention) upon such a figment." *Id.* at xi. *Cf.* Stephen R. L. Clark, *Vegetarianism and the Ethics of Virtue, in* FOOD, *supra* note 12, at 138; CLARK, STANDING, *supra* note 7, at 100. Clark maintains: "Bernard Shaw was mistaken if he seriously thought that any particular animal had a pleasanter or more fulfilled or longer life because he foreswore flesh; at best, some animal that might have been bred to feed him never was (but more likely, just as many animals were bred and slaughtered). His dietary choices did no good to any actual animal." Clark, *Virtue, supra,* at 139. On Clark's preferred account, "Shaw . . . was wrong to justify himself by the good he had notionally done to particular sheep or cattle, and optimistic even in supposing that his boycott of those goods would be a step on the way to . . . reform." *Id.* at 146.

47 CLARK, STANDING, *supra* note 7, at 100 (emphasis added).

48 I am concerned with *initiating the purchase* of meat rather than with *consuming* meat because the proposed boycott concerns the transmission of market signals. Consumption, per se, will not affect the market.

difference at all."[49] However, they argue, *some* acts of abstention may be enormously significant, depending on others' meat-purchasing choices. It may make a substantial difference if an individual vegetarian, "added to the others who are already vegetarians, reduces demand below the *threshold level* at which a new factory farm would have started up (or an existing one would have remained in production, if the industry is declining)."[50]

On SLIGHTLY MORE COMPLEX MARKET, which seems to be presupposed here, the growth in the number of animals killed can be represented by a step function. This number remains constant except at certain threshold points. Thus, the odds that a given purchase will result in the subsequent killing of an animal will typically be 0, because no increase will result from most purchases. The vast majority of purchases will have no marginal impact. However, a purchase will on rare occasion result in a threshold crossing, production levels will be ramped up, and many more deaths will occur.

If THRESHOLD is correct, the actor with perfect information, who knows that her meat purchase will result in harm to a single animal, and the actor with very imperfect information, who knows that her purchase might harm many animals or none, are in equivalent positions. While many individual purchases will have no direct impact on the meat market, I will have no way of knowing whether mine is one of those purchases. So I will need to assume that it might be. Even though I know SIMPLE MARKET doesn't describe the real world, I should behave *as if* it did.

Here's a highly simplified example. Industry analysts decide that, if 100,000,000 pounds of chicken are purchased in a given market during one year, they will give the green light to those who wish to open an envisioned factory farm. Deborah purchases a chicken burrito from TacoMax in early December. In virtue of her purchase, TacoMax's order to its supplier is such that total purchases in the relevant market exceed 100,000,000 pounds, with the result that the projected farm will open. If the farm opens, it will breed an average of, say, 100,000,000 chickens each year during its one hundred years of operation. Deborah obviously cannot know whether her purchase will cause the establishment of the farm. But she *can* know that there is a tiny risk that it will do so, and thus cause enormous attendant injury. Perhaps there is a 1/500,000,000 chance that a purchase in the given market during the relevant period will trigger the creation of the farm.[51] She will need to take this chance into account in making her purchasing decision: she will need to

49 Singer, *Utilitarianism*, *supra* note 39, at 335.

50 *Id.*; italics supplied.

51 *Cf. id.*; Matheny, *supra* note 42, at 295–6; Michael Almeida and Mark Bernstein, *Opportunistic Carnivorism*, 17 J. APP. PHIL 205, 205 (2000); Bart Gruzalski, *Why It's Wrong to Eat Animals Raised and Slaughtered for Food*, *in* FOOD, *supra* note 7, at 124.

Of course, it may not be the case that a vegetarian burrito Deborah might purchase instead at TacoMax would be in other respects the same as the chicken burrito. If it weren't the equivalent, farmers responsible for the products the vegetarian burrito might contain that would not have been

reason, in effect, as if there are small odds that her purchase will turn out to have caused the injuries resulting from the opening of the farm—say, the torture and killing of 10,000,000,000 chickens.[52]

Most of the time, to be sure, the consumer will certainly not injure any animal at all by purchasing meat. But she might sometimes bring about the deaths of enormous numbers of animals, and she has no way of knowing whether she will. So she should reason as if she were responsible for the number of deaths she might bring about, discounted by the likelihood that she will, in fact, bring that many deaths about. Thus, if there's a 1/500,000,000 chance that Deborah's purchase will be the one that triggers the establishment of the new factory farm, she should choose on the assumption that her purchase will cause the deaths of 10,000,000,000/500,000,000—that is, twenty—chickens.

C. *Muddying the Waters*

It's doubtful that SLIGHTLY MORE COMPLEX MARKET accurately describes the actual meat market. The real-world relationship between consumer choices and animal outcomes is fiendishly complex. Thus, SLIGHTLY MORE COMPLEX MARKET assumes a more direct relationship between production levels and consumer purchasing levels than an awareness of relevant market complexities renders likely. It isn't clear that meat production levels vary directly with consumer demand. The influence of other factors may substantially reduce the likelihood that consumer purchases are responsible for movements over thresholds (if there are thresholds). It is almost certainly impossible to perform the needed calculations at a level of precision needed to enable the threshold argument to succeed. Doubts about the existence of thresholds also call the argument into question, as does the idea that "ripples in the pond" disappear over time from a moral perspective.

1. Market Complexities

While it incorporates the recognition that there are limits to the impacts of individual consumer purchasing decisions, SLIGHTLY MORE COMPLEX MARKET still presupposes that production levels are determined by consumer purchases. So, for THRESHOLD, the principal reason individual meat-purchasing decisions generally exert no influence on production levels is simply the sheer *size* of the meat production market. Producers ordinarily don't register small changes in purchasing levels because production levels are so great. At some point, however, a change in

included in the chicken burrito might benefit from her decision not to purchase the chicken burrito, and this would presumably need to be taken into account. Thanks to Lee Reynolds for this point.

52 The example assumes that the average purchase is of something like one-third of a pound of chicken. Even if the relevant (actual) figure is less than the amount of flesh made available by the death of a single animal, as it likely will be, at least one animal will need to die to provide that amount of flesh.

purchasing levels will be just great enough for a producer to notice, and she will increase production levels. Meat production *does* vary directly with meat purchasing, just as on SIMPLE MARKET, even if production levels make large jumps rather than increasing gradually.

However, a more realistic understanding of meat production suggests that numerous factors apart from sheer market size intervene between the purchaser and the producer. The result is *both* that the average market impact of a consumer purchase is significantly less than SLIGHTLY MORE COMPLEX MARKET assumes *and* that, when it occurs, the impact isn't linear or even necessarily unidirectional.

Most importantly, production is ultimately a function, *not* of expressed demand but of *market strategy*. So it is simply not the case that production levels are functionally related only to, or vary directly with, purchasing levels. The other factors that determine production levels may include pricing strategies, subsidies,[53] the availability of other uses for factory farms' products, creative marketing responses to purchasing reductions, labor costs, supply expenses, logistical expenses, legal constraints, producers' tax strategies, the cost of borrowing, the behaviors of various markets, the alteration of farming methods to make up for profit reductions, and the state of the economy as a whole.[54] And if multiple independent variables account for production levels, the likelihood that a consumer's choices will affect these levels may be significantly lower than a simple model with only one independent variable might suggest. And, when a consumer choice *does* exert an effect, it need not be true that the effect will be an increase in production in response to an increase in the total quantity purchased.

Some of the operative factors (e.g., rising production costs, production control strategies designed to keep prices high) may serve to *keep* production from rising in direct response to consumer demand. And some may trigger increased production—including, if they occur, threshold crossings—*without* direct regard to individual consumer purchases. This is especially so given that "a vast market may already have built into it capacity for excess demand compared to the past, at least if projections for the number of people coming into the market exceed[] greatly projections for the number of people withdrawing from it, as is the case with the meat consumption market."[55]

53 A subsidy with the effect of stabilizing or increasing production levels may be triggered precisely because consumer purchases *decline*; *see* FREY, RIGHTS, *supra* note 12.

54 *Id.* at 208–214; Frey, *Utilitarianism*, *supra* note 36, at 121–23; Michael Martin, *A Critique of Moral Vegetarianism*, 3 REASON PAPERS 13, 27–28 (1976); Wenz, *supra* note 38; Philip Devine, *The Moral Basis of Vegetarianism*, 53 PHILOSOPHY 481 (1978). Thanks to Nathan Nobis for pointing me to more than one of these references and for enjoyable conversations. I am also grateful for opportunities to discuss these matters with Elias Rizkallah and Robert Beshara.

55 Frey, *Utilitarianism*, *supra* note 36, at 121. Note that, "[b]ecause beef is a perishable product, we consume what we produce. If more is produced, more is consumed. If less is produced, then less is consumed. As a result, per-capita consumption is more related to available supply than demand." Harlan Hughes, *The Role of Beef Demand*, BEEF, Feb. 1, 2002, https://www.beefmagazine.com/mag/beef_role_beef_demand.

Producers have some reason to produce at capacity. Momentum may prompt ongoing production increases. And substantial, ongoing fluctuations in demand and supply alike will often serve to render individual consumer choices inefficacious.[56] So not buying the industry's products might mean that consumption levels were lower but not that any fewer animals were slaughtered.

For simplicity's sake, I've assumed that the number of animals bred will vary directly with the amount of time the farm breeding the animals is in operation. But this is too simplistic. Production levels will probably not be consistent. And, if they're not, it won't follow that the number of animals that *would have been* bred for mistreatment and slaughter had a meat purchase not occurred will be significantly less, or less *at all*, than the number bred given the purchase's occurrence. And this may be the case even if, because of consumer abstention, a factory farm opens later than it otherwise would have.

Indeed, there is also quite possibly a small likelihood that *failing* to purchase meat will trigger a threshold-crossing production increase—if, for instance, a consumer's choice to abstain from purchasing a chicken burrito exerts an effect on pricing decisions that leads ultimately to a ramp-up.[57] Suppose, for instance, that a factory farm opens three months later than it would have had Deborah purchased a chicken burrito at TacoMax in early December. In this case, the farm's absence from the market for three months may lead to higher prices. Seeking to take advantage of these prices before the market settles in response to its arrival on the scene, the farm may produce furiously at first, meaning that *more* animals will be bred than would otherwise have been.[58]

Thus, while there may be *n* meat purchases in a given market when (presuming there are thresholds) a transition over a threshold occurs, it will not follow that the fact that there were *n* purchases *accounted* for this transition. Given the character of the relevant variables, what is almost certainly *more* likely than not in the world of my example is that, if a substantial ramp-up in production *does* occur, it will occur without regard to whether Deborah has purchased a chicken burrito. Lacking any evidence that overall production levels are less than they would have been had individual refusals to purchase meat industry products not taken place, we have no "way of estimating how many animals are saved from being

[56] Thanks to Elias Rizkallah for this point. David Gordon notes that there is reason to question the stronger claim, which I made in an earlier version of this paragraph, that producers are *always* motivated to produce at capacity, calling my attention to Ludwig von Mises, *Inconvertible Capital, in* Epistemological Problems of Economics 231 (3d ed., George Reisman trans., 2003).

[57] Thanks to Lee Reynolds and Nathan Nobis for insights related to this point.

[58] *Cf.* Devine, *supra* note 54. I have assumed that the injuries caused to animals being bred for mistreatment and slaughter will vary directly with the number of the animals bred. In reality, though, different production methods may cause more injuries than others at different stages of production processes. During a ramp-up period, for instance, more intensive and painful rearing methods may be used, so that delaying the start-up of a factory farm might result in particularly serious injuries for the affected animals. *Cf.* Frey, *Utilitarianism*, at 121.

reared [by these refusals], since we do not yet know that *any* animals *are* saved from being reared."[59]

2. Impossible Calculations

If SLIGHTLY MORE COMPLEX MARKET accurately represented the realities of meat production, the consumer wouldn't need to perform complex calculations. Even though she didn't know whether a given purchase would trigger a threshold crossing, she could reasonably treat the likely causal impact of an individual purchase as roughly equivalent to that of an actual purchase on SIMPLE MARKET. But SLIGHTLY MORE COMPLEX MARKET *doesn't* represent the realities of meat production. And this means that, to assess the causal impact of her choices, a consumer *would* need to perform complex calculations.

Performing these calculations will pretty clearly prove impossible.[60] The potential purchaser would need to be able to calculate the odds that her choice would result in a threshold crossing and to determine what the result of that threshold crossing would be. But the function in accordance with which the value of the number of animals bred can be expected to change is thoroughly unknowable,[61] as is the related function in accordance with which the kinds of injuries they are likely to suffer can be expected to change. It is uncertain whether anything like the list of salient variables I provided above is exhaustive (presumably it isn't), how to determine their values,[62] or how they are related to production levels and techniques. She has no idea of the relative magnitudes of any of the relevant variables to be related using the functions, or even of their signs. She also has no way of identifying the relevant thresholds (if there are any) or of determining how best to act strategically in light of her awareness of their existence.[63]

The consequences of any act—and certainly, therefore, of a meat purchase in a vast, impersonal global market—depend on factors quite apart from the choices of the actor, especially the acts of other agents.[64] To be sure, immediate-term and short-term consequences brought about directly by the agent can be predicted with relative accuracy. But those to which not only the agent but also others contribute cannot be.[65] The agent will be quite unable to estimate *these* consequences. Past experience, and assessment of the consequences of putatively similar acts, won't

59 Frey, *Utilitarianism*, *supra* note 36, at 121 (italics supplied); *cf. id.* at 122–3.

60 Calculation regarding the impact of consumer choices on the meat market are vitiated by unavoidable uncertainty; *see* CLARK, STATUS, *supra* note 7, at x–xi; Clark, *Virtue*, *supra* note 46, at 139. Clark is certainly not alone in seeing this as a serious problem for any position dependent on the calculation of consequences. *See* DONAGAN, *supra* note 17, at 199–209.

61 *Cf.* REGAN, *supra* note 7, at 223, 231.

62 *See* Raymond G. Frey, *Can Act-Utilitarianism Be Put into Practice?*, 11 J. VALUE INQ. 49–58 (1977).

63 FREY, RIGHTS, *supra* note 12, at 213–14. *Cf.* REGAN, *supra* note 7, at 225.

64 *See* A. N. Prior, *The Consequences of Actions*, *in* PAPERS ON TIME AND TENSE 65 (Per Hasle *et al. eds.*, 2d ed., 2003).

65 Frey, *Practice*, *supra* note 62, at 51.

help: the contributions of others to relevant outcomes may or may not be the same in one case as in others.[66]

Further, to determine the consequences of an act when others contribute to them, one will need to know how many others are contributing to various possible outcomes, and on what sorts of schedules, and one is almost certainly not going to be able to do this.[67] For instance: It may be that, for a threshold crossing to occur (if, indeed, there are thresholds), an appropriate number of consumers need to reach it *within a relatively narrow temporal compass*.[68] If crossing a threshold in tandem with others is important in bringing about the outcome in question, past experience can do little to help one determine whether one is or isn't at the threshold and whether others are or aren't at the threshold as well.[69] In short, then, there is good reason to believe that the purchaser cannot project the consequences of most actions to which others contribute with any accuracy; she may be ignorant even of a significant number of the individual consequences of her own actions;[70] and she thus cannot know the complete set of the consequences of any action with any accuracy. Not even rough calculations related to the causal impact of any purchase she might make seem realistically manageable.[71] She can reasonably expect, by Singer's own admission, that it is probable that her choices "will make no difference at all,"[72] and because she has no idea what the relevant thresholds might be, she can have no idea when they will, instead, make some difference.[73]

3. Ripples in the Pond

The issue of causal COOPERATION arises when we *can* identify some causal link between a choice on the part of the putative cooperator's and the relevant injury. The more attenuated the causal link between the choice and the injury, the more difficult it is to attribute any sort of responsibility to the agent. When causal COOPERATION is as remote as it is in the case of the meat market, it is unclear that the unintended consequences of an agent's choices are in any interesting sense her responsibility. Adherents of common-sense morality conventionally suppose that

66 *Id.* at 52–53.
67 *Id.* at 53.
68 FREY, RIGHTS, *supra* note 12, at 214.
69 Frey, *Practice*, *supra* note 62, at 54.
70 *Id.* at 57–58.
71 *Cf.* DONAGAN, *supra* note 17, at 199–205; PRIOR, *supra* note 64.
72 Singer, *Utilitarianism*, *supra* note 39, at 335.
73 It is possible, thus, that, as a result of making inaccurate (especially, perhaps, overly cautious) calculations, she might choose to decline the goods associated with meat consumption when a consequentialist would acknowledge that she was not required to do so. *Cf.* REGAN, *supra* note 7, at 225. Regan evidently intends this as, in effect, a *reductio ad absurdum* of Singer's argument, but I cannot see why it should be understood to be one. If the purpose of vegetarianism is, as it seems to be on the consequentialist view, to do something about the suffering of actual animals, then it will be morally obligatory only if it can be seen to have its intended effect.

"long-run consequences are like ripples in the pond; they die away," and thus "do not accept the . . . postulate that each of us is *responsible* for 'total' or 'overall' consequences, or for maximizing total or overall net good, or anything like that."[74] Absent a clear link between an agent's choices and various long-range outcomes, these outcomes can be seen as ripples in the pond, ripples less and less linked to her actions as they become more remote from those actions. When they aren't linked with her either by purpose or causal control, these outcomes might not plausibly be seen as the agent's responsibility at all.

4. Doubts about Thresholds

There is no link between most consumer meat purchases and injuries to actual animals. And THRESHOLD does not give us good reason to believe we should act *as if* such a link obtained even in its absence. The link between an individual consumer choice and a threshold crossing, if there are thresholds at all, will likely be much more tenuous than it would be were consumer meat purchases the only factors relevant to determining production levels; indeed, some delays in threshold crossings caused by abstentions from meat purchases might lead to *increases* rather than decreases in production levels, and thus to more injuries to animals. The needed calculations are impossible to perform, and intuitive estimates may not be sufficient. Given the distant connection between consumer choices and animal killings, they might be not regarded as responsible for these killings in accordance with the "ripple in the pond" postulate. And there may not be thresholds at all—the market for meat may not grow in stepwise fashion. It does not seem that THRESHOLD gives us much reason to attribute causal responsibility for meat market outcomes to consumers.

IV. ASSESSING MEAT INDUSTRY BOYCOTT PROPOSALS

In light of what we can reasonably conclude, per Part III, regarding the causal consequences of consumer meat purchases, I will employ the analytical approach described in Part II to clarify the moral status of proposals regarding boycotts of the meat industry. Assuming the correctness of AVOID, I will consider these questions:

- May one purchase meat for oneself?
- Must suppliers, retailers, and restaurants boycott the meat industry?

74 JOHN FINNIS, FUNDAMENTALS OF ETHICS 98 (1983). Finnis emphasizes that "[t]he 'ripple in the pond' postulate can be defended, not on an analysis of actual causal influences, but only on the basis of a theory of responsibility (*i.e.* a theory of practical reasonableness) which proportionalism [a category which includes consequentialism] radically rejects." *Id.* at 99. That is, talk about ripples in the pond is normative. This does not mean, of course, that Finnis would (perhaps he would, but nothing he says here suggests that), or that we should, reject a *but-for* analysis of causation (outside the context of a purposeful cooperative scheme), but, rather, that such an analysis cannot on its own settle questions about responsibility. To do *that*, we need to do normative theory.

- May one purchase meat ordered by someone else?
- May one initiate occasions for which others will purchase meat?
- May one consume meat which one has neither ordered nor purchased?
- May one purchase dairy products originating on factory farms?

A. *Purchasing Meat for One's Own Consumption*

A consumer trying to decide whether to purchase meat from a grocery store, meat market, or restaurant can determine whether she is required to join the meat industry boycott with reference to the criteria I noted in Part II.

1. *Acceptability*. Meat consumers often likely *do* endorse the activities of the slaughterhouses and factory farms responsible for the availability of their meals, even though of course it's not necessary that they do so. If they engage in purposeful COOPERATION with these facilities, of course, they violate the Principle of Respect.[75]

   The act of *purchasing* meat is not, in and of itself, a violation of AVOID. And it is not otherwise unreasonable apart from the fact that it potentially constitutes remote causal COOPERATION with the slaughterhouse.[76] The consumer is acting for the otherwise reasonable purpose of realizing goods including aesthetic experience, sensory pleasure, life and bodily well-being, and friendship.
2. *Magnitude*. The magnitude of the relevant side effects is potentially great: one or more creatures could be tortured or killed unjustly, depending on the effect of the market signals sent by a purchase. Slaughterhouse workers could be brutalized by their involvement in torture and killing.
3. *Likelihood*. The likelihood that a consumer's choice will actually cause any actual animal to be tortured or killed is very small.[77] The consumer's non-purchase is likely to have no impact on the volume or nature of the injuries effected by a factory farm or slaughterhouse. It will also likely have no effect on the experience of, for instance, slaughterhouse workers who are coarsened and distressed by their work.

75 It does not follow, of course, that they are therefore morally culpable. Most people in our society clearly do not see the wrongness of many of the meat industry's practices, are unaware of these practices. For reasons why this might be so, see, *e.g.*, FOX, *supra* note 13, at 39–51.

76 The expression "remote cooperation," derived from older Catholic manuals of moral theology, was intended as a label for the most indirect kind of cooperation; *see* GRISEZ, QUESTIONS, *supra* note 17, at 890.

77 If "we have no reason, absent some special consideration, to think that [the entry into the market of] a million [meat eaters] raises demand in such a way that it is to be met only by a further increase in the number of animals bred," Frey, *Utilitarianism*, *supra* note 36, at 121, then it seems even more unlikely that the addition of one consumer to the market will have a significant effect, much less one act of purchasing meat.

4. *Alternatives.* It is easy to eat a vegetarian diet, in the sense that flavorful and healthful vegetarian foods are readily available.[78] The consumer can often locate appealing alternatives to meat with relative ease. Many consumers will not experience these alternatives as satisfactory substitutes, however.

The availability of *alternatives* will frequently weigh in favor of not purchasing meat, because the consumer has an equally satisfactory alternative to meat consumption available: attractive meat alternatives will be readily available; further, the consumer will reap an economic—and probably nutritional—benefit, rather than suffering an economic loss, if she avoids purchasing meat. She may, however, regard a meat industry product she intends to purchase as such that no satisfactory substitute is available. The *magnitude* of the injury potentially resulting from a purchase is very great, while the *likelihood* is very low. The *acceptability* of the consumer's choice weighs in favor of the judgment that her purchase of meat need not be unreasonable. Whether her meat purchase is reasonable, all things considered (assuming she genuinely views the product she is intending to acquire as without an adequate substitute), depends, then, on whether she could fairly make the purchase in light of the goods realized by her choice and both the *magnitude* and the *likelihood* of possible injury.

How might she judge? Suppose someone acted in a way that subjected *her* or her loved ones to risk of harm. Suppose the harm was as severe as that typically suffered by an animal in a slaughterhouse. And suppose the risk that she would suffer this harm was no less than the risk that some animal would suffer a comparable harm *as a result of her purchasing decision.* Would she be willing to regard an act that imposed such a risk on her as acceptable?[79] If she would, then her own choice to purchase meat would likely be reasonable.

78 Contrary to Frey's claim that, were vegetarianism to become widespread or universal, "[t]he restaurant business and all those connected with the catering industry would suffer loss, probably catastrophically in the short term," since "it is hard to believe that all the restaurants of New York, London, Paris, and Alice Springs, with only non-meat dishes on offer, however varied, could stay in business" and since "what places there are will be, in essentials (grains, vegetables, etc.), alike." Frey, Rights, *supra* note 12, at 199. There is an immense variety of vegetarian food available, and had most people *chosen* to be vegetarians, (*i*) it is hard to see why consumers would shun restaurants in favor of home cooking because those restaurants failed to serve meat, which wouldn't be available at home either and (*ii*) the number of vegetarian consumers would prompt chefs to create more diverse vegetarian dishes than are currently available.

79 Note that what matters here is the restaurateur's willingness to accept the relevant risk. The Principle of Fairness is a test of internal consistency on the part of the reasoner. *Cf.* Finnis, *Commensuration, supra* note 21, at 228: "Is it fair to impose on others the risks inherent in driving at more than 10 mph or in planting trees near the roadside? Yes, in our community, since our community has by custom and law *decided* to treat those risks and harms as *not too great.* Have we a rational critique of a community which decided to limit road traffic to 10 mph and to accept all the economic and other costs of that decision? Or to have no trees along the road? . . . No, we have no rational critique of such a community . . . But we do have a rational critique of someone who drives at 60 mph but who, when struck by someone driving at 45 mph complains that that speed is per se negligent." *Cf.* Robert P. George, *Does the "Incommensurability Thesis" Imperil Common Sense Moral Judgments?*, 37 Am. J. Juris. 185 (1992).

To determine whether she would, she might think of this example. She might be concerned about the risks associated with highway driving, which can be very hazardous.[80] She might still opt to drive on a highway, judging that her use or nonuse of it was unlikely to make any but the smallest difference in the risk of serious injury posed to other drivers or to herself, even though her choice to drive might in a very rare case prove to be a cause of one or more accidents because of its contribution to overall traffic volume. The risk that she or those dear to her might be hurt increases marginally when she drives or when others drive. But she need not regard the act of driving as *unreasonably* risk enhancing. If she is willing to tolerate the level of increased risk associated with an individual driver's decision to enter a freeway, it would probably be reasonable for her to tolerate a similar level of risk that she might suffer the kind of harm to which an animal bred for slaughter might be subjected,[81] given the considerations regarding consumer impact noted in Part III. If so, her decision to purchase meat might well be consistent with the Principle of Fairness.

In short, the consumer would likely act unreasonably if she purchased a given meat industry product while regarding available alternatives as suitable substitutes. But she might do so reasonably if she did *not* regard them as substitutes and if she were willing to accept a general rule permitting a risk of injury of something like the kind and at something like the level created by her purchase.

Of course, this analysis assumes that the consumer's relationship with the meat industry is an arm's-length one. If the consumer and the industry formed a genuine community, this might alter the consumer's causal liability for the behavior of the

80 *See* Finnis, Ethics, *supra* note 74, at 91–92.

81 *Cf. id.* at 91–92: "If we have decided to build a highway through the desert . . . we can use cost-benefit computations to select among materials and methods of leveling and road-building. But it was not, and could not rationally have been, cost-benefit computations which guided our prior commitment to the level of economic activity (trade) and personal mobility which calls for highways of this sort. We know that the building and use of highways of this sort involves the death of tens of thousands of persons, and the horrible injury of hundreds of thousands more, each year. But we have not made any computation which shows that the goods participated in and attained by that level of trade and mobility exceed, outweigh, are proportionately greater, than the goods destroyed and damaged by that level, or any level, of deaths and injuries. Nor, on the other hand, could any computation yield the conclusion that the deaths and injuries are an evil which objectively outweighs, exceeds, etc., the good of mobility, etc. . . . The justification, and equally the critique, of any basic commitment [in light of which a choice like this might be assessed] must be in terms of the requirements of practical reasonableness, which give positive direction even though they do not include any principle of optimizing (i.e. of ordinal maximizing), and even though they permit indefinitely many different commitments (as well as, also, excluding indefinitely many other possible commitments!)." According to Department of Transportation data, "There were 34,439 fatal motor vehicle crashes in the United States in 2016 in which 37,461 deaths occurred. This resulted in 11.6 deaths per 100,000 people and 1.16 deaths per 100 million miles traveled. The fatality rate per 100,000 people ranged from 4.0 in the District of Columbia to 23.1 in Mississippi. The death rate per 100 million miles traveled ranged from 0.66 in Massachusetts, Minnesota, and Rhode Island to 1.88 in South Carolina." *Fatality Facts*, Insurance Institute for Highway Safety Highway Loss Data Institute, https://www.iihs.org/iihs/topics/t/general-statistics/fatalityfacts/state-by-state-overview.

industry; and it might also subject the consumer to some sort of shared, perhaps proportionate, moral liability for the industry's behavior. A community is created by the existence of a shared purpose.[82] Absent such a purpose, a community does not exist. And absent a community or, at any rate, *some* kind of genuine cooperative enterprise, shared moral responsibility is absent. Without these factors, it seems unreasonable to regard the consumer qua consumer as, apart from her actual causal responsibility, bearing some sort of proportionate responsibility for the behavior of the industry or of any firm.[83]

B. *Purchasing Meat for Commercial Use*

Someone involved in the commercial use of meat—a buyer for a grocery chain, say, or an executive at a restaurant—trying to decide whether to place an order with a slaughterhouse or an intermediate supplier confronts a related but somewhat different set of issues. She might reasonably think about her choice this way:

1. *Acceptability*. The act of purchasing meat is not, in and of itself, a violation of AVOID. The commercial purchaser is acting for the morally legitimate purpose of acquiring ingredients for food she will serve, in turn seeking to realize such goods as skillful performance, aesthetic experience, sensory pleasure, life and bodily well-being, and friendship (as well as the others that will be served instrumentally by her firm's receipt of consumer payments).

   Someone purchasing from a slaughterhouse may intend the slaughterhouse to kill, though it is of course possible that she does not. If she is engaged in purposeful cooperation with the slaughterhouse, she acts unreasonably. She and her firm might also in some cases, when a shared purpose and a coordinated, cooperative relationship can be specified, be reasonably regarded as forming an industry community with the slaughterhouse, and thus as bearing some proportionate responsibility for the particular injuries done by the slaughterhouse.

   If she purchases meat from an intermediate supplier, she need not necessarily have any particular view about the products it acquires. She need not intend that any animal be killed.[84] She might be equally happy if her firm were able to purchase genetically engineered lab-grown meat,[85] or perhaps its

82 *See id.* at 153.
83 On identifying groups, *see* JOHN FINNIS, NATURAL LAW AND NATURAL RIGHTS 147–53, 232 (1980).
84 On the technical issues related to intention raised by this claim, see, *e.g.*, DAVID S. ODERBERG, MORAL THEORY: A NON-CONSEQUENTIALIST APPROACH 105–26 (2000).
85 *See* PAUL SHAPIRO, CLEAN MEAT: HOW GROWING MEAT WITHOUT ANIMALS WILL REVOLUTIONIZE DINNER AND THE WORLD (2018); KOERT VAN MENSVOORT & HENDRIK-JAN GRIEVINK, THE IN VITRO MEAT COOKBOOK (2014). *Cf.* STEPHEN R. L. CLARK, BIOLOGY AND CHRISTIAN ETHICS 265 (2000) (making clear that Clark finds the idea of creating "pure beef" repugnant; he describes the relevant tissue as "muscular" and essentially cancerous).

equivalent.[86] She might be happy to purchase the meat of healthy animals whose deaths resulted from natural causes.[87] Thus, the killing of animals need not be integral to the proposal she adopts when purchasing meat in this case. The odds are good, of course, that she does endorse the killing of animals and that killing is integral to the proposal she adopts when purchasing; and, of course, if so, her purchase is inconsistent with the Principle of Respect.

Presuming this is not the case, however, then, apart from the issue of her causal cooperation, her choice to purchase the meat need not be unreasonable. Nothing else about the purchase, generically specified, need be unfair or otherwise inconsistent with the requirements of practical reasonableness.

2. *Magnitude.* The range of potential injuries to animals caused by the factory farm and the slaughterhouse as a result of the restaurateur's or grocer's order could be substantial, particularly given the likely quantity of the order. Slaughterhouse workers could also suffer moral injury.
3. *Likelihood.* Given the quantity of her order, the likelihood that the purchase will result in the killing of actual animals is not inconsiderable.[88] And her noncooperation could exert a small impact on the volume or nature of injuries effected by a factory farm or slaughterhouse.
4. *Alternatives.* Lab-grown meat, the meat of animals whose deaths resulted from natural causes, and numerous vegetarian and vegan substitutes are available, and can be expected to foster bodily well-being, aesthetic experience, sensory pleasure, and conviviality. Of course, the question of feasibility arises here, since the restaurateur or grocer may regard it as difficult to remain in business without serving meat. Consumers may regard the options other than lab-grown meat as not offering adequate substitutes with respect to aesthetic experience, nutritional value, and sensory pleasure.

The *acceptability* of the restaurateur's choice counts in favor of the view that she is not required to join the meat industry boycott when she doesn't embrace the purposes of the factory farm and the slaughterhouse. The availability of attractive *alternatives* weighs in favor of the restaurateur's not making meat purchases (though of course this depends on whether potential consumers understand these potential alternatives *as* alternatives).The *likelihood* that a restaurant's or grocery chain's purchase in quantity from a given supplier will result in injuries to actual animals and the *magnitude* of these injuries—which will ordinarily be death and will frequently involve maiming and torture—seem to count meaningfully, and in many or most cases decisively, against the restaurateur's or grocer's purchase of (non-

[86] *Cf.* Sapontzis, *supra* note 7, at 203–204 (discussing the possibility, now arguably obviated by the emergence of cultured or lab-grown meat, of developing, "through genetic engineering, food animals with naturally short life spans" that might in principle, even if doubtfully in practice, be consumed nonexploitatively after their natural deaths).

[87] *Cf. id.* at 206 (arguing for the limited moral appropriateness of eating scavenged food).

[88] Or it may not; *cf.* Frey, Rights, *supra* note 12, at 210–13.

lab-grown) meat—at least, presuming she is unwilling for someone to impose on her a similar risk of undergoing comparable torture and death. It seems probable that she should not purchase meat.

C. *Purchasing Meat for Consumption by Someone Else*

Perhaps the potential boycotter is buying someone else's meal and her dining companion chooses to order meat. Imagine, for instance, that Pat, a vegetarian, is considering whether to ask a co-worker, Chris, to share a meal for which, as the person issuing the invitation, Pat will pay. Pat knows Chris is a carnivore. Pat does not know whether Chris is likely to eat out or at home absent the invitation, nor does Pat know precisely how frequent Chris's meat consumption might be, though Pat is aware that Chris is a regular meat eater. But Pat *is* concerned that Chris will order meat should they eat together. Pat worries that the invitation to a paid-for meal may be a but-for cause of Chris's meat purchase, which might be a but-for cause of unwarranted injury to animals. There is a plausible argument for the conclusion that Pat is *responsible* for the putative injuries brought about by Chris's meat purchase—almost as if they had been brought about by a purchase initiated personally by Pat. So perhaps Pat is obligated to avoid issuing a dinner invitation, especially an invitation to a paid-for meal, to Chris. Call this, with a nod to Derek Parfit, the SOMEWHAT INTOLERABLE CONCLUSION.

The SOMEWHAT INTOLERABLE CONCLUSION will understandably strike many people as absurdly moralistic Especially in a cultural environment in which the vast majority of people eat flesh and more food dollars are spent on restaurant meals than on meals consumed at home, it would seem to place a significant, indeed appalling, constraint on people's personal choices. Sharing a meal is a millennia-old symbol of friendship and acceptance, and exclusion from table fellowship is, similarly, a common expression of contempt and rejection. An invitation to a meal is often an important means of initiating or cementing a friendship or a professional or romantic relationship. Especially when a relationship is casual, imposing a limit on what one's dining companion can eat or what one will pay for is likely either to preclude acceptance of one's offer or rule out the acceptance of other offers in the future. So there will be very good reason—for Pat and the rest of us—to resist the conclusion that Pat isn't morally entitled to invite Chris to a paid-for dinner.

Whether the SOMEWHAT INTOLERABLE CONCLUSION can, indeed, be successfully resisted can be determined as follows:

1. *Acceptability*. Pat is acting for good purposes: Pat is inviting Chris to a dinner at which a meat purchase that wouldn't otherwise have taken place may occur in order to foster the realization of friendship, or perhaps to further some instrumentally valuable professional good. Pat is purchasing meat to foster bodily well-

being, aesthetic experience, sensory pleasure, and the conviviality that restaurant meals can foster, to show generosity, to nurture a friendship or romantic relationship or family connection with a valued other, to cement a business relationship, or to assist a needy person.

To *intend* the maiming or killing of animals is, of course, to violate the Principle of Respect, but we may assume arguendo that Pat does not intend this. And, unintended consequences for animals and any specific commitments on Pat's part aside, the purchase appears consistent with the other requirements of practical reasonableness.

2. *Magnitude*. The killing or maiming of actual animals might result from the dinner invitation and meal purchase, as might moral injury to slaughterhouse workers.
3. *Likelihood*. It is unlikely that Pat's invitation and purchase will lead to harm for any animal even assuming a meat purchase wouldn't have happened except for the invitation to a paid-for meal, given the nature of the meat market.

   In addition, Pat's invitation and payment might not increase the likelihood of net harm to animals because Chris might purchase a meat meal even if Pat decides not to do so (either in the course of the dinner, or at an alternative meal minus Pat), or because Chris's total meat purchases would be the same whether Pat issued a dinner invitation or not. Perhaps, absent the invitation, Chris would have gone home and prepared a chicken-fried steak. Alternatively, perhaps Chris's meat consumption in a given month is relatively constant: Having meat while eating with Pat will mean *not* ordering meat on another occasion when it would otherwise have been purchased.

   The invitation to a paid-for meal also might not increase the overall likelihood of injury to animals because the shared meal might form part of an ongoing professional or personal relationship in the course of which Pat's influence could lead to a reduction in meat purchases by Chris. This may be because Chris might not wish to be offensive by consuming meat around Pat, because Chris might opt to purchase meals that Pat could share, or even because Chris, who wouldn't otherwise have done so, might come to see the desirability of a vegetarian diet as a result of Pat's influence. (Of course, this will be relevant only with respect to interactions that are expected to be repeated. And, even as regards these sorts of interactions, Pat can be confident neither that they *will*, in fact, be repeated *nor* that they will develop as hoped.)
4. *Alternatives*. Pat need not invite Chris to a meal at all, but this could represent a serious loss to both. Pat need not volunteer to pay for a shared meal despite inviting Chris, but etiquette ordinarily dictates that the person issuing a meal invitation take responsibility for the bill. And the decision not to purchase the meal might sometimes, however, have a negative impact on Pat's relationship with Chris. Agreeing to pay only when a dining companion orders a nonmeat meal can, under the right circumstances, have a useful symbolic effect.

> Appealing nonmeat alternative foods may be readily available, but it is not clear that the consumer's dining partner will necessarily acknowledge this. There may be some value in highlighting this fact, but *criticizing* the diets of others is *not* likely to affect their dietary choices and *is* likely to have an adverse impact on their relationships with the potential purchaser.

The *magnitude* of injury that might be caused by the purchase of meat is substantial. At the same time, there's no question apart from the issue of causal COOPERATION as regards the *acceptability* of Pat's choice to invite carnivorous Chris to dinner and to pay for Chris's meat. Realistic *alternatives* are lacking. And the *likelihood* that the invitation or payment will exert any causal impact on the meat market is minimal — not only because of the nature of the meat market generally but also because of the fact that Pat hasn't initiated a meat order and perhaps also because of some issues specific to the relationship between Pat and Chris. The relevant factors seem to render Pat's choice reasonable, provided the purchase is consistent, in the manner noted earlier, with the Principle of Fairness.[89]

It might sometimes be helpful, in an ongoing friendship, romantic relationship, marriage, or business relationship, to offer to pay only for a nonmeat meal (or only for the nonmeat portions of a meal) ordered by a dining companion, while declining to pay for meat. But this will only be the case in some instances, and will often be impractical and counterproductive.

D. *Occasioning Others' Meat Purchases*

Consider a similar case. Suppose someone considers inviting friends to a potluck, aware that one or more participants will likely prepare meat dishes (and will thus likely either purchase meat for the occasion or use meat which they have already purchased and which they will likely replace by purchasing more). Is the potluck organizer required to further the meat industry boycott by declining to issue such an invitation or by insisting that all contributions be vegetarian?

[89] Pat might also argue that the principles we internalize, the principles we make habitual, should be ones upon which we are actually likely to act. Heroic or saintly principles may be overly taxing and difficult to follow sensibly, and their adoption may lead either to the abandonment of morality entirely or to counterproductive exertions of one sort or another. Perhaps, then, it would be preferable for Pat to avoid subjecting choices about extending dinner invitations to moral scrutiny. Perhaps Pat would tend to respond resentfully to the demand that the consequences of individual invitations be assessed. Perhaps Pat would fumble things by attempting to corral unwilling omnivores into avoiding meat purchases. And so perhaps it would be better, all things considered, if Pat did not try to determine the consequences of an invitation to Chris, even ignoring the fact that these consequences are in fact and quite possibly in principle unknowable and that there is good reason to think they might involve minimal effects on actual animals. *See* R. M. HARE, MORAL THINKING: ITS LEVELS, METHOD, AND POINT 198–201 (1981). These sorts of considerations obviously wouldn't license someone in violating the Principle of Respect. They might, however, be relevant to determining what, for instance, the Principle of Fairness required in a given situation.

1. *Acceptability*. The person issuing the potluck invitation does not, *ex hypothesi*, embrace the purpose of harm to animals. Apart from the issue of COOPERATION and any specific commitments, the act of issuing a dinner invitation or calling for a potluck without insisting that all purchases be vegetarian is not, in and of itself, a violation of AVOID or of the Principle of Respect, the Principle of Fairness, or any other requirement of practical reasonableness. The person issuing the invitation is acting in order to realize various aspects of flourishing, including friendship—and does not embrace the purpose of injury to animals.
2. *Magnitude*. The potential magnitude of the harms that might result from others' meat purchases could be very great—including torture and death. Slaughterhouse workers might also be adversely affected.
3. *Likelihood*. The likelihood that slaughterhouses will kill more animals or that factory farms will abuse more because of *any* uncoordinated individual meat purchase is very small. So it is highly likely that the same number of animals would be bred to be mistreated, tortured, or killed whether or not the invitation was issued and a potluck participant purchased meat. The likelihood that others will acquire the *habit* of purchasing more meat because of the invitation or the organizer's failure to attempt to make the potluck meat-free is low and the effects indirect and diffuse.

   Some carnivorous dinner or potluck companions may surprise the organizer by failing to purchase meat. Some might well purchase meat in equivalent quantities whether or not one invites them to dinner or encourages them to participate in a potluck; there is no way of knowing whether they would do so only if asked to go to dinner or participate in a potluck, or whether they might eat less meat in other contexts because of having eaten it over dinner or at a potluck.

   In addition, avoiding the temptation to bully participants into not bringing meat might enhance the organizer's relationships with the other attendees, and so, potentially, her ability to encourage others to reduce their meat consumption. Neither narrowing the potluck invitation nor declining to issue it will likely prevent any harm, and some animals might not be injured because the invitation is issued.
4. *Alternatives*. Presumably in some cases the organizer could seek to discourage people from bringing meat to a potluck, though this may not be practical and might have disruptive consequences for her relationships with carnivorous invitees. (Meatless options may be nutritionally or aesthetically equivalent or superior, but not every participant will see these as perfect substitutes.) She might exclude carnivores from her invitation entirely, but this seems problematic for multiple reasons, including negative impacts on relationships, negative impacts on the carnivores themselves, and negative impacts on the chances that the carnivores, rendered more resentful by being excluded, will change their dietary habits.

The *magnitude* of the potential injuries will clearly weigh against issuing the invitation. But the *acceptability* of the invitation tends to weigh in favor of viewing it as a reasonable instance of causal COOPERATION. And the minimal *likelihood* that issuing the invitation would cause serious injuries renders the magnitude of the potential injuries non-decisive. *Alternatives* acceptable to one's preferred guests will often not be available. When a way of gracefully and unobtrusively reducing the likelihood that an invitee will purchase meat at dinner or for a potluck is available, the person who endorses AVOID and who accepts the NATURAL LAW account of COOPERATION will opt for this alternative. But, when it is not, presuming she can regard the relevant risk as acceptable in light of the Principle of Fairness, she will almost certainly be free to issue a potluck invitation anyway.

E. *Consuming Unpurchased, Unrequested Meat*

Suppose one is served a prepurchased dish, a dish whose contents one didn't specify (perhaps one is at a banquet) and which will be discarded if one doesn't consume them, only to discover that the dish contains meat.

1. *Acceptability*. If one opts to eat the meat, one will be acting for the acceptable purpose of consuming a putatively desirable meal, realizing various goods including life and bodily well-being, and perhaps also sensory pleasure and aesthetic experience. Certainly the act of *consuming* meat is not, in and of itself, a violation of AVOID or of any generic requirement of practical reasonableness.[90] The only obvious reason eating meat in this instance might be unreasonable apart from the issue of COOPERATION might be some particular commitment to oneself or promise to another, perhaps because of a public role or stance.
2. *Magnitude*. Whenever meat production levels might be affected, there is always the possibility that harms of great magnitude will be done to animals and that slaughterhouse workers will suffer moral harms. But consuming meat that one didn't request and that will be discarded if one doesn't eat it simply won't affect production levels even in principle.
3. *Likelihood*. The likelihood that the conceivable harms will occur is nil. Eating the meat is virtually certain to cause no injury.
4. *Alternatives*. One might decline to eat at all as an act of symbolic protest, but unless one is always required to protest what one regards as inappropriate, whether one *needs* to do so in any given case will be determined in light of one's commitments and the Principle of Fairness.

One might also request a nonmeat alternative; but alternative entrées may not be available in a fixed-menu setting (though one might still be able to request extra

[90] Of course, some specific commitment to oneself or promise to another might preclude consuming meat in this case or more generally.

portions of items that might otherwise accompany a meat entrée as substitutes for the entrée itself). Under some circumstances, of course, it might be undesirably complicating and rude to avoid eating or to ask for an alternative (though it is not clear that *anyone* is ever obligated, absent a specific personal commitment or interpersonal promise, to eat something she finds sensorily unappealing or does not want to eat for some other reason).

No animal will be harmed by the consumption of unrequested meat, and eating or not eating it will have no effect on the market signals transmitted to those who torture and kill animals. The proposed meat industry boycott makes sense as a matter of not *purchasing* the products of the industry, and so of not sending market signals that *cause* the torture and death of animals. It makes no particular sense as a matter of not *consuming* these products.

All of the relevant factors except the availability of *alternatives* weigh unequivocally in favor of the conclusion that the diner in this case does nothing inappropriate by consuming meat served her without her having ordered it. When there *is* value in making a symbolic protest or seeking to influence others by example, and when alternatives are available, however, it may be admirable for one to request a meatless meal. Apart from specific commitments or promises, one surely isn't required to do so. And, bracketing the issue of such commitments or promises, one will have no reason not to consume unrequested meat in virtue of the proposed boycott (though of course one may have other reasons not to do so).

F. Purchasing Ordinary Commercial Dairy Products

Given the connections between the meat and dairy industries, does a duty to boycott the meat industry translate into a duty to avoid purchasing ordinary commercial dairy products?[91]

1. Moral Concerns about Ordinary Commercial Dairy Products

There is no general moral argument for the view that obtaining milk from cows and eggs from chickens is inherently immoral.[92] It seems easy enough to imagine milk- and egg-producing practices that would not undermine the well-being of cows and

[91] *Cf.* CLARK, STANDING, *supra* note 7, at 23–24. The context here is Clark's analysis of the question whether those recognizing animals as morally considerable should occupy themselves defending prey animals from predators. On the issue of Christian missionaries' non-vegetarianism (and that of Jesus, which Clark explicitly acknowledges), see CLARK, STATUS, *supra* note 7, at 195–98.

[92] A fact certainly conceded by animal advocates; *cf.* SAPONTZIS, *supra* note 7, at 202–203; Evelyn B. Pluhar, *The Right Not to Be Eaten, in* FOOD, *supra* note 12, at 92, 96–97; FOX, *supra* note 13, at 146–47 (discussing the status of animals after a "shift to a completely vegetarian economy," and suggesting that "sheep could still provide wool, cattle milk, and poultry eggs").

chickens. Animals would be allowed substantial space for roaming;[93] no animals, including ones (like males) judged superfluous, would be killed or sent to slaughterhouses; bulls would be used for the insemination of cows; calves would not be weaned prematurely and would not be separated from their mothers.[94] Such practices would not violate AVOID.[95]

The difficulty, of course, is that very few dairy products are made in environments in which standards like these are respected. The substantial mistreatment of factory-farmed animals and the fact that killing so often accompanies the making of dairy products by factory farms makes factory dairy farming problematic.[96] Most commercially available dairy products come from factory-farmed animals. Even organic farming methods, while they involve greater respect for animals than do factory-farming methods, often involve some significant mistreatment of animals, and organically farmed animals are often sent to slaughterhouses. So even organic dairy farming is problematic. In short, dairy farms frequently violate AVOID.

2. Consumer Purchases

A consumer's purchase of ordinary commercial dairy products can be assessed under the following heads:

1. *Acceptability*. The act of purchasing milk or eggs is consistent with AVOID and (prescinding from the question of COOPERATION) with the general requirements of practical reasonableness. The purchasing consumer is acting for the morally acceptable purpose of realizing such goods as aesthetic experience, sensory pleasure, life and bodily well-being, and friendship. The individual consumer who purchases ordinary commercial dairy products need not engage in purposeful COOPERATION with those who mistreat, torture, or kill animals. She need not intend the harms these organizations perpetrate. She does not instruct or require

93 *See* ALASDAIR COCHRANE, ANIMAL RIGHTS WITHOUT LIBERATION: APPLIED ETHICS AND HUMAN OBLIGATIONS (2012). *Cf.* Hilary Peters, *Hilary Peters' E-Diary of Real Farm Food 2002–2005*, WARMWELL, http://www.warmwell.com/ediary.html (Oct. 7, 2002) ("At Church Farm, Friston, Saxmundham . . . [t]heir cows lead an independent existence, with a robotic milking parlour. This means they can come in and get themselves milked whenever they feel the need.").

94 The International Society for Krishna Consciousness may currently operate a dairy meeting these standards. Pravin K. Shah, *Cruelty Free Dairy*, DD-B, http://www.dd-b.net/~raphael/jain-list/msg02118.html, reports: "A friend informed me that the Dairy run by Hare Krishna religious group called Vaishnva Dairy that can be considered as close to cruelty free as possible. The cows are not confined to one place, no artificial insemination, no babies are shipped to veal factory, bulls are used for farming and mating." I last viewed this page on Jan. 23, 2005; the page doesn't seem to be in place at this point, and I'm not clear that Shah's spelling of the dairy's name is correct. While there appears to be no Vaishnva Dairy, more than one farm in India today carries the name "Vaishnavi Dairy," but it's unclear to me whether any of them is operated by ISKCON.

95 *Cf.* FOX, *supra* note 13, at 146–47.

96 *See, e.g.*, GARY E. VARNER, PERSONHOOD, ETHICS, AND ANIMAL COGNITION: SITUATING ANIMALS IN HARE'S TWO-LEVEL UTILITARIANISM (2012).

anyone to perpetrate them. She does not will, or will that others bring about, these harms in order to effect her nutritional or aesthetic goals, nor are they necessary consequences of the achievement of these goals.[97] So the ordinary purchaser does not violate the Principle of Respect.

2. *Magnitude.* In principle, the magnitude of the harm is substantial. Animals bred and mistreated on factory farms and ultimately consigned to slaughterhouses undergo a variety of injuries and are ultimately killed. Slaughterhouse workers suffer from their work as well.
3. *Likelihood.* It is quite unlikely that the market signals sent by consumer purchases will make a difference for any particular animal or group of animals even where the issue is purchasing *meat.* The odds that the individual consumer's purchase of *dairy products* will cause the death or torture of any particular animal are even lower than that her purchase of meat will do so.[98]
4. *Alternatives.* The consumer's alternatives may or may not be palatable. Some dairy products made by animals that have been and will be treated well are available, but not frequently and in large quantities in typical consumer outlets. Nondairy alternatives are available, and lab-grown dairy products doubtless will be soon. Nondairy alternatives are not perfect substitutes for dairy products, however—not only as regards flavor and texture but also as regards the potential health benefits some consumers reap from dairy products. But declining to eat any ordinary commercial dairy products will mean eating a vegan diet outside one's home under most circumstances, though cruelty-free products (as well as organic products and ones made by free-range animals) will sometimes be available. Since many meat-free products on offer in restaurants and grocery stores contain ordinary commercial dairy products, attempting to eat a vegan diet will often be difficult and inconvenient. Further, it will mean avoiding products which some people find conducive to their health (except when at home). And consuming dairy-free products can represent a significant aesthetic loss.

[97] Such a purchase at the consumer level is obviously quite different from a butcher's placement of a standing order with a slaughterhouse. Here, a purchase forms part of an ongoing transactional relationship that does involve instructions that more animals be killed.

[98] The dairy market is related to the meat market but is, of course, separate. It is comparable in scale. US milk production in 2018, for instance is estimated at roughly 217.9 billion pounds. *See Dairy Forecasts, in* OUTLOOK, *supra* note 37, at 26, 26. "In the semiannual publication *Dairy: World Markets and Trade*, USDA Foreign Agricultural Service forecasts that 2018 milk production for the top five major exporters (European Union (EU), United States, New Zealand, Argentina, and Australia) will total 652.6 billion pounds, 6.4 billion pounds higher than the December forecast and a 1.47-percent increase over 2017." Jerry Cessna & Jonathan Law, *Dairy, in* OUTLOOK, *supra*, at 8, 11. Egg production in the United States alone in 2018 was predicted to be 1,970 mil. doz. *See U.S. Red Meat and Poultry Forecasts, supra* note 37, at 25. In 2016, global egg production stood at somewhat under 74,000,000 metric tons. *See Global Egg Production from 1990 to 2017 (in 1,000 metric tons)*, STATISTA, https://www.statista.com/statistics/263972/egg-production-worldwide-since-1990/.

The consumer may have marginally less reason to avoid dairy products made by factory farms than she does to avoid the meat produced by such farms.[99] The *acceptability* of purchasing ordinary commercial dairy products and the *likelihood* that doing so will effect unwarranted injury, and thus the numbers actually likely to be affected, seem to weigh in favor of the judgment that the consumer's purchase of ordinary commercial dairy products need not be seen as an instance of material cooperation with the cruel and unfair treatment of animals. The *magnitude* of the relevant injuries would weigh heavily against any COOPERATION were the likelihood of harm not so low. Much of the time, the availability of *alternatives* will not weigh strongly against the purchase of such products, given the relative difficulty of obtaining cruelty-free dairy products or satisfactory dairy-free substitutes in restaurants and ordinary grocery stores.

The consumer might well analyze the relevant issues in light of the Principle of Fairness and find that, especially given the nutritional, aesthetic, and convenience-based reasons she might have for choosing foods containing dairy products, the very low risk that harm might result from her purchase of these products could be reasonably accepted. If she could accept a rule allowing the imposition on *her* or her loved ones of risks of harm equivalent to those her purchase would impose on animals—as she could, perhaps, accept the risk associated with others' decisions to drive—then she could reasonably accept this risk and purchase ordinary commercial dairy products or foods containing these products.

Of course, when satisfactory alternatives *are* readily available, she should opt for them, since doing so would reduce the already-low risk even more. Thus when she purchases dairy products, she has reason to opt for cruelty-free products over ordinary commercial dairy products when they are conveniently available. (Of course, most restaurants are unlikely to offer cruelty-free products, but when one is convenient and serves cuisine of the desired kind and quality, she has reason to patronize it.) Similarly, when cruelty-free products are unavailable, she has reason to choose nondairy alternatives—if they are conveniently available and competitively priced (as they may not be at many restaurants), if they are nutritionally apt, and if she experiences them as aesthetically satisfactory substitutes.

3. Commercial Purchases

Whether a commercial purchaser's choice to purchase ordinary commercial dairy products is reasonable depends on several factors:

99 Ironically, one might argue that if a boycott succeeded in eliminating the market for meat or milk, one result would be the more rapid killing of the animals resident on factory farms, since their ongoing maintenance would no longer be profitable. (I owe this point to Stephen Clark.) The example makes clear the need for a public policy response to this problem.

1. *Acceptability*. The act of purchasing milk or eggs is not, in and of itself, a violation of AVOID or of any requirement of practical reasonableness (bracketing the issue of COOPERATION). The commercial purchaser is acting for the morally legitimate purpose of acquiring ingredients for food she will serve, in turn seeking to realize such goods as skillful performance, aesthetic experience, sensory pleasure, life and bodily well-being, and friendship (as well as the others that will be served instrumentally by her firm's receipt of consumer payments). Commercial purchasers placing orders for commercial dairy products are presumably not asking that the animals that make the products they sell be killed or tortured (unless they judge that they prefer that these animals be mistreated and slaughtered in order to reduce the prices of dairy products). There is no *inherent* connection between abusive dairy farming practices and the availability of dairy products to grocery stores.[100] Such products could almost certainly be made available in a manner that doesn't involve injuring animals. Commercial purchasers do not, therefore, have the same kind of vested interest in abusive practices *associated with* the production of dairy products that they do in abusive practices *essential to* the production of meat. Thus, it is less certain that the commercial purchaser will be engaged in purposeful COOPERATION with slaughterhouses or with farms that engage in abusive practices. The killing and abusing of animals by others need not be integral to the proposal a commercial purchaser adopts when it purchases dairy products.
2. *Magnitude*. The magnitude of the potential relevant effects is considerable if they occur: animals may be bred and then mistreated before, if they are born on typical factory farms, being sent to slaughterhouses. The moral harms to slaughterhouse and factory farm workers are also considerable.
3. *Likelihood*. Because the commercial purchaser buys in volume, she may be able to influence the purchasing habits of her suppliers and so, indirectly, of dairy farms. Her decision not to order from a dairy farm because it mistreats animals, and to order from another because it does not, could help meaningfully to promote desirable behavior and discourage undesirable behavior. A given choice by a commercial purchaser may exert a small impact on any particular instance of harm by a dairy farm or slaughterhouse.
4. *Alternatives*. The commercial purchaser, buying in quantity, may be able to obtain dairy products made by animals that have been and will be treated well.[101] And she can acquire, prepare, sell, and serve some alternatives to dairy products if consumers find them appealing at the price at which she offers them.

100 Such practices do affect, of course, the *prices* of these products.

101 Locating such products requires some work. It's often easy enough to buy organic products, but it is clear that even these, even when labeled as "farmed free" (American Humane Association) or as "freedom foods" (RSPCA), aren't necessarily *cruelty-free*.

The *acceptability* of purchasing ordinary commercial dairy products and the *likelihood* that doing so will effect unwarranted injury count in favor of the reasonableness of the commercial purchaser's causal COOPERATION. The impact of the commercial purchaser's decision on dairy production might be significantly greater than any consumer's, and this might dispose the commercial purchaser to avoid purchase of such products if cruelty-free dairy alternatives that leave the range and appeal of the prepared foods on offer unaffected are available. If she can conveniently obtain cruelty-free products on reasonable terms, the commercial purchaser need not buy ordinary commercial dairy products and should instead buy from dairies that produce cruelty-free milk and eggs.

V. LIBERALIZING BOYCOTTS

The question whether one is required to join a boycott can arise in a variety of contexts. But it's very easy to assimilate the circumstances surrounding any proposed boycott to the kind envisioned in a scenario like SIMPLE MARKET. It's easy, that is, to act as if our purchasing decisions link us directly with other market participants and as if we are somehow responsible for the bad behavior of anyone with whom the market connects us.

There are small, local markets in which this can be the case. But we have every reason not to want to limit our interactions to the local and the personal. And this means that we will unavoidably engage in extended social cooperation with innumerable strangers, benefiting in innumerable ways from relationships with people we will never meet.

Liberals rightly celebrate this kind of social cooperation. But it is important to recognize that it poses moral challenges that cannot be resolved as if impersonal market transactions could be understood and assessed in the same ways as small-scale, face-to-face ones. The NATURAL LAW casuistry of COOPERATION can be used to analyze issues related to our participation in both kinds of transactions, but it won't yield the same sorts of results—nor should it, given the important differences between local and global markets.

I do not believe that we wrong animals if we receive services from them, as long as we compensate them and treat them with friendship and respect.[102]

[102] "Dogs, horses, cats and cattle are members of one and the same society with us—granted that they have not 'chosen' to be so, and may have radically different concepts of what society it is that they share in, but that is true of us as well. That is why I do not share the view of some animal liberationists that domestication is of its nature tyrannical and that all domestic 'pets' should be released to make their own ways in the world. That would, in my view, be as pointless and as cruel as it would be to throw out your children or refrain from disciplining and educating them on the specious ground that they have not 'chosen' to be born into our particular family and culture. I do not think it an infringement of liberty to educate and give moral training to a child or to a 'pet'. What is offensive is to deny to them the right to participate in the social order on such terms as allow them to form friendships and follow vocations in ways suitable to their age and kind. The ideal for which liberals are groping is not that of independent action without any obligation of care or cooperation, but the

In particular, we will surely have special duties of care, gratitude, and reciprocity to those animal species and individuals with which we have special relationships.[103] Certainly, humans have found it easy to ignore such duties: "others than I," as Stephen Clark observes, "have thought it a poor reward for the giver of wool and cheese to be killed and eaten when we have no need of flesh foods."[104]

Disregarding both general and special duties to animals, slaughterhouses and factory farms consistently violate AVOID. Many milk and egg products are made by organizations that do so as well. We thus have good reason to avoid *purposeful* COOPERATION with these organizations. But we may sometimes reasonably choose *causal* COOPERATION with them. On the liberal NATURAL LAW view I seek to defend here, DECLINE will follow from AVOID to the extent that we are required to boycott the meat industry because of the impact of our choices on the meat market. And the reality is that a global market like the market for meat is very unlikely to be sufficiently altered by a *consumer* buying choice to save any actual animal from torture and slaughter. Recognizing the possibility that meat purchases might sometimes trigger threshold crossings doesn't really change this picture.

Given AVOID, no one should purposefully kill a nonhuman animal for food or act with the purpose that someone else do so. Those who carry on the work of slaughterhouses always act wrongly. People who do not engage in *purposeful* COOPERATION with those who wrong animals may still choose unreasonably if they engage in *causal* COOPERATION. Thus, someone—like a grocer or restaurateur—who purchases meat in quantity may well act unreasonably by declining to participate in the meat industry boycott, given the potential extent of her purchase's impact and the fact that it is more likely to be filled by a single supplier.

By contrast, given the negligible market impact of an individual, isolated choice, the consumer who does not intend injury to animals is not required to participate in the boycott by declining to purchase meat in the global market in any particular case. (She would act wrongly if she purchased meat in a real-world setting like RUDIMENTARY MARKET or SIMPLE MARKET—as she might in some contexts. She would also act wrongly if she bought meat when what she experienced as a suitable substitute was on offer. And she would act wrongly if she imposed risks of harm through her purchases that she would be unwilling to accept for herself or her loved

open fraternity of mutually respectful well-wishers." CLARK, STANDING, *supra* note 7, at 106–7; *cf.* CLARK, BIOLOGY, *supra* note 85, at 290–300; CLARK, STATUS, *supra* note 7, at 73.

103 *Cf.* CLARK, STANDING, *supra* note 7, at 28–29: "Some non-human animals are members, though not citizens, of our immediate society, and have rights in law to our care and protection. They pay for those rights by the advantages we gain from them, and should certainly in natural justice be paid far more (or else pay far less). Some advantages we cannot seek from them without violating their rights as members of our society." And *cf.* HILL, *supra* note 7, at 168.

104 CLARK, STANDING, *supra* note 7, at 104–5; *cf.* PORPHYRY, ON ABSTINENCE FROM KILLING ANIMALS 3.19 (Gillian Clark, trans. & ed., 2000). Thanks to Stephen Clark for this reference; *see* STEPHEN R. L. CLARK, THE POLITICAL ANIMAL: BIOLOGY, ETHICS, AND POLITICS 141 n.48 (1999).

ones.) She need not participate in the boycott by refusing to purchase the meat ordered by her guests. She may likely issue potluck invitations to carnivorous friends. She may reasonably eat meat she has not ordered. And she may purchase ordinary commercial dairy products when what she takes to be satisfactory alternatives are not conveniently available.

One need not boycott all products whose producers do bad things. Declining to join in a boycott or participate in a protest is not the same thing as engaging in the objectionable activity being boycotted or protested. One is *required* to participate in a boycott only when not participating would mean purposefully embracing harm or actually causing it. Of course, that doesn't mean there's never a good reason to join a boycott when one isn't required to do so: someone might reasonably choose to be a vegetarian, for instance, not because doing so means avoiding harm to animals, but because of her decision's *symbolic* or *expressive* value.[105]

Thus, I do not eat animal flesh or purchase new leather shoes or jackets, because entirely satisfactory substitutes are frequently available and I want to protest the killing of animals by the meat industry. (I am also inclined to think that there is nutritional value in choosing a flesh-free diet.)[106] But I am quite aware that there are other convictions to express and other ways to spend my time that don't involve expressing convictions. And I recognize that actual animals will be saved, not in virtue of my participation in a causally inefficacious consumer boycott, but rather

[105] For a sensitive discussion (one which I appreciate but by which I am unconvinced) of the place of symbolic value in moral action, see ROBERT MERRIHEW ADAMS, FINITE AND INFINITE GOODS: A FRAMEWORK FOR ETHICS 124–28, 214–20 (1999). *Cf.* CLARK, STATUS, *supra* note 7, at 139 n.3 ("All those who disapprove of fox-hunting or vivisection . . . bear-baiting *et al.*, should indeed abandon flesh-eating in their own defence."); *cf. id.* at 45 ("[I]f we are to mean what we say in outlawing the unnecessary suffering of animals, we must become, at the least, vegetarians."); *cf. id.* at 52 ("[E]ven the minimal principle debarring the infliction of unnecessary suffering to animals must, in the present context, require us to become vegetarians, at the least, even if we allow the eating of meat to be an end of sufficient weight to act as the basis of our calculations. If, as seems more rational, we take merely the eating of food as our end, the argument is even simpler. Whatever the necessities of those with no other food available, we have no need of slaughter-houses."); *id.* at 183 ("Honourable men may honourably disagree about some details of human treatment of the non-human, but vegetarianism is now as necessary a pledge of moral devotion as was the refusal of emperor-worship in the early Church."). Someone might also hope that her choice to be a vegetarian might serve a pedagogical function (just as someone might recognize that boycotting a pharmaceutical product tested on animals before release to the market could have no effect on the means used to create that product—the testing will be complete before the product becomes available to consumers—but might nonetheless think that the company responsible for the product might rethink its approach to product development in the future).

[106] For population studies supportive of this claim, *see* GARY FRASER, DIET, LIFE EXPECTANCY, AND CHRONIC DISEASE: STUDIES OF SEVENTH-DAY ADVENTISTS AND OTHER VEGETARIANS (2003). Of course, alternative claims are also on offer, notably defenses of low-carbohydrate, high-fat diets that would be difficult for vegetarians to adopt. *See, e.g.*, GARY TAUBES, WHY WE GET FAT: AND WHAT TO DO ABOUT IT (2010); David K. Li, *Eating Cheese and Red Meat Is Actually Good for You*, NEW YORK POST, Aug. 29, 2018, *available at* https://nypost.com/2018/08/29/eating-cheese-and-red-meat-is-actually-good-for-you/amp/?__twitter_impression=true. Thanks to Sheldon Richman for opportunities to discuss these matters.

because of the adoption of moral norms and laws that prevent slaughterhouses and farms from torturing and killing animals.

Embracing the liberal spirit means recognizing the moral claims of the excluded, even as it also means avoiding moralism and celebrating the range of possible good choices. Liberals can draw on NATURAL LAW theory as they seek to identify and act on genuinely manageable, human responsibilities without being overwhelmed by crushing demands. We should challenge the torture and killing of animals. But we are not equally liable for all of the choices of the industries with whom our purchases may happen to connect us.[107] We are caught up in ambiguous webs of action and reaction, many of our actions have harmful consequences which in some cases we may reasonably accept, and we can't obsess about all of these consequences. Not all fights, not all *good* fights, must be fought all the time.[108]

Individual actors confronting vast, impersonal systems like the global market for meat face what may seem like overwhelming moral quandaries. More commonly, of course, given our capacities for deliberate attention and the extent to which our actions are causally efficacious, our moral concerns arise in the context of interpersonal interactions in which our purposes concern and our choices affect particular, identifiable others. A paradigmatic example of the kind of issue that arises in this sort of context is the question whether, and, if so, when, we may reasonably tell lies. I consider this question in Chapter 2.

107 *Cf.* HILL, *supra* note 7, at 166–69 (rejecting the demand for complete apparent consistency in human moral behavior), 184–86 (rejecting "the position of the moral 'hard-liner'" in favor of "compromise, example and gentle persuasion."); FOX, *supra* note 13, at 169–73, 178–80 (maintaining that "vegetarianism is a process that grows and evolves, an ongoing lifestyle choice that does not and need not follow a fixed pattern," *id.* at 171).

108 Frey seems to me to be right that moral goodness does not demand the puritanical avoidance of all association with institutions and practices to which one objects; *cf.* FREY, RIGHTS, *supra* note 12, at 227–42. But I am skeptical about Frey's proposal that the good person should press for substantial improvements in the lives of factory-farmed animals while remaining free to purchase meat, to the extent that this proposal is dependent on his view that it is not wrong, per se, to kill animals and that the imposition on them of unpleasant sensations, though these sensations deserve consideration morally, can be justified by the human benefits resulting from their imposition. And because, unlike Frey, I believe basic goods are incommensurable—I think we can more aptly justify rejecting a demand for complete purity in aretaic or (through something like the new natural lawyers' casuistry of cooperation) deontic terms.

2

Lies

I. LIBERALISM, NATURAL LAW, AND TRUTH

Liberalism rightly places a high value on truthfulness. A concern with flourishing is entirely consonant with this valuation. Accurate information plays a vital role in relation to both social cooperation and autonomous action; indeed, directly and indirectly, truth helps to make every variety of flourishing possible. Lies injure knowledge, practical reasonableness, and the intimate connection that is basic to friendship, and they have the potential to inhibit participation in other basic goods. And choosing truthfulness, difficult though it is, can enhance one's capacity to make good choices, respond sensitively to reality, and cement intimate relationships.

It seems clear that many lies are inconsistent with the requirements of practical reasonableness. A large number will violate the Principle of Fairness: I wouldn't want to be manipulated by being lied to in a given set of circumstances, so I act unfairly if I seek to manipulate you by lying to you in comparable circumstances. And others will be inconsistent with the Principle of Respect: when I lie in order to sabotage a friendship, say—whether as a means to some end or just out of malice—I always act wrongly.[1]

Liberals have generally sought to articulate humane moral visions in which the importance of truth is clearly acknowledged but in which restraints on lying do not bind absolutely, recognizing that some lies seek precisely to safeguard various basic aspects of well-being. It is also consistent with liberal values to recognize that some lies are trivial. Journalist Seymour Hersh, legendary for his exposure of official

[1] Even those who believe *some* lies may be reasonable nonetheless emphasize that there are multiple reasons to cabin acceptable instances of lying. For such reasons, *see, e.g.*, Sissela Bok, Lying: Moral Choice in Public and Private Life (1978); Jean-Paul Sartre, Notebooks for an Ethics 195–204 (1992) (maintaining that lying represents the objectification and subjugation of the other, so that, when I lie, I assert my authority over the other; and once I have conceded that I can lie, I imply that I am her or his master even if I do not exercise my imagined privilege); Bernard Gert, Morality: A New Justification of the Moral Rules 126–27 (1988); Leonard Nelson, System of Ethics 151–55 (1956); Charles Fried, Right and Wrong 54–78 (1978); Alan Donagan, The Theory of Morality 88–90 (1977); Alan Gewirth, Reason and Morality 198 (1978); T. M. Scanlon, What We Owe to Each Other 317–22 (1998); Lewis B. Smedes, Mere Morality 211–38 (1988); Alasdair MacIntyre, Ethics and Politics 101–42 (2006).

deception, emphasizes: "I happen to believe, innocently perhaps, that official lying or authorized lying or understood lying about military planning, weapons systems, or intelligence cannot be tolerated. I cannot look the other way."[2] However, Hersh observes:

> . . . I am in no way a fanatic or a prude about lying, and realize that human beings lie all the time. We all know the clichés about the big fish that one caught or the low golf score. My brother and I learned early in life that our mother lied repeatedly, especially about store-bought cookies she claimed to have baked. Not a big deal.[3]

Hersh even characterizes a lie he himself told in order, I take it, to avoid being whiny or ungracious as something done "in what I think was one of my finest hours."[4] Striking what is perhaps a complementary note, the insightful spiritual writer Hugh Prather maintains: "I want to be honest out of respect. And if I must lie in order to spare someone senseless pain, then it is my responsibility to lie so well that it won't be given a second thought."[5] It's interesting to ask whether Hersh and Prather are right; in any event, many people would, I suspect, echo their views.

While it values truth and truthfulness, NATURAL LAW liberalism, in particular, is neither moralistic nor rigoristic. Rather, NATURAL LAW theory understands moral principles precisely as guides to flourishing. On the NATURAL LAW view, as I've already stressed, morality is a second-order affair, regulating moral agents' choices with respect to flourishing (their own and others'). Flourishing is what matters. And concerns with values including the prevention of violence and the protection of privacy might dispose many people to think that a humane morality would treat some lies as permissible in the interest of flourishing.

It might seem as if defensive lying could be justified on the same basis as the defensive use of force, with the infliction of injury on one or more basic goods understood as incidental to reasonable defensive action. But orthodox NATURAL LAW theorists maintain that someone who lies necessarily chooses unreasonably. The liar purposefully or instrumentally injures both her own good and the good of the person to whom she lies.[6] Thus, on the orthodox NATURAL LAW view, lying is always wrong in principle, a violation of the Principle of Respect (which requires that one not attack one's own well-being just as it requires that one not attack another's).

I attempt here to suggest reasons to think that not every instance of lying—understood as *knowing false assertion*—need be unreasonable. The Principle of

[2] SEYMOUR M. HERSH, REPORTER: A MEMOIR 95 (2018).

[3] *Id.*

[4] *Id.* at 145.

[5] HUGH PRATHER, LOVE AND COURAGE 74 (2001). This doesn't mean that Prather was unaware of or blasé regarding the potential destructiveness of lying; *see, e.g.*, HUGH PRATHER & GAYLE PRATHER, NOTES TO EACH OTHER [22–25] (1990) (pages are unnumbered).

[6] *See, e.g.*, 2 GERMAIN G. GRISEZ, THE WAY OF THE LORD JESUS: LIVING A CHRISTIAN LIFE 407 (1994); CHRIS TOLLEFSEN, LYING AND CHRISTIAN ETHICS 107–8 (2014); Chris Tollefsen, *Lying: The Integrity Approach*, 52 AM. J. JURIS. 273 (2007).

Fairness and the Principle of Respect should provide appropriate and adequate grounding for limits on false assertion without yielding an absolute prohibition on lying. I begin by explaining why lying is always impermissible for the orthodox NATURAL LAW theorists (Part II). To be sure, some instances of verbal deception, even if not many, might be consistent even with orthodox NATURAL LAW theory (Part III), but these exceptions won't capture the concerns of those whose intuitions strongly suggest that some lies are morally appropriate. I explain why the in-principle rejection of the moral permissibility of all lies as purposeful attacks on self-integration might not survive careful scrutiny (Part IV) before summing up (Part V).

II. SELF-INTEGRATION, FRIENDSHIP, AND THE WRONGNESS OF LYING

The orthodox NATURAL LAW view is that any knowingly false assertion violates the Principle of Respect and is thus always impermissible. We have reason to object to lying because lies attack one or more basic goods, including knowledge, practical reasonableness, self-integration, and friendship.[7] The acknowledged injuries to the knowledge or practical reasonableness of the person to whom a lie is told might sometimes reasonably be accepted as side effects of reasonable acts, on analogy with the injuries brought about by the use of defensive force, so that in these cases lying need not be wrong, even if it injures the person deceived.[8] Nonetheless, on the orthodox NATURAL LAW view, lying is wrong in *all* cases because it necessarily involves purposefully injuring the liar's own self-integration and the good of sociality in the life of both the liar and the person to whom a lie is told.[9]

A. *Lying and Self-Integration*

Broadly speaking, self-integration is the good of *coherence* within a life, the good that obtains when the various aspects of oneself "hang together." This good may be characterized in such a way that lying necessarily injures it. Thus, John Finnis stresses that when I *assert* a proposition, I engage in "an act of self-disclosure." The division created by asserting a falsehood is the source of lying's moral wrongness:

7 *See, e.g.*, Mark C. Murphy, *Natural Law and the Moral Absolute against Lying*, 41 AM. J. JURIS 81, 86 (1996); JOHN M. FINNIS, AQUINAS: MORAL, POLITICAL, AND LEGAL THEORY 157–60 (1998); GRISEZ, LIFE, *supra* note 6, at 405–407; TOLLEFSEN, *supra* note 6, at 102–22.

8 *Cf.* GRISEZ, LIFE, *supra* note 6, at 407. Grisez does not say this explicitly. What I say in the text seems to me to be the most obvious way of making sense of Grisez's claim here that a lie doesn't always violate the rights of the person to whom it is told. Tollefsen suggests that telling a lie need not be an *injustice* to the person to whom it is told, though he nonetheless maintains that all knowing false assertions are wrong; *see* TOLLEFSEN, *supra* note 6, at 129–46.

9 *See, e.g.*, FINNIS, AQUINAS, *supra* note 7, at 157–60, 276; GRISEZ, LIFE, *supra* note 6, at 405–407; TOLLEFSEN, *supra* note 6, at 102–22.

> When one is lying, the mind one professes to reveal to those one is addressing is not one's actual mind. For one lies if and only if one asserts a proposition as true, believing it to be false, and thus communicating something about oneself . . . which is false even if the proposition asserted happens, contrary to one's belief, to be true. . . . The division of oneself—into the counterfeit self . . . fabricated externally by the false asserting, and the true self hidden interiorly—is fully effected in such an act of falsely asserting. . . . [T]he moral significance of the lie consists in its character precisely as false *self*-expression. . . . Its intrinsic moral significance is not so much in the fact (important as this typically is) that someone comes to believe the false proposition directly asserted. Its significance is rather . . . in this: what purports to be a relating of mind to mind and thus of person to person . . . is in reality made to be not that relationship at all but an act of *duplicity*, the presentation to another person of a pretended mind and heart.[10]

Lying and other kinds of deception "divide the inner and outer selves of those who engage in them, contrary to their own self-integration and authenticity. . . ."[11] Lying is uniformly objectionable because a person "cannot lie . . . without choosing the self-alienation which, opposed as it is to self-integration and authenticity, is sufficient to make lying wrong."[12] Lying involves "the duplicitous act of projecting for acceptance (belief) a phony self while actually remaining hidden behind one's pretended self-disclosure."[13] Acts of "intentional untruthfulness" can be seen to "express outwardly something at odds with one's inner self and attempt to lead others to accept it. Thus, they divide the inner and outer selves of those who engage in them, contrary to their own self-integration and authenticity . . . ."[14]

B. *Lying and Friendship*

A further NATURAL LAW argument maintains that a false assertion attacks the good of friendship—understood as including human social interaction generally. One aspect of this good, Chris Tollefsen maintains, is what he calls "communicative community."[15]

> [T]here is a shared order among participants in the paradigm case of the making and receiving of assertions, an order constituted at one level by the giving and receiving of meaning, and at a deeper level by the giving and receiving of the

10 FINNIS, AQUINAS, *supra* note 7, at 158. I take Finnis's exposition of Aquinas's account of the moral wrongness of lying to be at the same time an expression of Finnis's own position.

11 GRISEZ, LIFE, *supra* note 6, at 405.

12 *Id.* at 407.

13 FINNIS, AQUINAS, *supra* note 7, at 158. Finnis does not refer explicitly to self-integration here, but what he says—explicating, I take it, both his own view and Aquinas's—seems clearly consistent with the position taken explicitly by Grisez. Finnis does, at any rate, suggest that deception effects self-division. *Id.* at 157.

14 GRISEZ, LIFE, *supra* note 6, at 405; *cf.* TOLLEFSEN, *supra* note 6, at 103–14.

15 TOLLEFSEN, *supra* note 6, at 114–22.

asserter's self. At one level, then, the common good of such a communicative community is the sharing of meaning; at another level, it is the sharing of selves. It is this good that is mutually willed by the communicative agents.[16]

We need not, of course, actively seek to realize the good of communicative community any more than we need to seek actively to realize other goods.[17] But, as with other goods, we may not reasonably *attack* this good. Though the liar

> [since this begins in the middle, as it were, indenting the paragraph seems confusing], appears to make an offer to her hearer of communicative community, she at the same time blocks that community from coming to be by asserting that which does not, in fact, reflect her belief and her self. A liar thus creates the conditions under which something new—a realization of the basic good of sociality—would otherwise come to be, given her choice to assert, and then deliberately blocks that realization. And this seems to be an intentional act of damage . . . [to] the good of sociality.[18]

By making false assertions we actively *disconnect* ourselves from others, purposefully denying them access to ourselves, and so purposefully or instrumentally attack communicative community. Since purposefully or instrumentally attacking an aspect of a basic good is always wrong and since making a false assertion is effecting a purposeful attack on the good of friendship by attacking an aspect of it, communicative community, making a false assertion is always wrong, a violation of the Principle of Respect.[19]

III. ACCEPTABLE UNTRUTHS

Despite these seemingly rigoristic conclusions, even an orthodox NATURAL LAW analysis seems to leave room for pronouncing a limited number of untruths as consistent with the Principle of Respect (and, perhaps, the other requirements of practical reasonableness).

Suppose, for instance, that one is asked a question to which an accurate answer would be highly complex. One responds to the question with an assertion that is so lacking in nuance as to be false if taken literally. Here, one's goal is to avoid offering a complex answer. Now, it may be that the Principle of Fairness or another basic moral norm would rule out one's action as unreasonable. But it does not seem that one has violated the norm precluding *purposeful or instrumental* harm to any basic good. For the harm, if any, done to any aspect of well-being in this sort of case would seem to be a by-product of one's decision to avoid complexity. One's choice has not been *either* to attack, *or* to achieve some purpose of one's own *by means of* an attack

16 *Id.* at 115.
17 *See id.* at 119.
18 *Id.* at 120.
19 *See id.* at 119–22.

on, any aspect of one's own or another's well-being. Put another way, the success of one's action does not depend on the acceptance by the recipient of one's words of a false assertion as correct. (One's action in the kind of case considered here is sometimes said to be a matter of *economy* in truth-telling.[20])

Also germane is the fact that the context within which a verbal performance takes place can qualify something's status *as an assertion*. As Grisez notes, "there is no untruthfulness when entertainers create illusions, players in games bluff or opposing armies in war feint, and so on." This is because in these cases one is not, contextually, *asserting*. Rather, "deceptive acts are done but are neither intended nor understood as self-expressive, since everyone involved understands, and perhaps even agrees, that deception may be practiced."[21] It is interesting to ask how far this point can be extended. It seems as if it could allow for what might at least seem like knowingly false assertion in a number of cases.

There might be, for instance, cases in which clear standards of professional conduct permit professionals to lie to similarly situated professionals or to clients who have been put appropriately on notice. In such cases, the relevant professional standards would qualify the status of seeming assertions *as assertions*. A professional interaction of the right sort would in effect turn out to be relevantly similar to a game in which lying is permissible.[22] Also relevant might be cases in which the existence of relationships of hostility or conflict defeats otherwise reasonable expectations regarding truthfulness. Because of the context of utterance, someone might not believe that every communication she receives is necessarily a lie, but might nonetheless understand that her conversation partner is not necessarily telling the truth, with the result that her conversation partner would not be making a straightforward, unqualified assertion.

One might argue, for instance, that where the would-be murderer at the door *knows* that I know he is a murderer, he will not expect me to tell him the truth, so that an assertion made to him has more in common with a bluff in poker or a feint on a battlefield than with, say, the fraudulent manipulation of a machine shop's customer. An army on a battlefield does not wish to be misled by a feint, but it understands that the circumstances of hostility in which it finds itself make an expectation of clear and consistently truthful communication on the part of its adversary unreasonable. The same, one might think, should be true of the murderer.[23] Perhaps (I certainly don't assert this dogmatically) in the case of relationships like the one between Seymour Hersh and his brother on the one hand and their mother on the other there is, similarly, an implicit awareness of some communications as more ambiguous than their surface features might suggest: that they *might*, at least, be false will in such cases be mutually understood.

20 *See id.* at 157–59.
21 Grisez, Life, *supra* note 6, at 409.
22 *Cf.* Chapter 5.III.D and 5.IV.D, *infra*.
23 I owe this point to Charles Fried, Right and Wrong (1979).

But of course there are limits here. The same conclusion obviously doesn't follow when the issue is a communication with someone who does not realize that deception is to be expected. Because the moral wrongness of false assertion follows from its status as an attack on basic goods, it will not make a difference whether the person with whom one communicates *should* be aware that deception is to be expected. Rather, it must be the case, for the kind of exception Grisez notes to be relevant, that the actor reasonably believes it likely that the person with whom she is communicating actually *does* expect that deception is at least a possibility.

Suppose, then, that the would-be murderer at the door does not know that I realize he intends to kill or otherwise act in a way I might wish to resist. If I recognize that he does not, then, on the orthodox NATURAL LAW view, I may not lie to him, since he does not understand that deception is to be expected.

Perhaps, however, NATURAL LAW theory can accommodate a range of defensive lies. After all, on the NATURAL LAW view, one may kill without violating the Principle of Respect, provided death is a by-product or side effect of an action undertaken for another purpose—most commonly, to stop an unjust attack against oneself or another.[24] And it might seem as if the same kind of analysis could be used with respect to killing and knowing false assertion.

One could say, in parallel with what orthodox NATURAL LAW theorists say about killing: *if an act injures some basic aspect of well-being but injuring this aspect of well-being is part of neither the proposal one adopts in choosing nor a purpose for the sake of which one chooses, the act may be morally acceptable provided other relevant moral norms are observed*. If the NATURAL LAW justification of killing in self-defense is correct, some kinds of false assertion might be as well, given the parallel between physical and verbal defense.[25]

Intuitively, I think, we are inclined to regard causing someone's death as effecting one of the most serious sorts of injuries we can do her. So it may seem intuitively plausible that, at minimum, in any case in which it was appropriate to use force with foreseen but unintended lethal effect to repel an unjust attack, one might deceive to repel the attack, if deception appeared likely to be effective. After all, if one can avoid risking a violent confrontation with an attacker, a confrontation likely to be harmful to the attacker and oneself, would this not be preferable to using force? This seems especially reasonable when one cannot use force effectively, perhaps because of a vast disproportion between one's own capacity to use force and the attacker's. But

24 *See* THOMAS AQUINAS, SUMMA THEOLOGIÆ II-II q. 64 a.7; Germain Grisez, *Toward a Consistent Natural-Law Ethics of Killing*, 15 AM. J. JURIS. 64 (1970); Joseph M. Boyle, *Toward Understanding the Principle of Double Effect*, 90 ETHICS 527 (1980); John M. Finnis, Germain G. Grisez & Joseph M. Boyle, *"Direct" and "Indirect": A Reply to Critics of Our Action Theory*, 65 THOMIST 1, 43 (2001); FINNIS, AQUINAS, *supra* note 7, at 276–79; GRISEZ, LIFE, *supra* note 6, at 473, 482–85.

25 The analogy is hardly original with me; *cf.* Joseph M. Boyle, *The Absolute Prohibition of Lying and the Origins of the Casuistry of Mental Reservation: Augustinian Arguments and Thomistic Developments*, 44 AM. J. JURIS 43, 44 (1999) (on Scotus). It is one that Grisez and Finnis acknowledge, but which neither finds persuasive. *Cf.* GRISEZ, LIFE, *supra* note 6, at 407.

of course this won't matter if any false assertion, whatever its purpose or context, is wrong, as orthodox NATURAL LAW theorists maintain.

IV. DEFENDING DEFENSIVE DECEPTION

In Part IV, I explain why we might be warranted in declining to accept the orthodox NATURAL LAW theorists' view that false assertion is unavoidably an attack on the goods of self-integration and communicative community.[26] In each case, the question is how the bounds of the relevant good are best understood.

A. *The Limits of Self-Integration*

When self-integration is understood expansively, every false assertion is a purposeful or instrumental attack on this good. But the question is whether we should, indeed, understand self-integration in this way.

It seems to me that the orthodox NATURAL LAW theorist faces the following difficulty with respect to this good. (*i*) On the one hand, it can be understood as the attainment of emotional equilibrium and inner harmony. If it is understood in this way, acknowledging it to be such poses no difficulty for the view of false assertion I seek to defend. (*ii*) Alternatively, this good may be construed as constituted by the harmony of inner and outer. But, in this case, if we do not already find an exceptionless prohibition on all false assertions plausible, we will have little reason to affirm that self-integration thus construed is, in fact, a good.

The first interpretation is perhaps suggested by some of Grisez's language. He suggests that one way in which we "can infer the basic human goods" is by considering "the privations which mutilate them . . ." So, he suggests, "[w]e experience inner tension and the need to struggle for inner harmony," and self-integration is the good that answers to the need to which this inner tension points.[27] Similarly, "[v]arious aspects of the given self seem to be at odds with one another. There is a need to struggle for inner harmony. The objective sought is the integration of the competing components of the self. This good is quite appropriately referred to as 'self-integration' in its basic meaning of order within the self."[28]

[26] I don't attend to some other possible NATURAL LAW objections to lying here. For instance, I don't consider the possible claim that defensive killing and defensive lying aren't relevantly analogous quite apart from the putative fact that lying necessarily injures the liar's self-integration. This claim seems inconsistent with Grisez's own acknowledgment (which doesn't consider the possibility that lies might attack the good of friendship) that lying need not wrong the person being lied to, and the analogy between the two cases is, apart from the question of self-integration, so tight that to reject non-defensive lying as unjustly harming the person lied to would be to rule out the defensive use of force as illegitimate. I explore this and a number of other issues in *Toward a Consistent Natural Law Ethics of False Assertion*, 51 AM. J. JURIS. 43 (2006). I also don't consider Tollefsen's Augustinian suggestion that lies might be antithetical to both truth and religion; *see* TOLLEFSEN, *supra* note 6, at 122–29.

[27] 1 GERMAIN GRISEZ, THE WAY OF THE LORD JESUS: CHRISTIAN MORAL PRINCIPLES 123 (1983).

[28] *Id.* at 135.

The most obvious examples of dis-integration involve conflicting desires. And the language Grisez uses might suggest that *emotional* integration is what he has in mind. But if self-integration is understood as emotional integration, there is no reason why this should be opposed to false assertion. If one believes that a given instance of false assertion is justified, one's emotions, if properly educated, will not tilt against the act of false assertion; it will not be a source of emotional turmoil. If it won't, then, presuming self-integration is a matter of keeping the inner self together *emotionally*, it is unclear how false assertion need be seen as having any implications for this putative basic good. Self-integration as emotional coherence need not be inconsistent with (putatively justified) false assertion provided false assertion doesn't yield emotional turmoil. In any case, if knowingly making a false assertion *is* a source of emotional turmoil, the emotional turmoil will be a *side effect*, a foreseen but unintended consequence, of one's choice to make the assertion, so that causing it need not be inconsistent with the Principle of Respect.

If self-integration is understood as a matter of emotional balance, it is easy to see why a false assertion need not be an attack on this basic good. I may be upset by making a false assertion (though my desire in a given case may be precisely that my outer self *not* give accurate expression to my inner self), but my goal is not to bring about emotional upset, nor is the emotional upset a *means* by which I achieve my goal. I do not *will* any damage to the basic good of self-integration, understood as a matter of emotional harmony.

Of course, by referring to "various aspects of the self," Grisez might well have in mind outer behavior as well as inner judgment and disposition. Perhaps integrating outer behavior with inner judgment and disposition might be seen as valuable—but as *instrumentally* rather than intrinsically valuable. This kind of integration might be understood as a *means* of fostering friendship, community, and knowledge of the truth. Suppose this instrumental analysis is right. Then it seems as if there are two possibilities. (*i*) Self-integration *is* the relevant instrumental good. In this case, since its value is instrumental, self-integration isn't a basic good. (ii) Self-integration *isn't* the relevant instrumental good. In this case, even if lying amounts to an attack on the relevant good, it won't amount to an attack on self-integration. Thus (unless some other good is in play), lying won't violate the Principle of Respect.

But perhaps the claim is that the integration of inner and outer isn't instrumentally but rather intrinsically valuable. It is unclear just what it would mean to say that false assertion divides the inner and outer self. When the liar lies, her actions—the behaviors of her "outer self"—presumably reflect her intentions, the purposes of her "inner self." In what other sense, then, might false assertion effect a cleavage between inner and outer? Deception does, of course, involve a differentiation between what others understand one's public behavior to mean regarding one's mental state and what that mental state actually is. But this distinction is simply *constitutive* of false assertion; noting it does not give us new insight into the way in which false assertion might divide the self. And actions that aren't instances of false assertion, and that no one seriously regards as unreasonable, divide the inner and outer self in this sense—wearing a toupee, for instance.[29]

Aware that, even if reasonable, false assertion injures the deceived person, the deceiver might well feel inner tension in connection with a decision to deceive. But *whenever* an act has multiple consequences, one may regard it from diverse perspectives and experience inner tension as one contemplates its various effects. Even if the act is justified, one may still note with dismay its undesirable consequences. That one does so fails to show that the act was unwarranted.

Perhaps the relevant division is among "the moral reflection of individuals, their free choices, and the behavior by which they carry out their choices."[30] But, if one makes a *justified* choice to deceive verbally, then there will be no such conflict. Thus, whether a choice to deceive verbally might be justified cannot be determined in light of the possibility that, were it not, the deceiver's action might yield this sort of conflict. The notion that false assertion divides the inner and outer self seems simply to be a way of restating the claim that false assertion is wrong, not an explanation of this claim. If self-integration is a matter of rendering inner and outer consistent, it is hard to see when this would pose a problem except in connection with false assertion. The definition of self-integration as violated by a discontinuity between inner and outer seems tailor-made to provide a reason to reject false assertion, and to lack any other justification.

But perhaps there *is* an independent, non-question-begging understanding of self-integration.[31] Consider, for instance, the dilemma faced by a citizen of a dictatorship who is forced by social pressure and fear of reprisal to engage in public acts indicative of respect to the regime governing the country. The dismay such a person experiences at being forced to do this reflects the harm done when the inner self is divided from its outer expression, and perhaps this might be thought to point to the independent reality of self-integration as a basic good, understood precisely as involving, among other things, a unity of inner self and outer expression.[32]

Tollefsen's account is certainly defensible. But so are some alternatives. We can certainly agree that the subject in the envisioned case will be dismayed and troubled by the need to defer to a dictator. But her dismay can be explained phenomenologically without understanding communicative self-integration as a basic good. The grounds of her distress might include her dismay at being forced to do anything she doesn't want to do, at the regime's destructive actions, and at the support her seeming deference might be thought inadvertently to lend a government she wishes were overthrown. She may dislike being repressed; being required to support

[29] *See* Robert Merrihew Adams, Finite and Infinite Goods: A Framework for Ethics (1999).

[30] *See* Grisez, Principles, *supra* note 27, at 135. Grisez is here explicating the idea of *authenticity*, which it is simplest to see as identical with or as an aspect of self-integration.

[31] *See* Tollefsen, *supra* note 6, at 107–8.

[32] This example is Tollefsen's. *See* Tollefsen, *Integrity*, *supra* note 6.

a regime she regards as repugnant; her lack of political and social freedom. It needn't be, per se, the disconnection between inner and outer effected when she engages in ritual acts of loyalty to the regime to which she objects but the other ills of which engaging in these acts reminds her or to which they might lead. This analysis of course leaves open the possibility that it *is* the disconnection that's the source of dismay. But, if there are other possibilities, we may wonder why we ought to pick *this* interpretation.

Do "feelings of guilt and inner tension, the desire to be with those who agree with or support us, and our lip service, even in otherwise suspect ways, to honesty, authenticity, and integrity"[33] suggest that self-integration is a basic good? Either feelings of guilt are products of accurate judgments regarding our moral responsibility or they are not. They are troubling if they are not, but, of course, if they aren't, they tell us nothing about the way the world is. Feelings of guilt about lying, I believe, can be understood as resulting from the sense that one has ruptured a valued relationship or manipulated another person, or from the *belief* that one has done something wrong (rather than, necessarily, from any direct *awareness* of the wrongness of one's action). Felt tension is explicable in a variety of ways; certainly, it need not be a consequence of a perceived disconnection between inner and outer. The occurrence of feelings of tension can be seen as a pointer to the inevitable losses associated with choices among incommensurable goods made by finite agents. They need not be understood as telling us much of anything about the significance of the inner-outer divide.

Of course we seek friends who support us, but this need not be understood as a product of an impetus toward the integration of inner and outer. We certainly seek agreement from our friends because conflict can lead to relational ruptures, because we value acceptance and some people unfortunately find it hard to accept those with whom they do not agree, and because we hope for confirmation that our convictions are correct. Our lip service to honesty certainly reflects our concern about manipulating and being manipulated and about the cleavage between friends that dishonesty can create. Our reasons for favoring authenticity and integrity will be comparable to our reasons for endorsing honesty. The relevant phenomena don't provide overwhelming evidence that we do or should regard self-integration as Tollefsen understands it as a basic good.

Suppose we agree that "an agent whose inner life is at odds with her external actions is worse off both intra- and interpersonally."[34] Even if we do, the question remains whether this is so for intrinsic or instrumental reasons. Certainly, we might well say that someone who participates in the good of autonomy enjoys a better life, all other things being equal, than someone who does not. All other things being equal, an agent with genuine autonomy—here

33 *Id*. at 279.

34 *Id*.

understood as the capacity to give effect to her choices when doing so is consistent with her obligations to others—is better off than an agent who lacks autonomy. It does not follow, however, that autonomy is a basic good. The orthodox NATURAL LAW theorists maintain that it is not.[35] It's not clear that we should accept the judgment that, because a person is better off, all things considered, in a given situation, when she participates in a certain good, that good should therefore be regarded as basic. I am not sure why one could not say the same thing about self-integration that I think we'd want to say about autonomy. Why should we not regard self-integration as valuable in the same limited, relative way as autonomy?

It seems to me that the judgment that self-integration is a basic good is corrigible. It is possible to provide a competing and satisfactory account of the phenomena Tollefsen suggests point to its status as a basic good. And, if regarding it as a basic good leads to the conclusion that lies that do not wrong others are impermissible, it seems reasonable to count this as evidence precisely that self-integration thus understood is not a basic good. I am much more confident that I do no wrong by lying to the murderer at the door than I am that any particular moral theory is correct. It seems to me to be prima facie evidence of a problem with a theory that it yields conclusions that seem intuitively implausible (obviously, what I take to be a problem won't look like one to you if your intuitions differ on the relevant point). If the understanding that self-integration is a basic good yields such conclusions, then we have further reason to reject this understanding. We thus need not regard all instances of false assertion as morally impermissible.

It can plausibly be argued that false assertion need not impair self-integration understood *subjectively*, as a matter of emotional distress. If self-integration is understood objectively, it is less clear that there is any plausible way of characterizing self-integration as a good apart from a prior judgment that deception is always wrong. If it can be understood independently as involving a division between inner self and outer behavior, it is perhaps best seen as an instrumental good or as a derivatively valuable one like autonomy. Even if self-integration *is* injured when one engages in false assertion, it need not be the case that one intends the injury as ends or means. And if treating self-integration as a basic good really does have the implication that lies that do not wrong anyone other than the liar are impermissible, that might itself be an independent reason to reject the idea of self-integration as a basic good. The claim that false assertion constitutes an in-principle unwarranted attack on this basic good, ruled out by the Principle of Respect, thus seems difficult to sustain.

35 *See, e.g.*, TOLLEFSEN, *supra* note 6, at 140–41 (noting the importance of autonomy while affirming its purely instrumental value).

B. The Limits of Friendship

What about the claim that lying purposefully injures the good of friendship? A lie does damage the possibility of community in the moment. And I don't think we can be dogmatic about whether the argument against lying framed with reference to the good of friendship succeeds. But we might at any rate wonder about some possible difficulties. As with self-integration, so with friendship: if this good is understood broadly, making a knowing false assertion will mean purposefully or instrumentally attacking it. But the very fact that understanding it broadly would entail the implausible conclusion that all lies were morally impermissible is itself a reason to conceive of this good more narrowly.

Friendship in the focal sense of intimate, loyal, connection marked by overlapping identity is very obviously inherently valuable, a basic good. But it is less obvious that sociality in a highly inclusive sense is such a good, that any and all social connections should be seen as inherently worthwhile. No doubt other varieties of community than the intimate *are* intrinsically valuable—warm acquaintanceship, for instance, or shared membership on a football team—but we might reasonably view many as important only instrumentally.

To be clear: every *person* is inherently valuable. And that means that every person's good is to be treated with appropriate regard as the Principle of Respect and the Principle of Fairness are applied. It does not follow that there is a good of *sociality* that extends from friendship to all social interactions, that is realized in connection with all social interactions. One might think that, even if relationships more attenuated than friendship mattered, not all *interactions* mattered. On this view, while communicative community would matter intrinsically as an aspect of friendship, and perhaps as an aspect of other kinds of relationships, it would be only instrumentally valuable with respect to a broad range of non-intimate interactions. Purposefully injuring communicative community in those cases would not then violate the Principle of Respect.

Tollefsen offers considerations suggestive of the inherent worth of friendship.[36] But he does not offer any positive support for the notion that community in general, in a more extended sense, is intrinsically and not only instrumentally valuable. He does, however, offer support for the view that communicative community, in particular, is a form of the basic good of friendship.

> If, behind every initiative to communicate with another, there is always and only some further good being sought, then the claim about the goodness of such a form of community will seem less plausible. Yet sometimes, it seems, we communicate, and communicate honestly with another simply in order to realize the minimal form of community that communication itself enables us to do, as when we tell a stranger politely that we do *not* know the way and wish him luck in finding it. And when we do know, and answer the stranger truthfully, it is true that there are further

[36] *Id.* at 117.

> goods at stake for him, but it is not clear what further goods are at stake for us. Responding to the stranger's question is responding to something like an invitation to be a friend, albeit in a somewhat minimal way, and this gives us all the reason we need in order to answer.[37]

Telling the stranger I do not know the way instead of ignoring her need not be any sort of acknowledgment of communicative community as an instance of the basic good of friendship. To ignore the stranger, even if I lacked any information related to her query, would be to violate the Principle of Fairness. It would be to convey the false message that she was not worthy of a response, not morally considerable, or at least insufficiently considerable for me to acknowledge her. I would not want this insulting and confidence-undermining message conveyed to me or my loved ones in similar circumstances, so it could hardly be reasonable for me to convey it to the stranger.

In the case in which I answer the stranger truthfully, Tollefsen seems to be saying that there must be some good at stake for me and not only for the stranger. But, if this is so, if there must be some good for me, surely the good could simply be the good of practical reasonableness: I would, in the ordinary case, violate the Principle of Fairness were I to ignore the stranger's question or provide him knowingly with inaccurate information. After all, I would not be willing to embrace a norm in accordance with which I or my loved ones could be treated in this way. Of course I might view the encounter as an opportunity to develop a friendship, but I need not act unreasonably by not viewing it this way. I may decline the opportunity to develop a friendship without attacking the good of friendship.

In addition, it seems as if communicative community matters precisely when the establishment or maintenance of community of other sorts is possible: it's not, per se, valuable except as an *aspect* of other kinds of community. And this means that we will have reason to think differently about communicative community in a case in which the possibility of richer community has been foreclosed, at least for the moment—as by the intention to do something that is unreasonably harmful (whether or not under that description) or in virtue of some emotional or cognitive impairment. The bare possibility of communicative community with the Nazi at the door matters little, if at all, if there is no possibility of establishing any deeper, richer sort of community. If this is the case, if communicative community is not a basic good unless it plays an integral role in some other, richer, form of community, then one might think that an attack on communicative community with the Nazi fails to attack a basic aspect of well-being.[38]

37 *Id.* at 118.

38 David Gordon has suggested to me in conversation that we might also wonder whether the good of communicative community *just is* the good of not being lied to. If so, the question would be, as in the case of self-integration, whether we could motivate acknowledgment of communicative community *as* a good in a way that is clearly independent of concerns regarding lying.

If the good of friendship includes all sorts of actual or potential communities, including the potential community created by offering an assertion to someone else, then a false assertion will, indeed, constitute a purposeful or instrumental attack on this good. If, however, we understood the good of friendship more narrowly, so that much community outside the context of intimate relationships is instrumentally valuable, it need not. The possibility that communicative community is best understood as serving other goods, and especially richer varieties of community, offers further reason to avoid treating communicative community as if, *just as such*, it were an instance of the basic good of friendship. If it is not, then an attack on communicative community need not violate the Principle of Respect, and concern with communicative community need not render all false assertions unreasonable.

It will still be the case, however, that some lies *will* be instrumental or purposeful attacks on the good of friendship. I do not have in mind only those lies intended to attack friendship—as by misrepresenting one friend's loyalty to another. I mean, rather, any lie which is (*i*) told to someone with whom one participates in a genuine friendship or an appropriately comparable relationship and (*ii*) not told at a point at which the possibility of communicative community has, at least for the moment, broken down.

V. LYING LIBERALS?

The orthodox NATURAL LAW opposition to all lies *without exception* depends on its being the case that the liar always wrongly injures the goods of self-integration and sociality. If this turns out *not* to be the case, then telling lies in some conceivable circumstances will be reasonable—provided the lies don't violate the Principle of Respect, they don't amount to purposeful or instrumental attacks on other goods, and they aren't inconsistent with the Principle of Fairness.

By way of clearing the ground: it's worth noting that some verbal performances that could be read as assertions need not be. In many cases, that is, the context of an utterance will render what might seem to be an assertion ambiguous, so that it will not be understood as unequivocally presented as a truthful statement. In this case, if making the statement is consistent with the Principle of Fairness, it will not be objectionable even if one believes that all knowing false assertions are objectionable, because it won't qualify, quite, as a false assertion.

But knowingly making an unambiguously false assertion might itself sometimes be reasonable, presuming the choice to make it passes roughly the same test as the choice to kill. There is at least a reasonable case to be made that concerns related to self-integration and friendship don't preclude this kind of assertion, that the liar *doesn't* always purposefully injure the goods of self-integration or friendship. If so, knowingly making some false assertions will be consistent with flourishing, with living well; and they will, of course, if they are to be reasonable, serve to realize or facilitate other instances of flourishing.

I don't think we can be dogmatic about the moral status of lying. Whether it's the case or not that we may sometimes reasonably make knowing false assertions depends on how we draw the bounds of the goods of self-integration and friendship. If the reasons I have offered for narrowing these bounds are persuasive, then some lies may be permissible. If not, the orthodox NATURAL LAW view will likely prove correct. The counter-intuitive character of an absolute prohibition on lying gives us reason to wonder if a narrow view of these goods, which could obviate such a prohibition, is defensible and to ask whether there might be justifications for such a narrower and so more attractive view; but of course our intuitions might be wrong, our hopes misplaced.

With the reach of the basic goods of self-integration and friendship circumscribed as in my arguments in this Chapter, it is possible that at least some injuries done by lies to the basic goods including knowledge, practical reasonableness, and friendship may be reasonable just as the injuries done by the use of defensive force to the basic good of life and bodily well-being may be reasonable. However, even if a narrowing of the range of the relevant goods is defensible, an absolute prohibition on lying in some cases will still obtain. Just as purposeful or instrumental killing is always wrong, even though some defensive actions that happen to result in death may be reasonable, so purposeful or instrumental injuries to basic goods effected by verbal performances are always wrong, even though some defensive verbal performances that happen to result in injuries to such goods may be reasonable. Because the issue of injury to self-integration and the issue of *necessary* injury to friendship aren't on the table, it will be possible to justify defensive lying on analogy with defensive killing.[39]

While some lies may be reasonable, we would do well to form characters such that the thought of lying is repugnant to us. I would be delighted if lies as interpersonal lubricants—lies offering excuses for nonattendance at social events, lying compliments—vanished from our social repertoires: such lies disgust me. And the recognition that some lies are reasonable does not mean that we should treat it as a matter of indifference whether social institutions, practices, and norms encourage and presuppose regard for the truth. Quite the contrary. It is especially troubling when governments, unjust repositories of vast power and wealth, with immense capacities

39 Grisez maintains that the wrongness "of lying . . . [is not a function] exclusively . . . [of its] injustice to those deceived." Though lying is "always wrong," it "does not always violate any right of those deceived." GRISEZ, LIFE, *supra* note 6, at 407. Grisez's claim presupposes the notion that a lie purposefully attacks the good of self-integration (he doesn't consider Tollefsen's suggestion that a lie also purposefully attacks the good of friendship). If this notion is rejected, then what remains is the recognition that a lie "does not always violate any right of those deceived," and it may thus, when it does not (assuming that Grisez means by "violate any right of" mean "do any wrong to"), be permissible, since it does not necessarily wrong the liar herself. *Cf.* TOLLEFSEN, *supra* note 6, at 129–49.

for destruction and distortion, opt to lie. But avoiding lies, and fulfilling positive responsibilities to tell the truth, matters in other contexts, too. An appropriate concern with truth serves as one key constraint—not the only one—on the range of ways in which it is reasonable to assign grades to students. It is to this practice that I turn in Chapter 3.

3

Grades

I. LIBERAL GRADING PRACTICES

Liberalism emphasizes individuality and diversity. And so liberalism—social, even if, probably, not political—has implications for how students are evaluated.

So does NATURAL LAW theory. Academic evaluation is a matter of flourishing. Assigning grades is an exercise in practical reasonableness and skillful performance. It serves the good of knowledge on the part of the student who is evaluated and on the part of the others who receive the information academic evaluations provide. It may also facilitate the exercise of practical reasonableness by students and other consumers of evaluative information. It may also indirectly facilitate participation in various basic goods—as when a residency program selects for admission a medical student who is able to go on to perform lifesaving procedures effectively.

As individualists, liberals have good reason to assign grades (or the equivalent) *meritocratically*, rather than grading students in light of their social standing or group membership, and flexibly, given the different ways in which students can successfully demonstrate *subject-matter competence* (COMPETENCE). The Principle of Fairness and the Principle of Respect rule out alternative grading schemes that disregard individuality and merit and undermine the capacity of grades to convey accurate information.

A. *Grades in Court*

As every teacher knows, grades matter to students. It is not altogether surprising, then, that they sometimes bring concerns about their grades to court. Their challenges to institutional grading decisions have consistently been unsuccessful.[1] Courts have characteristically been unwilling to entertain such claims both because of their perceived triviality[2] and because of judges' lack of relevant "authority ... [and] expertise to prescribe academic standards ..."[3]

1 *See, e.g.*, Dilworth v. Dallas Community College Dist., 81 F.3d 616 (5th Cir. 1996), Attia v. Keller, 703 F.2d 558 (6th Cir. 1982), Raymon v. Alvord Independent School District, 639 F.2d 257 (5th Cir. 1981).

2 *Cf. Raymon*, 639 F.2d 257.

3 Axelrod v. Phillips Academy, 46 F. Supp. 2d 72, 82 (D. Mass. 1999).

On the other hand, "[n]o teacher has a fundamental right to hand in random or skewed grades . . ."[4] An educational institution has a legally recognized interest "in ensuring that its students receive . . . fair grade[s],"[5] and it is difficult to see why students might not be thought in principle to have a similar interest. Fairness issues arise with particular force when they concern, not subjective grading decisions made by instructors regarding individual student exercises, but rather general policies adopted by instructors and institutions. It would be unreasonable for a judge to assume under ordinary circumstances that she could improve on a teacher's judgment regarding the merits of an essay prepared for an English class. But it might be easier for her to assess the appropriateness of a policy calling for a reduction in the grade of any student who has, for instance, consumed alcohol; "[l]ess judicial deference, although still a considerable amount, is due those 'academic' decisions concerning academic and pedagogical policies of the university as to which reasonable educators can and do differ."[6]

In 1983, the Texas Court of Appeals rejected the claim that "the practice of reducing grades for non-academic disciplinary reasons was constitutionally unreasonable and impermissible."[7] But other courts have not viewed this practice so kindly. "The final grade constitutes a record that purports to measure academic attainment," wrote a dissenting judge in a 1976 Illinois case, *Knight* v. *Board of Education*. "[P]rospective employers as well as institutions of higher learning concern themselves with true academic achievement,"[8] he observed, and would thus, he implied, expect grades to serve as sources of academic information. Similarly, a federal district court concluded in *Smith* v. *School City of Hobart* that

> for college entrance and other purposes . . . [a substantial grade reduction for nonacademic reasons] would result in a clear misrepresentation of the student's scholastic achievement. Misrepresentation of achievement is equally improper and, we think, illegal whether the achievement is misrepresented by upgrading or by downgrading, if either is done for reasons that are irrelevant to the achievement being graded. For example, one would hardly deem acceptable an upgrading in a mathematics course for achievement on the playing field.[9]

Thus, the court found a "rule that calls for a grade reduction to discipline nonacademic conduct illegal, and null and void."[10]

While many courts may decline to hear grading-related cases, and while there is surely good reason for them to refuse to do so, legal disputes over academic

4 Wozniak v. Conry, 236 F.3d 888, 891 (7th Cir. 2001).

5 Keen v. Penson, 970 F.2d 252, 258 (7th Cir. 1992).

6 Thomas A. Schweitzer, *"Academic Challenge" Cases: Should Judicial Review Extend to Academic Evaluations of Students?*, 41 AM. U. L. REV. 267, 366 (1992).

7 New Braunfels Ind. School Dist. v. Armke, 658 S.W.2d. 330, 331 (Texas Civ. App., 1983).

8 Knight v. Board of Educ., 348 N.E.2d 299, 305 (Ill. App. 1976). According to the *Knight* majority, a policy that precluded instructor discretion might "justify court intervention." *Id.* at 305.

9 Smith v. School City of Hobart, 811 F.Supp. 391, 397–8 (1993).

10 *Smith*, F.Supp 391 at 399.

evaluation will undoubtedly continue.[11] A variety of legal theories support the conclusion that judicial assessment of some educational decisions is appropriate;[12] the law of contract has provided perhaps the firmest basis for students' claims.[13] A plausible contractual argument can certainly be made that "[a] registered student has a legally protected interest in his college education,"[14] and that when she enrolls, "a student . . . expects that the school [at which she registers] will treat her fairly," which means, among other things, that she will not be subjected to "arbitrary grading."[15]

B. *Grades and Norms*

The number of cases in which courts ought to entertain claims about academic evaluations is small. But normative questions about grading policies are frequent and unavoidable. Lawyers and judges may need only rarely to think critically and reflectively about the bases for these policies; instructors, institutions, and students need to do so far more often. My goal here is not to determine when legal issues related to grading deserve consideration by the courts but to articulate a normative framework that might reasonably guide assessments of the reasonableness of grading policies—by courts when courts should be involved, but, in any case, by instructors, students, and institutions.

My central contention is that an instructor has an obligation to grade accurately, to give to each student in a given course a grade that reflects the student's COMPETENCE rather than any other factor. She should do so in virtue of the ***principle of academic exclusivity*** (EXCLUSIVITY), which requires that she determine grades exclusively in light of as realistically accurate estimates of students' COMPETENCE as conveniently possible.[16] In this Chapter, I elaborate and defend EXCLUSIVITY,

11 *Cf.* Jayme L. Butcher, Comment, MIT v. Yoo: *Revocation of Academic Degrees for Nonacademic Reasons*, 51 C. W. RES. L. REV. 749 (2001); Curtis J. Berger & Vivian Berger, *Academic Discipline: A Guide to Fair Process for the University Student*, 99 COLUM. L. REV. 289 (1999); Dina Lallo, *Student Challenges to Grade and Academic Dismissals: Are They Losing Battles?*, 18 J.C. & U.L. 577 (1992).

12 *See* Berger & Berger, *supra* note 11, at 291 nn. 4–6 for a range of alternatives.

13 *See id.* at 291–92. Berger and Berger are concerned with discipline rather than grading and might well not support my conclusions.

14 *Id.* at 291.

15 *Id.* at 318.

16 This principle embodies (at least some of) what Gregory F. Weis calls "the conventional view of grading." *See* Gregory F. Weis, *Grading*, 18 TEACHING PHILOS. 3 (1995). The "conventional view," for instance, "takes no account of what the student has had to do, of how hard the student has had to work." *Id.* at 10. It also "ignores the classroom experience itself as a factor in a student's grade," *id.*, and thus implicitly precludes taking attendance and participation into account. My argument in this Chapter may be seen, in part, as an attempt to formalize this view and spell out its implications.

Weis's helpful essay also addresses other issues of interest discussed here, though I had completed most of my work on this Chapter before encountering it. Weis raises, for instance, the issue of "the audience" to which grades are determined, *see id.* at 6, noting, without endorsing, the idea I defend in the text that "the audience that will read . . . [a student's] transcript," *id.*, is the audience a teacher

explaining that it is rooted in two simple obligations. I suggest reasons we ought to be suspicious of two alternative positions, which I label *academic consequentialism* and *academic retributivism*. And I argue that EXCLUSIVITY renders a number of common grading practices inappropriate because these practices take into account factors other than COMPETENCE. Student behaviors and character traits unrelated to COMPETENCE may well be the business of educational institutions. But any institutional evaluation of student performance that does not directly reflect COMPETENCE should not influence students' *grades*, which should reflect COMPETENCE alone.

II. ACADEMIC EXCLUSIVITY

We can derive EXCLUSIVITY from the duty to avoid lying and from the need to respect the incommensurability of COMPETENCE and a variety of other factors that sometimes influence students' grades.

A. *Exclusivity and Truth-Telling*

There is a general obligation to avoid lying—knowingly making false assertions.[17] This obligation is rooted fundamentally in respect for a range of basic goods. Avoiding lies is a way of showing due regard for the goods of knowledge and practical reasonableness; it is, for instance, a way of permitting each person to make up her own mind about possible evaluations or courses of action. It is an expression in various ways of fairness. It is also frequently an expression of respect for the friendship or friendship-like relationship that obtains between the communicator and someone with whom she is communicating. And it matters for various other reasons, too. To the extent that we are obligated to avoid telling lies, then we are obligated to give accurate grades.

A student's grade is *accurate* to the extent that it permits someone to estimate what the student knows and what she can do—her COMPETENCE. It is *inaccurate* to the extent that it leads someone to believe that she knows more or less than she does or that she can do more or less than she can. A good grade is not justified by a student's

should consider when assigning a grade to the student. And he notes, as I do, the analogy between theories of grading and alternative—retributivist and utilitarian—rationales for punishment; *see id.* at 7–8. But where Weis seeks, rightly, to call our attention to the distinction between the conventional view and much actual educational practice, without taking sides in the conflict between this view and alternative positions, *see id.* at 12, I attempt here to offer a positive defense for a version of the conventional view.

17 *See, e.g.*, Chapter 2, *supra*; SISSELA BOK, LYING: MORAL CHOICE IN PUBLIC AND PRIVATE LIFE (1978); JEAN-PAUL SARTRE, NOTEBOOKS FOR AN ETHICS 195–204 (1992); BERNARD GERT, MORALITY: A NEW JUSTIFICATION OF THE MORAL RULES 126–27 (1988); LEONARD NELSON, SYSTEM OF ETHICS 151–55 (1956); CHARLES FRIED, RIGHT AND WRONG 54–78 (1978); ALAN DONAGAN, THE THEORY OF MORALITY 88–90 (1977); ALAN GEWIRTH, REASON AND MORALITY 198 (1978); T. M. SCANLON, WHAT WE OWE TO EACH OTHER 317–22 (1998); LEWIS B. SMEDES, MERE MORALITY 211–38 (1988); ALASDAIR MACINTYRE, ETHICS AND POLITICS 101–42 (2006).

hard work; a poor grade is not justified by a student's sloth.[18] More generally, a grade is not warranted by a judgment regarding a student's moral character, her helpfulness or respectfulness in class, or anything apart from her COMPETENCE.[19]

This is so because the primary *function* of a student's grade in a given course is to convey accurate information regarding the student's COMPETENCE. The consistant conveyance of this kind of information is beneficial to all those who become aware of students' grades (*transcript consumers*)—a class that of course includes students themselves.

The understanding that a grade should convey information about COMPETENCE follows from the role grades actually play in our society and the impersonal and generally inflexible ways in which they are ordinarily interpreted. Employers and educational institutions to which students apply clearly want to be provided with grades that accurately characterize students' COMPETENCE. Such grades allow them to make good decisions about applicants. A human resources specialist or a graduate school admissions committee chair reviewing a student's transcript will understand a grade as an index of academic performance.[20] While transcript consumers are certainly aware that educational institutions appropriately have a range of nonacademic concerns and while they realize that instructors sometimes award grades for

18 I disagree here with the variant of "luck egalitarianism" described and, on a qualified basis, defended by Francis Schrag, *From Here to Equality: Grading Policies for Egalitarians*, 51 ED. THEORY 63 (2001). For the luck egalitarian, because talent is a product of luck, we should minimize the effects of talent on social rewards. "[I]f a student who has produced a paper with enormous effort receives a higher grade than a student who has produced a paper with little effort, this is just *even when the second paper is higher in equality than the first* . . . ." *Id.* at 70. (Schrag ends the italicized phrase with a question mark.) According to Schrag, the luck egalitarian will emphasize that it is important to distinguish "grading the paper" from "grading the student." *Id.* at 70. But (and Schrag appears to be sensitive to this concern) we are interested in the paper precisely because we are interested in the student. A transcript consumer cares about a student's grade in a given class because she wants to know something about the student's COMPETENCE, not because she's interested in how much effort a student has expended.

19 As James Terwilliger, *Assigning Grades—Philosophical Issues and Practical Recommendations*, 10 J. RES. & DEV. EDUC. 21, 22 (1977), observes, a grade is not a reflection of "the amount . . . [of] 'effort' expended, the student's work habits, attitude, character traits (honesty, dependability, etc.) nor personality traits (cheerful, cooperative, etc.)."

It may be necessary to ask a student who is aggressive and abusive during a given class to leave the class temporarily or permanently or to spend time with a counselor if she wishes to remain in the class. If so, the point of doing so is not retributive: it is not to *punish* the student for being rude or unkind. The point, rather, is to protect other students' opportunities to learn. If the student continues to be enrolled in the class, then her grade, like that of every other student in the class, must reflect her COMPETENCE.

20 Schrag plausibly identifies as a desideratum "of any ethical grading policy" the requirement that "grades . . . not convey deceptive information to those who receive them." He explains: "Grades typically send signals to a variety of audiences in addition to the students themselves: prospective employers, college or graduate schools' admissions committees, and parents include the most important. Most readers of transcripts are likely to interpret grades and transcripts in fairly predictable ways. When, for example, a college admissions committee sees high school transcripts recording Jack as having earned a B in world history and Jason an A in the same class, committee members will infer that the quality of Jason's work was superior to Jack's." Schrag, *supra* note 18, at 68–9.

nonacademic reasons, they have, in general, no reason to suppose that any particular grade is other than what it appears to be: an assessment of a student's COMPETENCE.[21] And most transcript consumers other than students—and even sometimes students—lack personal opportunities to query instructors regarding particular grades. When assigning a grade, therefore, an instructor must assume that, absent specific personal information, those who become aware of it will assume that it is a compressed, summary evaluation of a student's COMPETENCE.

It ought to be possible to assess a student with respect to various factors other than COMPETENCE and to report the distinguishable results of a multifaceted evaluation of her performance in each of her classes. There is no reason such results cannot appear on students' transcripts. But these kinds of assessments aren't *grades*. Grades appear in general to be unidimensional, to offer academic rather than personal information.[22] And it makes sense that they are and they continue to be, since unidimensional grades are likely to be less subject to misinterpretation, to be less confusing, to convey information more clearly than grades intended to convey different kinds of information.

An instructor assigning a grade that does not reflect a student's COMPETENCE may not *intend* to deceive. She may not intend to convey an inaccurate message to others; she may do so believing that there is some chance that some transcript consumers will understand the grade as she intends it, as a response to something other than the student's COMPETENCE. Her *purpose* may be that all transcript consumers understand it this way. At minimum, though, if she does not intend to deceive, she must understand the risk that she will be misunderstood but be prepared to accept that risk because of some other good she seeks to achieve by assigning an inaccurate grade. However, the good she seeks to achieve will in general be dependent on the transcript consumers' misunderstanding of the grade she has assigned. The incorporation of factors other than COMPETENCE into grades works in the way deception in general works. That is to say, it works only because many, most, or all transcript consumers assume it isn't being done, or isn't being done frequently. Its effectiveness in influencing transcript consumers' attitudes is thus parasitic on the ordinary practice of COMPETENCE-based grading. And, as with other kinds of deception, this kind seems possibly to violate the Principle of Respect and the Principle of Fairness. To the extent that, in context, an inaccurate grade constitutes a false assertion, and to the extent that, within the strictures noted in Chapter 2, this particular false assertion violates the Principle of Respect, issuing an inaccurate

[21] Suppose a student, Alex, receives an F in a chemistry class because he may be responsible for an explosion in a chemistry lab. "Course grades . . . are normally based on knowledge of subject matter. Anyone who sees Alex's transcript will conclude that he failed to learn chemistry, not that he is being punished." KENNETH A. STRIKE & JONAS F. SOLTIS, THE ETHICS OF TEACHING 25 (1985).

[22] STEVEN M. CAHN, SAINTS AND SCAMPS: ETHICS IN ACADEMIA 107 n. 4 (1986) argues that "[t]hose who believe it important to recognize formally a student's level of effort or improvement should favor awarding supplementary grades for these special purposes rather than seeking to distort the recognized meaning of grades, thereby undermining their ordinary uses."

grade would qualify as in principle unreasonable. But even if, as seems likely, the Principle of Respect isn't dispositive here, the Principle of Fairness almost certainly is. An application of the Principle of Fairness—Would she be prepared for anyone else to suffer a comparable injury under similar circumstances because of the operation of a generalizable rule or norm permitting a choice like hers? Would she be prepared to suffer such an injury herself under comparable circumstances?—might well lead her to doubt that her action could be justified.

That it might doesn't depend on the existence of any legal or otherwise formal relationships between those assigning grades and those consuming transcript information. Issues of respect and fairness arise with respect to unknown and even in principle unknowable targets of our choices. Specific relationships determine contexts within which the Principle of Fairness must be applied, but it is applicable whether or not such relationships obtain.[23]

Giving an inaccurate grade would still be undesirable even if significant numbers of transcript consumers were aware that nonacademic factors might influence grades. These readers would still be uncertain *which* nonacademic factors were in play in determining the student's grade. They would not be able to use the grade to reach a sensible conclusion regarding the student's suitability for employment or admission. Of course, there is considerable variability in the meaning of grades; transcript consumers know they cannot assume that an A conferred at one institution means the same as one awarded at another institution. But there are limits: transcript consumers and instructors share enough assumptions about the meanings of grades that in the majority of cases transcript consumers can gauge the probable significance of students' transcripts.[24] If, however, it were generally accepted that grades reflected factors other than COMPETENCE to a significant degree, the already considerable variability in the meaning of grades would be compounded dramatically.[25] Transcript interpretation would be especially difficult because of the lack of a generally agreed-upon set of factors other than COMPETENCE that might contribute to the determination of grades. And those who did not share an instructor's or institution's judgments about these factors would have no way of discounting their influence when interpreting a grade shaped by such judgments.

[23] Thanks to David Gordon for insights related to this issue.

[24] Craig Kinzer (in personal communication) suggests that, in an ideal world, a transcript would therefore include the mean, median, mode, and standard deviation for each course, teacher, and department to which it refers, for a period from the year before to the year after the one in which any course to which it refers was taken. As he notes, this would, regrettably, be too much information to be contained conveniently in a conventional transcript. Of course, web-based delivery of academic information might make providing data like these possible. According to Cahn, ". . . at a number of colleges . . . transcripts now include not only a student's course grade, but also the average grade of all students in the course." CAHN, *supra* note 22, at 31.

[25] "It is sufficiently difficult to make sense out of a grade even when it is limited to achievement in the subject matter. It is impossible to interpret a grade if such factors as 'effort', work habits, citizenship, etc., are also considered. If there is a need to report upon such factors, this should be represented in a separate set of ratings." Terwilliger, *supra* note 19, at 29.

The interests of students, too, make it reasonable to want grades to represent students' COMPETENCE accurately. (*i*) Students benefit from grades when they receive accurate feedback regarding their COMPETENCE. Grades which correctly affirm that they already possess COMPETENCE appropriately reinforce and perhaps boost their self-confidence and self-respect. And grades which correctly indicate that they lack COMPETENCE appropriately point them toward needed improvements. Inaccurate grades either fail to do these useful things, or do them in manipulative and confusing ways.

(*ii*) Students also have reasons to want transcript consumers to receive accurate grades, grades on which these consumers can rely. An individual student might well desire that her transcript report across-the-board superb COMPETENCE. But such a report would be valuable to the student only if other transcript consumers treated it as an accurate source of information regarding her actual COMPETENCE. A student might enjoy the opportunity to free ride on instructors' general tendency to assign accurate grades, seeking special treatment. But it seems as if fair regard for the well-being not only of other transcript consumers but also of other students, and perhaps even, in other contexts, of the would-be free rider herself, would at least in most cases be inconsistent with endorsing the reporting of an inaccurately positive grade. (It is hard to imagine a case in which a student or another transcript consumer could possibly want an inaccurately *negative* grade recorded.)

The Principle of Fairness and, often enough, the Principle of Respect thus provide good reasons for instructors to ensure that grades convey accurate information about students' COMPETENCE.

B. *EXCLUSIVITY and Incommensurability*

A range of factors—effort, character, attendance, and so forth—sometimes treated as appropriate inputs into the grading process are *incommensurable* with COMPETENCE—and with each other. They are sufficiently *different* that it makes no sense to evaluate them using a single measure. There is nothing wrong with evaluating a student's character—moral or otherwise—and communicating the results of this evaluation to others; doing so may, in fact, be quite helpful to prospective employers and to other academic institutions. But an evaluation of a student's character is not the same thing as an evaluation of her COMPETENCE. Character and COMPETENCE are *incommensurable*. It is no more meaningful to collapse the two than it would be to add a student's height to her shoe size.[26]

[26] On incommensurability, see, *e.g.*, INCOMMENSURABILITY, INCOMPARABILITY, AND PRACTICAL REASONING (Ruth Chang ed., 1997); ELIZABETH ANDERSON, VALUE IN ETHICS AND ECONOMICS (1993); NOLA J. HEIDLEBAUGH, JUDGMENT, RHETORIC, AND THE PROBLEM OF INCOMMENSURABILITY: RECALLING PRACTICAL WISDOM (2001); JOHN M. FINNIS, NATURAL LAW AND NATURAL RIGHTS 113, 95–97, 110–18, 131–32 (1980).

Recognizing the incommensurability of COMPETENCE and character or moral conduct is no different from acknowledging that subject-matter mastery is not the same thing as friendliness, good looks, or the willingness to offer money or sexual favors. Money, sex, charm, and agreeableness are extraneous factors that shouldn't influence grades. They aren't the same thing as, and can't be combined with or collapsed into, COMPETENCE. These things are different, and they should be evaluated differently. Someone who believes that it is inappropriate to give a student a good grade because she is friendly on the view that friendliness isn't identical with, is no guarantee of, COMPETENCE is logically committed to the view that it is also inappropriate to give a student a good grade because she has performed an act of tremendous bravery on a class trip, or anywhere else. Taking incommensurability seriously means keeping evaluations of everything other than COMPETENCE distinct from grades.

Incommensurables can, of course, be compared using common measures. But these common measures aren't objectively required. There's nothing necessary about them. Adopting a set of common measures for a range of incommensurables is a matter of *choice*. Absent choices establishing common measures, the combination of other factors with COMPETENCE to generate grades is arbitrary and unjustifiable. Of course an individual instructor or institution might adopt some set of common measures. But the relevant weights will not in general be known or understood by transcript consumers. Certainly, there are not, and probably could not be, commitments adopted by all producers of transcript information that would allow for the commensuration of the relevant factors in a consistent manner. And, in any case, there would be no *reason* to adopt such common measures, even if the strategies used for combination were generally acknowledged: treating various incommensurable factors as distinct allows for much greater clarity, while combining them obscures COMPETENCE.

To be sure, the various factors that make up COMPETENCE in the context of a given *course* must be commensurated in a way that is in some respects arbitrary. However, when commensuration happens within a more narrowly defined universe, there may be more consensus about the importance of various factors, so that there will often be common expectations regarding the weights that should be assigned to particular categories. Performance with respect to different aspects of the subject matter of a given course will typically be much more highly correlated than will any aspect of course performance with some nonacademic factor. As a result, weights ordinarily won't matter enormously (provided factors that are less relevant to COMPETENCE are not weighted highly). And, in any case, an instructor might employ any one of many different sets of weights without creating inaccurate impressions. (Weighting busywork at 85 percent and a comprehensive final examination at 5 percent might lead to confusing or deceptive grades, of course.) The instructor's responsibility, of course, is to assign weights in ways likely not to prompt inaccurate judgments regarding students' COMPETENCE; provided she does so, she is surely free to employ whatever weights make sense to her.

C. Competence

Given EXCLUSIVITY, grades must reflect COMPETENCE.[27] Educational institutions are rightly concerned with all sorts of things other than COMPETENCE, and they can and should find a range of mechanisms designed to express their concerns. But these concerns shouldn't be expressed using *grades*.

A student exhibits COMPETENCE at a given level in a Calculus I course, for instance, if she understands the concepts explored in the course at the relevant level and has mastered the skill the course is designed to help her acquire at that level. She may lack or possess COMPETENCE whatever her actual academic *performance*; COMPETENCE is not the same as academic performance. This is so (*i*) because performance on some exercises has no tendency to tell us about COMPETENCE. But it is also true (*ii*) because, even if the exercises completed by most or all students do, indeed, provide useful information about COMPETENCE, an instructor may, in a given case, possess *other* evidence regarding COMPETENCE at least as useful as that provided by performance on any particular exercise or array of exercises.

Grades should be understood to reflect COMPETENCE because transcript consumers use them, in general, to assess COMPETENCE. Psychometricians speak of a person's "true score"—the score she would obtain on a perfect test of her ability or skill in or knowledge of a certain area. Someone's performance on an individual test is thought to approximate more or less closely to her true score depending on the test's accuracy. Her test performance is used, in effect, to estimate her true score.[28] By analogy, we may say that a transcript consumer hopes that, when she reviews a student's transcript, she is learning as much as possible about the student's true grades. She is not interested in information about the student's past academic performance for its own sake; she wants to know what she can expect from the student in the future. She is unlikely to be concerned about the vagaries of a student's performance on this or that exercise or in the course as a whole except as this helps her plan for the future. Thus, in turn, the instructor's goal should be the determination of a student's true grade, with the needs of transcript consumers in mind. Performance on a variety of individual exercises can be used to help the instructor identify the true grade. But what is of interest to the instructor should be the true grade itself.[29]

[27] Randall R. Curren, *Coercion and the Ethics of Grading and Testing*, 45 ED. THEORY 425–41 (1995), uses language that suggests the appropriateness of the expression "subject-matter competence," but I do not believe he ever employs this expression himself. He says, for instance, that a "student's act of signing up for . . . [a] course could be understood to entail an admission of subject-specific and level-specific noncompetence." *Id.* at 435.

[28] Thus, a "standard error of measurement" will be calculated for any typical widely used standardized examination in order to help anyone interpreting a score on the examination to estimate how close to the test-taker's true score her score in a given case is likely to be.

[29] It is therefore not quite correct to say that a grade "represents a value judgment concerning the relative quality of a student's achievement of course objectives during a specified period of instruction," Terwilliger, *supra* note 19, at 22, or that it "is intended to represent an expert's judgment of the quality

This obviously does not mean that grades can or should be determined in free-wheeling abstraction from academic performance. There are good reasons for using performance as a key indicator of a student's true grade and, indeed, for choosing only rarely to determine her grade in light of anything other than her aggregate performance on all assigned exercises.[30] No evidence regarding a student's COMPETENCE may be available apart from her aggregate class performance. Other bases for judgments regarding COMPETENCE may be available—but there may be good reason to be uncertain of their reliability or accuracy. Taking factors other than aggregate class performance into account, especially in an individual case, may require an inefficient use of an instructor's time. Perhaps most importantly, fairness—like the need to ensure that grades are useful to transcript consumers—requires that each comparable grade reflect a judgment regarding competence, understood in a consistent way, with respect to the same subject matter. Diversifying the ways in which instructors determine grades runs the risk of multiplying the meanings of grades in particular courses. Further, consistent standards make it easier for an instructor to avoid being swayed by biases that have nothing to do with a student's academic capacities, and such standards are easiest to apply to students' performance on ordinary course assignments. So there are good reasons to focus on aggregate class performance when determining grades. These reasons, though they are good, are not, however, decisive.

That grades ought to reflect COMPETENCE is a reason for an instructor to decline to take into account exercises unlikely to contribute to accurate measures of students' true grades. It is also a reason for her to be open to evidence that might lead her to give a student a grade different from the one she might assign if she attended only to aggregate class performance. At least, it's a reason for her to do so if this evidence is genuinely trustworthy and if she is willing to take comparable evidence into account when determining other students' grades.

Ordinarily, the instructor is entitled to assume that the same evaluative methods are appropriate for all students. But this is only a presumption. Suppose she has a particular reason to believe that, if she uses a technique other than the one she

of a student's work within a specified area of inquiry," CAHN, *supra* note 22, at 25. A student's grade ought not to be a reflection simply or primarily of her "achievement" or "work" per se, but of this achievement or work *as an estimator of* COMPETENCE. Cahn concedes as much when he says that "[s]tudents who receive C's in introductory physics are not C persons with C personalities or C moral characters, but individuals who have achieved only a *fair grasp of the fundamentals of elementary physics*," *id.* at 26 (my italics). Similarly, he notes that the fact that a student received an F in a course means that she "failed to master any significant part of it" and that "[a] person who requires two, three [,] or four attempts to pass calculus *lacks the mathematical or study skills* of someone who passes the first time . . ." *id.* at 27 (my italics). He suggests that the instructor who "grades on a curve" has confused "rank in class . . . with *mastery of subject matter*," *id.* at 29 (my italics). JOHN S. BRUBACHER, ON THE PHILOSOPHY OF HIGHER EDUCATION 108 (1982) may elide the two distinct ideas when he argues that "grades should be regarded not merely as motivators but as genuine measures of achievement in the mastery of the higher learning."

30 I use the expression *aggregate class performance* for this sort of performance.

employs to estimate the grades of other students, she can more accurately estimate a student's COMPETENCE than she could if she employed her conventional approach. It seems as if she should use the more accurate approach. The Principle of Fairness dictates that she treat like cases alike, but also that she treat different cases differently. If she can demonstrate that a particular student's case is relevantly different from the cases of other students, it may be reasonable—and perhaps even obligatory—for her to assess this student differently in order to ensure that the student's grade is an accurate estimate of the student's COMPETENCE. Of course, evidence suggesting that conventional evaluative exercises are inaccurate estimators of COMPETENCE will not always be available. Provided appropriate exercises are assigned, aggregate course performance can be a good, though not perfect, indicator of a student's COMPETENCE, and thus an appropriate determinant of a student's grade.

It's important to be clear that COMPETENCE is not the bare ability to recall facts or employ certain intellectual tools. An instructor may reasonably identify the ability to make use of relevant skills, information, or understanding in a particular setting as an element of COMPETENCE. Thus, while it may sometimes be appropriate to discount the effects of intense situational pressure on a student, accurately assessing COMPETENCE may sometimes require that a student's capacity to function under pressure be taken into account when grades are determined.

III. ACADEMIC CONSEQUENTIALISM AND RETRIBUTIVISM

A variety of conventional academic practices appear inconsistent with EXCLUSIVITY. These practices are likely to be defended using one of two possible theoretical approaches, which I term *academic consequentialism* and *academic retributivism*. As I explore particular issues in the ethics of grading below I will return to specific arguments proponents of each of these positions might offer for practices I believe to be unjustifiable. However, before I turn to specifics I want to make some more general observations about these approaches and to suggest why I believe neither is plausible.

A. *Academic Consequentialism*

Academic consequentialism is the application of consequentialism to grading. A consequentialist will be inclined to understand a grade in instrumental terms. She will understand it as a means of motivating transcript consumers of various sorts to view a student with favor or disfavor. And because of the possible reactions of transcript consumers, it will also serve as a means of motivating the student. The instructor's authority to assign grades gives her considerable leverage over a student's behavior, and, on a plausible consequentialist view, she ought to use it. Whenever doing so seems likely to prove effective, a consequentialist instructor ought to use the threat of a bad grade or the promise of a good one to prompt a student to behave in ways that benefit the student herself or others. And, similarly, she ought to use her ability to motivate transcript consumers by means of the grades she assigns to prompt them to respond aright to students.

Suppose, for instance, that a student from a wealthy family is experiencing academic difficulties at a university. Aware that a positive report from the student may lead her mother to be exceptionally generous when approached by university advancement personnel, a consequentialist instructor might conclude under some circumstances that, assuming the university serves the general good, it would make sense to use a grade as a means of increasing the student's satisfaction with the university and the consequent likelihood of a substantial gift from her mother.[31]

It's not certain, of course, what this instructor should do on consequentialist grounds. The circumstances may lead her to believe that, on balance, assigning an inaccurate grade to this student would be counterproductive. The consequentialist isn't committed to grading inaccurately. But there's no consequentialist reason why, in general, she shouldn't consider the possible impact of a grade on her university's bottom line.

This is, of course, just the sort of counter-intuitive example regularly canvassed in the literature on consequentialism. It will strike some readers as extreme; I have chosen it with the suspicion that most instructors will be disinclined to approve of using grades to increase donations. But I believe that rejecting academic consequentialism has implications for a variety of common academic practices.

There are, of course, good reasons for rejecting consequentialism generally.[32] Perhaps most fundamentally, consequentialism depends on the assumption that it is possible in some meaningful way to aggregate goods or preferences in a way that permits the global comparison of states of affairs. But if particular human goods and particular instances of human goods are incommensurable, so that this kind of

[31] Alternatively, suppose that an instructor wishes to benefit a socio-economically disadvantaged student. A good grade will help the student obtain educational and professional opportunities that will increase her socio-economic status. (An objector might suggest that in this case it's less likely that the general good would be served, since there's no guarantee that a benefit to this student would help others, while a donation to the university might be thought to foster the general good almost in the nature of the case.) Of course, deception in this kind of case can only be effective if it's not a standard practice.

[32] For criticisms of consequentialist approaches, see, *e.g.* ALASDAIR C. MACINTYRE, AFTER VIRTUE: A STUDY IN MORAL THEORY 61–63, 67–68, 185 (2d ed., 1984); FINNIS, LAW, *supra* note 26, at 111–19; JOHN M. FINNIS, FUNDAMENTALS OF ETHICS 80–108 (1983); JOHN M. FINNIS, JOSEPH M. BOYLE, JR., GERMAIN G. GRISEZ, NUCLEAR DETERRENCE, MORALITY, AND REALISM 177–296 (1987); GERMAIN G. GRISEZ & RUSSELL SHAW, BEYOND THE NEW MORALITY: THE RESPONSIBILITIES OF FREEDOM 111–14, 131–33 (3d ed., 1988); DAVID S. ODERBERG, MORAL THEORY: A NON-CONSEQUENTIALIST APPROACH 65–76, 97–101, 132–33 (2000); PAUL HURLEY, BEYOND CONSEQUENTIALISM (2011); NEL NODDINGS, CARING: A FEMININE APPROACH TO ETHICS AND MORAL EDUCATION 86–87, 151–54 (1984); BERNARD WILLIAMS, MORALITY: AN INTRODUCTION TO ETHICS (2d ed., 1993); Bernard Williams, *A Critique of Utilitarianism*, *in* J. J. C. SMART & BERNARD WILLIAMS, UTILITARIANISM: FOR AND AGAINST 77 (1973); Stephen R. L. Clark, *Natural Integrity and Biotechnology*, *in* HUMAN LIVES 58–76 (Jacqueline A. Laing & David S. Oderberg eds., 1997); Germain Grisez, *Against Consequentialism*, 23 AM. J. JURIS 21 (1978); ROBERT MERRIHEW ADAMS, FINITE AND INFINITE GOODS 298–300 (2000).

aggregation is impossible, consequentialism can't get off the ground. Consequentialism can also be criticized because it seems to be blind to distributional issues many of us think are morally significant; because it seems unable to take adequate account of special responsibilities and special relationships like friendship; because it instrumentalizes relationships, projects, and values we tend to think of as intrinsically valuable; and because it gives what many people think of as a poor account of promise-keeping and truth-telling.

The rejection of a consequentialist rationale for grading, in particular, will often be motivated by the intuition that assigning grades as a means of enhancing the general welfare flies in the face of the commitment to truth that is central to academic life. Truth-telling is central to and definitive of the practices of teaching, learning, and scholarship. Even those who do not believe, then, that consequentialism is a nonstarter as a moral theory may still be skeptical about the use of a general consequentialist rationale for assigning grades.[33]

The inappropriateness of academic consequentialism is especially apparent when the academic consequentialist seeks to maximize something other than the general welfare.[34] Restricted versions of academic consequentialism are problematic for (at least) the same reasons as general academic consequentialism. The most obvious sort of restricted academic consequentialism urges the assignment of grades in light of the probable value of the promise of good grades and the threat of poor grades to motivate student learning. An adherent of academic consequentialism reasoning this way might assign a grade to a student, not because the grade reflects the student's COMPETENCE, but as a means of benefiting the student. On another variant of restricted academic consequentialism, an instructor might assign a grade to a student as a means of benefiting some group of which the student is a member.

The instructor might seek to benefit the student herself by giving her a grade that suggests that she has *more* COMPETENCE than she actually does in order to improve her confidence and encourage her to remain in school and continue learning. The instructor might seek to benefit her by giving her a grade that suggests that she has *less* COMPETENCE than she actually does in order to encourage her to avoid what the instructor believes is irresponsible academic conduct that may limit her learning in other contexts. The instructor might seek to benefit a group of which the student is a member by giving her a grade that suggests that she has *less* COMPETENCE than she actually does in order to discourage other students from being, as the

33 A defender of consequentialism might point out that widespread assignment of grades for reasons unrelated to academic competence would diminish their usefulness. A consequentialist grader would obviously have good reason to proceed more frequently like a rule- or practice-consequentialist than like an act-consequentialist. However, given familiar difficulties with rule- or practice-consequentialism, the consequentialist grader might reasonably think about the specific consequences of particular grading decisions on occasion.

34 Again, intending to maximize the general welfare is like intending to draw a square circle: it's not doable even in principle. But it is surely possible to intend to do something impossible if one doesn't understand its impossibility.

instructor sees it, lazy and to encourage greater effort on the part of all students. In all of these cases—paralleled in standard consequentialist accounts of criminal penalties—the instructor's goal is academic in nature. She seeks to promote effective learning.

Like general academic consequentialism, restricted academic consequentialism is indefensible. It requires the same impossible commensuration of consequences on which consequentialism in general depends. The fact that the range of consequences the restricted academic consequentialist is prepared to consider is narrower than those the general academic consequentialist is prepared to consider doesn't change the fact that the categories and individual instances of human goods at issue in decisions about academic evaluation can't be nonarbitrarily measured on a common scale. And, like general academic consequentialism, restricted academic consequentialism violates the general requirement of truth-telling and falls foul of the academic incommensurability standard. Restricted academic consequentialism is designed to foster learning in the interests of truth. Ironically, and self-defeatingly, it leads instructors to deny the truth as a means of promoting the acquisition and dissemination of truth. In addition, it encourages an instructor to treat a student unfairly as a means rather than as an end when it prompts the instructor to determine the student's grade on the basis of the grade's likely effects on other students.

Not only does restricted academic consequentialism still yield some counter-intuitive results, there is little reason for someone not inclined to consequentialism in the first place to regard it as appropriate in an academic environment alone. A conventional consequentialist will make conduciveness to the general welfare the ultimate right-making criterion for her actions (she won't necessarily appeal to this criterion when making individual decisions, of course). She will wish to take all consequences into account (directly or indirectly). So she won't opt for a restricted version of consequentialism. And someone with principled objections to consequentialism in general won't be able to employ consequentialism as a normative defense for a particular approach to academic evaluation. An intuitionist moralist might not face a charge of personal inconsistency if she argued for the appropriateness of consequentialist reasoning under some circumstances and of deontological or aretaic reasoning under others.[35] But she will still need to confront the general positive objections to consequentialism. Others will be forced to choose between adopting general academic consequentialism (and consequentialism more generally), with predictable—and both implausible and undesirable—results, or rejecting consequentialism in favor of more satisfactory approaches to moral reasoning about, among other things, academic life.

35 The sort of intuitionist I have in mind is the sort best represented by W. D. Ross, The Right and the Good (1930); W. D. Ross, Foundations of Ethics (1938); Robert Audi, The Good in the Right (2006).

B. Academic Retributivism

Retributivism is the view that benefits and harms should be allocated to people, especially by the criminal justice system, in light of what they deserve. *Academic retributivism* is the thesis that a grade may rightly, at least in part, reflect a moral judgment regarding a student's conduct or character as it manifests itself in academic contexts. On the academic retributivist view, a grade may be in part a means of rewarding a student for morally good academic conduct and punishing her for morally bad academic conduct.

Academic retributivism is objectionable on several counts. Again, it leads to results inconsistent with the principle of academic incommensurability and the principle of truth-telling. I will explore the ways in which it does so in greater detail later in this Chapter. I want here to point out at a more general level that it can be rejected on the same basis as retributivism in general and that it leads to what seem like counter-intuitive conclusions.

A basic flaw in all forms of retributivism is that they transplant ways of reasoning that seem appropriate in the economic sphere into noneconomic sectors of our lives. If I unjustly cause you to lose something that is purely instrumental in value, purely monetary in worth, then I can compensate you for this loss by providing you with a replacement or substitute or simply by giving you the monetary equivalent of what I have caused you to lose. What matters is not that *I* have lost something in the process but that *you* have been made whole.

Retributivism transfers the logic of economic exchange into an arena in which it makes no sense. We speak of retribution as a matter of "paying back" someone who has done something harmful. But this is a case of metaphorical language doing work that ought to be done by careful philosophical argument. The idea of *punishment* for moral wrong means causing some harm to me because I have caused some putatively equivalent harm to you. But it is easy to see that, once stripped of the support provided to this idea by out-of-place economic metaphors, this idea is fundamentally nonsensical.

Suppose I tell lies about you to our mutual friends. The harm I've done to you and your friends is clear: I've disrupted your relationships. The logic of retribution suggests that I should suffer some harm as a result. It is obvious, however, that no harm I might suffer could itself restore your relationship with any friend from whom you've become alienated because of my deception.[36] And that means that you are no

[36] Of course, I am obligated to do my best to repair the breach I have caused. And in the course of doing this I may suffer injuries of one sort or another. But the notion that injuries *may* follow on attempts to redress wrongs is quite different from the notion that such injuries *should* follow or that their occurrence is or can be a constitutive part of what redressing the injuries *means*. Quite apart from repairing the breach, I might offer you something compensatory. And that you have what I've given you means that I don't have it; with respect to whatever it is, I'm worse off. But what makes you better off is that you have what I've given you, not that I don't.

better off because I've been harmed than you were when I hadn't been.[37] You haven't been paid back at all. If you believe or feel that you have, it's because you misconstrue a harm to you as, in this case, a benefit to me—as a consequence of the curious logic of retribution.[38]

It should be obvious that academic retributivism is indefensible for the same reason that retributivism in general is indefensible. The retributive punishment of students who have caused academically cognizable harms of one sort or another harms the students but does not itself *constitute* any sort of genuine benefit to those they have harmed.[39] This is true whether grading is used as a means of retribution—positive and negative—for moral conduct and character generally (*general* academic retributivism) or only for a narrower range of acts and character traits perceived to be directly relevant to the life of the academy (*restricted* academic retributivism).

General academic retributivism suffers from the incoherence of retributivism generally. It also leads to intuitively implausible consequences. On general retributivist grounds, it seems as if grades should respond to a range of virtuous choices by students. Perhaps, for instance, a student who saves a drowning boater on the school's lake might deserve higher grades. Perhaps a student who helps classmates study should be rewarded by receiving an A instead of an A-. And so on. General academic retributivism seems highly implausible because it links grades with choices with very limited connections, if any, to academic life. This would be enough to render it a nonstarter. But, of course, in addition it seems to encourage the communication of untruths about students' COMPETENCE and to exhibit disregard of individual merit; it is thus, obviously, quite difficult to square with the Principle of Fairness. Academic retributivism also seems to involve purposefully inflicting injury, and thus, where the contemplated injury is to basic goods (like knowledge), to violate the Principle of Respect.

37 *Cf.* STRIKE & SOLTIS, *supra* note 21, at 29: "Perhaps the weakest point in the retribution theory of punishment is the suggestion that the universe somehow requires that evildoers be punished with a compensating quantity of pain. . . . The retribution theory seems to require that we respond to one evil event by adding a second. . . . If we are to punish evildoers, ought we not to expect some good to result? Otherwise, does not punishment merely add gratuitously to the pain in the world?"

38 A policy or institution created with retributive rationales may sometimes be defended on consequentialist grounds. Retribution is seen, for instance, as deterring subsequent harmful conduct by others, as treating the punished person as an example to others. If the use of consequentialist arguments involves a repudiation of the previously advanced retributivist ones, then we do not need to attend to retributivist arguments for the policy or institution; those already outlined and subsequently elaborated against consequentialism will suffice. If, by contrast, the consequentialist arguments serve primarily to provide a cover for atavistic retributivist impulses, then the counter to retributivism I have offered here and on which I will expand below will show the policy or institution to be undesirable.

39 Again, these students may be harmed instrumentally, with the purpose of bringing about some benefit to others—perhaps the others they have harmed. But in this case they are being harmed on consequentialist grounds, and the standard objections to consequentialism will apply.

A defender of academic retributivism may be inclined to suggest that I have mischaracterized what the position actually looks like in practice. For the academic retributivist, the defender will say, there needs to be some sort of *equivalence* between a student's conduct or character and the way she is treated. She ought to undergo the sort of injury she has inflicted, receive the kind of good she has fostered. And the quantity of the relevant good or harm should be *proportional* to the good or harm offered or inflicted. The constraints of equivalence and proportionality seem to exert a measure of control over what retributivists might be prepared to argue and to help them avoid absurd conclusions.

But there are problems with this response. (*i*) Suppose an equivalence constraint limits academic retribution. Even so, the basic criticisms of general academic retributivism are still germane. Recall that these criticisms focus on the fact that general academic retributivism licenses the disconnection of grades from COMPETENCE and inaccurate communication with transcript consumers. These criticisms remain relevant even if the objection that general academic retributivism allows grades to reflect virtuous actions of all sorts—however nonacademic—ultimately fails. (*ii*) Individual harms and benefits aren't, as I've already noted, commensurable. Once we've left the monetary realm, it is impossible to say even that two instances of a given human good could be exchanged for each other. (*iii*) We don't ordinarily seek this kind of equivalence when we engage in retribution, academic or otherwise, or even imagine it to be possible.

The appeal to equivalence makes the most sense as a defense of execution as a judicial response to murder, though even here it doesn't succeed, of course, for the same reason that the idea of retribution generally doesn't hold water: the murderer's loss of life obviously does nothing for the victim or the victim's survivors.[40] Retribution makes no sense at all in other contexts. We don't lie to the academically dishonest; we don't see to it that late students are stood up. The punishments educational institutions seek on retributivist grounds to impose on students who cause academically cognizable injuries *aren't* in any obvious sense equivalent to those harms, even if we grant the retributivist's commensurability assumption. These practices can't, therefore, be plausibly defended on retributivist grounds. In any case, however, whatever the counter-intuitive character of the conclusions

40 Craig Kinzer (in personal communication) has suggested that an objector could argue that the beneficiary here is the community rather than the victim or her survivors. But it is not clear how best to make sense of this notion. If the idea is that the community is better off because a person with a propensity for violence has been eliminated, so that there is no possibility that she will harm anyone in the future, then the objector seems to be making a consequentialist argument, subject to the standard criticisms of consequentialism. (In any case, it is not clear why life imprisonment cannot, in principle, accomplish the same sort of risk reduction.) By contrast, if the objector believes that the community simply is *better* because someone who has caused someone else to lose something has lost something herself, I confess puzzlement. I do not see how the criminal's loss can be construed as *constituting* a gain for the community absent some doubtful economistic assumptions that seem inappropriate in this context.

to which academic retributivism might be thought to lead, the essentially incoherent and misleading character of academic retribution generally makes academic retributivism, general or restricted, an inappropriate basis for judgments about grades.

IV. ASSESSING COMMON ACADEMIC PRACTICES

Consequentialism and retributivism are unattractive guides to the ethics of grading. They give us no good reason not to affirm EXCLUSIVITY. This principle has implications for grading practices in a number of areas: basing grades on attendance and participation, on the bare completion of reading assignments, on homework of various kinds, or on participation in service-learning activities or in group work; discounting the credit assigned to putatively late work; policies governing grade changes; consistency in grading; institutional and instructor policies governing academic dishonesty; and the assignment of extra credit. In this section, I explain these implications and defend the conclusions I draw from EXCLUSIVITY about our grading practices. To the extent that I challenge these practices, I do not wish to deny that the goods they seek to serve are worth valuing. But instructors and institutions should employ other means to accomplish worthwhile goals.

A. *Attendance and Participation*

EXCLUSIVITY means that there is little or no reason for an instructor to take a student's attendance into account when assigning her a grade. Using participation to help determine a student's grade can, however, be consistent with EXCLUSIVITY.

A student attends a class session, if she does, for her own benefit and not the instructor's. And yet instructors frequently seem offended when students are absent, even though being absent is a student's own responsibility and a professor is (rightly) paid just as much whether a student opts to attend or not. That a student attends a lecture is not, in and of itself, a particularly good reason to believe that she possesses any particular level of COMPETENCE. It may be more likely, on the average, that a given student will be more competent with respect to the subject matter of a class if she attends it than if she does not. But attendance itself does not demonstrate COMPETENCE and absence provides little evidence of a lack of COMPETENCE. A student's presence at a class is not the kind of performance that could even *in principle* demonstrate that she is competent with respect to the subject matter of the class. At best, it can demonstrate a degree of exposure to the subject matter that might provide limited *support* for the contention that she has COMPETENCE. Whether she does or not can be assessed in a variety of ways other than noting her attendance or absence.

Either an instructor has reason to believe the evaluative instruments she uses to assess her students' COMPETENCE are reasonably accurate or she does not. If she believes they are, it is difficult to see why she could reasonably believe that altering grades based on sheer attendance would improve her ability to estimate her students' COMPETENCE. If she believes they are not, then she ought to replace them. She should not rely on attendance-based measures to improve her grades. Increasing or decreasing a student's grade because of her attendance record means implying, inaccurately, that she possesses a degree of COMPETENCE for which her attendance provides minimal evidence. It violates the expectation that instructors tell the truth.

An instructor is unlikely to think that attendance is an especially good indicator of COMPETENCE. She may take attendance into account for several reasons unrelated to COMPETENCE: (*i*) She may believe that attendance reflects habits and character traits likely to be of interest to transcript consumers which she supposes her grades should communicate. (*ii*) She may seek to offer students an incentive to develop these habits and traits. She may wish to offer students an incentive to attend because she believes attendance is crucial to learning. (*iii*) She may wish to punish students for what she believes is a morally irresponsible choice not to attend class and to avoid developing habits of punctuality and consistent attendance at scheduled appointments. (*iv*) She may believe that students who fail to attend her classes will waste her time and that of others by asking questions both in- or outside class that would have been answered had they attended class. She may believe that they will waste her time by submitting examinations or out-of-class assignments which she will be forced to grade even though their level of COMPETENCE is too low for the work they submit to be minimally satisfactory. She may also believe that those who attend but who arrive late will waste her time and the time of other students by disrupting her classes when they arrive. She might thus seek to use her grading scheme to discourage students from being late or absent. Most of these objectives are appropriate, but none is appropriately achieved *using grades*. None justifies violating EXCLUSIVITY by allowing a student's attendance to affect her grade.

(*i*) A grade, I have already argued, is not designed to reflect a variety of nonacademic character traits. Transcript readers have no way of knowing that the grade has been affected by these traits. And because they are so different from the COMPETENCE a grade is intended primarily to measure, it is meaningless, confusing, and unhelpful to combine them with COMPETENCE in determining a student's grade.

(*ii*) Attendance is surely often very useful for students. The desire for a good grade or the fear of a bad one may prompt a student to attend class. And offering credit of one kind or another for attendance will obviously not have the sort of effect on student behavior an instructor is likely to desire unless she fulfills her attendance-related promises or threats. If she intends to use her grading scheme as an attendance motivator, she must, in accordance with that scheme, give students who attend higher grades than they would otherwise have received in light of the available measures of their COMPETENCE and, conversely, give students who are late or who fail to attend lower grades. This sort of practice demands an academic consequentialist justification. But academic consequentialism in general is unwarranted. And in assigning grades for consequentialist reasons, an instructor violates EXCLUSIVITY. She fails to tell the truth about her students' COMPETENCE. Some students may receive poor grades because of their poor attendance. They may suffer later because they have acquired poor habits. But the goal of preventing these harms does not justify violating EXCLUSIVITY. In addition, her decision to award grades for motivational purposes is problematic because it is deliberately manipulative. The grades she assigns will be most useful as motivators if they are taken to reflect COMPETENCE and so not to have been awarded as motivational devices. Her choice makes sense only on the assumption that transcript consumers significantly misunderstand it.

(*iii*) The instructor is providing a service for which she will be paid whether students attend or not. Presuming the students are paying for their own enrollment directly or have accepted responsibility to repay loans that have enabled them to enroll, they wrong no one by not attending even if their failure to do so impedes their learning. And if they are able to learn in ways that do not require them to attend, they wrong no one even if others are paying. Students certainly don't wrong the instructor or other students by failing to attend, though in some cases they may wrong fee payers. But, whether or not failing to attend is wrong, assigning grades based on attendance certainly is. Doing so depends on the incoherent idea of retribution and involves misrepresenting students' COMPETENCE. Thus, it violates EXCLUSIVITY.

(*iv*) An instructor may be warranted in the belief that late or absent students will waste her time or the time of other students and that she can use the threat of poor grades to keep her time and that of her students from being wasted. But, again, consequentialist arguments of this sort don't work both because consequentialism is a nonstarter and because of the importance of truth-telling—in grading and in other contexts.[41]

Unlike attendance, a student's *participation in class discussions* can provide an instructor with useful information regarding a student's COMPETENCE. It is thus quite consistent with EXCLUSIVITY for an instructor to take a student's participation into account in determining the student's grade, provided she focuses on what the

[41] It would be consistent with EXCLUSIVITY for an instructor to require that a student drop a class if, whether because of perpetual absence or for some other reason, the student took up an excessive amount of her time and showed no promise of gaining satisfactory COMPETENCE before the end of the term during which the class was taking place. EXCLUSIVITY would require only that the student's transcript reflect the fact that she was forcibly dropped from the class and that the transcript make clear that any grade recorded was an estimate made at the time she dropped rather than a grade determined on the basis of a term's worth of assignments.

student's participation reveals about her COMPETENCE,[42] rather than on the fact or quantity of participation.

It would *not*, by contrast, be appropriate for an instructor to reward participation without attending to the content of what a student says as an index of COMPETENCE. If she does, she runs the risk of effectively rewarding a student for attendance alone, for the ability to raise a hand and speak—or perhaps for the virtuous habit of helping others learn—and thus of violating EXCLUSIVITY.

B. *Reading and Writing Assignments*

Some kinds of out-of-class writing assignments—ones calling for, say, the preparation of in-depth essays—can be immensely valuable both as opportunities for learning and as sources of information regarding COMPETENCE. By contrast, EXCLUSIVITY weights strongly against assigning grades on the basis of other kinds of out-of-class activities, notably repetitive skill-building exercises (instances of BUSYWORK). And it precludes taking into account the simple fact that a student has or has not read a body of assigned material at a particular time.

Given EXCLUSIVITY, a student's performance on an assignment should contribute to the determination of her grade for a course to the extent that it helps her instructor to estimate her competence. An assignment which allows more precise estimation of a particular aspect of a student's COMPETENCE should be preferred to one which allows less precise estimation of the same aspect of the student's COMPETENCE. It is doubtful, therefore, whether in light of EXCLUSIVITY it would ever be appropriate to give credit to a student simply for *reading* an assigned text, as opposed to, say, completing a review that shows critical engagement with the text.

The purpose of offering credit simply for reading a text would presumably be roughly the same as the purpose of offering credit for attendance—to prompt or reward good behavior or to discourage or punish bad behavior, with the hope that learning might be a collateral benefit. And the same sorts of arguments show why doing so is inappropriate. Negatively, these rationales are broadly consequentialist, and academic consequentialism is untenable. Positively, offering reading credit violates EXCLUSIVITY. Evidence that a student has read a text is evidence that she has been *exposed* to certain material, not that she has understood it or engaged with it critically. And, in most cases, evidence that she has not read a text is only

42 An instructor may believe—plausibly—that participation plays a vital role in facilitating the learning of others. She may also believe—plausibly—that a student is likely to read and think more carefully than she otherwise might when preparing for a class in which participation is required and that her subject-matter competence will consequently be enhanced. She may thus welcome a variety of positive consequences effected by a decision to award credit for participation, and EXCLUSIVITY gives her no reason not to do so. However, the potential value of these consequences gives her no independent justification for taking participation into account when she determines her students' grades and no basis for evaluating student participation, if she requires it, in a way that fails to focus on its value as a means of estimating students' likely subject-matter competence.

presumptive evidence that she has not been exposed to the relevant material, since she could have been exposed to it in some other way.[43] In any case, evaluative exercises that require that students *demonstrate* COMPETENCE give an instructor a much more accurate means of assessing COMPETENCE than the simple knowledge that a student has read a portion of an assigned text.

There is no hard-and-fast distinction between practice-oriented, skill-building homework exercises and other sorts of exercises. But it is clear that some homework exercises are designed primarily, even if not exclusively, to help students *acquire proficiencies* of various sorts rather than to enable instructors to *measure* students' COMPETENCE. Homework exercises in mathematics classes are obvious examples: a student practices problems of a certain sort repeatedly in order to learn how to approach an indefinite variety of possible future problems of the same sort. Whether she has in fact learned to do so will be estimated using examinations, which will ordinarily measure her abilities under monitored and time-controlled conditions.

In accordance with EXCLUSIVITY, an instructor should where possible avoid basing grades on students' BUSYWORK. Instructors should assign such exercises where appropriate. But it may often violate EXCLUSIVITY to use them when estimating students' COMPETENCE and so determining their grades. In most cases, a student's performance on examinations, papers, and projects will provide a much better basis for estimating her COMPETENCE than her BUSYWORK performance.

Information gained from students' performance on instances of BUSYWORK will often be, at best, superfluous. Consider four possibilities with respect to a given student: (*i*) the student does well on examinations, papers, and projects *and* on instances of BUSYWORK; (*ii*) the student does well on instances of BUSYWORK and poorly on examinations, papers, and projects; (*iii*) the student does poorly on instances of BUSYWORK (or does not complete them at all) and well on examinations, papers, and projects; (*iv*) the student does poorly on instances of BUSYWORK *and* on examinations, papers, and projects.

In cases (*i*) and (*iv*), the instances of BUSYWORK provide the instructor with no useful information as she determines the student's grade. The grade would be no different were she to disregard the BUSYWORK. In case (*ii*), the instructor has some reason to suspect that the student is cheating or is taking an inordinate amount of time to complete the instances of BUSYWORK. It is also possible, of course, that the student is a poor test-taker but is developing genuine COMPETENCE, which is revealed by her performance on the instances of BUSYWORK. But if the instructor believes that this is the case, she cannot reasonably do so primarily on the basis of the instances of BUSYWORK, the interpretation of which is in question. And she cannot do so on the basis of the student's overall examination performance, which

[43] Obviously, in a course in literature a student usually cannot be exposed to all of the relevant material except by reading the assigned text; digesting *Cliff's Notes* will tell a student something useful about *Huckleberry Finn*, but the student won't discover the delights of Twain's language or engage directly with his literary artistry.

is, *ex hypothesi*, poor. If, nonetheless, she *is* warranted in believing that the student is acquiring more COMPETENCE than the student's examination performance suggests, EXCLUSIVITY suggests that this belief might appropriately be reflected in the grade she assigns the student. But, in this case, what would prove decisive would be the fact that she has independent reason to believe the instances of BUSYWORK reflect the student's true COMPETENCE more accurately than do examinations, not the BUSYWORK itself.

In case (*iii*), the instructor has little or no reason to base the student's grade on her BUSYWORK performance, provided the instructor is confident that her examinations, papers, and projects enable her accurately to estimate the student's true grade. If they do, the student's BUSYWORK scores are superfluous and reducing the student's grade because of her BUSYWORK performance will violate EXCLUSIVITY, given that the grade will be a less accurate estimate of her COMPETENCE than it would be if her BUSYWORK performance were excluded from consideration.

It is possible, of course, that the instructor reasonably believes that her examinations alone do not allow her accurately to estimate a student's COMPETENCE and that it is not practicable for her to design them in such a way that they do so. If she reasonably believes this, and if she also reasonably believes that combining BUSYWORK performance with examination performance allows her to estimate the student's grade more accurately than would considering examination performance alone, she does not violate EXCLUSIVITY by taking BUSYWORK performance into account. It is also possible that exercises to be completed outside class are not instances of BUSYWORK at all, and are closer in nature to academic papers than to conventional homework exercises. It is unclear, however, what would provide evidence that taking instances of genuine BUSYWORK into account when determining grades yielded a more accurate estimate of COMPETENCE than not considering them,[44] particularly given the instructor's greater control over the completion environment of examinations. And it is crucial, in any case, to ensure that, in the rare cases in which instances of BUSYWORK are rightly taken into account, grades are not influenced by such irrelevancies as capable students' understandable lack of interest in completing BUSYWORK. Educational institutions rightly care about students' self-discipline, but students' character development is best encouraged in ways that do not affect their grades.

44 Where there is a significant disparity between a student's performance on a comprehensive final examination and her performance on prior examinations during a course, a similar problem may arise; if so, a similar analysis would apply in accordance with EXCLUSIVITY. If the final examination yields an estimate of a student's subject-matter competence that is clearly more accurate than one based on consideration of all examinations, the instructor should focus on the final examination when determining the student's grade. But there is a stronger case to be made for the view that performance on prior examinations is a useful contributor to an overall assessment of a student's subject-matter competence than there is for the view that BUSYWORK performance should play this role. And, indeed, there is reason to believe that a single examination is a less accurate estimator of students' subject-matter competence than an array of examinations or other controlled exercises.

Of course, instructors may tend to give students credit for their BUSYWORK performance, not because they believe that BUSYWORK performance is a good estimator of students' true grades but because they believe that by doing so they will encourage students to complete instances of BUSYWORK and thus to master relevant skills. But this sort of academic consequentialist reasoning falls foul of the criticisms of academic consequentialism I've already noted and will in some cases lead an instructor to violate EXCLUSIVITY. An instructor violates EXCLUSIVITY if, on the basis of a student's BUSYWORK performance, she gives a lower grade to the student than her examination performance suggests she should receive, not because she reasonably believes that the examination performance is an inaccurate estimator of the student's COMPETENCE but because the instructor wishes to maintain a system of incentives for other students to build skills by completing instances of BUSYWORK or for the student to develop better study habits.

EXCLUSIVITY underwrites a preference for examinations and essays, exercises that measure knowledge and skill rather than determination or a tolerance for boredom, rather than instances of BUSYWORK, as means of estimating students' COMPETENCE and so of determining grades. In accordance with EXCLUSIVITY, quizzes may also be taken into account in determining grades to the extent that they can serve as accurate snapshots of student performance rather than as motivational tools designed to spur students to prepare for class discussions or attend class. An instructor may welcome the positive motivational impact of the practice of administering regular quizzes; but this practice must be justified on other grounds—otherwise, it will in reality be serving inappropriate consequentialist or retributivist purposes.

C. *Service Learning*

Engaging in service activities can be a valuable way of learning about community problems, developing technical and managerial skills, and developing habits of compassion and generosity. It is perfectly reasonable that service activities might be among the learning experiences associated with a given course. But EXCLUSIVITY dictates that students be graded in light of their COMPETENCE, not their sheer *participation* in these activities.

The usual sorts of reasons may be given for awarding credit for service learning. Consequentialists will wish to encourage participation in service ventures and the development of useful habits. Retributivists will wish to reward the virtuous who participate and punish the vicious who do not. For the reasons I have already elaborated, these attempted justifications are unpersuasive.

Participation in a service activity connected with a given course may foster the development of COMPETENCE. But evaluative instruments should be employed to *determine* what COMPETENCE students possess. It cannot be *assumed* that they have done so simply because they have *participated* in service-learning activities, and it cannot be assumed that they have not because they have not participated. Structured evaluative instruments are likely to be far more effective at estimating students' COMPETENCE than the mere fact of *participation* in service-learning activities. EXCLUSIVITY dictates, therefore, that these evaluative instruments be used to determine students' grades.

Service learning as currently understood characteristically includes a reflective component. Students are asked to explore the meaning of the service activities in which they have engaged and to explain what their participation might have taught them. Provided such reflective exercises are taken seriously and actually provide evidence of COMPETENCE, instructors may reasonably consider them when determining grades. It will be important, however, not to give them undue weight, to evaluate them using standards different from those employed with respect to other evaluative instruments, or to use them in determining grades when they fail to illuminate students' COMPETENCE. Otherwise, it will be difficult to escape the conclusion that students are being rewarded simply for participating in or reflecting on service activities or punished for not participating or reflecting. It will thus be especially important to ensure that service-learning activities are incorporated into particular classes only when they foster the development of the *kind* of COMPETENCE the class as a whole is intended to foster. A calculus course, for instance, is intended to help students develop COMPETENCE with respect to calculus; a service-learning project in which students *taught* calculus to others might serve the course objectives, presuming the calculus they taught was calculus of the level addressed in the course itself. By contrast, teaching first-year algebra as part of a service project would be unlikely to foster the development of COMPETENCE at the relevant level with respect to calculus. The same would be true of an effort to clean up the home and garden of a retired mathematician. These sorts of activities are worthwhile, and institutions are certainly entitled to encourage them. But they shouldn't be encouraged by means of course requirements and grades.

To be sure, it is conceivable that some kinds of learning can happen only through doing. It may not be realistically possible for a student to acquire some kinds of habits and attitudes without participating in service-learning activities. But habits of compassion and generosity are quite different from COMPETENCE; this incommensurability makes combining them with measures of COMPETENCE to determine grades a dubious enterprise. Further, grades as conventionally understood do not measure or reflect habits of this sort, so taking them into account violates EXCLUSIVITY's truth-telling requirement. Grades are concerned with more narrowly cognitive capacities. It is reasonable for institutions and instructors to assess students' affective and moral development, but this assessment should be understood to be different from *grading*.

D. *Group Activities*

Students are sometimes asked to complete academic assignments in groups. Basing students' grades on group-produced work is often problematic.

This does not mean that it is always unreasonable to assign students to work *in* groups. Sometimes, especially in courses in management and leadership, instructors seek to enable students to learn how to interact effectively with others. In such cases, students must work in groups to acquire the needed skills. When this is the case, and when it is possible with some modicum of accuracy to assess students' interactions with others and their respective contributions to group projects, work done by individual students in groups may appropriately contribute to their grades. If it didn't, their grades would fail to communicate useful information regarding their COMPETENCE.

If it is not possible to assess students individually and reflect individual assessments in grades, however, performance on group assignments should not affect grades. Transcript consumers, after all, are not admitting or hiring or honoring the groups that undertook course assignments *as groups*; their concern is with the individual members of those groups. And students want feedback regarding their own COMPETENCE, not that of others. Students' different skill levels and contributions make uniform group-based grades unfair, even if all students contribute enthusiastically. But students are all too aware that free riding is common in groups, with underperforming students unfairly counting on high-performing ones to complete group assignments largely unaided. Wherever possible, then, instructors should decline to make assignments to groups and should decline to determine grades in light of group rather than individual performance.

While many dubious academic practices might be justified with reference to academic retributivism or academic consequentialism, both problematic theoretical accounts of grading parallel EXCLUSIVITY in counting against basing grades on group performance. The retributivist will note that group-based grades reward rather than punish the free rider, and the consequentialist will note the perverse incentives offered by group-based grading to the free rider.

E Late Work

In accordance with EXCLUSIVITY, a student's grade should not be reduced simply because the work on the basis of which her grade is determined was submitted later than the instructor preferred that it be submitted. EXCLUSIVITY licenses limited exceptions to this norm based on the need to avoid substantial inconvenience, to ensure the usefulness of evaluative instruments, and to facilitate the comparability of student grades.

The EXCLUSIVITY-based argument against lateness discounts is simple and straightforward. A grade is a rough measure of a student's COMPETENCE. The purpose of evaluative instruments is to help the instructor estimate a student's COMPETENCE. The time at which a student submits an exercise is often irrelevant to the significance of the student's performance on the exercise for an estimate of her COMPETENCE. A paper on Milton assigned at the beginning of the term and submitted on Thursday can provide the same sort of useful information about the author's COMPETENCE with respect to seventeenth-century British literature as a comparable paper assigned at the beginning of the term and submitted on Monday. To reduce the grade for the paper submitted on Thursday because of its arrival date would likely be to pave the way for an inaccurate assessment of the COMPETENCE of the student who submitted the paper. It would therefore violate EXCLUSIVITY.

Time may sometimes be relevant, of course. Grades within a given course should be comparable: a grade earned by one student should have the same meaning as the same grade earned by another student. Grades are certainly more useful to transcript consumers if they can facilitate comparative judgments among students. In some cases, treating work submitted at different times as comparable may reduce the cross-student comparability of grades for the course. The pressure to complete a project in a limited time, for instance, may have been a feature of the evaluative process for the course. If most students completed a project within forty-eight hours, a student who did so within seventy-two hours may need to be assessed differently. In most cases, time won't make a difference as regards cross-student comparability for a given course and term. But, in the rare cases in which it does, and if there is no other way to ensure comparability, it may be necessary for the instructor to discount work submitted after she has assigned grades, or employ an alternate means of assessing a student's COMPETENCE in addition to the late work, even though she should still take such work into account.

The potential justifications for lateness discounts will be similar to those typically offered for grade reductions based on attendance. They will be subject to the same sorts of rebuttals and will be similarly unsuccessful. Given both the implausibility of academic consequentialism and retributivism and the positive requirements of EXCLUSIVITY, academic consequentialist and retributivist arguments for lateness discounts fail. Encouraging student responsibility or punishing student irresponsibility does not warrant inaccurate grading.

However, accurate grading should not become a monomaniacal passion for any instructor. There are other things besides grading that rightly claim her time and attention. She is not obligated to subject herself to substantial inconvenience because her students have taken extra time to submit projects. She therefore has at least two options. (*i*) She is morally, and should be institutionally, entitled to delay her assignment of grades to students who have submitted exercises after she has requested that these exercises be submitted; she should not be obligated to assign grades to these students at the same time that she assigns grades to students who took her convenience into account when deciding when to submit *their* exercises. (*ii*) If grading an exercise would create a substantial inconvenience for her but there actually is, as there often will not be, a good reason for the grade to be submitted at the same time as all other grades, she is entitled to grade the exercise much more cursorily than she would have graded it had it arrived earlier.

She may rightly act in these and perhaps other ways to reduce unreasonable inconvenience created by students' late submission of exercises. What she may not do, at least ordinarily, is to reduce the grade on an exercise simply because the exercise is late. If an inaccuracy in a student's grade results from a cursory review of an exercise because the exercise was late, this inaccuracy may simply be an unintended by-product of the instructor's reasonable desire to avoid excessive inconvenience. By contrast, a lateness-based reduction in a grade for an exercise an instructor has chosen to inconvenience herself by evaluating with reasonable care is—even if it is also something else—an intentional act of deception, and thus a violation of EXCLUSIVITY.

F. Incomplete Conversions and Other Grade Changes

When faced with a request that she change one conventional letter grade to another or substitute a conventional letter grade for an I, an instructor must consider the probable degree of the inaccuracy, the likely cost to the student and to possible transcript consumers if the grade remains unchanged, and the inconvenience to herself. In accordance with EXCLUSIVITY, she may rightly refuse to change or convert a grade if leaving the grade untouched serves the interests of accuracy or convenience. However, EXCLUSIVITY precludes any *institutional* policy that, for punitive or motivational reasons, places any limit on an instructor's freedom to change a student's grade after she has submitted it or that requires that an Incomplete grade become an F after a specified deadline.

Given the invalidity of retributivist and consequentialist rationales for grade assignment, an instructor should never change a grade except in the interests of accuracy. The passage of time, often a key issue in disputes related to grade changes and conversions, may create accuracy problems for instructors because it may limit cross-student comparability of grades or instructors' capacities to use work completed in particular contexts to assess COMPETENCE.

Changing or converting a student's grade in a given course in light of her performance on assignments provided to the instructor after the end of the term in which she took the course will usually mean that the student has had more time to complete coursework than her classmates. In some classes, this may be irrelevant. In others, however, it may affect the accuracy of a grade. Cross-student comparability may be an issue. And an instructor may simply not accurately remember what standards she has employed to assess work submitted by other students. She may thus reasonably lack confidence that she can assess a newly submitted assignment for a given course using the same standards she used initially to determine grades for the course. Thus, she may reasonably be uncertain that a changed or converted grade in a given course will have the same meaning as an identical grade assigned at the end of the term during which the course took place. If she does, she may reasonably decline to consider the newly provided work. Alternatively, she may opt to discount it in some way to allow for any recall-related problems, or require an additional assignment.

Like the need for accuracy, the desire for convenience may rightly justify an instructor's refusal to change or convert a grade, within bounds set by the Principle of Fairness. An instructor is certainly entitled to avoid maintaining student-related records indefinitely (unless the records are the focus of legal or institutional controversy of which she has reason to be aware). Institutional policies should thus permit her to dispose of records related to a student's performance in a given course after a finite—and relatively short—period. If she is asked about a possible grade after this period and no longer has the necessary records, she may obviously be in no position to evaluate a student's request for a grade change or conversion. Similarly, if she reasonably believes the request is frivolous, she is justified in declining it without investigation.

By contrast, if the instructor does have access to the relevant records, if it is reasonable for her to believe that the student's request for a grade change or conversion might have merit, if she can evaluate the records accurately, and if she can do so without significant inconvenience, EXCLUSIVITY requires that she re-evaluate the student's grade and, if the currently recorded grade less accurately reflects the student's COMPETENCE, submit a new grade. Institutional policy should permit her to make a grade change or convert an Incomplete grade into a conventional grade at any time in the interests of accuracy, though it should not require her to disregard her reasonable concern for her own convenience.

Two kinds of institutional policies are called into question by EXCLUSIVITY: those that place time limits on grade changes and those that stipulate that grades may be changed only to correct clerical errors.

There is doubtless a presumption in favor of stable grades. A student needs to be able to assume that the grade she receives at the end of a class will continue to appear on her transcript. There is thus a not-inconsiderable reason to keep changes unilaterally initiated by instructors to a minimum, even if they are sometimes appropriate or even necessary. In addition, an institutional policy limiting grade changes or conversions protects instructors, reducing pressure on them to consider excessively demanding or unreasonable student requests. Nonetheless, EXCLUSIVITY requires policies that make accuracy possible.

Fairness to transcript consumers means providing them—where doing so is possible and convenient—with updated accurate information when such information becomes available. A student's expectation interest in stability does not trump a transcript consumer's interest in accurate information regarding the student's COMPETENCE or an instructor's responsibility to tell the truth. The presumption against instructor-initiated grade changes tells against such changes when they reflect, for instance, ongoing uncertainty—dithering, perhaps—on an instructor's part regarding how best to estimate a student's COMPETENCE. It does not tell against a change designed to ensure that a student's grade more accurately reflects her

COMPETENCE, provided there is good reason to be confident that the new grade *is* more accurate.

A rigid institutional policy that prevents an instructor from changing a grade after the passage of an arbitrary deadline does protect instructors from harassment by students. Nonetheless, such a policy deprives an instructor of the freedom to improve the accuracy of her grades. The cost of additional student harassment does not justify taking this freedom away from her because students and transcript consumers both have substantial interests in accurate transcripts. EXCLUSIVITY calls for a concern for accuracy that is not trumped by the institutional need for closure or instructor convenience. And an instructor who is confident in the grades she has given can convey this confidence to students as clearly and forcefully as she can describe a rigid institutional policy, and so forestall inappropriate demands for grade changes.

Some institutional policies prevent instructors from changing grades for reasons unrelated to clerical errors. Such policies may unnecessarily limit the accuracy of grades, and therefore violate EXCLUSIVITY. A student's grade should reflect the best available estimate of the student's COMPETENCE. There are a variety of ways of assessing COMPETENCE. And in a particular case an instructor may have access to information she did not have when she computed a student's grade that leads her to reassess the student's COMPETENCE. She may also find herself forced to reassess the procedures she has chosen to use to evaluate students' COMPETENCE. In either case, she should be free to change a grade.

At least two kinds of information might lead an instructor to assess a student's COMPETENCE differently from the way in which she did when she initially submitted a grade. The student might submit additional work—work that should have been submitted earlier or work that supplements the work the student did during the term in which she took the course in which she earned the grade at issue, and which provides better information regarding her COMPETENCE. Or the instructor might come to recontextualize the student's work as a result of learning about personal circumstances that affected the student's performance at the time she assigned the student's grade.

Post-term work may or may not be relevant. Regularly assigned work submitted after the date requested by the instructor probably will be: if it is taken into account, the student's aggregate class performance will look different, and the instructor may thus have good reason to alter her grade.[45] Substitute work, however, may not be relevant. Recall that a grade is not a reward for hard work. Doing additional work, even an infinite amount of additional work, does not itself warrant a higher grade. A grade is an estimate of COMPETENCE. So additional work justifies an improved grade only if it changes the instructor's assessment of the student's COMPETENCE. Giving a student a higher grade as a reward for *extra effort* violates EXCLUSIVITY.

45 Whether this is so or not will depend in part on the factors considered above in relation to late work.

Even if an instructor does not regard a grade change as a reward for extra work, however, taking additional work into account at all may seem to raise fairness or inaccuracy problems. Other students have been graded based on work submitted before grades were due; the student whose grade is being changed is not. But this is relevant to the fairness of the instructor's grade-assignment decision only if completion time affects cross-student comparability. If it doesn't, provided all grades submitted by the instructor reflect reasonable judgments about COMPETENCE, a grade change made in light of additional or substituted work need not be unfair.

Suppose the instructor comes to recontextualize a student's work because she discovers that the student was in the midst of a personal crisis at the time she completed the work on which the instructor based her judgment about the student's grade. She comes to believe, that is, that the student's work does not reflect the student's ability. This will not, in and of itself, be sufficient to tell her what the student's *actual* COMPETENCE is; it will simply tell her that she cannot trust her own earlier estimate. Recontextualization on its own will thus not warrant altering the student's grade. It may provide the instructor with a reason, however, to provide the student opportunity to complete additional work that will replace the work the student completed during the class in which she earned the grade she seeks to change or to assess the student's COMPETENCE in a new way. If she concludes, in light of additional or alternative work, that the grade she previously assigned to the student is inaccurate, EXCLUSIVITY dictates that she change it. On the other hand, the ability to respond to pressure may sometimes be a constituent of COMPETENCE. To the extent that it is relevant in a given case, no grade change may be appropriate, even if the student's performance is recontextualized.

An instructor may also come to conclude that some or all of her evaluative instruments or the way she made use of the information derived from them were such that she could not use them accurately to assess the COMPETENCE of some or all of the students enrolled in a given course. She has no obligation neurotically to explore this possibility; absent strong countervailing evidence, it is consistent with her duties under EXCLUSIVITY to take her own convenience as decisive. In some cases, though, she may believe that to grade accurately she must discount some of the instruments she has used to evaluate students in a given course or take them into account differently. If, for instance, she gave inappropriate weight to instances of BUSYWORK in determining her grades, she may realize that in so doing she assigned inaccurate grades to a variety of students. In accordance with EXCLUSIVITY, she should have the freedom to reconsider and revise her grades, if need be.

While EXCLUSIVITY requires that instructors be able to change or convert grades at will in the interests of accuracy, it also entails, however, indicating clearly when grades are changed. A student may have gained more COMPETENCE during the period since the completion of the term at which her initial grade was assigned. If this grade is changed, the student's transcript must make clear how much time has elapsed between the assignment of the initial grade and the grade change. Provided the student's transcript does make this clear, however, a grade change need raise no special accuracy problems.

Most grade changes should be made by instructors and only instructors. Respect for an instructor's freedom to assign grades reflects the instructor's knowledge of the subject matter of a course and of a subject area more broadly and of what she actually delivered in the course, as well as her acquaintance with students' behavior and circumstances, her awareness of appropriate expectations in the relevant field, and of her past experience issuing grades. It is a matter of regard for her as an independent professional. EXCLUSIVITY dictates, though, that institutional policies should permit the assignment of grades by others in rare cases. These might reasonably include (*i*) cases in which an instructor's death or serious illness prevents her from submitting grades and (*ii*) cases in which an instructor refuses to submit grades. Policies should permit others to alter grades in similar cases when information that would warrant an instructor in changing grades comes to light. Similarly, institutional policies should permit others to change grades when formal proceedings resulting from student grievances have revealed instructors' errors in grade determination and instructors decline to make appropriate alterations.

An instructor may sometimes be required by EXCLUSIVITY to give an Incomplete grade. If she lacks the information she needs to assess a student's COMPETENCE—if, for instance, the student has turned in too few assignments for her to estimate the student's COMPETENCE accurately—she cannot responsibly submit a grade for a student. And even if she is not required to give a student an Incomplete, she may have sufficient doubts about her understanding of the student's COMPETENCE to make acceding to the student's request for an Incomplete reasonable. Institutional policies should enable her to assign Incomplete grades, like other grades, at her discretion.

Such policies should allow her to convert an Incomplete she has assigned to a student into a conventional letter grade if she is able reasonably to assess the student's COMPETENCE. They should not require that the Incomplete become an F after a specified deadline. If they do, they clearly violate EXCLUSIVITY. An F grade for a course implies that the student is incompetent with respect to the subject matter of the course. But, in the case of an Incomplete grade, the fact of the matter is that whether a student lacks COMPETENCE is indeterminate. To imply that she is subject-matter incompetent would be inaccurate, and so a violation of EXCLUSIVITY. This principle requires that the Incomplete designation remain on the student's transcript until cleared.

The arguments against this position will, as usual, be consequentialist or retributivist. The retributivist will wish, unreasonably, to punish slothful students. The consequentialist will be concerned with motivating students to perform efficiently. It is no doubt good for students if they are encouraged not to wait indefinitely to complete course requirements. A student already taking a full load may be overwhelmed by the need to meet requirements for an uncompleted course from a previous term as well as for the courses for which she is currently registered. There are genuine costs associated with adhering to EXCLUSIVITY. The threat of an F is designed to motivate a potentially slothful student to complete work expeditiously. And there is no way for this threat to be effective unless it is carried out. But, when it is carried out, the instructor will be declaring, falsely, that she is confident that the student lacks COMPETENCE. A continued Incomplete grade, by contrast, will make clear that there is reason to be unsure whether she does or not, without giving transcript consumers any reason to overestimate or underestimate her COMPETENCE. And it will make it more likely that an instructor will have the opportunity to obtain the information she needs accurately to assess a student's COMPETENCE.

Policies that result in the automatic conversion of Incompletes to Fs create perverse incentives for instructors. Suppose an instructor knows that, if she does not act, a student who has received an Incomplete will latterly receive an F. In this case, she may be inclined to submit a passing grade for the student to prevent the automatic assignment of the F. But, since the fact that the student has received an Incomplete implies that the instructor lacks the information she needs adequately to assess the student's COMPETENCE, it follows that the instructor is not *able* properly to assign a grade. The odds are good, therefore, that the grade she assigns will be an inaccurate measure of COMPETENCE and that submitting it will violate EXCLUSIVITY. Eliminating automatic Incomplete-to-F conversion rules are thus also desirable because they will eliminate this temptation to inaccuracy.

As I noted earlier, however, it may sometimes be impossible for an instructor accurately to assess a student's COMPETENCE after a certain amount of time has passed. In this case, an Incomplete grade might simply become permanent. Because the Incomplete grade in a given course might reasonably be read as implying that there is still some possibility that a grade will be assigned for the course, it may be appropriate for institutions to assign a new Permanently Incomplete grade under such circumstances.

G. *Consistency*

The point is implicit in what I've already said, but it should be emphasized that an instructor is not obligated to employ the same grading methods for all those enrolled in a given course unless using varied grading methods would unduly impair cross-student comparability. Nor is an instructor obligated to avoid altering announced grading methods during the course of a term. Unnecessary consistency is less important than accuracy—conformity with EXCLUSIVITY. Perhaps a highly creative student can best respond to assigned material, not by writing a conventional academic paper, but by crafting a play, for instance. There is nothing wrong with assessing this student's COMPETENCE using an assignment crafted especially for her. At the same time, a student should not be entitled to complete an alternative assignment for any reason unless the instructor is confident that the student's

COMPETENCE *can* be assessed using this assignment in a manner that allows for cross-student comparability, and so ensures that the relationships among the grades for the course convey meaningful information.

Just as consistency among students need not be required if alternatives are consistent with EXCLUSIVITY, so consistency with a syllabus distributed at the beginning of a term need not be treated as essential. The Principle of Fairness will control here. Respecting expectations matters for its own sake: many people value predictability. And various sorts of investments of time and energy and money may have been made in light of announcements made at a course's inception. Disrupting expectations may thus in many cases be unfair. In some cases, however, it may be *essential*, as when an instructor recognizes that a grading scheme she has announced will result in systematic misestimation of students' COMPETENCE (as, for instance, by counting BUSYWORK performance toward students' grades unnecessarily).

H. Academic Dishonesty

In accordance with EXCLUSIVITY, an accurate grade is a more or less correct estimate of a student's COMPETENCE. An instructor may often be licensed to assume that, when a student fails to complete an exercise, the student has failed to do so because she lacks the knowledge or skills it is designed to measure. Absent alternative information, the failure to submit an exercise can reasonably be treated as evidence of a lack of COMPETENCE with respect to the subject matter of the exercise. That's why it's important to allow students to submit late exercises—so that instructors can acquire the most accurate possible information about their COMPETENCE. And it's also why instructors can reasonably treat the submission by a student of an assignment in fact completed by one or more other people as evidence of a lack of COMPETENCE on the part of the student with respect to the subject matter of the exercise. Work that is not a student's own cannot reasonably be used to estimate her COMPETENCE. Thus, EXCLUSIVITY directs an instructor to give no consideration to such work in estimating a student's COMPETENCE, and entitles the instructor to regard the submission of such work as evidence that the student has no competence at all in the relevant area.[46]

EXCLUSIVITY offers no justification, however, for *otherwise* penalizing the student simply because she submitted work she herself did not complete, for imposing consequences other than those that flow naturally from the refusal to treat work not completed by the student as providing any positive evidence of her COMPETENCE. If, of course, the instructor has reasonably assigned a sufficiently high weight to a given assignment or set of assignments that incompetence with respect to the skills or understanding the assignment or set of assignments is designed to measure means

[46] Perhaps it might on occasion be reasonable for an instructor simply to disregard an assignment entirely, not treating it as relevant either positively or negatively to the determination of a given student's grade. EXCLUSIVITY entitles an instructor to use what she takes to be the most effective approach to determining each student's COMPETENCE.

the student lacks satisfactory COMPETENCE, then the consequences for the student's grade may be quite serious. But this will be because of the instructor's reasonable belief regarding the student's COMPETENCE, not because of the student's moral wrongdoing.

Giving an academically dishonest student an F in a course for reasons not directly related to COMPETENCE could, of course, be justified on academic consequentialist or academic retributivist grounds. The academic retributivist will seek to punish the student for her immoral behavior; the academic consequentialist will seek to deter students from engaging in deceptive behavior. But neither the consequentialist nor the retributivist tells the truth by giving the student an F when her estimated COMPETENCE does not warrant one, and the moral values both seek rightly to take seriously are incommensurable with COMPETENCE. Adjusting grades in light of a student's immoral character or choices is thus inconsistent with EXCLUSIVITY.

There may be one sort of exception to this general rule. Recall that EXCLUSIVITY authorizes instructors to take their own convenience reasonably into account. It is unfair of a student who has already given an instructor reason to be suspicious of her honesty to expect an instructor to expend substantial extra time assessing the exercises she submits to determine if they are her own work. An instructor cannot regard concern for her own convenience as justifying her in refusing to make a good-faith effort to estimate a student's COMPETENCE. But if such an effort is rendered significantly more difficult by the student's own misbehavior, she may be authorized under EXCLUSIVITY to avoid the task of assessing all of the student's work in order to estimate the student's COMPETENCE, and so the student's grade.

Suppose the instructor knows that the student has submitted work not her own on more than one occasion. Suppose she has evidence that makes it reasonable to believe that the student has done the same thing on other occasions; she does not need to investigate every exercise—only a representative sample. Suppose, too, that she reasonably assumes that the student lacks COMPETENCE in many or all of these cases. And suppose that the student's presumptive lack of COMPETENCE in these cases means that she lacks COMPETENCE with respect to the subject matter of the course as a whole. In this case she might reasonably fail the student without an across-the-board assessment of the student's COMPETENCE.[47]

Given EXCLUSIVITY, it is not reasonable for an instructor to withhold all credit for an assignment unless she reasonably believes the *entire* assignment is not the submitting student's work or she cannot reasonably and conveniently determine

47 The appeal to convenience here and elsewhere is not an attempt to bring retribution in through the back door. The instructor who takes her legitimate convenience into account in deciding not to review all of an academically dishonest student's work need not be intent on causing the student purportedly compensatory harm for her dishonesty. The instructor's purpose may be only to reduce her own inconvenience; the harm to the student may be a foreseen but unintended by-product of her decision to minimize her inconvenience. *Cf.* Germain Grisez, *Toward a Consistent Natural-Law Ethics of Killing*, 15 AM. J. JURIS. 64 (1970); Joseph M. Boyle, *Toward Understanding the Principle of Double Effect*, 90 ETHICS 527 (1980).

which part is and which part is not the student's work. An assignment only partially a student's own work can still help an instructor to estimate her COMPETENCE, so she should take it into account in the interests of accuracy (within the limits of reasonable concern for the instructor's own convenience). An instructor is not obligated to make special effort to determine which elements of an assignment are and are not products of the student's work, but if she can do so easily she should take what the assignment tells her about the student's work into account when determining the student's grade. If not, of course, she is entitled to assume that none of the assignment is the student's work and that the student lacks COMPETENCE with respect to the area performance on the exercise is supposed to measure.

It is certainly appropriate for an instructor to give a student who has handed in work not her own an opportunity to submit substitute work, if an alternative assignment will make it easier for the instructor to estimate the student's COMPETENCE. An instructor may reasonably decline to consider additional work if doing so would cause her substantial inconvenience. It would be unfair of a student to avoid taking advantage of the opportunity for adequate evaluation provided by an instructor when she originally makes an assignment—by submitting work not her own—and then to demand that the instructor take extra time to evaluate her on the basis of work completed to replace an assignment for which she rightly received no credit.

Also given EXCLUSIVITY, it is unreasonable for an instructor to regard as an instance of academic dishonesty a student's submission of the same work in more than one course. There is nothing dishonest about submitting a paper to multiple instructors. If one gives a paper or project to an instructor, one represents it as one's own work; one is not ordinarily making any representation about the amount of effort one invested in preparing it. While many institutions regard multiple submissions as academically dishonest, it is hard to defend this judgment if a grade is understood to serve as an accurate estimate of COMPETENCE. Provided a paper or project genuinely reflects a student's COMPETENCE, an instructor may reasonably take it into account when determining a student's grade, whether it has been submitted to another instructor or not. A grade is not, again, a reward for effort, so the fact that a student who submits a paper or project to multiple instructors does not work as hard as another who does not is irrelevant.

An instructor might object that she should not give credit for a multiply submitted paper because her grades are comparative, and since students in general have had less time to invest in other projects for her class because of the need to produce a given paper or project, a student who reuses a paper or project prepared for another class has an unfair advantage over her classmates. However, comparisons among classmates can provide only a rough basis for grades; the instructor must be aware of the general population of students whom transcript consumers are likely to evaluate, comparing her students with them rather than with each other. The grade distribution for a class of exceptionally gifted or exceptionally untalented students surely ought to be quite different from the grade distribution for an ordinary class.

An instructor can't ensure intra-class comparability by prohibiting multiple submissions, since a student might submit for a given class a paper never used to fulfill a requirement for any other course which she had nonetheless written before the class began. Similarly, a student who had never received another instructor's formal evaluation of a paper or project might—and should—have drawn on the critical skills of others before submitting it for a class, asking for reactions from classmates or mentors. And even in the rare case in which an instructor might reasonably wish to take into account the amount of effort a student has invested in the preparation of a paper or project in order to compare her with her classmates, she can do so, not by labeling a student who submits a paper to multiple instructors dishonest but simply by asking whether a paper has been or will be multiply submitted and factoring this into the grade she assigns.

Academic dishonesty, like all or almost all dishonesty, is manipulative and an attack on personal relationships. It ought to be discouraged. But it should not be discouraged through grading practices that themselves are dishonest and unfair, that fail to respect EXCLUSIVITY's requirement that grades reflect COMPETENCE as accurately as possible.

I. Extra Credit

In accordance with EXCLUSIVITY, an instructor ordinarily has no reason to give extra credit work. If her evaluative instruments are adequate, then she does not need further exercises to determine students' COMPETENCE. And because a grade is not a reward for student effort or work, but an estimate of COMPETENCE, the sheer fact that a student has done additional work is no reason for her to receive a better grade than she would otherwise have been awarded. Indeed, allowing a grade to be influenced by extra credit can result in grade inflation that makes grades significantly less accurate, and so less useful to transcript consumers, than they would otherwise have been. Only in the event that an exercise is unnecessary to the accurate assessment of a student's COMPETENCE but nonetheless provides information that makes an instructor's evaluation of her COMPETENCE more accurate is taking the exercise into account appropriate.[48]

[48] This judgment at least raises questions about Schrag's proposal that instructors should allow "students to earn extra credit by choosing to expend additional effort on work that meets some minimal level of quality." Schrag, *supra* note 18, at 71. Increasing grades in response to student effort will often be deceptive and involve attempts to commensurate the incommensurable. As Schrag observes, until transcripts reflect effort or other factors in addition to COMPETENCE, "the egalitarian instructor must decide whether to give priority to supporting egalitarian justice or to avoiding deception." *Id.* at 73. Of course, extra work may sometimes signal that additional COMPETENCE has been acquired; if it does, a higher grade would obviously be appropriate.

V. GRADING LIBERALLY

Embodying liberal concerns with individuality and diversity, EXCLUSIVITY calls for instructors to grade with the goal of telling the truth to potential transcript consumers and to take seriously the incommensurability between COMPETENCE and other characteristics of students that become apparent in the course of teaching, evaluating, and otherwise engaging with them. In accordance with EXCLUSIVITY, an instructor should decline to take a student's attendance into account when determining her grade—though she may consider the student's class participation as a source of information about her COMPETENCE. She should not base her grades on activities that do not yield outcomes she can assess to estimate student performance, and she should give more weight to examinations and papers than to instances of BUSYWORK, ideally not taking instances of BUSYWORK into account at all when determining grades. She should not base individual grades on group performance. She may reasonably consider a student's engagement with her service-learning experiences as a source of insight into her COMPETENCE, but she may not base a grade simply on the student's *participation* in service-learning activities. She should in general avoid allowing the time a student's work is submitted to affect the student's grade. She should be free to make grade changes and replace Incomplete grades with letter grades at will and at any time if doing so will help to ensure that her grades more accurately reflect her students' COMPETENCE. Within the constraints set by the Principle of Fairness, she should feel free to vary her methods of evaluating individual students at her discretion and to alter methods of evaluation used for an entire class. And while she should refuse to consider work that is not a student's own in determining the student's grade, she should not use a grade as a means of expressing moral disapproval of a student's dishonesty or as a means of encouraging student honesty.

Many instructors grade in ways that aren't always consistent with EXCLUSIVITY. I suggest that this may reflect their implicit acceptance of two possible theoretical accounts of the logic of grading: academic consequentialism and academic retributivism. Neither of these approaches is more plausible than its nonacademic equivalent. Consequentialism is unworkable and incoherent; in addition, academic consequentialism leads to results, even in a narrowly academic context, which most academics are likely to regard as counter-intuitive. Retributivism unreasonably adds injury to injury. And academic retributivism violates EXCLUSIVITY's incommensurability requirement, since it attempts to make grades into expressions of moral judgment, despite the fact that moral worth is incommensurable with COMPETENCE. And of course academic retributivism, like academic consequentialism, leads to the submission and transmission of inaccurate grades.

Endorsing EXCLUSIVITY does not mean that the concerns which lead many instructors to grade as retributivists or consequentialists are illegitimate. It is important to motivate student behavior, to restrain dishonesty, and to reduce inconvenience. But it is also important not to do these things at the expense of accuracy and fairness. Thus, in particular, EXCLUSIVITY is also perfectly compatible with a strategy for student evaluation that involves retaining grades as measures of COMPETENCE while *also* involving assessments of students' effort and character. It would be possible to note on a transcript that a student was intelligent but lazy, say, or hardworking but a slow learner. It would be possible to indicate that the student performed well on examinations but wrote less satisfactory term papers, or vice versa. It would be possible to report that a student was academically gifted but personally immature and insensitive, inclined to make cutting remarks to others in class. Nothing prevents an institution from attaching to a student's transcript notations of all sorts related to students' characters. An institution could highlight a student's hard work in a given course, note that she suffered from exceptional personal stresses during a given term, or indicate that she was academically dishonest when preparing work for a particular course.[49] Providing such information separately would be more useful to transcript consumers than attempting to make *grades* communicate diverse and incommensurable sorts of information.[50] And it would remove the pressure on instructors to craft arbitrary ways of commensurating incommensurable factors when determining grades.

Respecting EXCLUSIVITY is also consistent with instructors' reasonable self-concern. An instructor can adhere to EXCLUSIVITY without inconveniencing herself excessively to accommodate students who have been slothful, for instance. While an instructor ought not to mislead transcript consumers, the Principle of Fairness does not obligate her to do anything and everything possible to determine the truth. Provided she does not use inaction for the sake of convenience as an excuse to *punish* students for wrongdoing or to injure them as a means of motivating them or others, she is certainly free to take her own convenience into account when determining when extra effort on her part is and is not appropriate.

EXCLUSIVITY challenges instructors and institutions to take accuracy seriously. It challenges instructors to grade students in ways that will be most useful to transcript consumers, and thus most fair to students themselves. It challenges instructors and institutions to respect the differences between academic and non-academic factors. It therefore calls them to exhibit in their grading policies and practices the commitment to truth and fairness that is at the heart of the academic

49 *Cf.* CAHN, *supra* note 22, at 107 n. 4 and Schrag, *supra* note 18, at 72 (noting that "grades that do count effort convey misleading messages to third parties and are reprehensible from the ethical point of view. My proposal to solve this problem cannot be adopted by the individual professor but requires institutional action, making the effort-based policy more transparent. For example, the transcript could indicate by an asterisk any grade earned by producing additional work not required of all students.").

50 It might even have a greater deterrent effect on irresponsible students. An academic dishonesty notation on a student's transcript may be far more threatening to her academic or professional future than a low grade. The proponent of EXCLUSIVITY can welcome this deterrent effect even though she does not regard deterrence as itself an appropriate basis for assigning grades.

enterprise. In so doing, it provides useful guidance for institutional decision-makers; in the limited number of cases in which courts appropriately engage with grading-related issues, this principle may help them to think more clearly about instructors' and institutions' policies and practices. Of course, courts will not typically be situated appropriately to second-guess instructors' and institutions' grading decisions. When they decide to review such decisions, however, EXCLUSIVITY may provide them with a useful basis for evaluating the accuracy and fairness of judgments about grades, and so for helping to ensure that grading practices embody and foster flourishing.

Academic institutions are committed to the quest for truth. So it seems to make particular sense to encourage participants in the lives of such institutions to seek and convey truth where the assessment of students' COMPETENCE is concerned. Legal and other ecosystems are valuable because they, too, facilitate the discovery and communication of truth even when the participants aren't *focused* on discovering and sharing the truth impartially. Liberals have rightly supposed that adversarial conflicts suitably limited and channeled in some contexts—in the marketplace, in the world of ideas and cultural products, in the courtroom—can be immensely productive of very valuable results.[51] Liberals believe that we have reason to appreciate ecosystems that provide room for conflict to take place in ways that generate broadly beneficial outcomes. But the worth of these ecosystems leaves open the question of how adversarial participants should understand and undertake their work. Zealous participants in such ecosystems sometimes suppose that particular loyalties—notably, attorneys' loyalties to clients—license them in actually attacking the truth, and in otherwise behaving in ways that would qualify as unreasonable in other contexts. I reflect on this understanding of adversarial advocacy and advocates' attitudes toward truthfulness in Chapter 4.

[51] *Cf.* GARY CHARTIER, AN ECOLOGICAL THEORY OF FREE EXPRESSION (2018).

4

Adversaries

I. LIBERALS IN COURT

The liberal tradition has rightly stressed the ways in which good outcomes should be sought through institutional design—through the fostering of the right sort of *ecology*—rather than by expecting or encouraging individual actors within a system to seek unconstrainedly good outcomes directly. In her role as a responsible member of a liberal society, someone can and should encourage good outcomes by supporting—behaviorally, rhetorically, perhaps financially—the right sorts of institutions, even as, in her role as a *participant* in particular institutions, she may and probably should opt for a narrower focus. Taking the Principle of Fairness seriously means recognizing that this sort of ecological approach can reliably bring about desired outcomes, and therefore supporting the rules, norms, and institutions that enable the relevant sorts of ecosystems to function effectively. Liberals have emphasized the merits of this two-level pattern of reasoning and action with respect to, among other things, markets, politics, expressive activity, scientific inquiry, and courts.

In particular, we rightly think and act on both levels where adversarial processes are concerned—in the legal system and elsewhere. There is good reason for everyone, in light of the Principle of Fairness, to support adversarial *processes* because of their effectiveness in protecting and fostering flourishing. Such processes help to safeguard all of the basic aspects of well-being at stake when people engage in legal and similar disputes, including the good of knowledge. And they also provide occasion for the development and display of the goods of practical reasonableness and skillful performance. At the same time, however, attorneys and others occupying adversarial roles have good reason to act in light of reasonable limits on their pursuit of their clients' goals, and we all have reason to favor norms, rules, and institutions that constrain how legal and other adversaries go about their business.

It is a truism that not everyone is fond of the legal profession. A lawyer joke is likely to elicit an appreciative laugh almost anywhere. Partly, no doubt, this is because lawyers are experts in the manipulation of a complex and sometimes arcane system of rules that can exert profound and often painful effects on people's lives but of which they may feel they have little mastery. In part, however, I believe it is also because of people's ambivalent responses to the practice of adversarial advocacy.

We expect an attorney to do battle for her client with the unswerving passion of a knight jousting for the honor of a patron in a mediaeval tourney. Like tournaments, our courtroom struggles may feel like ritualized sporting events, with temporary antagonists quite free to compare notes over drinks after they have retired from the field. While doing their jobs, however, lawyers may adopt the personae of fierce opponents, treating their clients' causes as righteous crusades.

We characteristically count on devoted, particularistic loyalty from our attorneys. We do not anticipate that our lawyers will question the appropriateness of the projects we ask for legal help in undertaking and we frequently assume that our advocates will disregard or perhaps even conceal evidence that might undermine our cases, shade the truth where necessary inside and outside the courtroom, and bully, humiliate, and browbeat in order to achieve the results we desire. At the same time, as the *targets* of lawsuits or as observers of the legal system, we may feel frustrated by what we may perceive as lawyers' disregard for the truth or as the system's tolerance for manipulation and deception.

Zealous advocacy is a duty of the lawyer in an adversarial system. But the performance of that duty can sometimes seem to entail choices that might be morally suspect. Does being an enthusiastic advocate require or permit such choices? Arthur Isak Applbaum argues that it does not. The requirements associated with professional roles, like those of attorneys, "can overwrite moral permissions, and become moral requirements. But role requirements cannot overwrite moral prohibitions and mint moral permissions."[1] I believe Applbaum is right.

In Part II, I detail one especially troubling and dramatic example of the moral quandaries faced by zealous advocates: the dilemma confronting Justice Department lawyers arguing that the Supreme Court should uphold the conviction of Fred Korematsu for violating the presidential order requiring the evacuation of Japanese Americans from the West Coast and effectively resulting in their internment—despite the knowledge that the evacuation program rested on demonstrable falsehood. In Part III, I explain the substance of Applbaum's argument. Though I find much of what Applbaum says appealing, in Part IV I consider some ways in which I think his understanding of adversarial ethics might be improved. In Part V, I sum up—and reaffirm my admiration for Applbaum's general approach.

II. BURLING, ENNIS, AND *KOREMATSU*

Lawyers tasked with defending the presidential order resulting in the evacuation and internment of Japanese Americans after the bombing of Pearl Harbor—as they laid

[1] Arthur Isak Applbaum, Ethics for Adversaries: the Morality of Roles in Public and Professional Life 248 (1999).

the groundwork for the government's response to the case against the internment program brought by Fred Korematsu—knew the order might have been based on inaccurate information. They realized that it might even have been enacted despite the knowledge that this information was inaccurate. They thus confronted a moral and professional challenge: how much of what they knew should they convey to the Supreme Court—and what other avenues might be available to them as they sought to address what they clearly saw as a potential injustice? Other lawyers encounter not dissimilar, if less dramatic, challenges in practice environments of other kinds. Their story provides a measure of narrative texture for otherwise sometimes abstract claims about adversarial ethics.

In 1944, General John DeWitt released a 618-page report on the evacuation and internment program, which he continued to treat as justified. DeWitt rested much of his argument for the internment on the claim that Japanese Americans on the West Coast were conveying sensitive military information to Japan's military or its intelligence services. Among the evidence he offered in support of this claim: numerous radio transmissions from the West Coast, intended for Japanese submarines, had been detected. Coincident with the implementation of the evacuation program, DeWitt said, the transmissions had largely ended.[2] Attorneys assigned to defend the internment program soon discovered that DeWitt's report was potentially inaccurate. They were forced to decide what to do about the inaccuracy.

A. *Problems with the DeWitt Report*

Expecting that the report would become an issue in the pending internment-related *Korematsu* case and skeptical about some of the assertions it contained, Attorney General Francis Biddle asked FBI director J. Edgar Hoover to assess it. He also requested that the Federal Communications Commission examine DeWitt's claims regarding radio transmissions from the West Coast near the beginning of the war. In his response to Biddle's request, Hoover denied DeWitt's contentions about the involvement of Japanese Americans in espionage. FCC chair James Lawrence Fly told Biddle "that DeWitt had been personally informed by the FCC that *not one* of the reports of illicit radio transmissions had been verified."[3] He concluded decisively that "the statements in [DeWitt's] Report indicating the existence of illicit radio signaling along the West Coast cannot be regarded as well-founded."[4]

Given Fly's analysis, there was no good evidence that illicit transmissions had occurred, despite what DeWitt had claimed. The probable invalidity of an assertion that had evidently played a key role in garnering support for the internment program might seem to make the program itself less defensible. And that DeWitt had been personally informed that the reports were ill-founded raised the question whether he

2 *See* Peter Irons, Justice at War 280–81 (1983).

3 *Id.* at 282.

4 *Id.* at 283 (*quoting* Fly to Biddle, April 1, 1944).

had promoted the program while knowing that a principal claim used to justify it was probably false—and that the program itself therefore rested on shaky ground.

The lawyers obviously faced a serious problem. They had no choice but to ask themselves both whether the evacuation and detention were defensible and whether they should acknowledge evidence that suggested this was not the case. "We are now therefore," wrote John Burling of the Justice Department's Alien Enemy Control Unit in a memo to Solicitor General Charles Fahy, "in possession of substantially incontrovertible evidence that the most important statement of fact advanced by General DeWitt to justify the evacuation and detention were incorrect, and furthermore that General DeWitt had cause to know, and in all probability did know, that they were incorrect at the time he embodied them in his final report . . . ."[5]

B. *Framing the Report in the* Korematsu *Brief*

An initial draft of the *Korematsu* brief, authored by Burling, clearly disavowed DeWitt's report. Burling's draft said the report had been relied on for information regarding the evacuation itself. He noted, however, that the report's claims about facts related to the justification for the evacuation were inconsistent with what the Justice Department knew. Unwilling to reveal the existence of the FBI and FCC reports, Fahy altered the draft to hide the direct conflict between the Department's understanding and that embodied in the report.[6] Burling appealed to Herbert Wechsler, who was responsible for the *Korematsu* argument in tandem with Fahy. Emphasizing the existence of "intentional falsehoods" in the report, Burling observed that DeWitt had attempted to defend it "by making important misstatements of fact."[7]

Faced with intense War Department opposition to the version of the brief Burling had prepared, Burling and Edward Ennis, also associated with the Control Unit, fought back with a stinging attack on DeWitt's report. The Justice Department, they argued, had "an ethical obligation to the Court to refrain from citing" the report.[8] Persuaded by their documentation of the War Department's duplicity, Fahy opted to include Burling's original, contested, language.[9] In the end of the day, however, Wechsler chose, with Fahy's approval, to replace it with truthful, but less direct language, noting only that the DeWitt report was being relied on solely with respect to details concerning the evacuation—but not explicitly denying the report's falsehoods.[10] Fahy himself opted for a version of the final *Korematsu* brief that committed the Justice Department to defending General DeWitt's detention

5 *Id.* at 285 (*quoting* Burling to Fahy, April 13, 1944).

6 *See id.* at 286.

7 *Id.* at 287 (*quoting* Burling to Wechsler, Sept. 11, 1944, File 146–42-7, DOJ).

8 *Id.* at 288 (*quoting* Ennis to Wechsler, Sep. 30, 1944, Box 3, Folder 3, Fahy Papers, FDRL).

9 *See id.* at 289.

10 *See id.* at 291–92.

order as justified,[11] even though the Department also had good evidence that a factual basis for the order was lacking.[12]

"[A]s an expression of institutional loyalty," the signatures of Burling and Ennis appeared on the *Korematsu* brief.[13] But the two Justice Department lawyers had felt sufficiently conflicted about the case that, even before the DeWitt report's inaccuracy became an issue, they had met with the American Civil Liberties Union's Roger Baldwin and Charles Horsky, expressing their support for an ACLU amicus brief in the case.[14] While it was inconsistent with Department policy for Burling and Ennis to give Horsky copies of the FBI and FCC reports, language in the ACLU brief he prepared suggests they likely showed him these documents as well.[15]

C. *Lawyers and the Adversarial Ethos*

The radical liberal will rightly challenge the legitimacy of the internment program and the authority and existence of the Department of Justice itself. But, even if we table various genuinely radical questions, the issues Department personnel faced in connection with the *Korematsu* case still prompt serious moral reflection.

- The Justice Department proceeded with the case against Fred Korematsu—although it knew the order Korematsu had disobeyed had been justified based on inaccurate factual assertions.
- The Department concealed its knowledge of the inaccuracy of these assertions in its Supreme Court brief.
- Burling and Ennis signed the brief despite their awareness that it concealed damaging information.
- Burling and Ennis cooperated with ACLU efforts to attack Korematsu's conviction although they had signed a brief calling for the Supreme Court to uphold that conviction.

Litigators confront dilemmas like those faced by Burling and Ennis on an all too regular basis, as loyalty to clients conflicts with respect for and fairness toward other participants in the legal system. A conventional, even if not universal, response is that, because an attorney's first responsibility is to her client, she is licensed in doing anything necessary to protect the client's interests (within, perhaps, the constraints set by narrowly interpreted rules of professional conduct).

This model has obvious implications for the behavior of Justice Department personnel in connection with the *Korematsu* case. The Department's loyalty to its client, the United States government, should have led it to defend Korematsu's

11 *See id.* at 297–98.
12 *See id.* at 292–95.
13 *See id.* at 302.
14 *See id.* at 268, 302.
15 *See id.* at 305.

conviction even in the face of evidence that the internment orders were unwarranted. It need not, and probably should not, have revealed to the Supreme Court the existence of this evidence. Burling and Ennis should have signed the *Korematsu* brief. And they should not have facilitated the preparation of the ACLU's amicus brief.

It is conclusions like this, which seem to flow from the adversarial ethic, that regularly trouble informed and sensitive observers. They might well shrink from the judgment that the Justice Department could not reasonably have asserted in its brief "that DeWitt 'in all probability' knew that his justification for evacuation and detention were 'incorrect'" because doing so would qualify as "a violation of legal ethics."[16] The norm of near-exclusive commitment to client welfare endorsed by most lawyers as almost self-evident can strike outside observers as morally dubious. Given the personal cost to Fred Korematsu and many others imposed by an unwarranted order, an observer sympathetic to the victims of the internment program and doubtful about its fairness might believe the Department was not behaving appropriately when it defended Korematsu's conviction and failed to provide relevant information to the Supreme Court. That Burling and Ennis doubted the truthfulness of the *Korematsu* brief might suggest that they should not have signed it—and that their cooperation with the ACLU was commendable rather than questionable.

The Principle of Fairness is quite compatible with particular concern for oneself, one's friends, one's teammates, one's associates.[17] But it certainly entails respectful concern of one kind or another with the flourishing of strangers and enemies as well as with the flourishing of intimates and allies.[18] And the Principle of Respect precludes injuring in the interests of this or that good cause. The Principle of Fairness entails a measure of openness to the other who falls outside our immediate sympathies, while, in accordance with the Principle of Respect, we will acknowledge that not doing harm is to be preferred, if we are forced to choose, to doing good. Decent people may therefore wonder whether, as sometimes seems to be claimed, lawyers' professional roles *really* exempt them from what might otherwise seem to be weighty moral responsibilities.

III. QUESTIONS ABOUT THE ADVERSARIAL ETHOS

Applbaum helps us reflect on this issue as he explores the moral significance of roles. In Part III, I elaborate his understanding of the conventional defenses offered for granting exemptions from otherwise binding moral norms to adversaries with some kinds of socially important responsibilities. I explain why he believes redescribing

16 Roger K. Newman, Hugo Black : A Biography 317n (1994). Newman refers the reader to Irons, who does not, I believe, make this judgment explicitly.

17 *See* John Finnis, Natural Law and Natural Rights 107–108 (1980).

18 *Cf.* Thomas Ogletree, Hospitality to the Stranger: Dimensions of Moral Understanding (1985).

adversarial practices is insufficient to render otherwise immoral conduct appropriate. I clarify his rebuttal to contentions that fair play considerations should license some violations of persons by occupants of legitimate adversarial roles. I also explore his critique of arguments that the legal system as a whole achieves its socially desirable ends most effectively if lawyers ruthlessly pursue clients' objectives with limited attention to the appropriateness of those objectives or to moral side constraints.

Applbaum assesses the merits of extreme adversarialism from a contractualist perspective. *To what sorts of standards would we agree*, the contractualist asks, *if we knew they would apply in the same way to everyone, including ourselves and our loved ones?*[19] Contractualism embodies a respect for particular persons that precludes harming them simply because doing so would promote some putatively good outcome. On contractualist grounds, Applbaum challenges a variety of commonly canvassed exceptions to general moral norms we are often encouraged to grant to occupants of particular adversarial roles.[20] Even those of us who aren't contractualists can expect to learn from his analyses: contractualism may generally be expected to reach the same conclusions as will NATURAL LAW theory when the Principle of Fairness is in view. The results may not be identical, and the Principle of Respect will impose further constraints on what adversaries may reasonably do. But Applbaum's arguments will prove helpful and illuminating even if we take his perspective to be incomplete.

A. *The Public Executioner as Exemplary Adversarial Professional*

Applbaum offers an especially stark example of adversarial professionalism: Charles-Henri Sanson, the public executioner of Paris both before and during the French Revolution. Applbaum explores a range of arguments that might be advanced in defense of Sanson's willingness impartially to kill the various legally condemned victims of the regimes he served, to do his putative duty with "the sensibility and self-image of a professional civil servant."[21] He does so through the device of a fictive debate between Sanson and one Louis Sébastien Mercier (an historical

[19] *See* THOMAS M. SCANLON, WHAT WE OWE TO EACH OTHER (1998).

[20] The notion of a role remains unanalyzed here. I take a role to be a socially defined practice with sufficient structure and definition that one who occupies it—whether by choice, by assignment, or in some other way (say, in virtue of a biological relationship)—is provided with significant guidance regarding her options and responsibilities and, in the case of more substantial personal and professional roles (pastor, life partner), her identity. A standard philosophical discussion of the idea of a role is DOROTHY EMMET, RULES, ROLES AND RELATIONS (1966).

Of course, the concept of a role may not always admit of precise application. Thus, for instance, whether one speaks of friendship as a role or an institution is partly, as Emmet reminds us, "a matter of terminology." While granting "the verbal point that 'friend' is a recognized social category," and thus on her definition a role, she notes the common conviction that "every friendship is unique, a matter of spontaneity and mutual affection and not of rules." *Id.* at 169.

[21] APPLBAUM, *supra* note 1, at 23.

contemporary of Sanson who was fortunate enough to escape decapitation). Sanson defends his vocation as one rooted in tradition and grounded in morally appealing "ideals and commitments."[22] Being a public executioner means practicing a craft that serves the interests of justice. To be sure, not every death sentence is necessarily just, but "the executioner must obey a division of labor between his office and the office of the tribunal."[23] The value of an orderly system of laws is so great that the wish to avoid individual violations of rights cannot justify upsetting it by refusing to do the duty imposed on Sanson by his public role.[24] The requirements of that role, rather than the personal judgments of "Charles-Henri, man and citizen," must determine Sanson's behavior when he acts as public executioner.[25]

We may rightly criticize the social definition of a given professional role—perhaps there is something wrong with the role of public executioner. (There is.) But, having granted that the role is legitimate *in principle*, we have no basis on which to question the performance of someone who simply does what the role demands.[26] Fulfilling the inherent requirements of his legitimate role makes Sanson a "good executioner," even if being a good executioner means doing things that might count as morally bad if done by someone not authorized to do them by an appropriate professional role.[27]

The defenses of the public executioner's role advanced by his imagined Sanson, Applbaum reminds us, are rather too close for comfort to those employed by contemporary professionals, including lawyers, for conduct that might otherwise appear morally inappropriate. Indeed, a

> visitor from another planet might be forgiven if he described ... [lawyers] as serial liars and thieves. He would observe that lawyers—good lawyers—repeatedly try to induce others to believe in the truth of propositions or in the validity of arguments that they themselves do not believe, and he would observe that lawyers—again, good lawyers—often devote their skills to advancing the unjust ends of rapacious clients. "Liar" and "thief," the good lawyer would retort, are either ignorant or malignant misdescriptions. But the arguments lawyers invoke to defend zealous advocacy echo all of the executioner's claims.[28]

B. *Role Definitions and Practice Positivism*

Though *Ethics for Adversaries* is concerned with professionals other than lawyers, Applbaum ensures that the legal profession is rarely far from the reader's mind. He

[22] *Id.* at 29.
[23] *Id.* at 31.
[24] *Cf. id.* at 38.
[25] *Id.* at 39.
[26] *See id.* at 39–40. Of course, it's not obvious that, even if the role were indeed legitimate, it would need to be defined in such a way that the executioner was obligated to give up her own judgment about when killing people was appropriate.
[27] *See id.* at 40–41.
[28] *Id.* at 42.

dives into the problems he has begun to examine in the Sanson-Mercier dialogue by exploring the concept of a *professional role*. What he says is of immediate relevance to lawyers, but it is perhaps ironic that, when he considers the Minnesota case of *Spaulding* v. *Zimmerman*,[29] he attends to the partial—almost adversarial—behavior of a *physician*. His purpose is to illustrate the possibility that roles can be variously defined.

In *Spaulding*, a physician under contract to an insurance company assessed Spaulding's health after Zimmerman, who was insured by the company, injured Spaulding in an automobile accident. The physician failed to tell Spaulding about an aortic aneurysm, with the result that Spaulding settled with the company for a small amount. When the aneurysm was later detected and corrected, the doctor's silence was exposed and the settlement agreement vacated.[30]

The *Spaulding* court maintained that standards of legal ethics did not compel the lawyer who negotiated the initial settlement on behalf of the company "to inform Spaulding that without treatment he could drop dead at any moment."[31] But what about the physician? Does not a *physician's* professional role carry with it the obligation to put patient welfare above profit?

Perhaps. But Applbaum concedes that there is nothing *necessary* about defining the physician's role in a particular way. It is easy to imagine a profession similar to doctoring but different from it—a profession for which Applbaum suggests the felicitous name "schmoctoring"—whose members are understood to have different duties, say, the maintenance of employer profit.[32] The position Applbaum labels "practice positivism," which he endorses, holds that professional roles are social creations. On this view, it's not *necessary* that particular characteristics be associated with *other* particular characteristics in a given practice or institution. There is no *essence* of medical practice such that one feature of the physician's role must be present in tandem with one or more others. Constellations of characteristics exhibited by particular practices or institutions are relatively contingent: other clusters are entirely possible. (Presumably there are limits here. The characteristics of human persons and societies are such that some features of an institution will typically be allied with others, with the result that there will only be a finite number of ways in which these characteristics can realistically be configured. Applbaum does not argue for completely untrammeled contingency, and of course he doesn't need to do so to make his point.)

Given practice positivism, it is not possible to determine the duties of a professional simply on the basis of the fit between her behavior and norms that might be thought to flow from the supposed essence of her profession.[33] The moral

29 Spaulding v. Zimmerman, 116 N.W.2d 704 (1962).
30 *See id.* at 710.
31 APPLBAUM, *supra* note 1, at 49.
32 *Id.* at 50–51.
33 *See id.* at 51.

requirements associated with a given professional role must be determined by careful moral analysis of the circumstances and characteristics of the professional occupying the role.[34]

C. Justifying Adversarial Violations through Redescription

On the basis of what they regard as role-based obligations, some lawyers might wish to reject Applbaum's characterization of certain forms of "zealous advocacy" as "lying"[35] or "deception."[36] Perhaps applying such moralizing labels to things lawyers do for their clients is a way of misdescribing these things. Applbaum disagrees: "it is the practice of lawyering [itself] that . . . [is marked by] misdescription."[37]

Thus, for instance, consider James Giffard, a lawyer attempting to secure a murder conviction designed to enable his employer to steal a substantial inheritance, who declared: "I make a distinction between carrying on a prosecution and compassing the death of a man,"[38] even though a conviction could have resulted in execution. Contrary to Giffard's apparent view, there are limits to my ability to characterize my actions. Declaring that my intention is not, as such, to bring about an injury in a way that would be wrong were it not for my professional role, but rather simply to fulfill a role-based obligation, is not on its own sufficient to absolve me from responsibility for having brought about the injury. Applbaum observes:

> Perhaps causing death by prosecuting or by executing are justified instances of causing death. But that is the conclusion of an argument about how to properly *evaluate* the richly described social practices of prosecution and execution. The redescriptive strategy seeks to preempt such an evaluation and bypass the hard work of moral argument by suppressing part of the true story. But this is itself a misdescription.[39]

Consider a more sophisticated redescriptive strategy, one suggested to Applbaum by the work of John Rawls and John Searle. Perhaps the way in which we describe a lawyer's practice is necessarily constituted by the social institution of lawyering. What a lawyer is *doing* can be accurately described only in terms derived from this institution, and it is only in light of the demands imposed by this institution that her actions may be criticized. One can criticize the institution, to be sure, and one can criticize a given lawyer's practice if it is *inconsistent* with her institutionally given role. But one cannot criticize her role-consistent actions directly.[40] And she is in no

34 *See id.* at 54–55.
35 *Id.* at 104.
36 *Id.* at 104.
37 *Id.* at 76–77.
38 Annesley v. Anglesea, 17 How. St. Trials 1139, 1248–49 (*quoted in id.* at 77 n. 2, *in turn quoting* David Luban, Lawyers and Justice 5 (1988)).
39 Applbaum, *supra* note 1, at 81.
40 *See id.* at 81–83.

position to do so *herself*; as long as she professes to be a lawyer, her duties follow from the social conventions that define lawyering.

Summarizing this envisioned stance, Applbaum concludes: "The lawyer who fails to advance the legal rights of clients who have evil purposes does not understand what it means to practice law."[41] Similarly, an attorney "advocating on behalf of a client who wishes to avoid paying an acknowledged debt cannot refuse to plead the statute of limitations and still call herself an advocate, or unless the defining rules of lawyering are changed, a lawyer who is not a diligent advocate for the legal interests of the client is not engaged in the proper practice of advocacy."[42] The action of a lawyer acting *as a lawyer* is simply different from an otherwise apparently similar act not performed in furtherance of a professional role. The meaning of the act depends on the institutional context in which it occurs; particular and unavoidable duties follow when an act is situated in the context of the practice of lawyering.[43]

But why should we accept this sort of argument, Applbaum plausibly wonders. It derives its force from the claim that role-specific actions performed by, say, lawyers are what they are *only* in virtue of their institutional setting. To criticize a lawyer's action, one must attend to the rules of lawyering, because only those rules can determine whether a given action is an instance of lawyering at all. As Applbaum observes, however, describing an action in terms of role-specific duties does not preclude *other* sorts of descriptions. One may be simultaneously carrying on a prosecution and "compassing the death of a man."[44] And the failure to describe away potentially objectionable features of role-specific actions means that an actor cannot be separated from her role in such a way that not she but the role is said to perform these actions.[45] A role-specific description of an act may be essential to understanding and assessing it, but this description need not be exhaustive. Even if we cannot criticize professionals "as ... lawyers, we can always evaluate them as persons."[46]

We can criticize a lawyer for adhering to the requirements of her role when doing so means engaging in morally problematic conduct. But internal criticism of professional roles is at least sometimes also possible, Applbaum acknowledges. Those participating in a practice or institution can challenge it as a whole from the inside when it is defined by incoherent requirements, perhaps ones that undermine the practice or institution itself.[47] Further, given that practices are social creations, it will often be implausible to maintain that a practice itself is defined so clearly that there cannot be legitimate disagreements about just what the socially constructed shape of an institution like lawyering actually *is*. Practitioners may

41 *Id.* at 83–84.
42 *Id.* at 85.
43 *See id.* at 89.
44 *Id.* at 91.
45 *See id.* at 97–98.
46 *Id.* at 98.
47 *See id.* at 101–102.

simply disagree about what a practice entails,[48] as Louis Brandeis did when he effectively redescribed lawyering by characterizing himself not so much as a client's representative but as "counsel for the situation," responsible for reaching a solution to a problem that was fair to all those concerned.[49] Further, part of occupying a given role may be the explicit *entitlement* to join in revising the social definition of that role. Thus, practitioners may also be free to challenge others' definitions of what is expected of them in their professional roles precisely in virtue of their authority *as practitioners*.[50]

D. *Justifying Adversarial Violations as Instances of Fair Play*

Even if role-based arguments do not justify what would otherwise appear as moral violations by lawyers, perhaps other arguments might. Perhaps, for instance, we might think of the legal system as a kind of game. Informed consensual participation in a game may imply voluntary acceptance of harms, or liability to harms, that would otherwise be unjustified. Perhaps, then, people cannot object if they are deceived, manipulated, or humiliated, insofar as deception, manipulation, and humiliation are expected behaviors within the game of the law.[51]

But people do *not*, as a general matter, actually consent to be deceived, humiliated, or manipulated in the context of the legal system. Nonlawyers may not be aware of what some insiders see as rules of the game. And involvement in the legal system by many people and institutions is anything but voluntary. People may be pressured to participate because the alternatives to participation are profoundly unsatisfactory (in the case of the legal system, say, the forfeiture of a range of claims that can be protected only by legal action).[52]

Can someone who hasn't consented explicitly be taken to have consented tacitly? Can her consent be inferred from her participation in the game or acceptance of benefits accruing from participation?[53] If such participation or acceptance of benefits is understood simply as good *evidence* for actual consent, then this putative evidence may easily be rebutted.[54] Someone may make it very clear that her

48 *See id.* at 102–103.

49 *See* Clyde Spillenger, *Elusive Advocate: Reconsidering Brandeis as People's Lawyer*, 105 YALE L. J. 1445, 1473–74, 1502 (1996) (detailing instances in which Brandeis acted on an unusually broad conception of the lawyer's role). Spillenger notes that the phrase was *attributed* to Brandeis, and was not, as has been alleged, spoken by him at his Supreme Court confirmation hearings (at which he was not present). *Id.* at 1504.

50 *See* APPLBAUM, *supra* note 1, at 103–104.

51 *See id.* at 113–15.

52 *See id.* at 116–17.

53 For skeptical assessments of the idea of tacit consent as a basis for a duty to obey the state, *see, e.g.*, CAROLE PATEMAN, THE PROBLEM OF POLITICAL OBLIGATION: A CRITICAL ANALYSIS OF LIBERAL THEORY (2d.ed., 1985); MICHAEL HUEMER, THE PROBLEM OF POLITICAL AUTHORITY: AN EXAMINATION OF THE RIGHT TO COERCE AND THE DUTY TO OBEY 22–35 (2013).

54 *See* APPLBAUM, *supra* note 1, at 118–19.

participation in the legal system is motivated by purely tactical considerations; she is, let us say, an anarchist who has chosen to rely on the legal system simply to preclude intrusive, abusive conduct by someone who is making a dubious legal claim against her.

Of course, in some instances one may be able to accomplish one's goals only by accepting the description of one's actions built into a given practice; Applbaum offers the examples of playing poker or playing football. One cannot simply accept one's cards and play a hand of poker while loudly proclaiming that one plans to pocket all the money on the table at the end of the hand merely because one has been dealt the four of spades. Full-scale participation in a voluntary practice like poker may be good evidence of consent to its norms. But this will not on its own be sufficient to justify subjection to these norms if participation is not intentional, free, and grounded in appropriate knowledge.[55]

Applbaum canvasses the possibility that a "fair play" argument,[56] related to but stronger than the argument from tacit consent, might do the trick. Perhaps other players are justified in imposing game-appropriate costs on free riders who reap benefits from the games in which they voluntarily participate, whether or not they have consented to the rules of the game.[57] Applbaum outlines a set of stringent conditions for harming a non-consenting "target" in a manner that might be justified by a fair play argument: (*i*) the rules of the game permit the harm, (*ii*) the rules permitting the harm and the game itself make possible advantages to players that would not be available in its absence (even if not necessarily the greatest conceivable advantages),[58] (*iii*) the acceptance of benefits must be voluntary (though this needn't mean there are no costs associated with exiting the game),[59] and (*iv*) the venture must be fair—the target must receive "a just share of the venture's benefits and burdens," the relevant institution must characteristically perform fairly with respect to all players, and the venture must not impose unfair costs on non-players.[60] Ultimately, Applbaum concludes, these sorts of considerations might conceivably apply to the dealings of informed repeat players with each other, but they provide little sanction for deceptive, coercive, or manipulative acts targeting others.[61]

55 *See id.* at 120.

56 On fair play, see, *e.g.*, Sivakumar Elambooranan, *An Analysis of the Fair Play Theory of Political Obligation* (1997) (unpublished Ph.D. dissertation, University of California at Santa Barbara); HUEMER, *supra* note 53, at 86–93.

57 *See* APPLBAUM, *supra* note 1, at 121–23.

58 *See id.* at 127–29. This standard may be too permissive.

59 *See id.* at 130–31.

60 *Id.* at 132–34.

61 *See id.* at 135. Applbaum grants that defending oneself or others, for instance, or avoiding less desirable injuries to some targets might justify imposing certain kinds of injuries on those targets, but it is difficult to see, he suggests that there is typically much room for the use of these justifications in ordinary business, legal, or political contexts. *See id.* at 136–74. Conceivably, for instance, "a truthful hostile witness can be described as a threat to the interests or liberty of a defendant, but she is not an

E. *Justifying Adversarial Violations Systemically*

Adversary institutions might be structured to take full advantage of partiality while, where necessary, correcting for its excesses and rendering some injuries acceptable.[62] Actors within such institutions, including the legal system, are likely to further public weal most effectively if they take full advantage of the opportunities afforded them by the law—not exceeding the legal bounds set on their actions but nonetheless "using any advantageous adversary tactic permitted by the existing rules." On the envisioned view, it is the rule-maker, rather than the adversary actor, who should be responsible for taking account of flaws in the rules and altering them if necessary.[63]

But many such violations simply would not pass the test of rational *ex ante* acceptability.[64] And the argument that adversaries can leave regulation to the law, on the theory that pursuing adversary strategies ruthlessly within the bounds set by the relevant legal rules will produce better outcomes than any realistic alternative, is implausible. Cost-effectiveness considerations mean that the rules governing adversary practices will help to foster good consequences, but will be unlikely to eliminate inefficiencies, much less neutralize the effects of various harms and rights violations in ways that would be satisfactory *ex ante* to the victims.[65] An adversarial professional who engages in deception, manipulation, or coercion, or who wrongfully injures in other ways, may argue that the institution within which she works is to blame, that she is merely a functionary playing her part in a system that, taken as a whole, is beneficial to everyone or almost everyone. But the wrongs for which she seeks to deny responsibility have still occurred.[66]

According to a great deal of conventional wisdom,

> the institution of zealous legal advocates is, on the whole, the best way to uncover the factual and legal truth, and so the best way to achieve just outcomes. The lawyer therefore is justified in playing the role of zealous advocate, even in those cases where such zealousness will not reveal the truth, or lead to a just settlement of legal disputes.[67]

This sort of analysis might perhaps justify deception, manipulation, and humiliation on the part of lawyers, Applbaum allows. But, even if it did, it would not provide any sort of moral justification for this kind of behavior on the part of other adversaries in contexts less clearly structured in ways designed to bring good out of misbehavior.[68]

unjustified threat, so the principle of self-defense does not justify discrediting her through humiliation and smear." *Id.* at 172.

62 *See id.* at 175–81.

63 *See id.* at 193.

64 *See id.* at 187.

65 *See id.* at 196.

66 *See id.* at 203.

67 *Id.* at 200.

68 *See id.* at 200–201.

IV. CONSTRAINING ADVERSARIAL EXUBERANCE

Applbaum has offered a thoughtful and persuasive defense of the basic conviction that "[r]ole requirements can overwrite moral permissions, and become moral requirements. But role requirements cannot overwrite moral prohibitions and mint moral permissions."[69]

The fruits of Applbaum's preferred contractualist procedure are, unsurprisingly, quite similar to the results of applying the Principle of Fairness. The most important difference between the NATURAL LAW approach and Applbaum's is that the Principle of Fairness is only one of several requirements of practical reasonableness. Choices that might be consistent with the Principle of Fairness might prove to be inconsistent with the Principle of Respect, or with a commitment to which one should adhere in virtue of the Principle of Commitment. And the Principle of Respect arguably renders some objections to bad behavior by adversaries more unequivocal than does contractualism. So, for instance, with respect to James Giffard's denial that he had sought to effect "the death of a man": Giffard's *purpose* in carrying on the prosecution seems to have been, precisely, to bring about "the death of a man" (this was certainly his client's purpose). He was, indeed, fulfilling a professional duty, but he was doing so by seeking someone's death. Acting on (what I take to be) Giffard's purpose was thus a violation of the Principle of Respect. Nonetheless, contractualism certainly captures a good deal of what we have in mind when thinking about the morality of professional roles.

For instance, it seems reasonable on NATURAL LAW as on contractualist grounds alike that rationales rooted in the reasonableness of self-defense would not permit lawyers or other practitioners of adversarial professions to deceive or otherwise violate the requirements of practical reasonableness. (Even if there are, as I suggest in Chapter 2 that there might be, reasonable lies, it is hard to imagine that ordinary adversarial interactions will be appropriate occasions for such lies.) More generally, while one's circumstances do affect whether what one does is fair, there are limits to how much the circumstance of occupying a professional role can change what does and doesn't count as consistent with the Principle of Fairness. There is relatively little to dispute, then, at the level of substance about Applbaum's argument.

I wonder, though, whether Applbaum concedes too much to adversaries in one arena: the law. In Part IV, I offer some criticisms of the limited exemption Applbaum seems to grant on behalf of lawyers to his general strictures on morally dubious adversarial conduct. I think we should give the settled expectations of clients and others regarding the behavior of the legal system and of advocates less weight in shaping advocates' moral judgments than he does. We can say more than he seems to want to about critiques by professionals of their professions and roles. I think we should make fair play considerations less dispositive than he seems to with

69 *Id.* at 248.

regard to deceptive choices by lawyers. And systemic considerations, which Applbaum suggests might sometimes justify zealous advocates' choices to injure, might provide significant reasons to *avoid* injury even in the few cases in which he thinks injury might be appropriate.

A. *Applbaum's Hesitancy about Condemning Some Adversarial Violations by Lawyers*

Applbaum refers throughout to a range of legal practices which he appears to find dubious and which seem to fall foul of his basic judgment that roles can generate additional obligations but not release us from existing ones.[70] Lawyers may sometimes act as liars and thieves.[71] "[G]ood lawyers certainly are serial *deceivers*—indeed, deception is one of the core tasks and skills of legal practice."[72] ABA rules forbid lawyers "from offering evidence they *know* to be false" but permit them to "offer evidence they reasonably believe is false."[73]

Applbaum emphasizes that it will not do to suggest that lawyers should be excused from ordinary duties of honesty because everyone involved in the legal process knows that advocates may seek to deceive in the course of pressing their clients' claims. In reality, lawyers are at great pains to establish their credibility. They *want* to be believed. They want to be trusted. They do not typically want to behave like people who expect to be regarded as advocates prepared to disregard or distort the truth.[74] And their effectiveness *depends* on their being believed. At the same time, however, they may trade on the appearance of trustworthiness to manipulate outcomes and seek verdicts they know are inconsistent with or unsupported by the facts.[75]

But Applbaum seems unwilling to conclude definitively that at least some conventional legal practices are morally unacceptable just because they are deceptive. To be sure, alluding to the case of the accident victim with the aneurysm concealed by the insurance company's physician on the advice of the company's lawyer, he grants that "[t]he success and stability of the institutions of insurance, lawyering, and doctoring do not depend on denying young Spaulding lifesaving information."[76] But when it comes to the deception that he regards as an ordinary part of lawyering, he is more careful, more qualified. "The lies lawyers tell and the deceptions they stage may be justified,"[77] he tells at the end of his initial reflection on the question, "Are

70 *See id.* at 104–8, 199–201.
71 *See id.* at 42.
72 *Id.* at 104.
73 *Id.* at 106 (*citing* ABA rule 3.3).
74 *See id.* at 107.
75 *See id.* at 108.
76 *Id.* at 171.
77 *Id.* at 108.

lawyers liars?" It might be reasonable to expect that his later reflections would resolve this question, but it is not clear that they do.

Thus, for instance, while fair play arguments do not justify imposing the costs of deception on ordinary litigants (and jurors?), perhaps, Applbaum suggests, they warrant deceiving other lawyers and some opposing parties who are those other lawyers' "corporate legal clients."[78] And there may, he thinks, be some validity to claims that the legal system really does its job most effectively when lawyers in their roles as zealous advocates "conceal incriminating information," "spin to juries stories they know to be false," or offer arguments "about the law in support of their ... [clients' cases] that they believe ... [are bad arguments] if they think ... [judges or juries] will believe ... [them]."[79] Whether this is so, he maintains, "is in part an assertion of fact, difficult to document, which may or may not be true."[80] At best, it does not apply outside the courtroom, where carefully equilibrated rules of procedure and evidence do not apply.[81]

It seems, however, that an attorney *is* sometimes free, or, indeed, required to disregard the purposes of the client or to decline to pursue those purposes in the manner preferred by the client. And, indeed, it may sometimes be unreasonable *not* to disregard clients' purposes or to decline to pursue them in particular ways. It is understandable that this possibility might make Applbaum nervous.

> The stable expectations of both principal adversaries and targets about the actions of professional agents . . . might be jeopardized if agents are permitted or required to act on their judgments about a client's moral purposes in particular cases of zealous advocacy, and such predictability is an important efficiency condition. So agents may have strong reasons to act as adversaries, and this is so even before considering reasons for action grounded . . . in obligations incurred by an agent to a principal, in an agent's permission to enable the principal's exercise of a right, or in some account of goods internal to a professional role.[82]

But the specter of James Giffard looms. The lawyer who could not tell the difference between prosecuting and "compassing the death of a man" reappears throughout *Ethics for Adversaries* as a cautionary tale, a particularly unpleasant example of undue professional detachment and overzealous advocacy.[83] It is thus surprising to find Applbaum so willing to countenance a moral division of labor that Giffard could have interpreted as licensing him to secure someone's conviction for murder and resultant death when he knew no murder had been committed and was aware of his employer's malicious motives.

78 *Id.* at 135.
79 *Id.* at 198.
80 *Id.* at 200.
81 *See id.* at 201.
82 *Id.* at 201.
83 *See id.* at 80–91, 90, 98, 247.

To be sure, Applbaum's justification is apparently offered in the hypothetical mode. And his prime purpose is to show that nonlawyers, and lawyers outside courtrooms, cannot avail themselves of justifications the virtues of the adversary system might make available to lawyers. Nonetheless, it is hard to escape the sense that he regards this sort of argument as having significant, whether or not decisive, force.

B. *The Extent of Professional Self-Critique*

Applbaum seems to hesitate where the possibility of radical critique by professionals of standards obtaining in their profession is concerned. It's not that he denies the possibility of critique: as I've already noted, he explicitly acknowledges it. But it's not clear to me that he's entirely comfortable with radical questioning of professional norms in ways that might warrant the refusal to adhere to those norms.

It's worth emphasizing that, from the outside, of course, we—people in general—can criticize the definition of a role or institution that permits, encourages, or requires unreasonable behavior (for an institution or role cannot exhaustively determine what counts as reasonable). And professionals don't disappear into their roles: they transcend those roles, and can thus stand outside them just as the rest of us can.

Applbaum allows for debates about just what a profession requires of its members. But he seems to want to limit the kind of critique he envisions to the question of what current standards *are*, not about what they *ought to be*. Thus, he insists that "genuine contestation is a claim in good faith about what shared meanings actually are, not a proposal for what they should be."[84] But how do shared meanings change if not in virtue of some people's direct criticism of how practices or institutions should function—including the internal criticism of participants (who are especially well equipped to understand an institution's dynamics)? Why should it not be the case that one of the ways in which any tacitly defined practice or institution may be revised is through changes in the expectations and behaviors of members of society, including those participating in the practice or institution? And should we be confident, in any case, that there really *are* shared meanings in a given contested area waiting simply to be interpreted? There may be considerable disagreement about just what a practice amounts to. Even if there weren't, however, moral evaluation of a practice is always, in principle, in order. And an understanding of a profession that treats it as licensing what would be immoral conduct when engaged in by someone occupying a different role is an understanding ripe for rigorous critique.

Occupying a professional role should equip one in more than one way to be a critic of one's profession. Thus, practitioners can and should challenge what

[84] *Id.* at 103.

should be expected of them *in their professional roles as practitioners*. Their skill as professionals and understanding of the current dynamics of the institutions in which they participate should enable them to object to others' characterizations of the meanings of their roles. And their internal perspectives on and insights into the purposes of these institutions should enable them to criticize client expectations as inconsistent with those purposes and should make them aware of what will serve those purposes effectively.

C. *Settled Expectations and Lawyers' Adversarial Violations*

Applbaum suggests that the need to protect settled expectations may provide some basis for a defense of otherwise unethical adversarial practices. I am unsure he is right.

Arguments to which the value of settled expectations is central have force in many areas of law and morals.[85] Rational action depends on our ability to plan, and we can hardly do so in the absence of some expectation of predictability and continuity in our lives. This is especially so if we have undertaken costly commitments of one kind or another on the basis of our expectations—a principal ground of the familiar "reliance interest" and its kin in the law of contracts.[86] But the force of such arguments notwithstanding, we may reasonably ask how far they take us here.

Lawyers' refusal to violate persons in otherwise impermissible ways could result in the disruption of two kinds of client expectations.

85 On expectations, see, *e.g.*, Stephen R. Munzer, A Theory of Property 223–24 (1990). Munzer suggests that there is "a strong though not invincible structural claim for [the] protection" of what he labels "rational" and legitimate interests. *Id.* at 223. An interest is *rational* if it is based on "appropriately accurate and detailed knowledge of the law," if the person or entity with the interest is capable of making "predictions on the basis of that knowledge," and if it reflects the capacity to understand and anticipate the relevant judgments of other involved actors. An interest is legitimate if it is grounded both in the particular laws relating to the relevant subject matter and in the underlying logic and normative assumptions of "the legal system as a whole." *Id.* at 223.

My claim is, to employ Munzer's categories (with allowances for the fact that many norms governing the legal profession are themselves quasi-legal or nonlegal), that (*i*) it is currently rational and legitimate for clients to expect their lawyers to engage in sharp, potentially dishonest practices on their behalf; (*ii*) a change in the public definition of the norms governing the legal profession would deprive these expectations of both rationality and legitimacy; (*iii*) the individual practitioner who explicitly disavows some adversarial norms in favor of ones calling for unequivocal honesty and greater compassion and a commitment to finding win-win solutions to legal conflicts has made it irrational for *her* client to predict compliance with these norms on her part, and has therefore rendered the client's expectation that she might conform with more conventional in-profession norms irrational (presuming the client must actually *make* predictions and not merely be capable of making them in the abstract); (*iv*) even if the explicitly nonconforming lawyer has not rendered the client's expectation interest in deceptive and other forms of sharp adversarial conduct unreasonable, this interest is weak enough that it should not receive the protection of the legal system; and (*v*) the client's interest in her attorney's engaging in unfair conduct on her behalf is unreasonable and thus deserves no protection.

86 And, more controversially, in the law of property. *See* Joseph William Singer, *The Reliance Interest in Property*, 40 Stanford L. Rev. 611 (1988).

Clients may expect that they will have the discretion to determine what projects their lawyers will further on their behalf. And of course the choice to pursue a particular project by any means may be morally dubious. No one really doubts that a lawyer is not entitled to take a case in the first place for any reason; and a lawyer's termination of work on a given case because of the morally dubious nature of the case needn't prove systemically disruptive and so inconsistent with the Principle of Fairness.

Clients may also expect to approve the strategies their lawyers employ to further their projects, while assuming that their lawyers will deceive or engage in other kinds of conduct that would ordinarily be unreasonable, to advance those projects. What clients expect of their lawyers will depend, in turn, on the standards of conduct for the legal profession generally acknowledged within the society to which the clients and lawyers belong, notably, though not exclusively, those endorsed by the legal profession itself.

Whether the profession should adopt standards prohibiting otherwise violative conduct by lawyers doesn't seem like a close question. If it did so, lawyers' refusal to engage in such conduct could hardly prove disruptive. This sort of refusal also presumably wouldn't prove disruptive if, quite apart from any formal action by the organized legal profession, instances of adversarial advocacy which directly wrong persons or further injurious projects are rare. Suppose they are. If so, settled expectations might not be substantially disrupted were attorneys to decline on a more consistent basis to use their professional skills and resources in ways that clearly involved or contributed to otherwise wrongful injuries, even if facilitating the infliction of those injuries is permitted under current law. To be sure, the more independent discretion lawyers expected to exercise, the more unpredictable the legal environment is likely to be for clients. But apart from clear instances of dishonesty or injustice, even lawyers inclined to use independent moral judgment would surely be disinclined to second-guess their clients—out of loyalty as well as self-interest. Even if lawyers employed independent moral judgment to assess their clients' projects and the methods they might use to promote those projects, there would surely be strong economic and social incentives against the undisciplined and idiosyncratic exercise of such judgment. A lawyer with a reputation for unpredictably obstructing clients' plans would doubtless find it difficult to attract and retain business.

Of course, many clients may expect lawyers to engage in conduct that would ordinarily be unreasonable. If so, pro-ethics changes in standards of professional conduct or the behavior of individual lawyers could yield potentially disruptive consequences for the legal system. Existing client expectations would sometimes likely be frustrated. On the other hand, once cultural and professional norms had changed, client expectations would have changed with them. If the legal system embodied a commitment to a new level of honesty and respect for persons that was generally acknowledged as setting the bounds for adversary practices, what clients anticipated would doubtless be different. A client who knew her attorney would not deceive a jury or "compass the death of a man" would hardly be surprised if the attorney failed to do so. Clients could thus continue to plan confidently in light of realistic assumptions about their attorneys' behavior. And provided attorneys advised clients about moral concerns but acted on their instructions except when requirements of honesty or respect were clearly violated, clients could still safely depend on their lawyers loyally to advocate their interests and further their projects.

Settled expectations aren't decisive. It's not reasonable for lawyers to violate moral requirements to further client projects, whatever clients expect. But changes in professional standards and in the social norms obtaining within the legal system could obviously prove helpful insofar as they reduced the gaps between moral requirements and client expectations. Such changes could preserve the predictability benefits of the current system while clearly precluding actions by a lawyer including:[87]

- making reckless, knowing, or purposeful misstatements regarding opinions, evaluations, and future intentions;
- offering evidence she reasonably believes, or should reasonably believe, to be false;
- withholding information the disclosure of which would likely preclude a fraudulent act by a client;
- withholding relevant information from a judge or jury;
- attempting to induce beliefs in a judge or the members of a jury which she knows or reasonably believes (or should reasonably believe) to be false; or
- offering arguments regarding the law which she reasonably believes to be inaccurate.

Professional standards and social norms should also acknowledge the *permissibility* of a lawyer's unwillingness to further client projects she believes clearly to involve the wrongful (even if legally permissible) infliction of injury and her refusal to pursue legal avenues otherwise permitted by the rules in contravention of her own deeply held conscientious convictions if the issues are clear-cut and have been explored in sustained, reflective dialogue with her client. It is perhaps not too much to hope that such dialogue would have the added benefit of challenging the client to rethink her own values and the consequences of her choices, and so play a limited but real role in enhancing public virtue.

It will be important, of course, for lawyers who believe it might be wrong in particular instances for them to act on their clients' preferences to recognize that their perspectives may be limited and that they may be tempted to arrogance and self-righteousness. The attempt to adopt a more detached and widely sympathetic perspective is surely beneficial, but the lawyer who makes this attempt can too easily

[87] *Cf.* Applbaum, *supra* note 1, at 107–8, 199–200.

come to behave as if she can take a God's-eye view of the situation. Precisely on moral grounds the lawyer who makes moral judgments about a client's *projects* (the problem is presumably less serious when the question whether to pursue a particular *strategy* in pursuit of a client project—the telling of a lie, say—is in view) must be aware of the limitations of her own perspective and of the need to be open to the perspectives of all relevant parties. The desire to control can easily masquerade as the impulse to foster moral rectitude, and this desire can and should be resisted. Genuine humility is essential if one proposes to be "counsel for the situation."[88]

Where professional standards and social norms concern a lawyer's subjective state, they will not always be readily enforceable (though doubtless on some occasions they will). But enforcement isn't my concern here (any more than it's Applbaum's, if I understand him). I'm interested in what it's reasonable for a loyal but decent advocate to do. The embrace of the kinds of standards and norms I've considered is appealing not only because it will sharpen individual lawyers' thinking about the issues they confront but also because it may be expected to promote a culture of fairness that overly zealous adversary practices may sometimes tend to subvert.

A decision by an individual attorney to take a moral position not generally endorsed by her professional peers could, of course, exert a disruptive effect on clients' expectations. And of course context will matter: sometimes, in virtue of the Principle of Fairness, expectations will mean that a lawyer may or even must choose differently than she would absent those expectations. On the other hand, this can hardly be the only consideration relevant even in relation to the Principle of Fairness; and the Principle of Fairness is of course not the whole of reasonableness. The responsible advocate will have no choice but to decline, on occasion, to make clearly unreasonable choices even in support of otherwise appropriate client projects. The real benefits to clients themselves as well as to real or potential targets of unreasonable conduct by clients can certainly warrant the exercise of attorneys' moral discretion in opposition to their clients' wishes (though of course lawyers must ordinarily be quite explicit about their choices, providing clients with opportunities to opt for new representatives at their discretion).

It is one thing to give a client the benefit of the doubt or to pursue her interests with zealous partiality. It is another to lie in negotiations or in the courtroom or to "compass the death of a man." No division of moral labor should license attorneys to deceive under ordinary circumstances or to violate persons in other, comparable ways. Attorneys or clients who would not want be willing to endorse rules or norms permitting themselves or their loved ones to be deceived, humiliated, or otherwise violated in particular circumstances cannot reasonably approve of strategies involving deceiving, humiliating, or otherwise injuring opposing parties or lawyers,

[88] *Cf.* Spillenger, *supra* note 49, at 1508–11 (criticizing Brandeis's immediate willingness to impose his own solution to a problem on others).

witnesses, jurors, or judges in comparable circumstances.[89] And of course some—many or all—lies will, in accordance with the Principle of Respect, be unreasonable whether or not consistent with the Principle of Fairness.

An individual lawyer could surely address the problem of settled expectations even in an environment in which unreasonable behavior is frequently expected of zealous adversaries by articulating them clearly to all prospective clients and to all attorneys with whom she did business. Some clients would doubtless decline her services, and some lawyers might be inclined to take advantage of her. But she might nonetheless be able both to behave reasonably in relation to the individual persons with whom she engages and to contribute by example to the transformation of clients' and other lawyers' perceptions of appropriate norms of professional conduct.

A lawyer cannot herself violate the requirements of practical reasonableness. But in some cases, while a client may choose to violate these principles, the lawyer may reasonably assist the client without embracing the client's unreasonable purpose. (The NATURAL LAW casuistry, discussed in Chapter 1 in connection with boycotts, that can be used to determine when COOPERATION in unreasonable injury is reasonable will be relevant here.) It may be permissible, or even required, as a matter of fairness for a lawyer who does not share a client's unreasonable purpose to assist the client in appropriately constrained ways. Thus, for instance, a lawyer may sometimes reasonably make choices that have the foreseen but unintended effect of facilitating a dubious project on the part of a client (say, the project of avoiding responsibility for causing a serious injury)—when the lawyer is herself doing something else (say, ensuring that the client receives a genuinely fair hearing in court).[90]

D. *Fair Play and Lawyers' Adversarial Violations*

A fair play argument seeks to show that someone may be subjected to the rules of a practice even when she *hasn't* consented. The fair play justification for what would otherwise qualify as immoral lawyering which Applbaum tentatively moots does not, however, succeed in warranting much, if any, lying or other injurious conduct by attorneys.

It seems as if, to be successful, a fair play argument needs to show *not only* that failing to subject the target to the rules of a practice *in general* would allow the target to reap unfair benefits from the practice *but also* that subjecting her to (at least

[89] On lying, *see, e.g.*, Chapter 2, *supra*; SISSELA BOK, LYING: MORAL CHOICE IN PUBLIC AND PRIVATE LIFE (1978); JEAN-PAUL SARTRE, NOTEBOOKS FOR AN ETHICS 195–204 (1992); BERNARD GERT, MORALITY: A NEW JUSTIFICATION OF THE MORAL RULES 126–27 (1988); LEONARD NELSON, SYSTEM OF ETHICS 151–55 (1956); CHARLES FRIED, RIGHT AND WRONG 54–78 (1978); ALAN DONAGAN, THE THEORY OF MORALITY 88–90 (1977); ALAN GEWIRTH, REASON AND MORALITY 198 (1978); T. M. SCANLON, WHAT WE OWE TO EACH OTHER 317–22 (1998); LEWIS B. SMEDES, MERE MORALITY 211–38 (1988); Alasdair MacIntyre, ETHICS AND POLITICS 101–42 (2006).

[90] *See, e.g.*, Robert P. George, *Reflections on the Ethics of Representing Clients Whose Aims Are Unjust*, 40 S. TEX. L. REV. 55 (1999).

something relevantly like) the *particular* rule one seeks to enforce against her is needed for this purpose. There's nothing unfair about accepting the benefits associated with participation in a practice while ignoring a convention associated with the practice that plays little or no role in making those benefits available. And this means that a fair play argument, unlike a consent argument, will likely need to show that the benefits are made available by the specific convention that permits deception or some other kind of injury, and not just in general.

It seems as if a fair play argument will justify deceiving and otherwise injuring unconsenting targets, even if they are the kinds of repeat players Applbaum envisions, only if there clearly are conventions permitting the relevant sorts of injuries. It won't be sufficient to show that some significant subset of lawyers might inflict such injuries or treat them as permissible. Rather, the infliction of these injuries will need to be part of the background against which legal practice takes place, something ordinarily assumed by at least most lawyers. Otherwise, it will be difficult to maintain that the infliction of these injuries, or the possibility that they will be inflicted, plays a crucial role in the generation of the benefits associated with adversarial legal practice. And it seems difficult to maintain that there are, indeed, such clearly accepted conventions within the legal profession.

Suppose there were a clear and generally accepted convention permitting deception and other injuries. The repeat players Applbaum suggests might reasonably be injured by zealous advocates would still be justified in doubting that the benefits of zealous advocacy depend on the possibility, much less the occurrence, of deception and other sorts of injuries. And it seems as if these injuries would need to yield these benefits if a fair play argument were to warrant their infliction. Given that the injuries are certain and the links between systemic benefits and the injuries unclear, treating the infliction of the injuries as permissible on fair play grounds seems questionable at best. Unconsenting targets might, indeed, argue that such injuries *undermine* the effectiveness of legal practice, by reducing trust and diverting energy, as well as by systematically tilting outcomes in favor of the dishonest and encouraging people who would prefer not to injure others to do so to level relevant playing fields.

E. *Systemic Consequences and Lawyers' Adversarial Violations*

Viewed in relation to the Principle of Fairness and the other requirements of practical reasonableness, these sorts of considerations seem likely to count not only against a fair play argument for the permissibility of deception (and other kinds of injuring) by zealous advocates but also against more general systemic arguments as well.

Applbaum alludes to Gresham's Law—"bad money drives out good"—in another context;[91] it is also worth considering here. Tolerating deception as a practice even in

[91] *See* APPLBAUM, *supra* note 1, at 236; the focus is on the role of political dissent in reducing the effectiveness of a democratic state.

limited contexts is the likelihood that it will lead to more deception. To the extent that permitting deception does yield consequences some or all players might regard as valuable, it does so, arguably, because deception is widespread. The less common and accepted deception is, the less particular players will be inclined to deceive in order to equalize their positions with those of other players they expect will deceive, too. Even if deception yields some good consequences, surely an environment free from deception is, all other things being equal, preferable to one in which people deceive each other. There is thus an argument that choosing to avoid deception, even if deceiving might be thought to produce certain benefits, conduces to the gradual creation of an environment from which deception is largely absent and which is thus, *ex hypothesi*, to be preferred.

Resisting the temptation to deceive and to engage in other kinds of single-mindedly adversarial tactics could have a related positive systemic consequence. The perception that lawyers are playing fair, that their commitment to advocacy does not inhibit their concern for people other than their clients, could ultimately benefit clients as well as opposing parties and outsiders. Negotiation plays a key role in resolving legal disputes. The likelihood that a win-win solution will emerge from a given negotiation depends in part on the degree to which negotiators regard each other as trustworthy, honest, and concerned for and open to those with other interests or perspectives. A general refusal on the part of lawyers to allow zealous advocacy to eclipse reasonable concern for non-clients would contribute to the perception that they were flexible, truthful, and reliable. It would thus make them more successful negotiators, with the result that in many cases they would be better able to reach solutions beneficial to their clients.

Doing the right thing does not always produce the results a client might prefer, of course, at least in a narrow sense. But (though truth-telling and the transcendence of narrow partiality properly reflect one's respect for oneself and those with whom one communicates) the systemic consequences of choosing reasonably are likely to be positive for clients as a class in ways that should discourage certain kinds of adversarial advocacy.

There is a further reason to wonder whether a professional rule permitting deception, even to fellow lawyers or of legally sophisticated opposing parties, can reasonably be regarded as generating "benefits and add[ing] value."[92] There is (because they are incommensurable) no objective metric for the relevant costs and benefits that would permit a cost–benefit analysis to be performed in the absence of people's specific commitments.

Are there, or could there be, the relevant sorts of commitments? The legal *system* isn't the kind of formalized cooperative venture in which the relevant sorts of commitments can be made. The organized legal *profession* might be such a cooperative undertaking, though I'm not sure it is. But, even if it were, members

[92] *Id*. at 126.

of the profession would surely find it politically difficult—both within and without the profession—to make the commitments needed to render deception reasonable. It would be difficult to make a case for a public rule permitting lying: members of the public would likely see this as more evidence of the profession's general untrustworthiness. And many members of the profession would likely not endorse the needed commitments.

After all, for many people, not being deceived, and so preserving the various aspects of well-being adversely affected by deception, will trump the aspects of well-being arguably promoted by a system permitting deception. Given their own individual preferences and commitments, they would presumably be disinclined to embrace a profession-wide commitment permitting lying under ordinary circumstances. And if many individual lawyers would not be willing to endorse such a commitment, it would be reasonable for lawyers *in general* to deceive other lawyers and corporate legal clients only if (*i*) a professional standard allowing deception were adopted in the face of the pro-honesty faction's opposition and (*ii*) such a standard could reasonably be taken to apply to the members of this faction despite their dissent. It is better to see such a rule as applying only to those who actually do embrace it directly or who embrace membership in a professional association that has embraced it.

There is, of course, no reason that this issue need be resolved on a profession-wide basis. The legal profession—like all other professions—should be disestablished.[93] Instead, then, of being forced by governmental licensing rules to belong to a single organized professional community, different lawyers might well, in the absence of such rules, affiliate with different such communities. And such voluntary professional groupings could and doubtless would adopt different standards. Members of professional associations publicly treating lying in carefully cabined contexts as professionally acceptable could, in virtue of their membership in those associations, be treated as having consented to being deceived by other lawyers in circumstances permitted by the applicable professional rules. And those choosing to be clients of such lawyers might be expected to agree that, if their lawyers could be deceived in the relevant contexts, so could they. It would be interesting to see how the market would respond to the availability of diverse lying-related options in the legal services industry.

V. ADVERSARIAL VIRTUE

Client loyalty is not an absolute. Good lawyers sometimes act contrary to their clients instructions and don't always treat their clients' well-being as supremely valuable. Applbaum helps us to see why this might be so. He argues persuasively for a deep and pervasive suspicion of the strategies people too often use to justify

93 *See* Clifford Winston et al., First Thing We Do, Let's Deregulate All the Lawyers (2011).

abusive adversarial practices, including ones engaged in by members of the legal profession. His careful examination of these arguments allows him to expose them as flawed and inadequate and thus to challenge legal professionals and others to more unequivocal commitments to reasonableness.

The Principle of Fairness and the Principle of Respect provide clear support for the kind of conclusion Applbaum wants to defend—*and* for the conviction that there are even fewer occasions for deception by lawyers than he supposes there might be and that lawyers should be free to, and sometimes simply should, decline to further clients' clearly wrongful projects. Adversarial contests can help to realize and facilitate advocates', clients', judges', and others' participation in various aspects of well-being. But no participant in the legal system or any other adversarial process can flourish by choosing to act unreasonably, even in pursuit of genuine goods. While acknowledging the appropriateness of constraints on adversarial practice may inhibit participation in some basic goods, it can't inhibit agents' all-things-considered flourishing, since choosing unreasonably directly undermines our capacities to live flourishing lives.

Burling and Ennis struggled honorably with the demands of justice and client loyalty. Their apparent willingness to provide back-channel support to the ACLU seems especially commendable, given the injustice of the internment program; but their overt resistance to their superiors' choices regarding the accuracy of the Justice Department's claims also merits our praise. Reflections like Applbaum's, and those his own thoughts help to inspire, might have helped Burling and Ennis as they considered their options with respect to *Korematsu*.[94] Such reflections would certainly have equipped them to see more clearly the utter flimsiness of arguments for adversarial advocates' connivance in injustice, and might have prompted them to take even more radical steps.

No philosophical text is likely to speak so directly to the particularities of a situation that it leaves the reader unequivocally certain what she ought to do. But lawyers who struggle with the demands of fairness and integrity as Burling and Ennis did will surely find Applbaum's reflections valuable. Lawyers would do well, I believe, to exercise more morally motivated restraint and more personal moral discretion than Applbaum's arguments might encourage them to do. But his systematic demolition of bad arguments for abusive adversarial partiality can and

[94] That the two were employed by the United States government raises other issues, of a sort to which Applbaum devotes considerable attention, *id.* at 207–39. I believe the best way to view this government, like all others, is as an exercise in stationary banditry—illegitimate, unnecessary, and dangerous. Thus, I don't think Burling and Ennis should have taken themselves to have any obligation to further the unjust purpose of legitimating and prolonging the internment—and they should, indeed, I think, have worked even more to undermine it. A criminal enterprise does not deserve the same sort of consideration as an ordinary client. But Burling and Ennis could, I believe, have reached the conclusion that they should have sought to challenge the internment and assist Korematsu without embracing anarchism simply by taking into account considerations like those noted here regarding lawyers' responsibilities for facilitating the realization of clients' aims.

should play a useful role in raising lawyers' awareness of the appropriateness of greater moral seriousness in the practice of their profession.

Apart from a case in which explicit consent obtains (and even explicit consent may not be morally decisive), it will be difficult to offer an ethical justification for lying in the context of ordinary legal practice. Some lies are inconsistent with the Principle of Respect. The Principle of Fairness, whether invoked in support of a fair play justification for deception or in support of a systemic one, seems likely to count against this kind of lying absent consent. And consent will presumably be available at best only in a limited range of cases.

While respecting truth and justice, lawyers can be aggressive advocates for their clients. Sometimes, however, lawyers and clients may find themselves at odds. And this may be the case with respect not only to the truth an attorney does or doesn't share in the courtroom but also to the truth she does or doesn't share in more intimate settings. One way to frame this issue is to talk about the issue of *privacy*: concern for a client's privacy (in one sense of that term) can prove to be, at minimum, a source of tension with a lawyer's regard for her own privacy (in another sense). I explore this possible tension in Chapter 5.

5

Lawyers

I. LIBERALISM, PRIVACY, AND LEGAL PRACTICE

Liberalism emphasizes, as I have said, the value of an ecosystem in which zealous advocacy for clients helps to ensure truth and fair treatment—concern for which flows from the Principle of Fairness. But while lawyers qua lawyers may be valuable as clients' agents, lawyers are also persons with lives of their own. Liberalism values those lives. Thus, it values the privacy of lawyers as well as their clients, among others—in the interests of various aspects of flourishing. And this means that liberal values can come into conflict in the context of legal practice. I consider the importance of lawyers' concern with one kind of privacy, client confidentiality, in Part II. I note the importance of another kind of privacy, jurisdiction over a private sphere of life, especially involving intimate relationships, for clients and lawyers alike in Part III. In Part IV, I highlight reasons to think that regard for privacy in these two senses might sometimes lead to conflict. I reflect on ways to address the tension created by concern for these two kinds of privacy in Part V.

II. CLIENTS' INFORMATIONAL PRIVACY

Lawyers are expected to protect the privacy of their clients. They must also be entitled to safeguard their own. The tension between expectation and entitlement becomes particularly clear, sometimes, in connection with the day-to-day realities of legal practice.

The American Bar Association's Model Rules of Professional Conduct stipulate that "a lawyer shall not reveal information relating to the representation of a client unless the client gives informed consent, the disclosure is impliedly authorized in order to carry out the representation or the disclosure is permitted" under the Model Rules themselves.[1]

Duties of confidentiality—which are, in effect, duties to protect clients' informational privacy—are drummed into law students' heads in clinical courses and in review sessions for the Multistate Professional Responsibility Examination. The honorable lawyer is repeatedly depicted as someone perhaps willing to keep

[1] Model Rules 1.6.

a client's secrets beyond the client's death. And it is easy to see why a deep-seated concern for clients' privacy might well be important. A client comes to a lawyer in a terribly vulnerable position. The exposure of the information she conveys to her lawyer—sometimes accidentally, often enough necessarily—could be humiliating, damaging, perhaps even life-threatening for her.

We care about privacy in this sense, *informational* privacy, for good and obvious reasons. Privacy is not an *intrinsic* good: at least in the vast majority of cases, I am not, as such, better or worse off because you know or don't know something, anything, about me. But privacy is frequently a valuable *instrumental* good. Information confers power. To know about your financial dealings, your family relationships, your sexual liaisons, your professional aspirations is, at least potentially, to possess substantial influence over you. Restrictions on access to information—protections of informational privacy—help to reduce the influence others have over people's lives.

The protection of informational privacy leads naturally, then, to privacy rules as applied to lawyer–client relationships. The lawyer already, in many ways, has more influence, more capacity to effect her will, than the client, in virtue of her professional expertise and judgment, her knowledge of the Byzantine intricacies of the law, and, very often, the emotionally distraught condition of someone seeking legal assistance. If there were a meaningful risk that the lawyer might use the information she acquired while representing the client to *injure* the client, the client's vulnerability would be enhanced even further. Client privacy rules serve to give the client the confidence that her vulnerability to her attorney will not be exploited.

There are, of course, legitimate questions about the scope of such rules, and about the ideal of client loyalty which they embody. A range of questions have been, and rightly will continue to be, asked about a lawyer's right or duty to violate a client's privacy when failing to do so would result in significant injury to a third party. But contained within our broader social notion of privacy *itself* is a tension between the lawyer's responsibility to protect a client's privacy and her legitimate valuation of her own, and it is to this tension that I want to attend.

III. PRIVACY AND THE PRIVATE SPHERE

The right to privacy, as it has come to be affirmed in American jurisprudence, certainly includes a right to informational privacy. But it includes considerably more than that. It is best seen as a right to make decisions regarding a legitimately private *sphere of life*. The right to privacy marks off a boundary of action and experience which the state, in particular, cannot transgress (except in the interests of protecting third parties). (Given their legislatively enshrined powers, bar associations, even if formally private, are in important senses state agencies.)

Justice Douglas's "penumbral" evocation of the right to privacy built on, among other things, the Fourth Amendment's prohibition of unreasonable searches and seizures.[2] Privacy doctrine is rooted in a sense of the (relative) inviolability of the home as a physical space. But as such doctrine emerged, from Justice Harlan's dissent in *Poe* to the majority opinions in *Griswold*, then *Roe*, then *Lawrence*, privacy doctrine has moved beyond a focus on the physical home to a focus on the protection of family, sexuality, and intimacy. These aspects of our lives seem to be interwoven deeply with our identities and to offer us distinctively valuable goods. From a NATURAL LAW perspective, they may be seen to implicate goods including friendship, aesthetic experience, play, practical reasonableness, and skillful performance—and, in particular, instances of these goods accorded very high priorities by many people. Interfering with them, then, appears especially violative.

It is not surprising, as a result, that the discussion of privacy jurisprudence in the United States came to include talk of "freedom of intimate association" as entitled to protection under the Court's privacy decisions. It would be too early to say that the initial promise of those decisions has been fulfilled with the elaboration of such a right, though the *Lawrence* and *Obergefell* decisions certainly move us closer toward its recognition. But the commentators' language has pointed, in any case, to a key dimension of privacy. One of the values our privacy jurisprudence seeks to respect is the right to maintain and nourish intimate relationships.

I have offered this brief constitutional excursus partly because our constitutional discourse makes clear the multiple, overlapping senses of privacy in play here. But we do not need constitutional jurisprudence to tell us about the importance of intimate connections in our lives. Nor do we need it to tell us about the significance of informational exchange in sustaining the private sphere where these relationships thrive.

Partners talk with partners. Lovers talk with lovers. Friends talk with friends. Parents talk with children. Talk is often the most crucial medium of exchange between intimates. If you lack knowledge of my inner life and of the details of my life apart from you, you do not really know me—I am a mere functionary, with whom you interact much as you would with a clerk in a government office or a salesperson proposing that you consider a new long-distance service. Broadly speaking, the closer we are, the more intimate we are, the more I know about you. And the less I know about you, especially when you deliberately choose to *keep* me from knowing things about you, the less connected, the farther apart, we are. Informational exchange is essential to intimacy.

We may reasonably expect that growing mutual knowledge will both (*i*) build upon and reflect trust and (*ii*) foster greater trust. You are unlikely to open up to me if you don't, in general, trust me. At minimum, you must be willing to take the risk of being vulnerable to me in order to see what will happen: your intimacy presupposes, if not trust, then at least the hope that trust will be validated and deepened. My greater knowledge of you makes it possible for me to injure you in ways I otherwise

2 *See* Griswold v. Connecticut, 381 U.S. 479, 482–86 (1965) (Douglas, J.).

couldn't; the ways in which I behave when you trust me can give you further reason to be more self-exposed and vulnerable, in an ongoing spiral of growing trust and growing disclosure. Of course there is no guarantee that intimates will not harm each other, and there is repeated evidence that, being flawed and fallible, they will. Nonetheless, we rightly experience reductions in informational privacy barriers as among the hallmarks of developing intimacy.

An entitlement to privacy—in the sense of a private sphere to which intimate connection is central—includes, then, the capacity to maintain a space in which privacy—in the sense of restraint on the sharing of information—is increasingly (even if never, of course, completely) transcended. If we respect the right to privacy, we respect the importance, indeed the centrality, of intimate relationships, the kinds of relationships the private sphere celebrated in American constitutional jurisprudence was meant, at least in significant part, to protect. And this means, in turn, that we value informational exchange among intimates, which ensures not only the vitality, but, indeed, the very *existence* of the private sphere.

IV. TENSIONS IN LAWYERS' LIVES

But if this is the case, then, we can begin to see the tension—in the setting of the attorney-client relationship—between two facets of privacy. The client understandably wishes to prevent the exploitation of her vulnerability by her attorney. She wants, quite reasonably, to know that her lawyer will not use the access to leverage-conferring information facilitated by the attorney–client relationship to take advantage of her. Thus, her concern for *informational privacy*.

At the same time, like the client, the attorney has a life that extends beyond the confines of the attorney–client relationship. The attorney is, in a word, *human*. And it is the interests of, at least, all humans which are safeguarded by a right to privacy understood as the right to create, maintain, and nourish a *private sphere* of life.

The attorney can exercise the right to privacy in this sense only if she can, indeed, maintain rich, close connections with intimates. There is no way to guarantee that she will be able to do this, of course—perhaps she is too socially clumsy or mean-spirited or driven to be able to sustain such connections. But she certainly cannot exercise this right if she is barred from engaging in the kinds of informational exchanges that ensure that at least some of those with whom she interacts will be, not strangers, but friends.

The attorney must, that is to say, be able to talk freely with those with whom she enjoys intimate relationships. And to do this, she will need to talk freely about her work. It is not only the work-obsessiveness of our culture that makes this unavoidable. It is also the simple fact that work consumes an inordinate amount of our time and emotional energy. Your understanding of who I am and what I experience would be sadly impoverished if it did not include an understanding of the events, feelings, and people associated with my work life. And talking about her work obviously involves talking about her clients—the legal issues they confront, but also what interacting with them in person is like, how they treat her, how she views and feels about them, what moral challenges dealing with them forces her to ponder, and so forth.

Thus the tension: the client seeks to ensure that her informational privacy is protected in order to reduce the risks associated with the vulnerability created by the attorney–client relationship; the attorney (like the client) needs the opportunity to maintain a private sphere, a sphere of intimate relationships in which the exchange of information, including information about work-related experiences, and so, potentially, about the client, plays a central role.

V. THINKING ABOUT THE TENSION

Knowledge is valuable to lawyers, their clients, and to others. Sharing information regarding clients with friends, family members, and professional colleagues can offer those with whom sharing takes place the inherently valuable good of knowledge. It can be an instance of play. It can deepen friendship (as withholding information can build or strengthen barriers, and so undermine friendship). It can help to develop practical reasonableness and the capacity for skillful performance (not only in general with respect to professional practice but also with regard to the resolution of significant practical dilemmas). It can offer opportunities for aesthetic experience (as a story well told frequently can). Rules that preclude this kind of sharing thus interfere in serious ways with aspects of well-being that can reasonably be understood under the umbrella of privacy.

On the other hand, constraints on the sharing of information can reduce the risk that clients' adversaries—commercial, legal, personal—will use information to purposefully, instrumentally, or incidentally interfere with the clients' flourishing or opportunities to flourish. And they can make it more likely that clients will share unreservedly with their lawyers and will thus receive excellent legal services.

Confidentiality rules thus both threaten and foster flourishing. There is no simple analytical resolution of this tension. Such a resolution must begin, it seems to me, with the twofold presupposition that attorneys must not harm their clients and that attorneys must not be expected to abandon their humanity in order to practice law. This means, then, not only that attorneys must not themselves exploit their clients, but also that they must ordinarily restrict access to information about those clients when they reasonably believe that doing so is necessary to ensure that others will not act exploitatively. Being an attorney's intimate—or anyone else's—does not entitle one to information acquired for the purpose of unreasonably injuring another. This means, then, that there will be some unavoidable limits on the attorney's right to privacy—the right to maintain a private sphere.

At the same time, the client cannot reasonably expect that, absent such risks, her attorney's refusal to exploit her vulnerability should entail that the attorney will abandon or substantially constrict her right to privacy in this sense when doing so is unlikely to harm her client. The lawyer's personal life is not only separate from her professional life; it is also, we may assume, prior to, and ultimately more significant to her than, her professional life. Her personal concerns do not license harm to her client. But her responsibility not to use her client's disclosures to harm her client does not, cannot be understood to, require her to abandon the personal sphere that ultimately provides her own life, like her client's, with much of its *raison d'être*.

A lawyer might not find privacy in the sense of maintaining a space for intimate connection crucial, just as a client might not find informational privacy crucial. A lawyer, in any case, will need to make decisions about what is appropriate in light especially of the Principle of Commitment and the Principle of Fairness. Her commitments will help in important ways to set the importance of her intimate connections in her life, as also the priority she as a professional gives to client services. The Principle of Fairness will be relevant to the ways in which her tacit and explicit promises to intimates constrain her options in relation to clients. And this principle will also, of course, crucially determine the obligations generated by her agreements with her clients, as also by the expectations created by her conduct.

My point here is not to prescribe ways in which lawyers should understand themselves as professionals or what priority they should give to intimate connection. I simply want to emphasize that friendship is a genuine good, that this good is served by intimate disclosure, and that expectations regarding professional probity should not be supposed automatically to trump concerns with the maintenance of intimate relationships. Flexible norms that protect client interests but that arguably allow more room for discretion than current rules could appropriately acknowledge the value of privacy for attorneys.

The tension between the right to privacy understood as the right to maintain informational privacy and the right to privacy understood as the right to maintain a private sphere comes clearly to expression in the lawyer-client relationship. Both faces of the right to privacy are important. To maintain both, the attorney needs great sensitivity to the requirements of practical reasonableness, to the priorities established by her commitments, and the obligations created by her agreements and by the vulnerabilities brought into being by her conduct. This kind of sensitivity can allow her to respond appropriately to her own needs, to those of intimates, and to those of clients.

Obviously, the tension between privacy in the two senses with which I'm concerned here will matter in different ways for different attorneys and different clients. There is no reason for a uniform set of standards, even a uniform *presumption*. Lawyers and clients can negotiate about privacy and take positions that make sense to them (though I think it would in general be unreasonable for a client not to acknowledge the value to a lawyer of maintaining a private sphere sustained in part through informational exchange with intimates). The attempt to create uniform requirements is unduly complicating. Of course, this matters primarily because bar associations in particular states, while nominally private, occupy cozy relationships with the governments of those states, relationships that allow them to exercise monopoly power over the practice of law in their states. As a result, bar association ethics rules are not simply norms embraced by particular voluntary associations, but rather limits on people's abilities to engage in voluntary transactions with willing clients. For the failure to abide by these rules can result in disciplinary actions including suspension from membership, and someone suspended from membership who nonetheless practices law can be subjected to legal penalties for engaging in "the unauthorized practice of law." A bar association is a legally created cartel. Ending the monopoly status of bar associations would open the way for different attorneys, and different communities of attorneys, to explore alternate standards of behavior and test them in the marketplace.[3]

A liberal understanding of the legal profession will be one that allows for diversity, for a profusion of different options. But it would make sense, in any case, for the kinds of non-monopolistic lawyers' associations that could be expected to flourish in a liberal order to avoid treating a privacy rule as capacious as the existing ABA rule as a default. That's because adopting such a default rule seems *symbolically, expressively*, problematic. It appears, that is, to send the message that the lawyer's private, intimate sphere doesn't deserve consideration in the way the client's informational privacy does. By not establishing a default rule that favors either the privacy of the client or the privacy of the attorney, a lawyers' association would leave attorneys and clients free to find arrangements that worked for them.

While attorneys and clients may sometimes embrace different objectives as regards the release of information, the legal system within which lawyers qua lawyers and clients qua clients function tends to value adversarial legal practice as a way of maximizing the information available to judges and juries and other legal decision-makers. Legal institutions rightly value the availability of information. But there are sometimes also reasons for such institutions to abstemiously deny themselves access to information. This is particularly true when the information is demonstrably irrelevant, or even prejudicial. I consider one such case, the potential use of victim impact testimony in parole hearings, in Chapter 6.

[3] *Cf.* Clifford Winston et al., First Thing We Do, Let's Deregulate All the Lawyers (2011).

6

Victims

I. LIBERAL QUESTIONS ABOUT THE VICTIM ROLE

Radical liberalism rejects retributive and deterrent punishment and the institution of incarceration.[1] But it certainly leaves room for *internal* criticism of institutions and practices that don't reflect the kind of radical challenge to the existing system of criminal justice radical liberals would prefer to advance.

Thus, while I view the current practice of imprisonment with skepticism, I believe it is also perfectly reasonable to argue that, as long as this institution persists, if the option of releasing incarcerated persons on parole is to be made available, as it should be, parole decisions should not be based in any way on victim impact statements. That they should not be is an important implication of the Principle of Fairness—in a legal context, of *due process*. In addition, because such statements are more often than not used to enhance sentences, even if they might be used in some cases to reduce them, excluding them from consideration is also a reflection of the liberal concern (itself an implication of the Principle of Fairness) to make legal proceedings more *humane*—to ensure that they pose as little risk as possible to the flourishing of those in the custody of the legal system. Avoiding harsh sentences is a way of increasing the likelihood that people will be able to participate in varied opportunities for flourishing and fulfillment.

The institution of parole permits the conditional release of an incarcerated offender before the completion of her sentence.[2] It subjects her to the supervision of the justice system between the time of her release and the conclusion of her sentence, with the understanding that she may be returned to prison if she violates the conditions of her parole. Rehabilitation is arguably the parole system's primary

[1] *See* GARY CHARTIER, ANARCHY AND LEGAL ORDER: LAW AND POLITICS FOR A STATELESS SOCIETY 263–302 (2013).

[2] On the parole system, *see* JOAN PETERSILIA, REFORMING PROBATION AND PAROLE IN THE 21ST CENTURY (2001); HOWARD ABADINSKY, PROBATION AND PAROLE: CORRECTIONS IN THE COMMUNITY (13th ed., 2017); TODD R. CLEAR & HARRY R. DAMMER, THE OFFENDER IN THE COMMUNITY (2000); NEIL P. COHEN, THE LAW OF PROBATION AND PAROLE (2d ed., 1999); LEANNE FIFTAL ALARID, COMMUNITY-BASED CORRECTIONS (12th ed., 2018). Parole differs from probation: probation serves as an alternative to incarceration; by contrast, parole reduces an offender's time in prison while leaving her in the custody of the justice system after release. On probation, see Joan Petersilia, *Probation in the United States*, 22 CRIME & JUST. 149 (1997).

purpose.[3] Once relatively popular among penologists,[4] the institution of parole has come under increasing attack as ineffective and overly lenient,[5] and opportunities for parole have been significantly reduced.[6]

The decision to grant a prisoner's application for parole is characteristically affected by factors including the time the prisoner has already spent in prison, her behavior while incarcerated, and any limits imposed by law.[7] Also relevant in many American jurisdictions are the perspectives of victims, who play increasingly important roles because of the activism of the "victims' rights" movement.[8] In the vast majority of states, the victim[9] is entitled "to be heard regarding parole decision making—in writing, orally, or both,"[10] and in 1997 members of the United States Congress discussed a proposed constitutional amendment guaranteeing this right at

3 For a judicial account of the parole system's function, *see, e.g., In re Lee*, 177 Cal. 690, 692–93 (1918) ("It is generally recognized by the courts and by modern penologists that the purpose of the indeterminate sentence law, like other modern laws in relation to the administration of the criminal law, is to mitigate the punishment which would otherwise be imposed upon the offender. These laws place emphasis upon the reformation of the offender. They seek to make the punishment fit the criminal rather than the crime. They endeavor to put before the prisoner great incentive to well-doing in order that his will to do well should be strengthened and confirmed by the habit of well-doing. Instead of trying to break the will of the offender and make him submissive, the purpose is to strengthen his will to do right and lessen his temptation to do wrong."). *Cf.* Morrissey v. Brewer, 408 U.S. 471, 482 (1972): "The parolee has been released from prison based on an evaluation that he shows reasonable promise of being able to return to society and function as a responsible, self-reliant person."

4 *See, e.g.*, DAVID J. ROTHMAN, CONSCIENCE AND CONVENIENCE: THE ASYLUM AND ITS ALTERNATIVES IN PROGRESSIVE AMERICA (1980); Walter J. Dickey, *Sentencing, Parole, and Community Supervision, in* DISCRETION IN CRIMINAL JUSTICE: THE TENSION BETWEEN INDIVIDUALIZATION AND UNIFORMITY 135 (Lloyd E. Ohlin & Frank J. Remington eds., 1993).

5 *See* Joan Petersilia, *Parole and Prisoner Reentry in the United States*, 26 CRIME & JUST. 479, 479–83, 492–95 (1999); Mistretta v. United States, 488 U.S. 361, 363 (1989); FRANCIS A. ALLEN, THE DECLINE OF THE REHABILITATIVE IDEAL 6–7 (1981); JOHN O. SMYKLA, PROBATION AND PAROLE: CRIME CONTROL IN THE COMMUNITY (1984).

6 *See* Petersilia, *supra* note 5, at 495–97.

7 *See* COHEN, *supra* note 2; Martha Worner, Pennsylvania Board of Probation and Parole v. Scott: *The Taking of a Parolee's Fourth Amendment Right to Privacy*, 51 BAYLOR L. REV. 1115, 1121 (1999).

8 *See* Lynne Henderson, *Revisiting Victim's Rights*, 1999 UTAH L. REV. 383 (1999); Lynne Henderson, *The Wrongs of Victim's Rights*, 37 STAN. L. REV. 937 (1985).

9 I assume throughout for simplicity's sake that a crime involves only one victim and one offender. A parole system will face additional difficulties when it attempts to take victim testimony into account in a case in which there are multiple victims with conflicting perspectives or preferences.

10 Peggy M. Tobolowsky, *Victim Participation in the Criminal Justice Process: Fifteen Years After the President's Task Force on Victims of Crime*, 25 N.E. J. CRIM. & CIV. CON. 21, 91 (1999) (footnote omitted). *Cf.* Frances P. Bernat *et al.*, *Victim Impact Laws and the Parole Process in the United States: Balancing Victim and Inmate Rights and Interests*, 3 INT'L REV. VICTIMOLOGY 121 (1994); Mark W. May, *Victims' Rights and the Parole Hearing*, 15 J. CONTEMP. L. 71 (1989).

According to Tobolowsky, states with explicit guarantees of opportunities for victim input into parole decisions include Arizona, Arkansas, Delaware, Idaho, Massachusetts, Nebraska, Rhode Island, and Virginia; *see* Ariz. Const. art. II, §2.1; Ark. Code Ann. §16-93-206 (Michie Supp. 1997); Del. Code Ann. tit. 11, §§4350, 9416 (1995); Idaho Const. art. I, 22; Mass. Ann. Laws ch. 127, §133A (Law. Coop. 1989 & Supp. 1997); Neb. Const. art. I, §28; R.I. Gen. Laws §12–28-6 (1994); and Va. Code Ann. §53.1–155 (Michie Supp. 1997). Tobolowsky (the source of many of the specifics to which I allude here, and whom I thank for these references) notes that, in Oklahoma, a victim who has not been made aware of

the federal level.[11] Statements by victims appear to be quite influential on parole decision-makers, and appear significantly to reduce the likelihood that offenders will be paroled.[12]

We might justifiably be troubled by the influence of victims on parole decisions for a variety of reasons. Whether they occur in the context of the sentencing process or in the setting of the parole review process, victim impact statements, the most common media of victim input, can—troublingly—"legitimate popular notions of revenge, victimhood, and pain."[13] The use of confidential protest letters in hearings reviewing parole applications from women imprisoned for killing their batterers may be troubling on Equal Protection grounds.[14] But I wish here to focus on another fundamental problem: *the use of such statements in parole decisions appears largely pointless on most plausible theories of criminal justice*.[15] Alternative theoretical accounts of the criminal law often yield conflicting results.[16] In this case, however, there is significant overlap in the conclusions to which a variety of alternative theoretical positions lead.

My procedure in what follows is simple. I successively elaborate rehabilitationist and incapacitationist (Part II), retributivist (Part III), correctivist (Part IV), and consequentialist (Part V) accounts of incarceration and parole.[17] I suggest that each school of thought I consider (though not every strand within each school)

a parole hearing for an offender responsible for harming her can ask that a parole board reassess a decision made at such a hearing; *see* Okla. Stat. Ann. tit. 57, § 332.2 (West Supp. 1998).

11 See Robert P. Mosteller, *Victims' Rights and the United States Constitution: An Effort to Recast the Battle in Criminal Litigation*, 85 Geo. L.J. 1691, 1695–96, 1714 (1997).

12 Edwin Villmoare & Virginia V. Neto (U. S. Dep't of Justice), Victim Appearances at Sentencing Hearings Under the California Victims' Bill of Rights 43 (1987); William H. Parsonage *et al.*, *Victim Impact Testimony and Pennsylvania's Parole Decision Making Process: A Pilot Study*, 3 Crim. Just. Pol'y Rev. 187, 194 (1992).

13 Elizabeth E. Joh, *Narrating Pain: The Problem with Victim Impact Statements*, 10 S. Cal. Interdis. L. J. 17, 18 (2000).

14 Jennifer S. Bales, *Equal Protection and the Use of Protest Letters in Parole Proceedings: A Particular Dilemma for Battered Women Inmates*, 27 Seton Hall L. Rev. 33 (1996).

15 *Cf.* Michael S. Moore, *Victims and Retribution: A Reply to Professor Fletcher*, 3 Buff. Crim. L. Rev. 65, 65–66 (1999): "[T]he role of the victim of crime . . . is to be ascertained by thinking through the theory of punishment. One's theory of punishment has to make room for victims if they are going to have some role that is justified in the criminal process."

16 Paul H. Robinson, *Criminal Law Scholarship: Three Illusions*, 2 Theoretical Inq. L. 287 (2001), maintains that these theories are often cited by decision-makers in ways that leave their interrelationships unclear and suggest that less principled reasons are actually responsible for the decisions of legislators and judges. As Robinson puts it: "The fact is, the various purposes listed frequently conflict with one another. When they do, the decisionmaker is free to select that purpose that justifies the result he or she prefers for whatever reason, even an inappropriate one. The result is a system that has the appearance of being based upon principle, a system in which decisionmakers can give sound reasons for their decisions, but that allows them uncontrolled and undisclosed discretion." *Id.* at 294. The point to make here, then, is that there seems to be significant overlap in the conclusions to which alternative theories of criminal justice appear to point with respect to the role of victim testimony.

17 I do not intend to suggest that no other position is conceivable. In particular, there is no discussion here of restorative justice. This is because there is no particular reason why a proponent of restorative justice should, as such, favor incarceration at all. Proponents of restorative justice might well favor

would have reason to regard parole as appropriate. Allowing victim input to influence parole decisions, however, appears largely pointless from the perspective of almost all of the approaches I examine.

There might be some limited reason for allowing victim impact testimony to be taken into account on consequentialist grounds, and one variety of correctivism, *subjective correctivism*, might offer strong support for the consideration of such testimony. The consequentialist reasons for allowing victim testimony to make a difference in parole decisions don't seem especially strong even if one grants the reasonableness of consequentialism. And subjective correctivism is an unattractive basis for a system of criminal justice. It seems reasonably clear, then, that, absent some alternative justification, victim testimony should not be allowed to influence parole decisions (Part VI).

II. REHABILITATION AND INCAPACITATION

For a rehabilitation theorist, imprisoning an offender will likely serve two functions.[18] First, prison will provide a controlled environment in which representatives

incarceration as a means of incapacitating habitually dangerous offenders. Perhaps they might justify incarceration on other grounds. But it is not clear that their perspective on parole will differentiate them from other theorists for whom incarceration should play a role in the criminal justice system and the process of crime control.

On restorative justice, *see, e.g.*, John Braithwaite, *Restorative Justice and Social Justice*, 63 SASK. L. REV. 185 (2000); John Braithwaite, *Restorative Justice: Assessing Optimistic and Pessimistic Accounts*, 25 CRIME & JUST. 1 (1999); Daniel W. Van Ness & Pat Nolan, *Legislating for Restorative Justice*, 10 REGENT U.L. REV. 53 (1998); Gretchen Ulrich, *Widening The Circle: Adapting Traditional Indian Dispute Resolution Methods to Implement Alternative Dispute Resolution and Restorative Justice in Modern Communities*, 20 HAMLINE J. PUB. L. & POL'Y 419 (1999); Frederick W. Gay, *Restorative Justice and the Prosecutor*, 27 FORDHAM URB. L.J. 1651 (2000); Robert F. Schopp, *Integrating Restorative Justice and Therapeutic Jurisprudence*, 67 REV. JUR. U.P.R. 665 (1998); Walter C. Long, *Karla Faye Tucker: A Case for Restorative Justice*, 27 AM. J. CRIM. L. 117 (1999); Joan W. Howarth, *Toward the Restorative Constitution: A Restorative Justice Critique of Anti-Gang Public Nuisance Injunctions*, 27 HASTINGS CONST. L.Q. 717 (2000); Mary Ann Yeats, *"Three Strikes" and Restorative Justice: Dealing with Young Repeat Burglars in Western Australia*, 8 CRIM. L.F. 369 (1997); William Haft, *More Than Zero: The Cost of Zero Tolerance and the Case for Restorative Justice in Schools*, 77 DENV. U.L. REV. 795 (2000); Robert D. Enright & Bruce A. Kittle, *Forgiveness in Psychology and Law: The Meeting of Moral Development and Restorative Justice*, 27 FORDHAM URB. L.J. 1621 (2000); Willie McCarney, *Restorative Justice: An International Perspective*, 3 J. CENTER CHILDREN & CTS. 3 (2001); Charles W. Colson, *Truth, Justice, Peace: The Foundations of Restorative Justice*, 10 REGENT U.L. REV. 1 (1998); Robert Yazzie, *"Hozho Nahasdlii"—We Are Now in Good Relations: Navajo Restorative Justice*, 9 ST. THOMAS L. REV. 117 (1996); Jennifer J. Llewellyn & Robert Howse, Institutions for Restorative Justice: The South African Truth and Reconciliation Commission, 49 U. Toronto L.J. 355 (1999); Lawrence W. Sherman, *Domestic Violence and Restorative Justice: Answering Key Questions*, 8 VA. J. SOC. POL'Y & L. 263 (2000).

18 Given the assumptions that undergird the contemporary criminal justice system, rehabilitative approaches deserve renewed attention. On the general issues, *see* Edward L. Rubin, *The Inevitability of Rehabilitation*, 19 LAW & INEQ. J. 343 (2001). On the empirical question of rehabilitation's effectiveness, *see, e.g.*, ANN CHIH LIN, REFORM IN THE MAKING: THE IMPLEMENTATION OF SOCIAL POLICY IN PRISON 39–41, 103–108 (2000); STAN STOJKOVIC & RICK LOVELL, CORRECTIONS: AN

of the public can help the offender develop a satisfactory character. Second, the shock and unpleasantness of imprisonment will serve as a spur to self-examination and growth. The memory of prison's awfulness and the desire to avoid future imprisonment can help a prisoner to develop appropriate habits. It is not just that, as the specific deterrence theorist supposes, the prisoner will seek to avoid extrinsic consequences. Rather, she can come to choose and affirm for their own sakes habits developed initially to avoid discomfort. A parole system fits naturally within a rehabilitative framework, but allowing victims to influence parole decisions does not.

For the rehabilitationist, the prime function of incarceration is that it provides a setting in which the rehabilitative process can be effectively completed. For the incapacitationist, by contrast, it serves first to protect the members of the public from the harms to which the offender might be thought likely to subject them. The incapacitationist's focus on future dangerousness is the reflex of the rehabilitationist's focus on character development. Both are likely to favor confining the offender for the same period—until she is prepared to be reintegrated safely into society.

A. *Rehabilitation and Parole*

In a penal system designed to foster rehabilitation, parole will serve multiple functions. The possibility of parole will serve as an extrinsic motivator for habits the rehabilitation theorist hopes the prospective parolee will internalize. And it will serve to mark the point at which the justice system concludes, tentatively, that an offender can no longer benefit from the educational environment putatively provided by prison. Once the rehabilitative function of imprisonment has been served, the pure rehabilitation theorist will see no reason, at least in principle, for further incarceration. She may recognize, however, that judgments about the extent of an offender's rehabilitation are highly fallible. She may therefore conclude that it is

INTRODUCTION 215–17 (2d ed. 1997); EFFECTIVE CORRECTIONAL TREATMENT (Robert Ross & Paul Gendreau eds., 1980); Francis T. Cullen & Paul Gendreau, *The Effectiveness of Correctional Rehabilitation: Reconsidering the 'Nothing Works' Debate*, *in* THE AMERICAN PRISON: ISSUES IN RESEARCH AND POLICY 23 (Lynne Goodstein & Doris Layton MacKenzie eds., 1989); Paul Gendreau, *The Principles of Effective Intervention with Offenders*, *in* CHOOSING CORRECTIONAL OPTIONS THAT WORK 17 (Alan T. Harland ed., 1996); Ted Palmer, *Programmatic and Nonprogrammatic Aspects of Successful Intervention: New Directions for Research*, 41 CRIME & DELINQUENCY 100 (1995); Ted Palmer, *The Effectiveness of Intervention: Recent Trends and Current Issues*, 37 CRIME & DELINQ. 330 (1991); D. A. Andrews et al., *Does Correctional Treatment Work? A Clinically Relevant and Psychologically Informed Meta-Analysis*, 28 CRIMINOLOGY 369 (1990); Paul Gendreau & Robert R. Ross, *Revivification of Rehabilitation: Evidence from the 1980's*, 4 JUST. Q. 349 (1987); Robert Martinson, *New Findings, New Views: A Note of Caution Regarding Sentencing Reform*, 7 HOFSTRA L. REV. 243, 250 (1979) (thanks to Rubin for these references). Despite the good intentions underlying these views, I think we should be skeptical about them, primarily because they afford too much power to those responsible for rehabilitating others. *See, e.g.*, C. S. Lewis, *The Humanitarian Theory of Punishment*, 6 RES JUDICATÆ 224 (1953); CHARTIER, ANARCHY, *supra* note 1, at 298–99.

more reasonable to release the offender on parole, with the possibility of renewed confinement, than to assume unquestioningly that the offender has been successfully rehabilitated and has no further need of any kind for the supervision of the justice system. A parolee can continue to benefit from the support offered and the discipline imposed by the parole system as she makes the transition to ordinary life.

The only relevant difference between rehabilitationist and incapacitationist approaches to parole may be that the rehabilitationist assumes that, at least in many cases, positive character change is possible and, indeed, likely, while the incapacitationist need make no such assumption. Proponents of the two approaches may sometimes differ, then, with respect to the question whether parole is likely to be granted; the incapacitationist might suppose, in principle, that some offenders, even those incarcerated for relatively minor crimes, might be too likely to injure others again to be safely released (though of course this risk might be worth taking if the offender is anticipated only to commit a minor crime after release). But, despite the differing assumptions rehabilitationists and incapacitationists might make about human nature, and so about the *appropriateness* of granting parole in particular cases, they will have the same general view of the *function* of parole in general.

B. *Rehabilitation, Incapacitation, and Victim Testimony*

The rehabilitationist will see victim testimony as relevant to parole decisions to the extent that it enables decision-makers to assess offenders' progress toward rehabilitation. The incapacitationist will see it as relevant to the extent that it helps decision-makers assess offenders' future dangerousness. Ordinarily, then, such evidence will be useful only if the victim is able to offer insights into the offender's character and state of mind at the time she is considered for parole. Except where she has had significant contact with the offender after confinement, the victim will have nothing of value to contribute to a parole decision.

Might information that an offender's character was especially bad at the time of the offense suggest that the change in character needed to justify release was substantial? And might this not be relevant because, given the magnitude of the needed change, the parole board could justifiably require more evidence that it had taken place than in a case where the offender didn't have far to go to meet the bar?[19]

The rehabilitationist might not think these considerations provided decisive reason for victim testimony to be be taken into account. On grounds of fairness, she might well think that subjecting some offenders to higher standards than others was objectionable. She might doubt that knowing about the offender's character at the time of the offense would facilitate the formation of an accurate judgment regarding the offender's current character. She might think, rather, that it made the most sense to trust those providing evidence regarding an offender's current

[19] Thanks to the estimable David Gordon for raising this question.

behavior and apparent character (who would not themselves necessarily know what the offender's character at the time of the offense was). I am doubtful that this issue would appropriately be reached, in any case. The possibility that the victim could offer evidence related to character change on an offender's part would offer little reason for a rehabilitationist (much less an incapacitationist) to give special weight to victim testimony, for two reasons.

(*i*) Victim testimony about this topic will be superfluous, and, indeed, its inclusion may actually reduce the likely accuracy of parole decisions. The original trial record, which will be available to parole decision-makers, should adequately document the offender's state of mind at the time of the offense. And the victim's recollection at the time of the parole hearing is likely to be of limited value, given not only the passage of time but also the impact of the victim's own subsequent thoughts and feelings and the behavior of others on the victim's memories. This is especially troubling given the absence of cross-examination.

(*ii*) The proffered argument for the inclusion of victim testimony misunderstands the rehabilitationist's position. The rehabilitationist is not typically interested, per se, in the relative moral progress of the offender. The function of parole is not to reward the offender's effort or self-discipline. Instead, it is to allow a prisoner to regain her freedom once she has met an *appropriate minimum standard* of character development. The rehabilitationist is interested in helping the offender reach a baseline level of responsibility, not in using confinement as an opportunity paternalistically to supervise her progress toward moral excellence. Information about the offender's character at the time of her offense may prompt sympathy or admiration, but it will not enable a decision-maker to determine whether or not the offender has been rehabilitated successfully or whether she still needs to be incapacitated to protect the public. In addition, knowledge of the offender's behavior at the time of the crime won't typically provide information about her character, which would require more than the snapshot the victim will often be able to put on display.

In most cases, victim testimony will offer limited insight into the rehabilitation and future dangerousness of an incarcerated offender. As a general rule, therefore, rehabilitationists and incapacitationists will have no good reason to regard such testimony as relevant to parole decisions.

III. RETRIBUTION

Retributivism is the thesis that wrongdoers are duty bound to suffer for their wrongs.[20] Retributivists don't agree about the appropriate extent and nature of

[20] *See* Michael S. Moore, Prima Facie *Moral Culpability*, 76 B.U.L. Rev. 319, 330 (1996). There has been a remarkable resurgence of enthusiasm for retributive conceptions of criminal justice in American courts and legislatures during the last three decades. For a detailed critical analysis of the

offenders' just suffering.[21] And there is no consensus among retributivists about the precise justification for retribution,[22] though they commonly maintain that retribution restores a just order of things that an offender has in some way disrupted. But there is a general consensus that, at least in the context of criminal law, the experience of punishment by the offender *constitutes* the good the criminal law seeks to effect, rather than contributing instrumentally to its achievement. And there is a similar consensus that liability to punishment is, at least ordinarily, a function of moral culpability and that the magnitude of punishment should vary with the magnitude of moral wrongness.

A sensible retributivism will acknowledge that there is no means of commensurating offenses and punishments, so that a given punishment cannot be identified as *the* suitable response to a given offense.[23] But there will be for at least one sort of retributivist a natural fit between the punishment of imprisonment and almost any conceivable crime. For the fundamental wrongness of a crime, that which makes it criminal, may be seen as an unjust self-assertion to which an excessive claim and exercise of personal liberty are essential. Because crime involves asserting and acting with too much freedom, the restriction of freedom intrinsic to incarceration may be seen as restoring the balance of justice disrupted by criminal conduct.[24] Confinement need not be the only punishment a retributivist deems appropriate, but it may well occupy a central place in her penal armamentarium.

After elaborating a likely retributivist account of parole, I will argue that retributivists have no reason to allow victim testimony to influence parole decisions. Both retributivists concerned with offenders' acts and retributivists concerned with offenders' characters will regard victims as unlikely to be able to contribute meaningfully to parole decisions.

ways in which judicial activism led to a restoration of retribution as a legitimate central purpose of the justice system, *see* Michele Cotton's intriguing essay, *Back with a Vengeance: The Resilience of Retribution as an Articulated Purpose of Criminal Punishment*, 37 AM. CRIM. L. REV. 1313. For a provocative, if not always persuasive, argument that retributivism shares many of the faults its proponents attribute to consequentialism, *see* Russell L. Christopher, *Deterring Retributivism: The Injustice of 'Just' Punishment*, 96 NW. U.L. REV. 843 (2002).

21 I use the words "suffer" and "suffering" for convenience here. But I realize that these words might suggest that retributivists believe offenders should suffer subjective distress. However, the kind of suffering in view here need not involve such distress, which will be neither necessary nor sufficient from a retributivist point of view. Indeed, John Finnis, *Retribution: Punishment's Formative Aim*, 44 AM. J. JURIS. 91, 97 (1999), passionately rejects the claim that "the essence of punishment is the infliction of pain."

22 For alternatives, *see, e.g.*, Jeffrie G. Murphy, *Moral Epistemology, the Retributive Emotions, and the "Clumsy Moral Philosophy" of Jesus Christ, in* THE PASSIONS OF LAW 149, 153 (Susan A. Bandes ed., 1999).

23 *See* Finnis, *Retribution*, *supra* note 21, at 103.

24 *Cf.* Finnis, *Retribution*, *supra* note 21, at 101: "The precise benefit or advantage whose fair distribution it is the primary and shaping purpose of punishment to uphold is the advantage of freedom, in one's choosing and acting, from external constraints including the constraints appropriately imposed by laws made for the common good."

A. *Retribution and Parole*

Retributive punishment may be concerned with the acts or with the characters of offenders. If the focus is on acts, a penal sanction will be justified to the extent that it appropriately rights the wrong done by an individual offense. Punishment will be fitting if it matches the criminal act committed by the offender. Presuming a punishment was set fittingly in the first place, it is unclear that the act-retributivist has any reason to endorse the granting of parole—in effect, a mid-course change in sentence. If a term of incarceration was appropriately determined in the first place, then it seems to follow that subsequently reducing it by granting parole would be unjust from a retributive perspective.

It won't do to note that a term of incarceration might have been *defined* in advance as variable in virtue of a possible grant of parole. An act-retributivist will have no reason to define a term of incarceration as variable in this way. What might cause the term to vary? The discovery of new information regarding the original offense might have this effect, but an adjustment on the basis of such information would reflect a reassessment of the justice of the initial sentence, not a response to ongoing good behavior. Paroling an incarcerated offender is a response to observed features of the offender's character and behavior during the time she is incarcerated, and these are simply irrelevant from the perspective of the strict act-retributivist.

To be sure, the act-retributivist can, as I have already noted, emphasize that the sentencing authority possesses a significant measure of freedom in *determining* a sentence and might therefore, arguendo, be free during a prisoner's term of confinement to alter her punishment. But the sentencing authority will be free to do this, on act-retributivist grounds, only if it determines that the original punishment was not, in fact, a just response to the conduct that led to the offender's incarceration. A strict act-retributivist will therefore have no rational basis for endorsing a parole system at all and will not, therefore, face the question of the role of victim testimony in parole decisions in the first place.

For a character-retributivist,[25] what merits retributive punishment (or doesn't, as the case may be) is the offender's character. Unlike an act-retributivist, a character-retributivist may well have some reason to support the institution of parole. Characters change over time. People grow. An offender's character at the time she

[25] I believe Jeffrie Murphy deserves credit for introducing the term "character retributivism" into discussions of criminal justice. *See, e.g.*, JEFFRIE G. MURPHY, GETTING EVEN: FORGIVENESS AND ITS LIMITS 43 (2003).

Character-retributivism is not, of course, the only theory of criminal justice to which character is central. For a good example of a contemporary Aristotelian approach, see Kyron Huigens, *The Dead End of Deterrence, and Beyond*, 41 WM. & MARY L. REV. 943 (2000). My sense is that other character-focused theories of criminal justice would need to reach roughly the same conclusions about victim involvement in the parole decision-making process as character-retributivists. For doubts about approaches that see character as a basis for determining criminal guilt, *see* Benjamin B. Sendor, *The Relevance of Conduct and Character to Guilt and Punishment*, 10 N.D. J. L. ETHICS & PUB POL'Y 99 (1996).

commits a crime may be such that she merits a certain sentence, but to impose the same sentence on her at a later time, when her character is significantly different, may violate the retributive norm of respect for the retributivist principles of proportionality and respect for desert.[26] For instance, then, on character-retributivist grounds, "[t]he repentant person has a better character than the unrepentant person, and thus the repentant person ... simply deserves less punishment than the unrepentant person."[27] Granting the option of parole may thus be an appropriate expression of character-retributivism.[28]

B. *Retribution and Victim Testimony*

Retributivism makes wrongs done to victims central in the determination of appropriate punishment. But retributive theorists agree that victims have no appropriate role in sentencing. Even the victim-oriented retributivism of George Fletcher allows no space for victim involvement in sentencing, and so, presumably, parole.[29] Other retributivists, like Michael Moore and John Finnis, are, if anything, more unequivocal in their rejection of a specific role for victims in sentencing.[30] From a characteristically retributivist perspective, Moore maintains, an offender's "duty to suffer ... is not linked primarily to the wrong done to some victim in the actual world."[31] Thus, "retributive justice does not merely demand that victims of wrongdoers be given *the right to make* their offenders suffer; rather, retributive justice demands that culpable wrongdoers *suffer*, irrespective of whether or not those they wrong wish it."[32] Because "doing justice is the essence of retributive punishment[,] ... victims have neither any moral right nor expertise to say how our legal institutions should achieve such justice."[33] Similarly, for Finnis, punishment "cannot rightly be imposed on behalf of the victim as such, but only on behalf of the community of citizens willing to abide by the law," since on Finnis's view the function of punishment is precisely to re-establish justice among citizens by eliminating the effects of the offender's unjust self-assertion. Thus, according to Finnis, "[a]ny practice of giving victims some role

26 For a parallel argument with respect to the commutation of capital sentences on character-retributivist grounds, see B. Douglas Robbins, *Resurrection from a Death Sentence: Why Capital Sentences Should be Commuted Upon the Occasion of an Authentic Ethical Transformation*, 149 U. PA. L. REV. 1115 (2001).

27 MURPHY, GETTING EVEN, *supra* note 25, at 50; *cf.* Robbins, *Resurrection*, *supra* note 26, at 1162–64.

28 Of course, by the same token, it seems as if the significant degradation of an offender's character during incarceration should perhaps incline a character-retributivist to favor the extension of her term of confinement. This possibility raises questions beyond the scope of this Chapter.

29 George P. Fletcher, *The Place of the Victim in the Theory of Retribution*, 3 BUFF. CRIM. L. REV. 51, 52 (1999).

30 As Moore puts it bluntly, ". . . I think victims should and must be ignored if you are claiming to be doing retributive theory." Moore, *Victims*, *supra* note 15, at 67.

31 Moore, *Culpability*, *supra* note 20, at 330.

32 Moore, *Victims*, *supra* note 15, at 78 (my italics).

33 *Id.* at 88.

in criminal proceedings other than as witnesses, amongst other witnesses, to the fact of the offense must be highly questionable."[34]

If there is no persuasive reason for a retributivist to involve victims in the sentencing process, there will, a fortiori, be no such reason to involve them in the review of parole applications. The same basic reasons offered by retributivists for excluding victims from the sentencing process—the distinction between retributive punishment and revenge, the irrelevance of victim attitudes once the facts of the case have been determined, the focus of retribution on the public rather than on the individual victim—will all militate against giving victim testimony any weight in parole decisions.

The one exception, from the perspective of the character-retributivist, will be in the rare case in which a victim possesses independent evidence regarding the development of an offender's character after incarceration. Perhaps, as a result of ongoing post-incarceration contact with the offender, the victim might sometimes be in a position to testify to the state of the offender's character at the time she applies for parole. But this kind of testimony would be worth including whatever its source; its relevance wouldn't depend on its being provided *by a victim*.

Act-retributivists will likely regard the institution of parole with suspicion, as inherently anti-retributive. Character-retributivists will have reason to regard parole as appropriate. But retributivists of all stripes, even those who wish to enhance the role of victims in the criminal justice system, adhere to a theoretical position that leaves no place for an independent role for victims in the process of determining appropriate criminal sentences. Victim impact testimony will similarly be irrelevant in most cases to the adjudication of requests for parole. It will be unable to provide new insight into the offender's culpability at the time of the crime or crimes responsible for her incarceration—the only concern of the act-retributivist.[35] And it will be unlikely to provide useful information regarding the development of the offender's character after incarceration. The retributivist will not, therefore, see testimony from the victim qua victim as relevant or appropriately considered in the context of the parole process.

IV. CORRECTION

Corrective justice is ordinarily thought to provide norms especially for tort and contract law. The focus here is on the responsibility to provide compensation for harms. But some theorists disposed to make the interests of victims central to the

[34] Finnis, *Retribution*, *supra* note 21, at 102–3.

[35] Some scholars who defend the value of victim-impact statements maintain that they provide additional information regarding crimes not otherwise available to parole decision-makers, including insights into the specific consequences of crimes for victims; *see* Bernat *et al.*, *supra* note 10, at 134–35. But the fact that such statements have not been tested at trial militates strongly against their admissibility.

processes of criminal justice have attempted to adopt corrective justice models for use in a criminal law context.[36] Such theorists reject the common view of crimes as primarily directed against the state or the body politic and instead focus on the actual harm to the victim.[37] From their perspective, the criminal law should entitle the victim to compensation for any wrong she has suffered. For some proponents of corrective justice approaches to criminal law, this will mean that victims should receive monetary restitution of some kind—or, perhaps, some kind of appropriate nonmonetary compensation. From their perspective, measures taken to correct an injustice must conform to an objective standard. Call proponents of this perspective *objective correctivists*. On an alternative view—call it *subjective correctivism*—what corrects the injustice done by a criminal act is being given the *right* to determine what consequences should befall the offender. It is also possible, presumably, to imagine a hybrid variety: *mixed correctivism*. For the mixed correctivist, objective standards will determine the maximum to which the victim is entitled from the offender. The hybrid correctivist will maintain, however, that if the victim doesn't *want* this maximum, it would be cruel and inefficient for the justice system to require it of the offender.

I argue in this section that correctivists of all stripes can legitimately endorse a parole system. But objective and mixed correctivists will not regard victim testimony as a useful contributor to parole decisions unless they regard the harms for which the criminal justice system is to provide a sort of restitution as capable of being reassessed after trial. Subjective correctivists will regard victims as appropriately determining whether incarcerated offenders should be paroled, but, I will argue, subjective correctivism has little to recommend it as a theory of criminal justice.

36 *See, e.g.*, Jeffrie G. Murphy, *Getting Even: The Role of the Victim*, *in* RETRIBUTION RECONSIDERED: MORE ESSAYS IN THE PHILOSOPHY OF LAW 61 (1992) For another version of correctivism, arguably more at home in the context of restorative justice, *see* RANDY E. BARNETT, THE STRUCTURE OF LIBERTY: JUSTICE AND THE RULE OF LAW 158–60, 177–85 (2d ed., 2014); Randy E. Barnett, *The Justice of Restitution*, 25 AM. J. JURIS. 117 (1980); Randy E. Barnett, *Restitution: A New Paradigm of Criminal Justice*, 87 ETHICS 279 (1977). The correctivist position described in this section is not intended to be understood as identical with that of Murphy or any other scholar but as an elaboration of a tendency in criminal law theory. On the general structure of this sort of approach, *cf.* Moore, *Victims*, *supra* note 15, at 75–76.

37 Moore asks of Fletcher's victim-oriented retributivism a question he would presumably want to ask of correctivism as well: "Can such an engine of victim vengeance still be retributivism? It doesn't look retributive; it looks compensatory to the victims. Punishment in such a scheme turns on the victims deciding what they want, not on what justice demands." Moore, *Victims*, *supra* note 15, at 76. But it is not clear that there is any necessary link between the idea of compensation and the idea of victim choice. Presumably it would be just as possible (or impossible) to determine the compensation to which a victim was objectively entitled as it would be to determine the demands of abstract justice apart from the issue of victim entitlement. We do not, after all, in tort law—the natural home of corrective justice—give victims the right to determine what counts as appropriate compensation; we assume that it will be possible to identify what sort of compensation is reasonably appropriate using objective standards.

A. Correction and Parole

Different varieties of correctivism will offer different accounts of the function of imprisonment, and thus of a parole system.[38] Correctivists may sometimes see imprisonment as a means by which a prisoner can make amends to the victim, offering her own suffering as a kind of restitution to the victim. For the objective correctivist, imprisonment will be selected by a court as a suitable means of correcting the injustice created by an offender's wrongful act, of offering restitution of this (odd) sort to the victim (perhaps from among a portfolio of punitive options). Given the fittingness of this determination, it might seem as if the objective correctivist, like the act-retributivist, would have no basis for regarding a parole system as appropriate. But, in fact, such a system might be appropriate for more than one reason on correctivist grounds.

The judgment that a given sentence is appropriately restitutive might be predicated on assumptions about a prisoner's likely suffering during incarceration that turned out to be inaccurate. If the prisoner suffered more than anticipated, a correctivist might conclude that she had provided the necessary sort of compensation to her victim more rapidly than had originally been projected and therefore that she deserved early release on this basis alone. Moral reformation might bespeak inner pain that might add to the pain a correctivist would think it appropriate to take into account.[39] And the sheer fact of moral transformation, whether or not accompanied by pain, might be seen as a compensatory offering to the victim of which a correctivist decision-maker should take account. For an objective correctivist, then, parole would be appropriate when an incarcerated offender suffered more or when her character changed more than anticipated during incarceration.[40]

For a subjective correctivist, like her objective counterpart, there need be no particular preference for incarceration over other corrective mechanisms. But a

38 Correctivists could presumably endorse the equivalent of parole—a tentative reduction in sentence, conditioned on good behavior and subject to revocation—in the case of a sentence other than incarceration. Suppose a court-imposed monetary restitution as a sentence. There might be circumstances under which the requirement to make restitutionary payments was temporarily suspended for one reason or another or in which the amount of restitution was reduced. Most, at any rate, of what I say here would be relevant to correctivist accounts of parole equivalents for persons serving non-carceral sentences.

39 *Cf.* Robbins, *Resurrection*, *supra* note 26, at 1162–64 (discussing ways in which remorse and penance make punishment less necessary). According to Robbins, "Punishment of the body, in a retributive scheme, is prorated by the wrongdoer's self-imposed punishment of the mind." *Id.* at 1162. The same point could presumably be made in correctivist terms.

40 Perhaps, from an objective correctivist standpoint, a variety of punishment options will be available in a given case, with none more apt as a means of compensating the victim than any other. In this case, a decision-maker might be free to alter the punishment imposed on an offender. But if, on correctivist grounds, it turns out to be appropriate for a decision-maker to release an offender earlier than expected on the theory that a shorter sentence was as adequately compensatory as the one originally imposed, this shouldn't be seen as a judgment about the appropriateness of *parole*, but rather about the rightness of making a new assessment of the offender's conduct and the punishment rightly flowing from it.

victim might opt for imprisonment as the offender's punishment. On a subjective correctivist view, the function of parole in such a case will be to allow the actuation of the victim's wishes as they are refined during the period of the offender's incarceration. On a mixed correctivist account of criminal justice, the victim could presumably opt at trial for any sentence (whether of imprisonment or of any other sort of acceptable punishment) within the relevant limits. But at a parole hearing she could then opt to reduce the sentence further at her sole discretion. For mixed correctivism, the purpose of parole would be to effect the victim's wishes as they take shape while the offender is confined, but only within the upper limits set by an objective standard of justice.

B. *Correctivism, Victims, and Parole*

Objective, subjective, and mixed correctivists will obviously differ about the relevance of victim testimony to parole decisions. An objective correctivist will regard such evidence as largely irrelevant. By contrast, it will be the *only* relevant evidence for subjective and mixed correctivists.

For the objective correctivist, the amount of restitution exacted in compensation for a crime will be a function of the nature of the crime and the relevant legal standards. There will either be a single right answer or else a relatively limited range of possible right answers to the question, *What kind of restitution is appropriate here and now? Has the offender or has she not provided appropriate compensation to the victim?* The relevant standards and the facts about the offender's crime and her suffering and reformation since incarceration will be objective. As a result, there will be no particular role for a victim qua victim in determining whether parole is appropriate in a given case, since the victim qua victim would have no special evidence regarding an offender's suffering or character change (or, indeed, the suffering or character change anticipated at sentencing).

On the subjective correctivist view, the victim will have complete authority to determine the outcome of any parole request. She will be free to approach any such request *de novo*, taking into account only those factors that she regards as significant. When someone was imprisoned in accordance with subjective correctivist legal norms, the facts that might dispose an objective correctivist to grant parole would be relevant to a parole decision regarding a particular offender to the extent that they were relevant to the victim of the criminal conduct responsible for the offender's incarceration. The victim will be free, however, to regard any other consideration as relevant—or irrelevant. Her wishes will be unequivocally determinative. She can, presumably, accept money from the offender in exchange for early release, forgive the offender without any regard to her repentance or reformation and authorize her release, or decline to endorse the offender's parole application despite unequivocal evidence of the offender's suffering or reformation.

In a mixed correctivist system of justice, a victim will not be free to impose just any sentence she likes on the offender. Similarly, she will not be free to direct parole decision-makers to disregard facts that make parole appropriate on an objective correctivist view. Under mixed correctivism, then, a parole decision-maker will be free—will, indeed, be required—to ignore the victim's wishes if the relevant objective factors are such that the offender can reasonably be thought to have provided appropriate compensation to the victim. On the other hand, of course, the victim *will* be free to authorize parole at any time in the absence of the factors needed to satisfy the objective compensation standard—for any reason she finds appealing.

From an objective correctivist perspective, victim testimony and victim preferences are irrelevant to a parole decision. Subjective and mixed correctivists, however, will see not only victim testimony but victim preferences as exceptionally—sometimes decisively—important determinants of such decisions. Subjective correctivism, however, is an implausible account of criminal justice. It is subject, first of all, to the objections that might confront any form of correctivism. It assumes that it is possible to equate harms and benefits experienced by one person with harms and benefits experienced by another, when they might reasonably be thought to be incommensurable. And it assumes that a loss to the offender *counts* in some way as compensation of, or the "payment" of restitution to, the victim, even though it confers *no benefit* on the victim—and thus appears indistinguishable from revenge. But subjective correctivism faces another and, as it seems to me, fatal problem. Suppose the correctivist is right that the economistic metaphors she favors are appropriate in the moral context of criminal law. Suppose that criminal law ought to look a great deal like tort law or contract law. Suppose that remedies in criminal law should be modeled on those available in tort and contract law, with the minor difference that damages are paid in the coin of suffering rather than in money. If all this is true, there is nothing that justifies the correctivist in supposing that criminal "damages," unlike those available in tort or contract law, should be subjectively determined.

The correctivist needs objectivity for the same reasons we need objectivity in the context of tort and contract law. If damages of a given magnitude really *are* objectively required, then of course it would be unfair and inaccurate to award damages at some other level. And even if they are not objective, the need for predictability and fairness supports an objective standard. Further, to make the victim the sole judge of what counts as an appropriate criminal sanction would be to make corrective criminal justice especially indistinguishable from revenge, something the correctivist—and the rest of us—might be thought to want to avoid.

The correctivist—whether subjective, mixed, or objective—might attempt to defend the appropriateness of victim influence on parole decisions by proposing a redefinition of the harms criminal penalties are supposed to correct. Act-retributivism focuses on the wrongness of the individual criminal choice. This choice must have consequences in the public world, of course, to merit punishment by the state, but it is the choice itself that is central. The criminal's choice is judged against the standard of what it would have been reasonable for her to choose at the point at which she opted to engage in criminal conduct. The retributivist will thus have relatively little reason to suppose that the unpredictable, lingering after-effects of a crime alter its moral character.[41] She assumes that the extent and intensity of a given wrongful harm is in principle fixed at the time it is inflicted or soon thereafter. A crime's after-effects will be of even less interest to the character-retributivist, for whom the criminal character manifested in the criminal act is the focus of retribution. But it might be thought that for the correctivist, who is concerned with securing redress for the actual harm the criminal has inflicted on an actual victim, the after-effects of a crime might well help to determine the appropriateness of a criminal sanction. Perhaps the effects of some harms continue, unpredictably, for indeterminate periods after their infliction. Perhaps an injury that at first seemed minor has done lasting, devastating damage that could not adequately have been anticipated at trial. Perhaps, alternatively, an apparently overwhelming injury has proven relatively minor in its effects. If the function of confinement is to require the offender to suffer as a means of compensating the victim for her suffering, then, the correctivist might argue, the offender's suffering should reflect the actual harm to the victim, not merely the harm initially ascertainable at trial. Thus, new evidence about a victim's suffering should have the potential to influence a decision regarding parole for the offender who caused the suffering.

Of course, corrective justice ordinarily does not work this way. In the context of tort law, for instance, a victim ordinarily has a single bite at the proverbial apple. For the sake of administrative convenience, fairness, and predictability, we do not retry tort cases when unexpected harms emerge after trial. The same kinds of considerations might well militate against taking into account evidence of the ongoing, unexpected effects of a crime after trial, even for a correctivist. Certainly, to revisit the issue of liability during confinement—which is effectively what the correctivist would be asking the justice system to do—would raise serious moral and evidentiary questions.

Perhaps, given their focus on the harm suffered by the victim, correctivists wish to recast criminal liability in such a way that negligence is the minimal state required

[41] Well, some retributivists, anyway. See Moore, *Victims*, *supra* note 15, at 85–88. His extended argument for taking into account the specifics of harm to victims—by means of victim impact statements—*at trial* might suggest Moore would be open to this sort of analysis. He explicitly rejects the view that "culpability alone . . . counts in determining desert, maintaining instead that the amount of harm caused determines the seriousness of the wrong done and that the amount of wrong done does affect desert . . . if there is an accompanying culpable mental state that has as its content that wrong doing." *Id.* at 87. "A lot of the detail of the harm to ... [a particular] victim may not have been foreseen or foreseeable by . . . [a particular] defendant. Holding him more blamable because of these details nonetheless does not violate our culpability limitation." *Id.* at 88. I'm not sure whose intuitions are in view here. In any case, even if retributivists accept Moore's account of the reach of the culpability principle, they might still be persuaded by the arguments I offer below to regard allowing harms not determinable at trial to influence parole decisions as a dubious practice.

for conviction for most crimes. But given the moral outrage that forms the backdrop to correctivist arguments, it seems unlikely that correctivists wish to abandon the culpability principle altogether. And to eliminate the requirement that a criminal undertake a wrongful act knowingly or intentionally in order to be liable for a serious offense would be to evacuate the law of the capacity to make the kinds of moral distinctions essential to the public condemnation of immoral behavior the correctivist is likely to encourage. Presuming the correctivist wishes to retain the culpability principle, it appears as if the offender should not be held accountable for effects of her criminal conduct she could not reasonably be expected to have anticipated. If she were not, then the option of taking into account claims regarding post-trial harms would not be available with respect to any conviction for a crime requiring a *mens rea* of purpose or knowledge, and perhaps recklessness. In this case, victim testimony would be rightly considered only during parole hearings focusing on offenders guilty of offenses involving negligence—not the serious violent crimes whose victims are likely to be especially interested in expressing themselves during parole hearings.[42] Even then, the culpability principle would require that post-trial harm be considered only in a case in which a trier of fact had expected an offender reasonably to have anticipated certain risks or had, at any rate, determined that she had, in fact, taken these risks recklessly into account. In such a case, if the harm the offender risked causing did not materialize by the time of trial but became apparent during confinement, the correctivist could argue that the fact that this harm emerged too late to be considered during trial should not enable a lucky offender to avoid liability.

Whether or not the correctivist accepts the culpability principle, however, there are serious evidentiary problems posed by the introduction of evidence regarding harms not apparent at trial. To the extent that harms occurring since trial but significantly before a parole hearing takes place are at issue, the reliability of victim memory becomes an important question. In the context of a parole hearing in which evidence of post-trial experiences of harm resulting from the conduct occasioning the trial was considered, it would also be necessary to determine whether the original trier of fact had or had not taken into account the possibility of the harms being alleged at the parole hearing. It would also be necessary to demonstrate that the harms being alleged actually resulted from the conduct for which the offender has been convicted. The absence of adequate standards of evidence and proof would obviously make it unfair to consider claims of post-trial harm, and the introduction of the procedural safeguards required to avoid inaccurate judgments about post-trial harm would create a substantial administrative and fiscal burden. Despite the fact that unforeseen consequences are in view, what amounted, in effect, to a second criminal trial related to conduct for which the offender has already been convicted would also raise obvious double jeopardy problems.

[42] The exception, of course, would be a murder conviction for conduct causing death and characterized by extreme reckless indifference to the value of human life.

Acceptance of the culpability principle would rule out appeals to all post-trial harms by victims in parole hearings. Acceptance of the culpability principle plus a rigorous *mens rea* requirement for serious crimes would require that only harm resulting from an offense for which recklessness or negligence was the required *mens rea* be considered at a parole hearing. This, in turn, would significantly limit the opportunities for victim participation in parole hearings. Abandoning rigorous *mens rea* requirements would tend to evacuate the criminal law of the moral content the correctivist clearly wants it to have. And even for correctivists prepared to abandon the culpability principle and rigorous *mens rea* requirements, the evidentiary difficulties associated with taking evidence of post-trial experiences of harm into account provide reason for parole decision-makers not to take such harms into account.

A correctivist argument for victim input into parole decisions is difficult to sustain. Unlike subjective correctivism, objective and mixed correctivism provide no support at all for allowing victims to influence parole decisions. At least, they do not unless correctivists wish to argue that the criminal law should allow for the punishment of offenders for offenses that are, in effect, redefined or re-evaluated after trial, for harms that are in some important sense measured after or understood to occur after trial. Given the difficulties with correctivism generally, and with subjective correctivism in particular, as well as the unattractiveness of a possible correctivist argument for allowing post-trial experiences of harm to affect parole decisions, correctivism provides little justification for permitting victims to influence parole decisions.

V. CONSEQUENTIALISM

Consequentialist criminal law theorists understand the generalized prevention of crime as the principal purpose of the criminal justice system. Modern criminal law consequentialism characteristically features at least two elements: deterrence and norm reinforcement.[43]

Deterrence means, roughly, making people aware that the extrinsic consequences experienced by convicted criminals will be so undesirable that they will tend to avoid engaging in criminal conduct.[44] Criminal sanctions are calibrated to affect the behavior of those who become aware of them in ways that will reduce the incidence of crime. The imagined rational calculator of classical consequentialist theory must

[43] In the broad sense, of course, theories concerned with rehabilitation and incapacitation are consequentialist—they are focused on the future rather than, like retributivist and correctivist theories, the past. But their focus on the behavior and character of the individual rather than on the societal incidence of lawful and criminal conduct differentiates them from the approaches I have labeled as consequentialist in this section.

[44] This is a description of the general deterrence approach. A deterrence theorist can argue, of course, that the criminal law system should incentivize the individual criminal to avoid repeating her criminal conduct as well as encouraging potential criminals to avoid criminal behavior in light of the unpleasant consequences suffered by others. But the issues raised in connection with a focus on special rather than general deterrence are not sufficiently different to deserve separate treatment here.

be thought of as performing a kind of cost–benefit analysis. On one side of the scale, she will place the cost of committing a contemplated criminal act—not only the costs borne, or likely to be borne, on the immediate occasion of the act's commission but the extrinsic consequences imposed by the justice system—multiplied by the likelihood of apprehension. On the other side, she will place the value of the pay-off resulting from the criminal act multiplied by the likelihood of the act's success in realizing the desired pay-off. She will therefore choose the option with the higher value.[45]

But consequentialists also concern themselves with the ways in which the law expresses and supports social norms. It shapes popular attitudes and values: if for no other reason than to avoid cognitive dissonance, people may tend to internalize the attitudes implicit in the law, at least if the legal system as a whole appears reasonably fair. The law's expression of society's condemnation of criminal behavior underscores the sense that there exists a societal consensus in opposition to such behavior. Because people tend to accept and follow norms more readily if they believe others do so as well, legal condemnation of criminal conduct encourages compliance with the law. And when the criminal law as a whole seems essentially fair, compliance with its dictates is more likely.[46]

Consequentialists have a variety of reasons for endorsing a parole system. There are limited reasons for a consequentialist to regard victim input into the parole decision-making process as appropriate, but there is good reason to think that these reasons would not be decisive from a consequentialist perspective.

A. *Parole and Consequences*

Because of its concern with deterrence, a consequentialist system of justice will seek to adjust the extrinsic consequences imposed by the state for criminal behavior and the likelihood of apprehension so that the probable cost of committing a crime will clearly outweigh the benefit to be obtained as a result of committing it. The consequentialist might thus be thought to have some doubts about the

[45] I'm attempting to describe the relevant calculations as I take the consequentialist to understand them. My own view, as I've noted before, is that consequentialism is untenable as a criterion of moral rightness or obligation. The various costs and benefits are incommensurable, and thus can't be traded off against each other in objective fashion: only a set of prior commitments can establish the weights of the various factors and thus enable the relevant trade-offs to be made, and there is no one set of rationally required weighting commitments. We may be able to guess at the potential criminal's priorities, and how she will therefore proceed, but there is no single rational way for her to do so. I'm bracketing these external criticisms of consequentialist approaches throughout this discussion.

[46] Dan M. Kahan, *What Do Alternative Sanctions Mean?*, 63 U. CHI. L. REV. 591, 602–604 (1996). *Cf.* Alex Geisinger, *A Belief Change Theory of Expressive Law*, 88 IOWA L. REV. 35 (2002). For an empirical and social-theoretic critique of the approach to criminal justice articulated in Kahan's article, *see* Bernard E. Harcourt, *Reflecting on the Subject: A Critique of the Social Influence Conception of Deterrence, the Broken Windows Theory, and Order-Maintenance Policing New York Style*, 97 MICH. L. REV. 291 (1998).

appropriateness of any sort of parole system. She might wonder whether the provision of parole as an option makes it more difficult to incentivize a potential criminal's behavior appropriately. The criminal will know that she will be able to reduce the extrinsic consequences of her crime by means of her good behavior while in the justice system. It will therefore be open to her cynically to plan to make her crime pay by acting in ways she knows will yield the reward of parole. The consequentialist will emphasize, more generally, that eliminating the option of parole will tend to increase the predictability, and thus the effectiveness, of the criminal justice system. Inflexible sentencing "would make the punishment more automatic than it is now; and punishment is more deterrent the more automatic it is."[47]

But the resourceful consequentialist need not be overly troubled by the possibility that rationally calculating criminals might be able to take advantage of a parole system. She may simply argue that, where parole is available, initial sentences should be longer than they would otherwise be and that parole procedures should be rendered as rigorous as practically possible. Thus, she can keep the presumptive cost to the would-be criminal imposed by the justice system at an appropriately high level. Insincere good behavior will be unlikely to result in early release, not least because it will probably be detected, and the prospective felon will be forced to take into account the prospect of an unpleasantly long sentence if her attempts to feign good behavior are unsuccessful. Provided appropriate safeguards are in place, the consequentialist will have little reason to oppose a parole system as such on deterrence-related grounds.

A concern with norm reinforcement is also consistent with the operation of a parole system. Just as many consequentialists see imprisonment as expressing society's condemnation of morally inappropriate behavior, so parole represents a societal affirmation of morally desirable behavior. A parole system could be thought, of course, to imply that society does not take seriously the norms it seeks to enforce by means of criminal sanctions. But at least as long as the standards for parole are high, it need not convey this message. And a parole system's active encouragement of positive behavior can be seen as sufficiently important to outweigh, in consequentialist terms, any negative effects that might result from the failure to require a prisoner to serve the entirety of her sentence.[48]

Because of the differences between life in prison and life in ordinary society, there is no guarantee that behavior during incarceration will, in fact, predict behavior after release.[49] However, the fact that in-prison behavior itself may not be a good predictor

47 Ernest van den Haag, *The Criminal Law as a Threat System*, 73 J. Crim. L. & Criminology 769, 774 (1982).

48 Of course, the sentence will ordinarily be understood to include the possibility of parole in the first place, so it is not clear that this need be a serious concern.

49 See James B. Jacobs, *Sentencing By Prison Personnel: Good Time*, 30 UCLA L. Rev. 217, 264–5 (1982). As Jacobs notes, "Prison is a quintessentially abnormal environment . . . ." *Id.* at 264.

of behavior after release does not mean that parole decision-makers have no way of predicting such behavior. A combination of pre-incarceration behavior, behavior during imprisonment, testimony reflecting the evaluations of professionals and others who have interacted with a prisoner, and general information regarding the deterrent effects of particular sentences might provide insights into future dangerousness sufficient to enable a parole board to make a reasonable decision regarding the merits of a parole application on consequentialist grounds. Even if a parole board were unable to make such a decision, however, this need not lead a consequentialist to reject the idea of parole out of hand. The consequentialist might regard the incentivizing effects of a parole system as sufficiently useful as a source of good behavior in prisons to justify its continuation even in the face of uncertainty unless the expected recidivism rate were very high. And, even in this case, the other factors weighing in favor of a parole system might warrant its maintenance.

Suppose, then, that there are not insuperable *objections* to parole from a consequentialist perspective. A consequentialist might approach the question of parole in at least two ways—in relation primarily to prisoners' behavior *while incarcerated* or as part of a *package* of criminal justice strategies.

(*i*) The consequentialist might think of parole primarily as a means of encouraging prisoners to behave well while incarcerated. This would be a matter both of deterring bad behavior and of reinforcing norms calling for good behavior. The institution of parole would be seen as affecting the behavior of prisoners in roughly the way that the system of criminal sanctions shapes the behavior of members of the public at large. In this case, she might believe that the existence of the institution of parole would have no discernible effect on the deterrence of crime. Her argument would presumably be that, before incarceration, one cannot predict in one's own case whether one will be paroled or not with any great degree of accuracy, that a rational calculator would thus not take the potential availability of parole into account when deciding whether or not to commit a crime, and that the appropriateness of a parole system could thus be assessed in relative isolation from the rest of the criminal justice system. Call this an *insulated deterrence* account of parole.

The proponent of insulated deterrence could also, as a consequentialist, consider other factors in justifying her support for parole. Since all welfare matters to her, and since prisoners are presumably better off released from prison than incarcerated, she will obviously prefer early release, all other things being equal, to imprisonment. She will also welcome the benefits potentially accruing from the parolee's capacity to contribute to the economy and society more readily after release. And she will presumably regard the diminished drain on public resources effected by the release of paroled prisoners from incarceration as a reason in favor of a parole system.

At the same time, of course, she will need to take into account the potential costs of early release. Most obviously, these will include the costs resulting from crimes committed by parolees. She will also need to take into account the lack of confidence in the justice system that may result if members of the public see parole as unfairly benefiting criminals. Similarly, she will need to consider the possibility that a poorly administered parole regime might encourage cynical manipulation of the justice system by criminals. None of these considerations need dispose her to reject a parole system as inappropriate. They will, however, encourage her to be careful.

(*ii*) Without ignoring the benefits relevant from the standpoint of insulated deterrence, a consequentialist might also attempt to think of parole as an element of a (relatively) complete package of criminal sanctions. She might offer a *comprehensive* story about parole. In this case, she would argue that a system of criminal sanctions that allowed for the possibility of parole would be more effective at reducing the societal incidence of crime than would one from which parole was absent.

Perhaps the most obvious reason she might do so is this: members of the public are not, as a rule, consequentialists.[50] They may tend to be more concerned with the personal culpability and future dangerousness of prisoners than with general deterrence. *They* will thus be inclined to believe that reformation on the part of an incarcerated person makes her or him an appropriate candidate for early release from prison. If the justice system does not appear to be responsive to their concerns, it will strike them as harsh and inflexible. They will repose less confidence in societal institutions of justice, and the justice system as a whole may thus enjoy less support. If it does, it will be less likely to fulfill its function of reducing the incidence of crime, since would-be criminals

50 See Paul H. Robinson & John M. Darley, *The Utility of Desert*, 91 Nw. U. L. Rev. 453 (1997) (arguing on utilitarian grounds for broadly retributivist criminal law norms). According to Robinson & Darley: "The criminal law's moral credibility with the community, we argue, requires a distribution of liability that follows the community's perceptions of principles of deserved punishment and requires a separate and distinct criminal justice system, a system which can demonstrate its exclusive focus on blameworthiness and can effectively convey the special condemnation of criminal conviction. This credibility is risked when the legal system criminalizes actions that the community regards as not criminal or does not criminalize actions that the community regards as serious moral violations that deserve criminal condemnation." *Id.* at 488. The injustice of imposing serious penalties for conduct that is not, in fact, immoral or that, even if immoral, does not warrant forcible interference should certainly give proponents of this approach pause, it seems to me.

Andrew Strauss has provided an extended critique of the Robinson-Darley model in *Losing Sight of the Utilitarian Forest for the Retributivist Trees: An Analysis of the Role of Public Opinion in a Utilitarian Model of Punishment*, 23 Cardozo L. Rev. 1549 (2002). Strauss believes that "[t]he power of the law to influence the community's norms of conduct"—to reshape them over time—is significantly greater than Robinson and Darley suppose. *Id.* at 1595. If he is right, of course, then the consequentialist will have less reason to attempt over the long term to shore up public confidence in the criminal justice system by ensuring that it behaves in ways with which retributivists are likely to be comfortable. As a result, a consequentialist system of justice will have less reason over time to take victim testimony into account even if at some point social norms might encourage consideration of such evidence.

will find it easier to dismiss it as unworthy of their loyalty and other members of society may not cooperate with it at crucial times.

The consequentialist could also focus on a variety of other societal benefits resulting from a parole system. She could maintain that a parole system allows the maintenance of a system of general deterrence while adjusting the outputs of the system in ways calculated to lead to social benefit.[51] She might also focus on the post-release behavior of the paroled criminal. The parolee might regard the justice system as less harsh, and thus as more worthy of her cooperation, if paroled. Her gratitude for the opportunity to leave prison, and her perception that the justice system was sensitive to her individual needs, might incline her to behave in more desirable ways if paroled than if kept in prison and then released. In addition, given the deleterious behavioral consequences of imprisonment, the consequentialist might consider the possibility that the parole of some prisoners, at any rate, might reduce recidivism. The former prisoner under the supervision of a parole officer might be less likely to internalize criminal habits than would a resentful prisoner associating almost exclusively with other criminals.[52] Finally, of course, she might judge that it was welfare-enhancing to allow genuinely reformed prisoners to leave prison. She might judge that the prisoners themselves would surely be better off outside and that they need not be expected to pose significant dangers to those outside. And she might judge that releasing them early only after parole hearings would leave the

[51] Such an arrangement runs the risk of being deceptive. *See* Franklin E. Zimring, *Making the Punishment Fit the Crime*, 6 Hastings Ctr. Rpt. 6, 14 (1976): "a parole system allows us to advertise heavy criminal sanctions loudly at the time of sentencing and later to reduce sentences quietly." Zimring's claim need not be understood as a defense of the parole system on the basis that it is usefully deceptive (as van den Haag, *supra* note 47, at 780, maintains). It can be seen as a means of rendering the justice system flexible and responsive to individual needs in ways that members of the public might often be expected to support, at least in the abstract. At the same time, of course, there is no reason why a consequentialist as such need have any objection in principle to deception, and so to deception of the public by the state.

[52] The failure to acknowledge a range of other social benefits that might result from a parole system and to assume that deterrence is the only reasonable consequentialist strategy for crime control seems to account for the narrowness of Ernest van den Haag's critique of the institution of parole. *See* van den Haag, *supra* note 47, at 777–78; he argues, in effect, that the possibility of parole will always reduce the deterrent value of sentencing. The more certain a sentence, the greater its deterrent value. But his argument may fail satisfactorily to take into account the other factors consequentialists might consider relevant to the determination of sentencing guidelines. Perhaps this is because of his assumption that "crime rates . . . depend on the expected net benefit of crimes to perpetrators, not on rehabilitation or on incapacitation of convicts. The crime rate can be reduced only by deterrence. Therefore, the rehabilitation of individuals cannot be the social purpose of sentencing." *Id.* at 779. But there is no reason for consequentialists to accept van den Haag's conclusion. Rehabilitation has never been understood as designed solely or even primarily for the benefit of the individual offender: its purpose is just as much the benefit of others as the redemption of the individual criminal. I think van den Haag dismisses any potential social benefit derivable from rehabilitation much too quickly. I think it's also significant that he ignores the value of norm reinforcement and the other benefits I've just enumerated.

deterrent efficacy of imprisonment in place—since it would send the message that only genuine behavior change would be rewarded with early release.

The consequentialist could reasonably argue that the appropriateness of a parole system could be considered in isolation from other aspects of the criminal sentencing process. She could also argue, however, that parole might play a positive role in the process of crime reduction more generally. It is thus open to the consequentialist to consider the value of allowing victim impact evidence to affect parole decisions within the terms of her overall theory of criminal justice.[53]

B. *Consequentialism, Parole, and Victim Testimony*

A consequentialist would have little reason to believe that victim testimony should influence parole decisions, though she might believe it should play a limited role.

If the primary function of a parole system for the insulated deterrence theorist is to incentivize *prisoner* conduct, then most victim testimony will be of little value from her perspective in determining the appropriateness of parole. Any evidence relating to the severity of the harm inflicted by the prisoner or her state of mind at the time of her criminal act will be irrelevant, since the focus of the parole hearing from the standpoint of the insulated deterrence theorist will be to encourage appropriate post-conviction behavior and to discourage inappropriate post-conviction behavior.

A victim who has had ongoing opportunity to observe a prisoner's behavior after confinement might be able to offer independent testimony regarding this behavior, whether the victim takes the behavior to be positive or negative. The insulated deterrence theorist could see it as reasonable to take this sort of victim testimony into account in order to prompt desirable behavior on the part of the prisoner and others aware of her circumstances. Where the victim had established a positive relationship with the offender, the victim might be in a position to encourage appropriate behavior on the part of the offender after release and not disappointing the victim might in this case be important to the offender. But of course these sorts of considerations would not count in favor of giving victims *as such* special rights to give evidence at parole hearings. Non-victims might also have relevant information and have established relationships with offenders that might facilitate desirable post-release behavior.

For a proponent of a comprehensive consequentialist theory of parole, there would be some argument for taking victim testimony into account. Any reason

53 Of course, in principle, the deterrence theorist could reject the parole system as incompatible with her general theoretical position while accepting that, given its existence, she had good reason to offer policy prescriptions likely to maximize its contribution to deterrence. Since, however, *ex hypothesi*, the deterrence theorist in this case will regard parole as unhelpful, these prescriptions will presumably serve primarily to reduce its availability. She will therefore have little interest in discussing alternate parole policies to the extent that they do not make parole less available.

someone might offer from a non-consequentialist perspective for doing so could be taken on board by the consequentialist to the extent that it reflected an individual *preference* whose satisfaction she might seek to facilitate. Given that preferences are exogenous for standard consequentialism, she might reasonably take any and all preferences into account. She might do so as well, again, to maintain confidence in and support for the justice system. To the extent, at any rate, that popular sentiment favored the use of victim testimony, she could see a system that took such evidence into account as designed to ensure the popular endorsement of the justice system needed to ensure its effective functioning. On the other hand, however, recognizing what she would likely take to be the bad consequences of acting on some popular preferences, the consequentialist would not seek to reinforce such preferences over the long haul but rather to discourage them over time, so she would not wish to give excessive weight to every popular sentiment.

The other reasons a consequentialist might advance in support of the establishment or maintenance of a parole system would not seem to dispose her to give victim testimony significant weight, except—perhaps—in cases in which the victim has actual knowledge of the offender's behavior and mental state after conviction. Again, though, the consequentialist will presumably suppose that anyone, and not only victims, with such knowledge should be allowed to testify and that there is no special consequentialist reason to give victim testimony extra weight.

Perhaps there's an additional reason, however, for a consequentialist to give victim testimony special weight. On average, presumably, victims will be more likely than not to discourage the granting of parole. A consequentialist might argue that, while parole is necessary as a safety valve designed to mitigate the effects of effectively deterrent sentences, the involvement of victims in parole hearings will serve predictably to reduce the likelihood that offenders will be paroled. The justice system will still incorporate the practice of granting parole, which will yield the benefits consequentialists might reasonably be thought to desire; but offenders will know that they will need to demonstrate especially high standards of good behavior in prison to outweigh the effects of the negative testimony of their victims. So the consequentialist who reasoned this way might think that the use of victim testimony in parole decisions will tend to reduce the apparent leniency of the parole systems and will actively encourage good behavior on the part of inmates.

While the use of victim testimony might indeed serve this role, it clearly also poses problems from the standpoint of the consequentialist. All other things being equal, she will regard incarceration as undesirable. She will acknowledge the injuries such sentences impose on inmates themselves. While she hopes that sentences of appropriate length will help to deter criminals, and will not want to see them arbitrarily reduced, she is also aware that their net social benefit is uncertain. Being incarcerated for a longer period may increase the likelihood that a person will be acculturated as a criminal. It will also likely breed resentment that may issue in criminal behavior on release. And it will reduce the chances an offender would otherwise have to contribute meaningfully to society after release, both because release will happen later and because the offender may be more damaged when finally released. The consequentialist cannot, therefore, regard lengthier sentences as unqualifiedly good.

The consequentialist will want to ensure that sentences are sufficiently long and unpleasant to deter crime; to emphasize that incarcerated offenders will need to demonstrate genuine behavior change if they are to qualify for parole; and to release offenders as soon as possible to permit them to contribute more effectively to societal well-being. Using victim testimony to—on average—decrease the likelihood of parole will not make much contribution to the achievement of her goals. Sentencing guidelines or the exercise of judicial discretion might, for the consequentialist, prove more effective, predictable, and reliable at the job of ensuring deterrent sentences than the use of victim testimony to shape parole decisions. The consequentialist will trust research-based expert opinion to yield good decisions; victim testimony, by contrast, will typically be uninformed, unlikely to contribute to rational or predictable sentencing.

Parole guidelines requiring exemplary conduct on the part of prisoners if they are to qualify for parole will be sufficient to encourage them to behave appropriately while incarcerated. And, except when victims have independent information regarding the dangerousness of offenders, their likely negative testimony will, if anything, make it less likely that a parole board will return an offender to society at a point at which she *could* safely begin to make an effective contribution to social welfare. Further, if victim testimony is allowed to play a significant role in sentencing, an incarcerated offender may often conclude that she has no chance of parole. She may therefore conclude that she has *less* reason to behave well while in prison, since she has little or no chance of early release, *whatever* she does during her incarceration. Including the testimony of victims qua victims, or giving victim testimony extra weight, in the parole process could thus actually result in worse behavior on the part of inmates.

The proponent of a comprehensive consequentialist approach to criminal justice will also be concerned about assigning any special role to victim testimony in the parole process because it might tend to legitimize retributive attitudes unlikely to yield good consequences. Given the norm-reinforcing potential of assigning special roles to victims, the comprehensive consequentialist will likely want to avoid supporting the assignment of such roles.

Most testimony by victims will likely be directly related to the severity of the crimes experienced by the victims. Victims are not likely to be consequentialists, and their inclusion in the sentencing and parole processes will generally be motivated primarily by retributive, corrective, and expressive concerns, not by consequentialist ones. An insulated deterrence theorist of parole will regard all victim testimony as irrelevant. A more comprehensive consequentialist account of parole theorist will offer relatively little reason for the justice system to allow victim testimony significant weight in shaping parole decisions. The consequentialist can reasonably argue that any information a victim could provide regarding the severity of a crime will already have been taken into account during sentencing. She will ordinarily be disposed, therefore, to regard post-conviction victim testimony as relevant only when it illuminates an offender's current character and future dangerousness, and to deny that a victim should be more entitled than anyone else to offer such testimony or that victim testimony should be given extra weight. She might consider the possibility that, for systemic reasons, it could make sense to provide some room for the consideration of such evidence. But she would have good reason to conclude that the relevant systemic goals could be better served in other ways.

VI. VICTIMLESS PAROLE DECISIONS

Every broad theory of criminal law that can justify the practice of incarceration can also justify the institution of parole. By contrast, despite widespread provision for victim input into parole decisions, the practice of permitting and encouraging such input is remarkably lacking in justification. Its appeal to legislators is perhaps best seen as a product of an inchoate and ill-considered intuition that it will provide a legally regulated mechanism by which victims can take partial revenge on those who have harmed them. In any case, in light of most popular theoretical accounts of criminal justice, this practice appears unproductive—even counterproductive.

Victim input makes no contribution to the achievement of the rehabilitationist goals of encouraging behavior change and ensuring that only those who have been satisfactorily rehabilitated are released. It does not help significantly to reduce the risk that offenders who pose a significant risk of future danger to others are incapacitated rather than being released on parole. It does little to help ensure that offenders will be punished—by being subjected to prison terms of appropriate length—for their bad choices or bad characters, as a retributivist will believe it should. It plays little role in accomplishing consequentialist goals: deterring future crimes by offenders or others or in supporting positive social norms—so that, given its likely negative results, the consequentialist will, at minimum, have quite limited reason to support it. And it can make no contribution to the objective and mixed correctivist goal of "paying back" victims through offenders' suffering for crimes of impartially ascertainable severity. Only the subjective correctivist, for whom victim preference *determines* appropriate compensation for a crime, can make a great deal of sense of the role currently afforded victims in parole hearings in many jurisdictions. (The subjective correctivist will believe, implausibly, that victims should have the sole authority to determine sentences and determine whether parole applications should be granted. But she will at least be able, unlike other theorists, to explain why victim input into parole decisions might appear reasonable.)

Despite the implausibility of subjective correctivism, the fact that the victim might have new evidence related to the *original crime or crimes*, or be in a position to offer a new perspective on old evidence, might still make her perspective of interest to a retributivist or to an objective or mixed correctivist. But without the imposition of costly due process standards, and the effective conversion of a parole hearing into a new trial, the introduction of this sort of evidence should not be allowed. Similarly, in the rare case when she had access to information related to an offender's *post-conviction* behavior or character, rehabilitationists, incapacitationists, and consequentialists might all find this information of value. But they would have no reason to give her testimony regarding the offender's rehabilitation and potential for future dangerousness any more weight than they would give evidence from any other person with relevant knowledge. She might, that is, be entitled to be heard, but no more so than anyone else with information likely to contribute to a more accurate assessment of the offender about whom she might wish to testify.

Giving victims *as victims* influence over parole decisions is inconsistent with the most popular plausible—and implausible—accounts of the purposes of the criminal justice system. Despite its widespread popularity in many American jurisdictions, it is an inappropriate practice likely to lead to results that advocates of diverse perspectives on the criminal law have good reason to find unattractive. There is no justification for giving victims' perspectives any weight in parole decisions. Declining to do so appropriately fosters the flourishing of potential parolees and—given that unreasonable choices don't facilitate, and, in fact, undermine, flourishing—of institutional designers and other participants in the legal system.

The rejection of a role for victim impact testimony in parole decisions makes sense because of a concern to treat those being considered for parole humanely and to view them fairly and so as individuals. (Fairness dictates that we treat like cases alike, but also that we treat different cases differently, and this means taking individual variations into appropriate account.) The requirements of practical reasonableness that underlie these concerns are among those that give rise to the wider liberal ethos, with its commitments to both individualism and cosmopolitanism (itself an expression of fairness and individualism).

It is in light of these commitments that liberalism encourages us to view particular people *as* particular people rather than as representatives of generic collectivities and to acknowledge the importance of maintaining the social space needed for the expression of individual diversity. They prompt us to acknowledge the absence of any deep reason to view people differently as regards their moral standing and capacity to enrich others' lives in virtue of their presence on one side or another of arbitrary lines on maps.

Thus, liberal values weigh strongly against any sort of nationalism, which treats the subjects of particular states as belonging to common tribes and which encourages them to embrace a solidarity that has no ultimate foundation apart from the fact that the rulers of particular states can treat their subjects as engaged in common projects and that the rulers of other states may share this arbitrary assumption. Nationalism is pernicious. It ignores individual people's different concerns, commitments, circumstances, and lifestyles, and views arbitrary, imposed commonalities as salient features of their identities. And it encourages the members of particular national groups to treat nonmembers inhumanely. Like the determination of sentences in light of victim testimony, nationalism is neither fair nor humane. It is thus not an appropriate partner for liberalism. This is true even of an optimistic nationalism designed to promote (some) liberal values. This kind of nationalism is the focus of Chapter 7.

7

Believers

I. AMERICAN FAITH AND THE FUTURE OF LIBERALISM

Richard Rorty advanced an optimistic version of modern liberalism rooted in a vital sense of American possibility—in something we might call "the religion of America."[1] Rorty's brand of liberalism responds creatively to genuine challenges. But civic religions, even secular ones like the religion of America, are troubling, and there are reasons for preferring radical to Rortyan liberalism.

Political commentators rediscovered Rorty's *Achieving Our Country* in the wake of the 2016 US presidential election, after realizing that Rorty's critical evaluation of the American Left's focus on cultural politics might well lead alienated white blue-collar voters, among others, to support a would-be strongman like Donald Trump.[2]

Natural law liberalism is a position on the political Left. The Principle of Fairness offers good reason for concern at exclusion, subordination, and deprivation rooted in social class, ethnicity, gender, and a range of other factors. Liberal natural law theory thus shares key concerns that animate Rorty's analysis. It doesn't follow, however, that Rorty's arguments should be accepted *in toto*—not his diagnosis of the problem on which he focuses, not his proposed policy solutions, and not his approach to religious themes.

[1] *See* Richard Rorty, Achieving Our Country: Leftist Thought in Twentieth-Century America (1997). Note that Rorty talks about "leftist" politics, but he is not especially concerned with radical socialists, with communists, or with anarchists, though they are perhaps included within what he calls "the Left." He is focused primarily on modern liberals, on the New Left of the 1960s, and on academic radicals, most of whom probably share something like Rorty's own meliorist social democratic politics. I will sometimes refer to "the Left" where Rorty does, and sometimes elsewhere; but I do not think it is unreasonable to see him as pitching an understanding of what I've called modern liberalism.

[2] *See, e.g.*, Conor Friedersdorf, *The Book That Predicted Trump's Rise Offers the Left a Roadmap for Defeating Him*, The Atlantic, July 6, 2017, https://www.theatlantic.com/politics/archive/2017/07/advice-for-the-left-on-achieving-a-more-perfect-union/531054/; Sean Illing, *Richard Rorty's Prescient Warnings for the American Left*, Vox, Jan. 12, 2018, https://www.vox.com/policy-and-politics/2017/2/9/14543938/donald-trump-richard-rorty-election-liberalism-conservatives; Edward Helmore, *"Something Will Crack": Supposed Prophecy of Donald Trump Goes Viral*, The Guardian, Nov. 19, 2016, https://www.theguardian.com/us-news/2016/nov/19/donald-trump-us-election-prediction-richard-rorty; Jennifer Senior, *Richard Rorty's 1998 Book Suggested Election 2016 Was Coming*, New York Times, Nov. 20, 2016, https://www.nytimes.com/2016/11/21/books/richard-rortys-1998-book-suggested-election-2016-was-coming.html.

Rorty was notoriously skeptical of traditional religious beliefs. They were, he believed, "too childish to be discussed seriously."[3] And injecting them into public debate seemed likely to frustrate the pluralistic dialogue needed for us satisfactorily to resolve our social, political, and economic problems.[4]

But even if "we have got rid of theology,"[5] we apparently can't quite do without religion, at least of a sort. This seems, at any rate, to be one theme in *Achieving Our Country*.[6] Rorty sees the Left as having pessimistically withdrawn from practical political engagement. And he sees this withdrawal as grounded in an ideology he characterizes in religious terms.

Natural law theory itself doesn't entail support for some particular variant of religious belief. And it rules out the use of force on behalf of particular religious views. At the same time, the basic good of harmony with reality comprehensively understood—we might call this *religion, meaning,* or *harmony*—is one natural law theorists appreciatively acknowledge. So natural law theory offers more than one reason for us to take Rorty's analysis seriously: not only the grounding it provides for concern with many of the issues that animate him but also its acknowledgment of the value of this good.

More broadly: natural law liberalism endorses many of Rorty's goals, even if not necessarily his preferred means. Thus, I join him in rejecting unjust privilege and in favoring inclusion. The concerns of radical natural law liberalism thus overlap in significant measure with Rorty's opposition to what he liked to label *selfishness* and *sadism*, labels for, respectively, economic inequity and cultural exclusion, to the extent that both are inconsistent with the Principle of Fairness.

In this Chapter, I attempt to engage with Rorty's advocacy of a kind of nationalistic civic religion in *Achieving Our Country*. I begin by reflecting on what he sees as a crippling source of inertia on the part of Americans on the Left: the abandonment of practical politics in the face of guilt and pessimism rooted in what he sees as a mischievous religious vision (Part II). In place of this vision, Rorty offers his own alternative, a kind of civic religion centered on American possibility—a civic religion well worth questioning (Part III). The possibility of raising critical questions requires us, I suggest, to move beyond the kind of immanent critique Rorty sometimes seems to see as the only sort of possible critique (Part IV). There are reasons, I suggest, some but not all related to the importance of critique, to embrace a more positive view of the potential of spiritual traditions distinct from his preferred Americanism (Part V) and to reject Rorty's proposed dichotomy between freedom and social justice as foundational societal values (Part VI). Rorty's insights are worth

3 Richard Rorty, The Consequences of Pragmatism: Essays, 1972–1980 at 24 (1982) (*quoted in* Nicholas Lash, Easter in Ordinary: Reflections on Human Experience and the Knowledge of God 201 (1988)).

4 *See* Richard Rorty, *Religion as Conversation-Stopper*, Common Knowledge, Spring 1994, at 1.

5 Rorty, Consequences, *supra* note 3, at 34 (*quoted in* Lash, *supra* note 3, at 201).

6 Rorty, Achieving, *supra* note 1.

acknowledging, but his version of Americanist liberalism is ultimately unsatisfactory (Part VII).

II. RELIGIOUS VISION AS A SOURCE OF MISCHIEF?

Rorty's focus is on what he views as a crisis of self-definition faced by the American Left since the 1960s. Leftists embraced, he believes, an increasingly pessimistic theology, central to which was a secular analogue of the idea of original sin, according to which American society was irredeemable. In Part II, I explain why he believes this is the case and ask whether he's right. I suggest that the "theology" of the cultural Left may not be the sole or even the principal source of mischief.

A. *The Retreat to Theory*

The progressive tradition Rorty associates with Walt Whitman and John Dewey was passionately critical of many aspects of American life. But it was critical in the name of a conceivable and achievable future. It was not burdened by a crushing sense of American guilt or moral brokenness that rendered hope impossible. James Baldwin's continued embrace of such optimism gives Rorty his title. Unwilling to forgive the United States for its treatment of African Americans, Baldwin nonetheless held out the hope that Americans might yet "... end the racial nightmare, and achieve our country, and change the history of the world."[7]

According to Rorty, this optimistic, progressive tradition, with its hope of fulfilling America's promise—achieving our country—ran aground in the '60s. The "reformist Left," comprising liberals and socialists alike—"all those Americans who, between 1900 and 1964, struggled within the framework of constitutional democracy to protect the weak from the strong"[8]—ran out of steam. Characterizing the Left as "by definition ... the party of hope,"[9] Rorty nonetheless argues that, despite the success of the anti-war movement and the initial victories of the civil rights struggles, the Left gave up on America. American progressives—horrified by "the Vietnam War"—came, he says, to affirm what he curiously characterizes as "the old religious idea that some stains are ineradicable."[10] Though the peace movement succeeded in derailing the war machine, Rorty suggests, Vietnam exposed the worst side of American culture. That exposure led the Left to withdraw from the task of public policy formulation and advocacy. Rather than continuing to press for real, even if incremental, changes, progressives retreated behind the walls of the academy, turned from economic issues to cultural ones, and began to engage in increasingly arcane theorizing.

7 *Quoted in id.* at 13.
8 *Id.* at 43.
9 *Id.* at 14.
10 *Id.* at 95.

What Rorty calls the "cultural Left" has, he emphasizes, enriched our common life. Challenges to what he terms the *sadism* that stigmatizes the Other in virtue of such characteristics as ethnicity, gender, sexual orientation, or religious affiliation have made a genuine and important difference.[11] "The American academy has done as much to overcome sadism during the last thirty years as it did to overcome selfishness in the previous seventy. Encouraging students to be what mocking neoconservatives call 'politically correct' has made our country a far better place."[12] But intellectuals on the Left have failed to address the problem of *selfishness*, the challenge posed by economic injustice. And they have proved generally unwilling to advance concrete public policy proposals, opting instead to offer highly abstract subversions of what they take to be the dominant ideology. "Leftists in the academy have permitted cultural politics to supplant real politics, and have collaborated with the Right in making cultural issues central to public debate."[13] "The Foucauldian academic Left in contemporary America is exactly the sort of Left that the oligarchy dreams of: a Left whose members are so busy unmasking the present that they have no time to discuss what laws need to be passed in order to create a better future."[14]

People on the Left now seem inclined, Rorty suggests, to the tragic view that it is "a fundamental moral fact that the commission of certain acts . . . is incompatible with further self-respect."[15] A crippling focus on national sinfulness makes the quest for real social change seem a dubious enterprise at best. If we are all enmeshed in networks of oppression that distort our understanding and cripple our efforts to effect change, then perhaps people who think of themselves as members of "a saving remnant"[16] have few options beyond the attempt to unmask oppression by exposing its inner contradictions. If change is impossible because American culture is in the grip of irresistible evil, patient efforts to change laws or organize social movements will be futile. Evil can be theorized, but it cannot be overcome.

Such gloomy religious visions should be rejected, Rorty argues, because embracing them cuts the nerve of political action. Leftists must abandon their sense of hopelessness and move from theory to practical politics. The Left must devote more

11 Stigmatization based on class has not tended to evoke the same kind of attention from the cultural Left. Rorty notes acidly that "[n]obody is setting up a program in unemployed studies, homeless studies, or trailer-park studies, because the unemployed, the homeless, and residents of trailer parks are not 'other' in the relevant sense. To be other in this sense you must bear an ineradicable stigma, one which makes you a victim of socially accepted sadism rather than merely of economic selfishness . . ." (80). *Cf.* Social Class and State Power: Exploring an Alternative Radical Tradition (David M. Hart *et al.*, eds., 2018).

12 Rorty, Achieving, *supra* note 1, at 82.

13 *Id.* at 14.

14 *Id.* at 139.

15 *Id.* at 32–33.

16 *Id.* at 8.

time to crafting and advancing policy proposals,[17] and less time to offering Lacanian accounts of the power relations implicit in Michael Douglas films.

Those who see how much improvement American institutions need will have no doubt about the value of careful legal, political, economic, and social analysis. I am doubtful, however, not only about a number of Rorty's specific policy prescriptions but also about his diagnosis of the Left's ineffectiveness. He suggests that the tendency to focus on sadism rather than selfishness reflects the religious conflict to which he alludes throughout the book. But presumably the evils that result in sadism are deeply rooted in American society, just like those that give rise to selfishness. An obvious question is whether someone could consistently regard original sin as so crippling as to render the *economic* order beyond change while working actively to transform *cultural* life in tangible ways. It seems as if Rorty is attributing a not-altogether-plausible schizophrenia to Americans on the Left. Might it be easier to understand the Left's failure to mount a frontal assault on American economic institutions in terms other than Rorty's? I suspect that the Left's continuing engagement with cultural politics—an engagement reflective of at least limited hope in the possibility of change—points to a flaw in Rorty's sin-based analysis and suggests that we should look elsewhere if we want to understand the absence from the scene of broad-based movements for justice among leftist intellectuals.

B. Sources of Retreat

I suspect that the retreat from active political struggle, at least against Rortyan selfishness, is rooted in factors other than widespread belief in ineradicable American sinfulness. While self-righteous critics might attribute the change to a "culture of narcissism,"[18] this seems unlikely: after all, people need to step outside their own concerns in order to respond to sadism just like they need to do so in order to respond to selfishness.

Some people may have bowed out of the political arena because of the perception that American institutions were quite unresponsive to pressure from protestors and politicians alike. When John Lennon announced that he didn't want to change the world, it wasn't, I think, because he felt overwhelmed by America's sinfulness. The sexual explorers of California's Sandstone and the visionaries of the Esalen Institute were not, I think, immobilized by a sense of the inescapability of evil. My intuition is that they attributed not so much malice as impassibility to American cultural

[17] Despite Rorty's positive use of "reform" and its cognates, I'm confident that he wasn't concerned exclusively with electorally or legislatively oriented political reformism. I believe he would have agreed that the sorts of campaigns he envisioned could be undertaken appropriately not only within but also outside existing political structures; protestors as well as legislators (some people, of course, are both) can take part in campaigns.

[18] *See, e.g.*, Christopher Lasch, The Culture of Narcissism: American Life in an Age of Diminishing Expectations (1979); Barbara Ehrenreich, The Hearts of Men: American Dreams and the Flight from Commitment (1983).

institutions. They focused on what they believed they could change, their own lives and the lives of those in their immediate orbits, rather than on institutions that seemed impervious to their influence. The problem was not that The System was evil but that it was inert—a product not of oppressive malevolence but, rather, of impersonal, inexorable institutional processes.

Also important, I suspect, was the lack of a theoretical framework useful for confronting the economic concerns Rorty seeks to capture under the heading of "selfishness." Marxism, which had offered a critical perspective on these issues, appeared increasingly to have been discredited—as economically unsound, philosophically dubious, and linked not only with an implausible understanding of historical change but also with inescapably totalitarian politics. At the same time, while market economics seemed reasonable, and likely inescapable, culturally visible interpretations of pro-market theories seemed to treat a range of socio-economic inequities as inevitable. The sort of approach Rorty attempts to defend, featuring not only a generous welfare state, substantial regulations, and high minimum wages[19]—but also, perhaps, protectionist measures, didn't seem unequivocally appealing. And this left the Left without a great deal to say about economic issues.[20]

The middle- and upper-class Americans who had played a disproportionate role in leading the protest movements of the '60s grew more and more involved and invested in the economic and political power structures of their country—comfortable and co-opted in ways that made it difficult for them to criticize those structures. The association of social-democratic policies with the intergenerational perpetuation of poverty made it hard for politicians and activists to defend familiar positions.[21] And the racialized politics of poverty made it easy to paint concern with deprivation as a matter of siding with feckless members of racial minority groups against increasingly beleaguered blue-collar whites.

The turn to cultural politics may also be a result of the split in the New Deal coalition brought about by the Vietnam War. Notoriously, American hard hats were put off by what they saw as the moral laxness and anti-Americanism of many representatives of the anti-war movement, and many undoubtedly had mixed reactions to the New Left's racial and sexual politics. Splits within the Democratic

[19] A particularly doubtful idea. *See, e.g.*, Daniel Shaviro, *The Minimum Wage, the Earned Income Tax Credit, and Optimal Subsidy Policy*, 64 U. Chi. L. Rev. 405, 406 (1997) ("Most economists of all ideological persuasions have long agreed that . . . [the minimum wage] is self-defeating: it destroys jobs in the low-wage sector of the economy and thus hurts many of the people it is intended to help.").

[20] The sort of natural law anarchism I seek to defend here offers an alternative rooted in the thought of the nineteenth-century individualist anarchists—an alternative that endorses markets while suggesting that it is precisely the distortion of markets by state-secured privilege that accounts for structural poverty and underwrites workplace subordination. *See* Markets Not Capitalism: Individualist Anarchism against Bosses, Inequality, Corporate Power, and Structural Poverty (Gary Chartier & Charles W. Johnson eds., 2011); Gary Chartier, Anarchy and Legal Order: Law and Politics for a Stateless Society (2013).

[21] For one influential exposition of this view, *see* Charles Murray, Losing Ground: American Social Policy 1950–1980 (1984).

coalition occasioned by the liberation movements of the sixties and the perception that the agendas of these movements conflicted with traditional religious beliefs led many people, intellectuals and blue-collar workers alike, increasingly to ally with the political Right.[22] Lacking the influence derived from participation in a broad-based political movement, members of Rorty's cultural Left may have felt disinclined to take some risks to which they might earlier have been drawn. And the split over cultural issues during and after the war years may have made them wary of attempts at coalition building.[23] This hardly shows that a confident political movement on the Left is impossible. And inactivity resulting from the current lack of an effective coalition hardly seems tantamount to a dismissal of the American project as irredeemably depraved.

Rorty's dichotomy focuses on cultural concerns and socio-economic ones. While he notes the importance of the Vietnam conflict in the shift he seeks to analyze, he doesn't note the Left's growing disengagement from issues of war and empire after Vietnam. When Bill Clinton became the first representative of the Vietnam generation to occupy the White House, he sponsored a brutal imperial adventure in the Balkans with very little criticism from the Left.[24] In general, the Democrats resisted attempts to challenge war, an embodiment of both sadism and selfishness, on moral grounds, though they sometimes raised pragmatic fiscal and geopolitical worries. I suspect this tendency reflected the fact that people who had been outsiders during the 1960s were by now significant players within the Establishment, and found it difficult not to adopt the Establishment's prevailing perspectives. It was also likely a consequence of perceived political risks. Republicans had repeatedly painted Democrats as unable to defend America; Democrats responded by returning to the hawkishness of Cold War liberalism.

I am not sure, in short, that a defeatist belief in original sin lies behind the lack of a sustained commitment to practical economic, social, and political change on the part of the American Left.[25] Other factors seem as capable of explaining how things have developed. Similarly, I am unsure that what people committed to positive social change need is the religion of America.

[22] *See, e.g.*, KENNETH L. KARST, LAW'S PROMISE, LAW'S EXPRESSION: VISIONS OF POWER IN THE POLITICS OF RACE, GENDER, AND RELIGION (1993); THOMAS BYRNE EDSALL WITH MARY D. EDSALL, CHAIN REACTION: THE IMPACT OF RACE, CULTURE, AND TAXES ON AMERICAN POLITICS (1991).

[23] Rorty notes this split, referring to the point at which "intellectuals began to lose interest in the labor unions, partly as a result of resentment over the union members' failure to back George McGovern over Richard Nixon in 1972," RORTY, ACHIEVING, *supra* note 1, at 77, but he does not comment on the possibility that the split might be integrated into an historical narrative different from his.

[24] A welcome exception has been Noam Chomsky. *See* NOAM CHOMSKY, THE NEW MILITARY HUMANISM: LESSONS FROM KOSOVO (1999); NOAM CHOMSKY, YUGOSLAVIA: PEACE, WAR, AND DISSOLUTION (2018).

[25] Another complicating factor: sometimes, the ideology Rorty attributes to "the cultural Left" involves ineradicable guilt, sometimes pervasive tendencies toward evil. How we think about and respond to the two must obviously be quite different. How we address the fact of guilt, if it is a fact, will involve a change in self-understanding. But such a change is unlikely by itself to eliminate injustice sedimented in social institutions.

III. THE RELIGION OF AMERICA

Rorty complains about the "quasi-cosmological" character of the cultural Left's rhetoric. The sort of religion it embraces, he fears, encourages it to submit to necessity rather than remaining open to the possibility of being surprised by hope. Thus his objection to Marxism: it employs theory, rather than careful, attentive, ongoing observation, as a basis for historical predictions and leads us to ignore the surprises of history. A grand theoretical framework squelches novelty. But Rorty counters the cultural Left's pessimism with an alternative religious vision, one which maintains that there is no way of getting away from contingency and particularity—and that emphasizes the celebration of American possibility.[26] He argues for a new literary canon, highlighting the inspirational—in effect, religious—value of great works of literature, pragmatically defined as those which do, in fact, inspire.[27] And he suggests that a religious stance which is hopeful about American possibility must take the place of one preoccupied with America's irredeemable sinfulness. Will the religion of America Rorty defends do the critical work he wants it to do?

A. *An American Faith*

Rorty maintains that James and Dewey, whose putative positions on this issue he evidently shares, regarded pragmatism as "compatible with religious belief—but only with a privatized religious belief, not with the sort of religious belief that produces churches, especially churches which take political positions."[28] At the same time, he remembers approvingly that the leftist movement made the American university into a church of a sort, and he clearly favors cultural institutions that transmit American civic religion.

As Rorty conceives of it, American civic religion must be rooted in hope—not in divine providence but in the self-fulfilling belief in a possible American future in which justice and inclusive community are realized. Dewey and Whitman, the great exemplars of the stance he articulates, "hoped to separate the fraternity and loving kindness urged by the Christian scriptures from the ideas of supernatural parentage, immortality, providence, and—most important—sin."[29] "They both hoped that America would be the place where a religion of love would finally replace

26 "As long as . . . the American Left remains incapable of national pride, our country will have only a cultural Left, not a political one." RORTY, ACHIEVING, *supra* note 1, at 38.

27 *See id.* at 125–40.

28 *Id.* at 142 n. 8. On the (de)politicization of faith, *see, e.g.*, ROBERT AUDI & NICHOLAS WOLTERSTORFF, RELIGION IN THE PUBLIC SQUARE: THE PLACE OF RELIGIOUS CONVICTIONS IN POLITICAL DEBATE (1997); KENT GREENAWALT, PRIVATE CONSCIENCES AND PUBLIC REASONS (1995); KENT GREENAWALT, RELIGIOUS CONVICTIONS AND POLITICAL CHOICE (1988); STEPHEN L. CARTER, THE CULTURE OF DISBELIEF: HOW AMERICAN LAW AND POLITICS TRIVIALIZE RELIGIOUS DEVOTION (1993); STEPHEN L. CARTER, THE DISSENT OF THE GOVERNED: A MEDITATION ON LAW, RELIGION, AND LOYALTY (1998); STEPHEN L. CARTER, GOD'S NAME IN VAIN: THE WRONGS AND RIGHTS OF RELIGION IN POLITICS (2000).

29 RORTY, ACHIEVING, *supra* note 1, at 15–16.

a religion of fear."[30] They hoped, Rorty says approvingly, to break "the traditional link between the religious impulse, the impulse to stand in awe of something greater than oneself, and the infantile need for security, the childish hope of escaping from time and chance. . . . They wanted . . . [a] utopian America to replace God as the unconditional object of desire."[31] "Dewey wanted Americans to share a civic religion that substituted utopian striving for claims to theological knowledge."[32] Together with Whitman, he wanted America to rejoice in its capacity for continuous, self-surpassing improvement.

B. Questioning "America"

The ideal Rorty articulates here is obviously attractive. But perhaps it offers too much—unintentional—support for American pride of the wrong sort. And it leads to an unreasonable willingness to treat America—whether understood as polity, as geography, or as population—as exerting a special moral claim on Americans.

As I have emphasized, NATURAL LAW theory is antithetical to nationalism. The failure to embrace the NATURAL LAW perspective—simultaneously cosmopolitan and localist, but definitely non-nationalist—can be a source of multiple problems. One is the temptation to treat genuinely fundamental criticism as effectively impossible. Dewey, Rorty tells us, "abandoned the question 'Why should one prefer democracy to feudalism, and self-creation to obedience to authority?'" in favor of the question "Given the preferences we Americans share, given the adventure on which we are embarked, what should we say about truth, knowledge, reason, virtue, human nature, and all the other traditional philosophical topics?"[33] But what if certain features of American politics and policy need to be questioned?

Take the (ab)use of American military power as a key example. Rorty notes that he inherited from his parents the conviction that identifying with the Left meant being an anti-militarist. He observes, however, that he celebrated and celebrates America's decision to enter the war against Hitler. He fails to acknowledge thoughtful criticisms of American participation even in this "good war" by both realists and radical leftists.[34] And he never explains on what basis, if any, he abandoned his earlier belief, nor explains what the contours of his new position might be. The result is that his endorsement of the Cold War—grounded in his thoroughly justified skepticism of Leninism, Stalinism, and Maoism—comes to seem more unqualified than it

30 *Id.* at 17. *Cf.* JOHN DEWEY, A COMMON FAITH (1934).

31 RORTY, ACHIEVING, *supra* note 1, at 18.

32 *Id.* at 38.

33 *Id.* at 28.

34 *See, e.g.*, BRUCE M. RUSSETT, NO CLEAR AND PRESENT DANGER: A SKEPTICAL VIEW OF THE UNITED STATES ENTRY INTO WORLD WAR II (2d ed., 1997); Howard Zinn, *Holy Wars*, DEMOCRACY NOW, Jan. 8, 2010, https://www.democracynow.org/2010/1/8/howard_zinn_three_holy_wars; Howard Zinn, *Three Holy Wars:* The Progressive's *100th Anniversary Conference*, HOWARDZINN.ORG, May 2, 2009, https://www.howardzinn.org/three-holy-wars-the-progressives-100th-anniversary-conference/.

doubtless is. Rorty is hardly blind to the abuses perpetrated around the world in the name of American foreign policy. But, despite the utter awfulness of Stalinism, we can still ask whether viewing Cold War America simply as "the nuclear superpower which halted the spread of an evil empire ruled by a mad tyrant"[35] might obscure the underside of American foreign policy.

Or consider the problem of global poverty—seemingly linked all too closely to the choices of American political and military leaders. War, political meddling, restrictions on trade, restrictions on immigration, and misplaced aid all contribute to the unnecessary persistence of poverty. Changing these features of American policy won't just enhance the well-being of people around the world; it will yield obvious economic benefits for ordinary Americans. A genuine, peaceful, noninterventionist cosmopolitanism can be expected to be beneficial across the board. But Rorty hesitates. He plausibly identifies globalization as a major unresolved issue to be confronted by people who care about a better future—despite the fairly clear evidence that markets spread prosperity widely.[36] He is unsure, however, how to resolve some of the tensions potentially associated with cosmopolitanism

To put the problem in terms somewhat different from Rorty's: The Principle of Fairness—expressed in liberal universalism and a commitment to equality and inclusiveness—seems to entail an openness to economic policies suited to raising the living standards of people around the world through the opening of borders and the elimination of trade restrictions. But articulating this position runs the risk of linking genuine liberals with those who use the rhetoric of freedom to support rigged trade agreements and cronyish deals with authoritarian governments. On the other hand, resistance to so-called neoliberal policies might prompt openness to industrial policy, protectionism, and border regulation. But articulating *this* position runs the risk of linking liberals not only with bad economics and ethics but also with populist demagoguery.

Achieving Our Country pointedly delineates what Rorty sees as the difficulties created by globalization. And he suggests persuasively that the issue of how best to respond to the globalization of the economy "will be the most deeply divisive that the American Left will face in the twenty-first century." He goes on, soberly: "I wish that I had some good ideas about how the dilemma might be resolved, but I do

35 Rorty, Achieving, *supra* note 1, at 63.

36 *See, e.g.*, Jay R. Mandle, Globalization and the Poor (2003); William Easterly, The Tyranny of Experts: Economists, Dictators, and the Forgotten Rights of the Poor (2015); William Easterly, The Economics of International Development: Foreign Aid versus Freedom for the World's Poor (2016); Jagdish Bhagwati & Arvind Panagariya, Why Growth Matters: How Economic Growth in India Reduced Poverty and the Lessons for Other Developing Countries (2014); Charles Kenny, Getting Better: Why Global Development Is Succeeding—and How We Can Improve the World Even More (2011). *Cf.* Deirdre N. McCloskey, Bourgeois Dignity: Why Economics Can't Explain the Modern World (2010); Deirdre N. McCloskey, Bourgeois Equality: How Ideas, Not Capital Or Institutions, Enriched the World (2016); Bas van der Vossen & Jason Brennan, In Defense of Openness: Why Global Freedom is the Humane Solution to Global Poverty (2018).

not."[37] But his discussion of the issue seems unfortunately weighted in favor of the nationalist alternative.[38] He obviously—and rightly, as we can see all too clearly in the age of Donald Trump—fears that economic insecurities brought about by globalization could lead to the rise of populist demagogues who might roll back the gains made during the last three decades by the cultural Left while leaving selfishness unchecked at home or abroad.[39] He seems to hint that he fears that preventing this nightmare scenario from becoming reality might, at least to some extent, justify protectionist and kindred strategies, though he does not argue for them unequivocally.

A genuinely inclusive liberalism cannot afford to be blind to the pragmatic concerns Rorty's observations rightly put on the table: freedom to work and freedom to trade can yield short-term disruption. At the same time, however, it is important not to overstate the point. Immigrant labor boosts overall economic productivity, and free trade makes the poorest consumers better off. A range of domestic policy changes could address economic vulnerability in the United States without interfering with anyone's economic freedom.[40] And attempts to "level the playing field" by requiring that workplace standards be uniform across the planet will serve primarily to keep overseas workers in poverty while disadvantaging consumers in the developed world.[41]

Rorty is no jingoist. He is unequivocal, for instance, that the "Vietnam War . . . is an atrocity of which Americans should be deeply ashamed."[42] Indeed, he expresses the (worrisome) "hope that the United States of America will someday yield up sovereignty to what Tennyson called 'the Parliament of Man, the Federation of the World.'"[43] But his decision to treat American ideals as to some degree given and his focus on the importance of national loyalty and self-respect may sometimes incline him to give nationalism a pass.

Rorty approvingly cites Whitman to the effect that we Americans "are the greatest poem because we put ourselves in the place of God . . . . Other nations thought of themselves as hymns to the glory of God. We redefine God as our future selves."[44] Thus, "[b]oth Dewey and Whitman viewed the United States as an opportunity to

37 Rorty, Achieving, *supra* note 1 at 148–49 n. 8. *Cf.* Richard Rorty, *Moral Universalism and Economic Triage*, UNESCO Philosophy Forum 1996, http://pp.kpnet.fi/seirioa/cdenn/rort.html.

38 See both his discussion of the importance of national pride and his implicit suggestion that American workers will be able to support progressive causes only if globalization has not robbed them of economic security.

39 Rorty, Achieving, *supra* note 1at 90–91.

40 *See* Markets Not Capitalism, *supra* note 20.

41 *See* Benjamin F. Powell, Out of Poverty: Sweatshops in the Global Economy (2014).

42 Rorty, Achieving, *supra* note 1, at 56. The Vietnam War was certainly an atrocity. And those who promoted and executed it certainly ought to be ashamed. But it is unclear to me why those who did not support it, and why those who were not even born, or were not American citizens, when it occurred should feel ashamed by it.

43 *Id.* at 3.

44 *Id.* at 22.

see ultimate significance in a finite, human, historical project . . . ."[45] What is wrong with thinking and talking in this way is not that it somehow offends the ego of a touchy divinity but that we are ultimately incapable of managing the task of being God. No finite reality, even one capable of continuous improvement (and is any finite reality capable of *limitless* progress?) can fail sometimes to disappoint us. No finite reality can serve as a center of loyalty that relativizes all of our other loyalties. No finite reality can avoid becoming tyrannical if accorded ultimate significance. To give unqualified loyalty to America is to transform it into an idol. Despite Rorty's genuine commitment to serious social criticism and his sensitivity to the value of justice beyond American borders, his project still seems to run the risk of excessively valorizing the American project. What we need, I think, is just the sort of vision of which Rorty seems suspicious—one on the basis of which American practice and ideals can be evaluated.

IV. TRANSCENDENCE AND CRITIQUE

The possibility of critique depends on the ability to step outside the story of America. The optimistic and positive vision of Dewey and Whitman merits our qualified affirmation. But social criticism depends on convictions that are more than merely American. It depends on a sort of *realism* with which Rorty is uncomfortable.

Rorty's dismissal, with Dewey, of "the idea that there ... [is] a reality 'out there' with an intrinsic nature to be respected and corresponded to" as "a relic of Platonic otherworldliness"[46] leaves open the question whether his position can take adequate account of what is radically different. You don't have to believe that we have unmediated access to Platonic universals to believe that reality is more than we can assume or conceptualize, that other people resist reduction to the limits imposed by our categories. And such a belief is crucial if adequate social criticism is to be possible. Only if our criticisms are more than what we take to be arbitrary preferences, only if there is more to the oppressed person than the system of oppression has put inside her, is there any warrant—logically or psychologically—for criticizing that system.[47]

Rorty genially relegates the "quasi-religious form of spiritual pathos" with which philosophers like Derrida and Levinas respond to the obscurity and incomprehensibility of reality, our inability to master it, our sense of being infinitely responsible, "to private life." "When we take up our public responsibilities," he says, "... the infinite and unrepresentable are merely nuisances."[48] It is certainly possible for appeals to the infinite and unrepresentable to justify moral and political paralysis. But I think they are better read as reminders of our limitations *precisely in the face of*

45 *Id.* at 17.
46 *Id.* at 29.
47 *See, e.g.*, Wendy M. Farley, Eros for the Other: Retaining Truth in a Pluralistic World (1996).
48 Rorty, Achieving, *supra* note 1, at 96–97.

otherness—an otherness that must be acknowledged if the dominance of the selfish and the sadistic is to be resisted. Critique depends on our accountability to a reality that is more than our, or anyone's, preferences, on the capacity of reality to surprise us at a deep level.

Though he enthusiastically endorses the dedication to "achieving our country" suggested by Baldwin's call to remain engaged in political struggle, Rorty curiously implies that there is no reason to describe this call as more justified than the alternatives. He suggests that while Baldwin chose to be an agent, a participant in shaping America's future, Elijah Muhammad opted "to be a spectator and to leave the fate of the United States to the operation of nonhuman forces." Then, he goes on: "I do not think there is any point in arguing that Elijah Muhammad made the right decision and Baldwin the wrong one, or vice versa. . . . Both decisions are intelligible. Either can be made plausible. But there are no neutral, objective criteria which dictate one rather than the other."[49] Similarly, he maintains:

> For Whitman and Dewey, a classless and casteless society ... is neither more natural nor more rational than the cruel societies of feudal Europe or of eighteenth-century Virginia. All that can be said in its defense is that it would produce less unnecessary suffering than any other, and that it is the best means to a certain end: the creation of a greater diversity of individuals ... To those who want a demonstration that less suffering and greater diversity should be the overriding aims of political endeavor, Dewey and Whitman have nothing to say. They know of no more certain premises from which such a belief might be deduced.[50]

He is confident, similarly, that "[f]or purposes of thinking about how to govern our country, we do not need to worry about the . . . grounds of normativity . . . . For those purposes, we can give both religion and philosophy a pass. We can just get on with trying to solve what Dewey called 'the problems of men.'"[51]

There are, as Rorty would be quick to acknowledge, multiple ways to read passages like these. He may wish simply to maintain that there are no universally acknowledged *procedures* for resolving substantial moral and political disputes. This claim, which seems unexceptionable, need not trouble anyone. A claim can be both justified and true whether or not everyone agrees that there is a way of justifying the claim or that the claim really is true. "[J]ustification," as Rorty elsewhere observes, "is relative to time and place," while "truth is not. . . ."[52] But the reader may be tempted

49 *Id.* at 13.

50 *Id.* at 30.

51 *Id.* at 97. Apparently, however, among the problems of men is not the problem of which goals merit our pursuit or the problem of what makes for a fulfilled and flourishing life. At least in some moods, Rorty seems to see ethics as a matter of realizing our desires in tandem with others' realization of theirs; *see, e.g.*, Richard Rorty, *An Ethics for Today, in* An Ethics for Today: Finding Common Ground between Philosophy and Religion 7, 15 (2011).

52 Richard M. Rorty, *Realism and Reference*, 59 Monist 321, 321–22 (1976). *Cf.* Richard M. Rorty, *Pragmatism, Davidson and Truth, in* Truth and Interpretation: Perspectives on the Philosophy of Donald Davidson 333 (Ernest Le Pore ed., 1986); Richard M. Rorty, Philosophy and the Mirror

to conclude that, for all his evident passion for justice, Rorty inclines to the view that the moral and political norms he endorses are finally arbitrary. And of course there are pragmatic reasons for not viewing them this way, since viewing norms this way, whatever an ironist might prefer to believe, undermines our ability to embrace, inhabit, and deploy them.[53]

This seems to pose a problem for Rorty's political commitments. I am not sure we can credibly seek justice or affirm its worth if we "see everything around us and within us as one more replaceable social construction."[54] It seems to me that Rorty runs the risk of making a commitment to particular ideals simply another preference, to be affirmed or rejected as a matter of taste. If it is simply that, then there is no reason (apart from random inclination) that we, or Rorty, or anyone else should prefer liberalism, say, to monarchism. Rorty is perfectly willing to speak of some outcomes as better or worse;[55] he is no nihilist. But it is hard to see just why he should not be, apart from his own humane temper. It seems to me that the kind of critique he wants to offer seems more plausible if offered from the perspective of something like natural law theory.

Rorty's sin-based analysis of the Left's retreat from the political field reflects his contention that competing religious visions lie at the root of the split within the progressive movement and his general suspicion of grand visions—"metanarratives"—of the sort he tends to associate with religious traditions like Christianity and Marxism. Thus, he criticizes Marxism for its religious character,[56] and maintains "that, in committing itself to what it calls 'theory', ... [the cultural] Left has gotten something which is entirely too much like religion." This error, he indicates, takes the form of coming "to believe that we must place our country within a theoretical frame of reference, situate it within a vast quasi-cosmological perspective."[57]

Thus, he would likely be quick to respond to any demand for warrants by reminding us that none of us occupies a God's-eye point of view beyond all traditions and communities, from which she could survey the American project and assess it. And he would be right. But the ability to engage in credible social criticism does not depend on the accessibility of such a point of view. It depends on the active

OF NATURE 176, 180 (1979). Thanks to JEFFREY STOUT, ETHICS AFTER BABEL: THE LANGUAGES OF MORALS AND THEIR DISCONTENTS 24–28, 93–94, 244–55 (1988) for sensitizing me to the distinction between justification and truth, for making me aware of its presence in Rorty's work, and for providing me with these specific references and the passage quoted in the text.

53 *See* MARCEL LIEBERMAN, COMMITMENT, VALUE, AND MORAL REALISM 132–33, 197–98 (1998) (*quoted and cited in* WILLIAM D. CASEBEER, NATURAL ETHICAL FACTS: EVOLUTION, CONNECTIONISM, AND MORAL COGNITION 157, 184 n.7 (2003)).

54 RORTY, ACHIEVING, *supra* note 1, at 96.

55 *See id.* at 28.

56 *See id.* at 46.

57 *Id.* at 95.

confrontation of rival traditions and ongoing, piecemeal critical reflection.[58] This means, in turn, that two things are necessary: encounters with quite different projects, and the assumption that—even though we always encounter reality using our own metaphors and concepts and assumptions—reality is not identical with what we can understand and describe, and thus stands in judgment on our claims.

Providing theoretical warrants for critical analysis of American life need not mean returning to just the sort of foundationalism Rorty and others have rightly sought to dislodge from its place in our affections. We don't require a clear and complete account of our circumstances in order to make the judgments and choices we need to make as persons and groups. We do not require a bottom-up rational justification of our moral or scientific practices in order to work or love or understand. But understanding our critical engagement with contemporary social and political reality within a broader framework can be thoroughly useful: such a framework can help to situate and undergird our reflection and action. It need not be this sort of foundationalist or procrustean theoretical construct. It can even be a story.

Rorty makes no bones about his fondness for stories. He urges that we look to great works of literature for inspiration, maintaining that a fluctuating, multiple, diverse array of stories should inform our imaginations. It is arguable, though, whether such an approach, while appealing, is sufficient. For sometimes our purposes must be ordered—to assume some consistent and coherent relation to each other. The various stories on which we draw for inspiration need to be connected with each other, their perspectives assessed and evaluated. The episodes of one's own life must be integrated into a unified story, and the story of that life as a whole into a more inclusive narrative.

Rorty himself has already offered just such a story: the story of America as a community brimming with possibility and leaping toward an unimaginable future, a story peopled with saints like James and Whitman and Dewey. This story provides context and trajectory for the moral and political claims he advances. It integrates and unifies the campaigns for which he calls. But this story, valuable as it is, is perhaps inadequate on its own. It doesn't seem inclusive enough.

Rorty is convinced that "you cannot urge national political renewal on the basis of descriptions of fact. You have to describe the country in terms of what you passionately hope it will become, as well as in terms of what you know it to be now."[59] The problem here is that, unless the commendation of the ideal has some warrants, it becomes simply an exercise in manipulative persuasion no more credible than the pronouncements of the White House press secretary or the CIA. What we think and

58 On pragmatic critical reflection, *see, e.g.*, Stout, *supra* note 52. On the confrontation of traditions, *see, e.g.*, Alasdair MacIntyre, Whose Justice? Which Rationality? (1988); Alasdair MacIntyre, Three Rival Versions of Moral Inquiry: Encyclopædia, Genealogy, and Tradition (1990). *But cf.* MacIntyre's more recent reflections on what seems a lot like human nature: Dependent Rational Animals: Why Human Beings Need the Virtues (1999).

59 Rorty, Achieving, *supra* note 1, at 101.

say regarding the course our society should take must be understood as *fitting*, as a matter of more than our own aspirations. Our convictions must be *appropriate*. If they are not the sorts of things about which we can reason at all, if only on an ad hoc basis, if they are not the sorts of things that could be true or false, then they can hardly claim our loyalty.

We must genuinely believe that it is a good thing to craft a community in which the strong do not oppress the weak and in which ethnicity, gender, and sexual orientation provide no basis for exclusion. To suppose that it is, we do not have to provide a fully worked out theoretical underpinning for our claims, but we have to have—and those with whom we communicate have to have—some sense that we are responding aright to the reality of women or gays or African Americans or entrepreneurs, and not merely articulating our own arbitrary or private preferences.[60] This entails abandonment of the subjectivism or emotivism that dispenses with meaningful talk of truth about moral and political ideals.

We cannot regard normative assertions as our own ultimately arbitrary creations, as matters of preference, and still take them very seriously. Either the phenomenology of moral experience will need to be transformed radically or we will be forced to refuse our assent to debunking accounts of moral language and moral truth.[61] But if such understandings of morality are inadequate, then we will need to believe that our moral claims really are capable of being objective and true. An account in virtue of which this can be the case seems likely to be more adequate than Rorty's alternative, in accordance with which it is hard to see social criticism as more than simply an expression of our arbitrary preferences.

V. POLITICS AND SPIRITUALITY

A credible spirituality provides a perspective that allows not only American practice but also American ideals to be the object of critical scrutiny. Spiritual beliefs and practices can prompt a healthy awareness of our limitations and, indeed, our brokenness, an awareness that may prove to be a useful element in a proper response to our society's inequities rather than simply a debilitating source of inertia, especially if linked with an understanding of forgiveness more radical than the one Rorty seems to envision as possible. And a chastened belief in providence may offer a basis for the hope that radical social critique seems to demand.

At their best, the religious and spiritual traditions of which Rorty is skeptical offer useful reminders of the limits of political institutions. He dismisses conventional religious belief as an attempt to gain an impossible purchase on eternity. But

60 See Gary Chartier, Comment, *Righting Narrative: Robert Chang, Poststructuralism, and the Limits of Critique*, 7 UCLA Asian Pac. Am. L.J.105 (2001).

61 We can affirm moral truth without any sort of robust moral ontology; *see, e.g.*, Annette *Bryson, Non-Inflationary Realism about Morality: Language, Metaphysics, and Truth* (2017) (unpublished Ph.D. dissertation, University of Michigan).

traditional religious suspicion of idolatry served to undercut just that sort of attempt. If idolatry is to be avoided, then no representation of the divine can be final, no claim to possess unmediated absolute truth plausible, no social institution beyond criticism. Indeed, the rejection of idolatry entails precisely the responsibility to attend with infinite patience to the particularity of creatures, not to subsume them within categories that obviate attention to their distinctive reality.

A. *Brokenness is Real*

Talk about sin can be a source of unbearable guilt and hopelessness. It can be used destructively to stigmatize choices that in fact realize or promote flourishing. It can be used to convey an indefensible sense of inherited guilt—people cannot reasonably be held responsible for actions by others which they neither intended, effectively enabled, nor cheered, but some understandings of sin allow for this kind of faux responsibility. And it can seem wrapped up with belief in an arbitrary divine tyrant, in William Blake's Nobodaddy.[62] And so there may be good reason to avoid using the word "sin." But an awareness that we've made and continue to make serious mistakes, sometimes knowingly and willingly, that we don't have it all together, that we are sometimes our own worst enemies—these facts about ourselves seem well worth acknowledging.

This kind of recognition is a useful source of modesty. It challenges our pretensions. It need not lead to fatalism or resignation. But it can and should make us sensitive to the possibility of deep and pervasive distortions in laws, institutions, and social practices.

Rorty criticizes a sense of sin that he seems to think entails a belief in complete human powerlessness in the face of evil. If it did entail this, an increasing awareness of distortion and destructiveness in American life might be paralyzing. But to believe that brokenness is pervasive and that it conditions and shapes the background to our choices is not necessarily to regard any given instance of brokenness as essential, necessary, or inevitable.

To be sure, a conservative account of human nature and society might maintain that evil's inevitability makes positive social change impossible. Moral brokenness always has the potential to get in the way of movements toward justice. And the fact that we are not angels should make us doubtful not just about the potential knavery of market actors but also of politicians and generals and bureaucrats.

That recognizing the pervasiveness of power need not lead to inertia is as evident from the career of Michel Foucault himself as from that of any philosopher of the century. Foucault combined a sense of the omnipresence of systems of domination and a passion for highly abstract theory with a commitment to practical engagement

[62] *Cf.* Gary Chartier, The Analogy of Love: Divine and Human Love at the Center of Christian Theology 177–89 (2d ed., 2017).

in ongoing struggles on behalf of prisoners, immigrants, and dissidents. If the ideology of the cultural Left were so clearly inimical to action, then a figure to whom Rorty refers repeatedly as a prime exponent of that ideology might reasonably be expected to wallow in passivity. Foucault did nothing of the sort.[63]

There is no conflict between acknowledging the pervasive effects of oppression and working to challenge them. Indeed, acknowledging that those effects are felt in our own lives as well as in the behavior of The System can be a helpful pointer to the unsustainability of self-righteousness. In this sense, an awareness of sin may be an ally, not an enemy, of effective social criticism.

B. *Rediscovering Grace*

Rorty puzzlingly alleges that those "who take ... [the] notion [of sin] seriously find Dewey and Whitman childlike, naïve, and dangerous... . For such people, it is a fundamental moral fact that the commission of certain acts ... is incompatible with further self-respect."[64] Dewey believed, according to Rorty, that even if one has done something horrible, one should "attempt to live so as never to do such a thing again" rather than regarding oneself as irredeemable. Those "who take the notion of sin seriously ... view ... [this notion] as merely the light-minded, Californian view that one should treat any crime one happens to commit as a useful learning experience."[65] By contrast, for Rorty this attitude is crucial to an effective commitment to social change. Thus, when he says that American progressives "reinvented

63 Foucault's own sense of the pervasiveness of power did not lead him to abandon the possibility of critique any more than the possibility of action. In an interview, Michel Foucault, *The Ethics of the Concern for Self as a Practice of Freedom, in* ETHICS: SUBJECTIVITY AND TRUTH 281 (Paul Rabinow ed., 1997), in which he explores a range of related issues, Foucault maintains: "[W]hen I talk about power relations and games of truth, I am absolutely not saying that games of truth are just concealed power relations—that would be a horrible exaggeration. My problem . . . is in understanding how truth games are set up and how they are connected with power relations. . . . [T]he medicalization of madness . . . was connected with a whole series of social and economic processes . . . but also with institutions and practices of power. This fact in no way impugns the scientific validity or the therapeutic effectiveness of psychiatry: it does not endorse psychiatry, but neither does it invalidate it. . . . [M]athematics . . . is linked . . . to power structures, if only in the way it is taught, the way in which consensus among mathematicians is organized, . . . determines what is good (true) or bad (false) in mathematics. This in no way means that mathematics is only a game of power, but that the game of truth of mathematics is linked in a certain way—without thereby being invalidated in any way—to games and institutions of power. It is clear that in some cases these connections are such that one could write the entire history of mathematics without taking them into account. . . . [I]n any case, one simply cannot say that games of truth are nothing but games of power." *Id.* at 296. Responding to an interviewer's observation that someone "who has the capacity to formulate truths also has a power, the power of being able to speak the truth and to express it in the way [she or] he wants," Foucault says: "Yes, and yet this does not mean that what the person says is not true, which is what most people believe. When you tell people that there may be a relationship between truth and power, they say: 'So it isn't truth after all!'" *Id.* at 298.

64 RORTY, ACHIEVING, *supra* note 1, at 32.

65 *Id.* at 33.

the old religious idea that some stains are ineradicable,"[66] he does so by way of emphasizing that in so doing they had taken a step toward passivity, toward abandoning America as beyond hope.

I confess a measure of puzzlement. If Rorty is right that James Baldwin regarded America as unforgivable while nonetheless holding out hope that it might be transformed,[67] then perhaps contemporary American advocates of positive social change might regard the stain of the nation's evil as ineradicable while still holding out hope for change. But, more fundamentally, I am unclear why Rorty supposes that actual religious traditions regard some actions—collective or individual—as "incompatible with further self-respect," as justifying "bottomless self-disgust" or the decision to become merely "a horrified spectator of . . . [one's] own past."[68] While Rorty refers to unforgivable sins, it is curious that he never alludes to the possibility that those who suppose some sins to be unforgivable aren't retailing an old *Christian* idea at all.[69] Perhaps Rorty's cultural Left needs not so much a diluted sense of sin as an enhanced understanding of grace.

On what I would take to be an understanding shared within multiple spiritual traditions, moral failure never needs to have the last word regarding anyone's status, self-understanding, or capacity for goodness. Indeed, believing in grace means believing that love and acceptance envelop us before, during, and after any particular instance of wrongdoing.[70] It is perfectly possible, then, to be fully aware of having failed, even of having failed monstrously, without being crushed by a sense of guilt.

To the extent that Rorty is correct that the cultural Left regards America as unforgivable, he's wrong that their attitude is evidence that academic leftists have "gotten religion." The problem, rather, is that they haven't got the right sort. They haven't fully apprehended the possibility of radical grace, radical forgiveness. Multiple sets of spiritual beliefs convey the message that it is possible in the face of horrific evil to do precisely what Rorty suggests Deweyans ought to do: refuse to be overwhelmed or to retreat from agency to spectatorship.

Recognizing the possibility of grace may make it easier to face truly awful personal or national evil. Certainly, a vision of divine care, of a divine embrace, provides some *content* for the idea of an ultimate security that secures my identity and value as a person and not merely this or that relationship with some finite other.[71] And embracing a vision of grace means that it may be possible for an offender to be

66 *Id.* at 95.

67 *See id.* at 12, 13.

68 *Id.* at 33.

69 *Cf.* L. GREGORY JONES, EMBODYING FORGIVENESS: A THEOLOGICAL ANALYSIS (1995); Marilyn McCord Adams, *Forgiveness: A Christian Model, in* CHRISTIAN THEISM AND MORAL PHILOSOPHY 77 (Michael Beaty *et al.*, eds., 1998); L. WILLIAM COUNTRYMAN, FORGIVEN AND FORGIVING (1998); EDWARD M. FARLEY, GOOD AND EVIL: INTERPRETING A HUMAN CONDITION (1990).

70 *See* JACK W. PROVONSHA, YOU CAN COME HOME AGAIN: AN "UN-THEOLOGY" OF THE ATONEMENT (1982).

71 *See* FARLEY, GOOD AND EVIL, *supra* note 69, at 144–46.

more honest with herself about her brokenness and to retain hope in divine love than she would otherwise be. She can face the radicality of her own moral brokenness, or her nation's, while knowing that she need not depend on herself or her nation for redemption.

Rorty sometimes talks as if the principal problem with the cultural Left's recovery of the idea of original sin were that sin can't be *forgiven*. It is clear, though, that his concern is not only with the view that America's abuses make national self-respect impossible but also with the conviction that these abuses point to the existence of structures of abusive power that make real social and political change *impossible*. Thus, Rorty's envisioned campaigners need a doctrine of providence as well as a doctrine of forgiveness.

C. *Providence and Hope for America*

The commitment to doing justice Rorty seeks to foster depends on hope. Describing the Left as "the party of hope," he sees a sense that change is still possible, that all is not lost, as crucial to the transformative project he advocates. And he seems to me to be right. But it is not so obvious that the basis for hope he offers is particularly secure or that it is even altogether supportive of his socio-political agenda.

Hope in American possibility might be understood in at least two ways. It could depend on the broadly empirical claim that the American tradition just is the sort of tradition that is capable of self-correction and change. This cannot be the simple and relatively trivial claim that the future is open, that change is possible. It must be the claim that positive self-transformation is a recurrent feature of American life. Otherwise, it would provide no particular basis for hope.

This claim is not self-evidently false. It may be that American national culture, marked by a refusal to look backward, an almost pathologically futuristic orientation, is especially open to the possibility of change. And perhaps American ideals are such that the change to which America is prone tends to be positive. It would certainly be possible to tell a story of America's development that emphasized the progressive realization of ideals of equality, freedom, and justice. However, despite the evident power of these ideals in American history, it is clear that they have been realized fitfully and that America's movement toward an increasingly just community is anything but rectilinear and unimpeded. Hope in America is not positively irrational, but the continuing unjust treatment of women, poor people, and diverse ethnic and sexual minorities should, at minimum, give us pause.

Indeed, hope *for* America of a broadly empirical sort always runs the risk of becoming hope *in* America—an excessive confidence in America's innate goodness. This sort of hope is not objectionable because it flies in the face of a gloomy doctrine of original sin, but for the very practical reason that it may tend to cut the nerve of social criticism. It may tend to lull us into a false sense that America is fundamentally all right. The liberal need not and should not be a merchant of gloom: she has no investment in a particularly negative assessment of American life. But she cannot allow herself to depend on the conviction that the state of America's soul is healthy. She must be prepared to face the possibility, at any rate, of radical sinfulness.

In any case, Rorty seems really to have in mind a different sort of claim, one that doesn't depend on any empirical judgments about the actual state of America. Confident in the relative malleability of history, he wishes to suggest that hope in America may become self-fulfilling. If we hope in America, we may bring that for which we hope into being. Hope will energize and empower us for struggle, prompt us to discern new and untried possibilities. According to "the civic religion of which Whitman and Dewey were prophets," Americans

> were supposed to love our country because it showed promise of being kinder and more generous than other countries. As the blacks and the gays, among others, were well aware, this was a counsel of perfection rather than description of fact. But you cannot urge national political renewal on the basis of descriptions of fact. You have to describe the country in terms of what you passionately hope it will become, as well as in terms of what you know it to be now. You have to be loyal to a dream country rather than to the one to which you wake up every morning. Unless such loyalty exists, the ideal has no chance of becoming actual.[72]

And, again, this is not an absurd claim. But we may nonetheless wonder just how much difference our hope alone will make. We may wonder whether, if we are dependent solely or primarily on the power of our own hope to bring its object into being, we might not do well to tend our own gardens and leave the public square to the snake. Hope is an uncertain basis for itself.

So there is reason to be doubtful about a purely immanent account of hope for America. By contrast, the idea of providence—which Rorty hopes to do without—offers the basis for a hopeful engagement with American life that remains open to the possibility of a better future. But it does so without undercutting criticism of the current state of American life by resting its confidence in that possibility in an overly optimistic assessment of the American present. A plausible account of providence will not understand divine action as unilaterally eliminating injustice. Views of providence in accordance with which the good is realized always and everywhere are simply incredible. On the other hand, however, a credible account of providence which enables us to see the possibility that divine purposes might genuinely be realized in history can indeed be articulated.[73] If we can see grace at work in and through the circumstances of history, we can find reason to be confident that

[72] Rorty, Achieving, *supra* note 1, at 101.

[73] *See, e.g.*, Arthur Peacocke, *God's Interaction with the World, in* All That Is: A Naturalistic Faith for the Twenty-First Century 45, 45–47 (Philip Clayton ed., 2007); Langdon Gilkey, Reaping the Whirlwind: A Christian Interpretation of History 303–306 (1976); Keith Ward, Divine Action (1990); Peter C. Hodgson, God in History: Shapes of Freedom (1989); John B. Cobb, Jr., *Natural Causality and Divine Action, in* God's Activity in the World: The Contemporary Problem 101 (Owen C. Thomas ed., 1983); Philip Clayton, God and Contemporary Science 188–269 (1997).

providence will continue to challenge Americans to realize what is best in their ideals—and, where necessary, to abandon and replace those ideals with more appropriate ones. And so we can be confident that advocacy of justice places us in an important sense with the grain of history, with the grain of the universe, rather than in tragic conflict with the way things are.[74]

Hope in providence is linked, for Rorty, with "the infantile need for security, the childish hope of escaping from time and chance."[75] By contrast, American faith, which passionately embraces temporality, is forgetful of eternity.[76] "Neither Dewey nor Whitman . . . was committed to the view that things would *inevitably* go well for America . . . . The price of temporalization is contingency. Because they rejected any idea of Divine Providence and any idea of immanent teleology, Dewey and Whitman had to grant the possibility that the vanguard of humanity may lose its way . . . ."[77] But an adequate account of providence need not understand history as scripted in advance, with the outcomes of our choices determined by an implacable divine will. Rorty seems to pose a stark dilemma: either providence or contingency, either God or a fruitful chaos. It is unclear that the God of classical theism can be dismissed as readily as many modern critics believe as the enemy of time and chance. But even if classical theism deserved to be criticized in this way, a variety of contemporary understandings of God and the God–world relationship would leave ample room for contingency.[78] A conception of providence as involving the interplay of divine and human freedom makes it possible to hope for order and direction in human lives and in human history without assuming that divine grace somehow cancels human freedom or annuls the unpredictability and vulnerability of human life. It is possible, then, to take human temporality seriously while also anticipating continuing providential activity in history.

VI. FREEDOM AND SOCIAL JUSTICE

Natural law liberalism calls for us to act fairly in institutional as in other interpersonal contexts, and to make fair contributions to institutions that themselves involve

[74] Rorty notes that Dewey and Whitman sought to craft an American religion unsullied by belief not only in providence but also in life beyond death. I have focused here on providence as a source of hope because, among other things, I believe providence offers a sense of meaning for and in history and thus can play an especially crucial role in relation to efforts for social change. But hope for life beyond death however conceptualized is obviously significant for political struggle as well: hope undermines fear, and thus deprives the tyrant and the torturer of one of their most potent weapons. *See, e.g.*, HODGSON, SHAPES, *supra* note 73, at 324–31; John B. Cobb, Jr., *The Resurrection of the Soul*, 80 HARV. THEOLOGICAL REV. 213 (1987).

[75] RORTY, ACHIEVING, *supra* note 1, at 18.

[76] *Id.*

[77] *Id.* at 22–23.

[78] *See, e.g.*, KEITH WARD, RATIONAL THEOLOGY AND THE CREATIVITY OF GOD (1982); PETER C. HODGSON, WINDS OF THE SPIRIT: A CONSTRUCTIVE CHRISTIAN THEOLOGY (1994); DAVID RAY GRIFFIN, REENCHANTMENT WITHOUT SUPERNATURALISM: A PROCESS PHILOSOPHY OF RELIGION (2001).

participants in acting fairly and extend the reach of their fairness. In this sense natural law liberalism embodies a conception of social justice.[79] But natural law liberalism provides no support for Rorty's proposal that we substitute "social justice for individual freedom as our country's principal goal."[80] This is true both because a key function of justice is precisely to safeguard freedom and because—this is, as I've already suggested, the key insight of radical liberalism—institutional arrangements that safeguard freedom can effectively address societal ills.[81]

A. *Justice, Social and Otherwise*

Primarily, justice concerns what people may reasonably claim by force. In this sense, justice demands that people avoid attacking others' bodies or interfering with their justly acquired possessions. This is the kind of justice a reasonable legal system can be expected to safeguard. I'll call this *political justice*.

Justice is sometimes understood more broadly as having to do with the whole realm of interpersonal moral responsibility. This means it includes requirements that can reasonably be implemented by force and those that can't be, and, in the latter category, requirements to benefit or avoid harming specific people. (It might not—usage is fuzzy—be applicable to the realm of open-ended requirements to confer benefits—but not to any particular beneficiaries.) An obligation to keep a promise to one's spouse, to avoid spreading vicious rumors, or to give money in support of a worthwhile cause could be seen as a matter of justice in this broader sense, even though not, at least ordinarily, a matter of justice in the narrower sense. I'll refer to justice in this broader sense as *moral justice*.[82]

Social justice refers to multiple, arguably incompatible, things. It's a curious expression, both because justice *couldn't* be asocial—since it's a matter of how we treat others—and because justice is a characteristic of actions rather than states of affairs.[83] But it seems to be used, roughly, to refer to institutional responses to widespread ills. Social justice might thus be seen to be a matter of such things as relieving poverty, facilitating access to basic services, and promoting dignity in the workplace. Obviously, these sorts of goals can be undertaken as a matter of individual obligation or goodwill, but talk about *social* justice will be appropriate when they are addressed institutionally or structurally or cooperatively. It is thus

79 *Cf.* Michael Novak et al., Social Justice Isn't What You Think It Is (2015); Gary Chartier, Book Review, 21 Indep. Rev. 302 (2016).

80 Rorty, Achieving, *supra* note 1, at 101.

81 *See* Chartier, Anarchy, *supra* note 20, at 320–77.

82 The distinction between political and moral justice I make here parallels the Aristotelian distinction between general and special justice, to which Roderick Long alludes in the course of noting the availability of the idea of social justice to an anti-statist position like the one he and I share: see Roderick T. Long, *Proletarian Blues*, Austro-Athenian Empire, Nov. 25, 2006, http://aaeblog.com/2006/11/25/proletarian-blues/.

83 *Cf.* John Finnis, Natural Law and Natural Rights 170 (1980) (dichotomizing the two somewhat less starkly than I do); 2 Friedrich A. Hayek, Law, Legislation, and Liberty 62–196 (1976).

characteristically assumed that social justice in this sense can and should be achieved by the state, acting on behalf of the entire society.

Despite the characteristic association in both popular and scholarly conversations between the idea of social justice and action by the state, it is entirely reasonable to think about social justice in a different way. Social justice can be achieved without the state through a variety of institutional and structural changes: by eliminating state-secured privilege, remedying past injustice, empowering people to create wealth through trade and to share it through a variety of non-state institutions, and contributing to the enhancement of a society's underlying structure of pre-political rules. Achieving social justice can reasonably be understood to be in part a matter of political justice and in part a matter of moral justice. Eliminating privileges and other unreasonable restraints on freedom and providing remedies for past acts of violence are crucial instances of political justice, while people's assumption of shared responsibility for each other is a crucial instance of moral justice.

Rorty seems to assume that social justice requires action by the state. But social justice can be achieved by a just legal order and active community institutions without the involvement of the state, and freeing people from the shackles of the state can be a means of actively fostering social justice. Commitment to a free society is thus quite compatible with a commitment to social justice.

B. *The Impact of Freedom*

States consistently create cartels and monopolies that benefit the wealthy and well connected. Liberating people from systematic aggression can foster social justice for three distinct but related reasons: (*i*) Free people can be productive in ways that can be widely beneficial, generating wealth that will be shared as the process of extended social cooperation through exchange goes on. (*ii*) Systematic aggression not only hobbles productivity but also creates structural poverty while actively dispossessing people and redistributing resources to the wealthy and well connected. And (*iii*) free people can organize themselves into mutual aid networks and societies in ways that can offer remedies for economic vulnerability. The first two means of fostering social justice are kinds of political justice, while the last is a kind of moral justice.

Leaving people free, against a background of robust protections for just possessory claims, to produce and exchange goods and services fosters productivity for at least two reasons. Giving people freedom mobilizes the collective intelligence of society as a whole, something no top-down control mechanism can do: the system, as it were, possesses knowledge, in distributed form, that no individual could have. In addition, allowing people to internalize the benefits and requiring them to internalize the costs of their choices prompts them to be efficient and careful. This need not be because they seek to further their own individual interests—what matters is that they can pursue goals they value, whatever those goals are. Because liberation fosters productivity then—provided productivity gains aren't captured by means of arbitrary, politically secured privileges—when freedom is fostered, wealth can be dispersed, and everyone can benefit. On its own, of course, the production and dispersion of more wealth need not affect everyone equally; but it can certainly be expected to benefit all active participants in the economy, including the working poor, as well as their dependents. It can create more long-term wealth for everyone.

As I emphasized, freedom can foster productivity in an environment undistorted by privilege. But privilege is, indeed, a persistent problem. States tend to constitute and serve the interests of an exploitative ruling class. They do so, in particular, by creating and maintaining unjust privileges.

Perhaps the most serious, destructive variety of privilege is protection for titles to assets secured through acts of blatant dispossession. Land theft has represented a massive redistribution of resources from ordinary people to privileged elites throughout the world—in Europe, in the Americas, in Africa.[84] Peasants who *should* have enjoyed the law's protection of their rights to own and freely dispose of the land they worked were converted into dependent tenants. And their successors in interest have been consequently disadvantaged in ongoing ways in relation to those able to benefit from large-scale robbery. Land engrossment has both benefited the cronies to whom engrossed land has been distributed and hampered the efforts of those who might otherwise have homesteaded it to improve their economic positions. Slavery has destroyed the lives of generations of those enslaved, wounded their descendants economically, socially, and psychically, and helped to increase the economic, social, and political influence of slave-owners and their successors in interest. Massive tax-funded subsidies and bailouts have redirected resources to well-connected military contractors and financial institutions, among others, enriching them while depriving others of resources.

Privilege protects these acts of violent redistribution. But it also fosters structural poverty and enriches the wealthy and well connected in multiple, and arguably more subtle, ways: limits on the work people can do (from licensing requirements to zoning rules) and constraints on the cost of housing and workspace and, more broadly, on access to resources (from building codes to measures that engross or otherwise encumber undeveloped land to tariffs to sales taxes to unjust intellectual property privileges) increase the cost of working for oneself, raise the cost of housing, food, and other sorts of consumption, and drive people into stultifying and often low-paying corporate employment.[85] People who can care for themselves find it more difficult to do so, and also more difficult to help support those unable to be self-sufficient—children, the disabled, and the elderly.

[84] *See* Kevin A. Carson, *The Subsidy of History*, The Freeman: Ideas on Liberty, June 2008, at 33, *available at* https://fee.org/media/5291/0806freemancarson.pdf.

[85] *Cf.* Charles W. Johnson, *Scratching By: How Government Creates Poverty As We Know It*, *in* Markets Not Capitalism, *supra* note 20, at 377, *available at* https://fee.org/articles/scratching-by-how-government-creates-poverty-as-we-know-it/.

At the same time, these privileges disproportionately channel wealth to those who benefit from them—those who can afford licenses, those who want to build homes in accordance with legal requirements, those who can charge more for properties they sell or rent because of zoning rules. Ongoing privileges distort the economic environment and, not surprisingly, boost the incomes of those able to lobby and otherwise manipulate politicians in a position to secure them, even as they foster and perpetuate the poverty of others.

Rectifying the problem of ongoing, structural privilege is, on the surface, relatively straightforward—a just legal system can simply decline to enforce rules that secure unjust privileges—though there is obviously the question of how best to deal with those, and the predecessors in interest of those, who have been victimized by structural privilege. There is unlikely to be a simple, straightforward program for rectifying acts of large-scale violence, but, at minimum, stolen land can be returned to just possessors when they can offer reasonable evidence for the legitimacy of their claims to title;[86] and assets acquired with clearly stolen wealth can be treated as without legitimate owners and ripe for homesteading.[87] Remedying injustice in this way can create new opportunities for ordinary people to acquire the resources they need to care for themselves and others while empowering those impoverished because of state-perpetrated and state-sanctioned theft.

It can also foster greater dignity in the workplace. State-secured privilege helps to concentrate investable wealth, and thus make it harder for people to work for themselves or in partnerships or cooperatives with others (because, for instance, of the risks associated with unemployment when people can't easily care for themselves when not working for others). It therefore channels people into subordinative paid employment. It also helps to protect the economic viability of large, hierarchical organizations.[88] Eliminating privilege and remedying injustice will thus make it easier for people to find the resources they need to craft humane work environments, reduce the pressure for people to work for others, and reduce the viability of corporate hierarchies as alternatives to empowering workplaces.

In addition, because small, flat work groups related by contract can mobilize workers' local knowledge and incentivize them, as owners rather than employees, to care about long-term firm success, fostering the emergence of such work groups by eliminating the props for conventional, hierarchical workplaces can boost productivity in the economy as a whole and increase workers' incomes. Freeing the market can thus make workplace dignity possible; and, if productivity is the goal, as it presumably should be, actively foster its achievement as well.[89]

86 *See, e.g.*, Murray N. Rothbard, The Ethics of Liberty 63–76 (1982).

87 *See, e.g.*, Karl Hess, *Where are the Specifics?*, *in* Markets Not Capitalism, *supra* note 20, at 289; Murray N. Rothbard, *Confiscation and the Homestead Principle*, *in* Markets Not Capitalism, *supra* note 20, at 293.

88 *See* Kevin A. Carson, Organization Theory (2008).

89 *See id.*

Commitment to a free society need not involve any rejection of shared responsibility for risk and vulnerability. Statists often assume that only state action can ensure that people assume this kind of responsibility. However, the performance of mutual aid societies and similar organizations, at present largely (albeit not exclusively) crowded out by state action, suggests that people can care for each other in viable ways without state involvement and that they can be expected to take responsibility not only for those who can themselves help to sustain systems of mutual aid but also for those who are unable to do so. And, of course, the elimination of state-secured privilege could be expected both to reduce the incidence of economic vulnerability and to facilitate the maintenance of thriving mutual aid networks. Eliminating this kind of privilege while also remedying state-perpetrated and state-tolerated wrongs—ending, rather than strengthening, the state—could *both* counteract the effects of upward redistribution by the state to its cronies *and* "let the free market eat the rich."[90]

The elimination of market-distorting privilege can foster increased productivity. It can help to lift out of economic insecurity those who have been victimized by aggression. And it can help to equip people to take collective responsibility for each other's well-being in periods of vulnerability and loss. Eliminating privilege isn't a matter of encouraging charity, per se, though that may happen as well: it is a matter of changing *the rules*, altering the basic structure of society.

So the redistribution of wealth need not be the work of any sort of state apparatus seeking to bring about an overall desired pattern of wealth and income. It can instead be the work of consensual institutions in a stateless society. It can be accomplished by genuinely open markets liberated from state-secured privilege, by the legal institutions of a stateless society as they eliminate state-secured and state-tolerated privileges and the effects of past injustice, and by solidaristic community institutions.[91]

The various sorts of wealth redistribution that would occur in a stateless society wouldn't *ensure* that any problem associated with poverty in a particular case wouldn't occur or would be satisfactorily remedied (any more than activities or structures of any other sort could realistically be expected to *ensure* that such problems wouldn't occur or would be dealt with appropriately).[92] These sorts of redistribution *would*, however, foster or involve substantial responses to the problem of economic insecurity. If pursuing social justice is a matter of seriously addressing socio-economic vulnerability and exclusion at the structural level, then the kinds of redistribution that could be bedrock features of a stateless society incorporating genuinely open markets should be seen as ways of pursuing social justice.

90 *See* Jeremy Weiland, *Let the Free Market Eat the Rich*, *in* Markets not Capitalism, *supra* note 20, at 301.

91 *See* Chartier, Anarchy, *supra* note 20, at 328–50.

92 *See* David Schmidtz, *Guarantees*, *in* Person, Polis, Planet: Essays in Applied Philosophy 174 (2008).

C. *Freedom as a Path to Social Justice*

Respecting freedom—avoiding aggression against people's bodies and their justly acquired possessions—is both an aspect of political justice and a means of implementing the demands of moral justice. It is thus a path to social justice.

Talk about social justice can sometimes be confusing because it may seem to assume the necessity of mandating a society-wide pattern of wealth distribution and the legitimacy of state action to achieve this pattern. But the underlying concerns that motivate talk about social justice can be met without either. Eliminating state-secured privilege and remedying state-perpetrated and state-tolerated dispossession can play a vital role, in tandem with the operation of diverse community institutions, in addressing the challenge of poverty and fostering social inclusion and participation.

State-secured privilege deprives people of opportunities to work and dramatically increases the liabilities associated with being poor and the costs of obtaining significant goods and services, including housing and medical care. And a history of violence engaged in by the state and its cronies lies behind the existing distribution of wealth. As a result, ending state-effected violence and state-secured privilege could play a vital role in ending economic vulnerability and insecurity. It will also free people—both by eliminating the drain on their resources brought about by state predation and by increasing economic productivity—to care more effectively for each other. These structural changes can help to redistribute wealth, as can the operation of open markets. And community-based noncommercial institutions can also contribute to this process. Thus, key structural changes involving the expansion of freedom can contribute effectively to enhancing the well-being of the economically vulnerable and promoting greater economic security. These changes are crucial instances of social justice in both the political and moral senses. Contrary to Rorty's assumption, therefore, freedom can be seen as a precondition to and a means of achieving social justice rather than as an alternative to it.

VII. TOWARD RADICAL LIBERALISM

In *Achieving Our Country*, Rorty makes his case with predictable clarity and wit and enlivens his argument with his reminiscences as a child of the Old Left. Discovering that the thoroughly secular Rorty is the grandson of Social Gospel theologian Walter Rauschenbusch helps to put his almost-religious vision of America in perspective. And learning that his parents broke with the Communist Party in the '30s after the repressive character of Stalin's regime became evident makes his commitment to Cold War liberalism more intelligible. Rorty has sometimes been accused of being a relativist with no basis for opposing tyranny. But moral passion is certainly evident throughout (whether it is always rightly directed is, of course, another matter). We can be confident that, were Rorty still alive, some of his passion would be directed at Donald Trump, whose rise he eerily foretold.

As both candidate and president, Trump has proven to be profoundly illiberal—in his assertion of untrammeled presidential authority, his rejection of freedom of expression, his support for ethnonationalism, his interference with free trade. Rorty's fear that economic and cultural insecurity could enable the rise of a demagogue seems disturbingly well founded.

And Rorty's words rightly remind liberals that they can hardly meet contemporary political challenges, including the challenge of Trump, by retreating into the realm of cultural theory. But I don't believe they should respond to the threat of demagoguery by embracing a liberal version of solidaristic nationalism, either. This isn't quite what Rorty has called for. But it's not a stretch to imagine modern liberals reading or rereading *Achieving Our Country* and concluding that that's precisely what's needed.[93]

Critics of Trump don't need to steal his clothes. What's needed instead is a confident reassertion of liberalism—not a meliorist, establishmentarian liberalism, but a genuinely *radical* liberalism that embraces free trade, open borders, and the rejection of war and empire not as self-immolating gifts to the rest of the world but as sources of *shared* benefit that enrich and empower and dignify both Americans and those with whom they interact across our planet.

Liberalism is about creating space for the expression and development of the diverse forms of flourishing, fulfillment, well-being, welfare. A nationalistic civic religion, and, indeed, any sort of civic religion, runs the risk of interfering with people's capacities to make their own practical choices, including ones about their relationships with ultimate reality. It also runs the risk of licensing active interference with people's flourishing in various ways—through warfare and empire-building abroad and through interference with freedom—including the freedom exercised in peaceful social cooperation through consensual exchange—at home.

I am not confident that Rorty's diagnosis of the American Left's lack of political engagement is accurate. And I wonder whether, without intending to do so, he runs the risk of placing an ironic imprimatur on America. Liberalism needs, it seems to me, more than Rorty offers: a more confident affirmation of moral truth, a more pronounced distance from the American project, a more radical hope, an alternative conception of the relationship between freedom and social justice that doesn't cast the American state in the role of savior. In short, liberalism needs to be radical. We will be able, I believe, to achieve our country only if we look beyond our country.

93 Leftist nationalisms continue to be defended; *see, e.g.*, Francis Fukuyama, Identity: The Demand for Dignity and the Politics of Resentment (2018); John B. Judis, *What the Left Misses about Nationalism*, New York Times, Oct. 15, 2018, https://www.nytimes.com/2018/10/15/opinion/nationalism-trump-globalization-immigration.html.

The failure to do so, as I have suggested, makes it very easy to take an unduly sanguine perspective on war and empire. This is perhaps especially true in the context of a self-consciously liberal case for an interventionist foreign policy. In Chapter 8, after considering general reasons to opt for anti-interventionism and anti-imperialism, I consider one such liberal case, the one advanced by Peter Beinart.

8

Interventions

I. LIBERALISM AND WAR

War attacks and undermines all of the aspects of flourishing—life and bodily well-being, of course, but also every other aspect as well. Liberals of earlier generations were predictably, even if not uniformly, opponents of war and empire.[1] This is hardly surprising, given liberalism's general preference for peaceful, voluntary cooperation as the heart of social life, its commitment to the equal moral status and authority of persons, and its enthusiasm for global trade and cultural exchange. The outstanding English liberal Richard Cobden, who saw his passionate advocacy of free trade as intimately linked with a commitment to peace, publicly and strenuously opposed war with France and Russia and challenged English military violence against the Chinese. The American liberal Moorfield Storey, among the founders of the National Association for the Advancement of Colored People, led in the establishment of the Anti-Imperialist League. *The Nation*'s founding editor, Oswald Garrison Villard, objected publicly and at personal cost to American involvement in European war.

And of course there have been more recent adherents of the liberal tradition who have found war and empire deeply repugnant. The New Left of the 1960s incorporated, and was to a significant extent birthed by, the growing anti-war movement. George McGovern enthusiastically mounted a pro-peace, anti-empire presidential campaign. More recently, modern liberal Dennis Kucinich and classical liberal Ron Paul have both strongly defended the cause of peace. But this sort of liberalism has become increasingly uncommon across the political spectrum in the United States. Opponents of war and empire have been sidelined in favor of politicians who, confident in the capacity of state power in the hands of experts, simultaneously embraced economic and social intervention at home and military (sometimes in tandem with economic and social) intervention abroad.

The earlier liberals, I believe, had it right. Liberals should embrace a policy of *noninterventionism*, of using a government's military capability only to defend the state the government putatively serves. And natural law theory grounds a sturdy

[1] I am grateful to Jeffrey Cassidy for comments on an earlier version of this Chapter.

rejection of militarism and imperialism that can help to refine and defend noninterventionism. (It also provides reasons to endorse noninterventionism in the economic sphere, but that's another matter.) Natural law theory is not pacifist, but it provides a basis for rigorous constraints on the use of force and tight limits on the decision to engage in warfare. There's no such thing as "liberalism in one country." The liberal recognition of the equal authority and moral status of persons, and of the value of global trade and cultural interchange, makes liberalism inherently cosmopolitan. And it undermines any attempted liberal defense of war and empire that involves applying different standards to people based on their geographic locations.

In this Chapter, I seek to explain briefly what natural law limits on violence, war, and empire might look like and why they might be reasonable (Part II) before going on to outline Peter Beinart's argument, in *The Good Fight*,[2] for a contemporary interventionist liberalism (Part III). Beinart's thoughtful and well-developed proposal offers an intriguing liberal alternative to noninterventionism. I seek to take stock of Beinart's project (Part IV) before going on to highlight some critical concerns with this project (Part V) and briefly considering the development of liberal interventionism in the period following the release of *The Good Fight* (Part VI). I conclude by reaffirming liberal noninterventionism in the face of Beinart's alternative (Part VII).

II. VIOLENCE AND EMPIRE

The late philosopher Sydney Allen once groused at me: "Your religion is pacifism!" I did not and do not think that embracing either liberalism or natural law theory entails a commitment to complete nonviolence. But I do believe we should endorse stringent limits on violence and warfare and that we should entirely reject the pursuit of empire.[3] In brief, in the foreign policy arena as also (in another sense) domestically, liberals should be noninterventionists.

A. *Principled Limits on the Use of Force*

Given the Principle of Respect, it is unreasonable, ever, to injure another purposefully (as a matter of sadism, say) or instrumentally (perhaps in order to induce her to behave as one desires). One may do something that *in fact* injures another; but one

[2] *See* PETER BEINART, THE GOOD FIGHT: WHY LIBERALS—AND ONLY LIBERALS—CAN WIN THE WAR ON TERROR AND MAKE AMERICA GREAT AGAIN (2006). My concern is with this book as an attractive, if ultimately unpersuasive, case for a particular vision of liberal foreign and military policy, as a winsome example of an alternative standpoint within the liberal tradition, rather than as a window on Beinart's own views. Thus, I do not seek to determine to what extent, if at all, Beinart's current position differs from the one expressed in *The Good Fight*.

[3] For the roots of the moral analysis that follows, *see, e.g.*, Germain G. Grisez, *Toward a Consistent Natural-Law Ethics of Killing*, 15 AM. J. JURIS 64 (1970); JOSEPH M. BOYLE, *Toward Understanding the Principle of Double Effect*, 90 ETHICS 527 (1980); JOHN M. FINNIS, JOSEPH M. BOYLE, JR., & GERMAIN G. GRISEZ, NUCLEAR DETERRENCE, MORALITY, AND REALISM (1987).

does so in a manner consistent with the Principle of Respect only if the injury is unintended (even if anticipated). When one makes another's death, in particular, an end or a means, one identifies with the harm one does. Though personal life is inherently valuable, one irrationally treats it as if it were not. And one adopts the identity of a killer.

> If one intends to kill another, he accepts the identity of killer as an aspect of his moral self. If he is to be a killer through his own self-determination, he must regard himself in any situation as the lord of life and death. . . . Others' natural attitudes toward their own lives must be regarded as an irrational fact, not as a starting point for reasonable community.[4]

Because the Principle of Respect excludes bringing about death sought as an end in itself, it rules out killing in revenge. But it also excludes killing for instrumental reasons, as when people are killed to terrify others into submission.

However, because "when one knowingly brings about bad effects in carrying out some choice, one need not intend them,"[5] a just combatant can reasonably use lethal force while not viewing herself "as the lord of life and death." Provided "one intends not the death of another but only the safety of . . . [one's] own life, then one need not identify . . . [oneself] as a killer."[6] In this case, the combatant "need not regard death (even the attacker's) as if it were any sort of good."[7] One does not identify with an attack on the inherent good of personal life when one brings about another's death as a foreseen but unintended side effect or by-product of an action which one undertakes for another purpose—as, to defend oneself or another against an unjust attack. (And a soldier who is part of a military entity engaged in the unjust use of force, who has not surrendered, but who happens not to be engaged in active combat at the time an attack takes place, remains an attacker.) One might seek to stop an attack and, in the course of doing so, injure the attacker, but this injury, even if *foreseen*, need be neither the goal of one's action nor a means to that goal. One might "perform[] an action directed at resisting and reducing unjust force, an action which unavoidably results in the injury or death of another person"[8]—acting "to stop the [unjust] attack, accepting as a side-effect the attacker's death"[9] without intending "to kill . . . as a means to an end."[10] A would-be assassin might intend "that Hitler be incapacitated from participating in the ongoing Nazi tyranny whose murderous violence he directed." The assassin might detonate a bomb in the same way that

4 Grisez, *Ethics*, *supra* note 3, at 76.

5 John M. Finnis, Germain G. Grisez & Joseph M. Boyle, *'Direct' and 'Indirect': A Reply to Critics of Our Action Theory*, 65 Thomist 1, 7 (2001).

6 Grisez, *Ethics*, *supra* note 3, at 76; *cf.* John M. Finnis, Aquinas: Moral, Political, and Legal Theory 276 (1998).

7 Grisez, *Ethics*, *supra* note 3, at 78; *cf.* Finnis, Aquinas, *supra* note 6, at 276.

8 Germain Grisez & Russell Shaw, Beyond the New Morality: The Responsibilities of Freedom 151 (3d ed., 1988).

9 Finnis et al., Deterrence, *supra* note 3, at 312.

10 Grisez & Shaw, *supra* note 8, at 151.

a soldier might fire "a rifle or [throw a] grenade to stop the assault of enemy soldiers, or a howitzer to disrupt enemy formations assembling far behind the lines."[11]

This principle is not only a basic requisite of justice; it is vital to a meaningful response to terrorism. For one might reasonably define terrorism (in which state actors as well as non-state actors can engage) as causing or threatening to cause serious injury for political purposes. While the morally responsible soldier (who need not be a state actor) uses force to stop unjust force, the terrorist injures purposefully or instrumentally—either in a project of revenge against an enemy population viewed as collectively guilty or in order to frighten people into capitulating to her demands. A consistent prohibition on purposeful killing allows a clear moral line to be drawn between the activities of terrorists and the activities of soldiers making just use of potentially lethal force.

In addition, even if causing injury in a given case is consistent with the Principle of Respect, it may not be consistent with the Principle of Fairness. This principle requires that the force used against an unjust attacker be no more severe than is needed to end her attack. Suppose one kills an attacker whom one could (and reasonably believed one could given the constraints of the situation—obviously, fairness does not require that one transcend the split-second nature of much of the decision-making required in violent situations) incapacitate without killing. In this case—even if one does not, in fact, violate the Principle of Respect by intending her death as a means or embracing it as one's purpose—one exhibits unreasonable, perhaps reckless, disregard for the value of life. If one would not endorse a rule permitting similar heedlessness in one's own case or the cases of those one loves, one's use of force is unfair.[12]

Harm to a combatant may be an entirely anticipated but still unavoidable and unintentional by-product of repelling an unjust attack. In much the same way, harm to one or more noncombatants who aren't purposefully targeted may be a side effect of the use of force designed to stop an unjust attack. However, even if the person using force is seeking to stop someone else's unjust use of force, she must still ask whether the unintended but foreseen harm done by her own use of force is fair. If those she might unintentionally injure were her loved ones or fellow citizens (or were she herself among them), would she endorse a rule permitting the imposition of the kind of risk to which people are subjected by her own attack? She ignores the Principle of Fairness when she imposes more risk on some people, whether or not they are purposefully targeted, than she would be prepared to impose on those near and dear to herself. To impose risk unfairly is implicitly to treat the lives of one's own

[11] Finnis, Aquinas, *supra* note 6, at 291.

[12] Thus the inappropriateness of George W. Bush's stance as described by Beinart: "America wouldn't send police to apprehend the terrorists; it would send soldiers to kill them." Beinart, Fight, *supra* note 2, at 112. If it is genuinely possible to apprehend someone using law enforcement methods—and often, where heavily armed terrorists are concerned, it obviously will not be—then it would surely be wrong to kill them instead.

compatriots, one's own loved ones, and oneself as categorically or qualitatively superior in value to those one is prepared unintentionally to harm—arbitrarily, without rational justification.

Thus, it's inconsistent with the requirements of practical reasonableness (and, to be clear, with traditional just war norms more generally) to treat any and all collateral damage as acceptable. One may be engaged in an important mission. But that fact in and of itself doesn't excuse causing injuries unfairly. The importance of one's objective doesn't, can't, justify monomaniacally ignoring moral constraints on one's pursuit of that objective. It seems all too common for military personnel to breathe a sigh of relief when they announce that they have not *targeted* noncombatants, as if the lack of targeting alone made any harm that nonetheless *resulted* for noncombatants acceptable. But in fact the imposition of collateral injuries will be reasonable, if at all, only when consistent with the Principle of Fairness.

Both the Principle of Respect and the Principle of Fairness (and perhaps other requirements of practical reasonableness as well) are relevant to decisions to undertake programs of violence in the first place. "It is only those," wrote General William Tecumseh Sherman, "who have neither fired a shot nor heard the shrieks and groans of the wounded, who cry aloud for blood, more vengeance, more desolation." "War," he famously concluded, "is hell." And this means that the decision to engage in systematic violence must be made, if at all, only within narrow constraints and after sustained deliberation.

The most commonly canvassed alternative to principles like the two I have outlined here is some form of consequentialism.[13] But utilitarianism is not a satisfactory approach to moral decision-making. It is often thought to yield results inconsistent with our considered moral intuitions, and it lacks any inherent principle of distribution that would ensure its fairness. Both of these criticisms might, of course, turn out to be unsustainable: perhaps our considered moral intuitions are flawed, perhaps utilitarianism doesn't actually yield the imagined problematic results,[14] and perhaps fairness simply does not have basic moral status. But utilitarianism (like its various

[13] On the untenability of consequentialism, *see, e.g.* ALASDAIR C. MACINTYRE, AFTER VIRTUE: A STUDY IN MORAL THEORY 61–63, 67–68, 185 (2d ed., 1984); JOHN FINNIS, NATURAL LAW AND NATURAL RIGHTS 111–19 (1980); JOHN M. FINNIS, FUNDAMENTALS OF ETHICS 80–108 (1983); FINNIS ET AL., DETERRENCE, *supra* note 3, at 177–296; GERMAIN G. GRISEZ & RUSSELL SHAW, BEYOND THE NEW MORALITY: THE RESPONSIBILITIES OF FREEDOM 111–14, 131–33 (3d ed., 1988); DAVID S. ODERBERG, MORAL THEORY: A NON-CONSEQUENTIALIST APPROACH 65–76, 97–101, 132–33 (2000); PAUL HURLEY, BEYOND CONSEQUENTIALISM (2011); NEL NODDINGS, CARING: A FEMININE APPROACH TO ETHICS AND MORAL EDUCATION 86–87, 151–54 (1984); BERNARD WILLIAMS, MORALITY: AN INTRODUCTION TO ETHICS (2d. ed., 1993); Bernard Williams, *A Critique of Utilitarianism, in* J. J. C. SMART & BERNARD WILLIAMS, UTILITARIANISM: FOR AND AGAINST 77 (1973); Stephen R. L. Clark, *Natural Integrity and Biotechnology, in* HUMAN LIVES 58–76 (Jacqueline A. Laing & David S. Oderberg eds., 1997); Germain Grisez, *Against Consequentialism*, 23 AM. J. JURIS 21 (1978); ROBERT MERRIHEW ADAMS, FINITE AND INFINITE GOODS 298–300 (2000).

[14] Since it does not genuinely offer a determinate decision procedure, it can be made to yield almost any results by someone with appropriate rhetorical skill.

siblings and cousins) suffers from a much more serious defect: it is simply incoherent.

For utilitarianism not only entails that we can predict the future with reasonable accuracy, which we cannot; it also requires that we pick the best available option. However, the diverse and incommensurable character of the various goods embodied in every situation makes it impossible to rank-order states of affairs in the way utilitarian optimization would require us to do. Thus, utilitarian calculation serves, not as a means of actually assessing policy choices, but as an exercise in rationalization. It could not be otherwise, for the kind of calculation it purports to involve is impossible. Of course we can make judgments about efficiency in the context of goals we have already adopted; but we cannot compare macro-level goals in the same way. Instead of asking us to make reasonable *choices*, utilitarianism asks us to select among *states of affairs*. It asks us to abandon the perspective of agency, to stop asking who we are and become in and through our choices, and instead to take up a purely technical stance as persons who seek to manipulate the levers of history. And it is, finally, an exercise in *hubris*: by making each of us responsible for history, it invites every moral agent to take up the role of an imagined all-determining God, a role for which none of us is satisfactorily suited.[15]

B. *Reasons to Avoid War*

Even in cases in which individual uses of force are consistent with the Principle of Respect and the Principle of Fairness, these principles tightly cabin reasonable decisions to go to war. Acting in a manner consistent with these principles will mean avoiding war in almost all cases.[16]

This is true even when there might appear to be objective justifications for the use of force. Such justifications are unlikely to play the same role in politicians' own deliberations as they do in politicians' public rhetoric: the actual reasons for going to war may be much less admirable than the factors adduced in morally uplifting speeches. In addition, a consistent bright-line rule against non-defensive uses of military force by states might be expected to avoid the many injuries associated with war more effectively than case-by-case decision-making.

It is important to recognize that, while state actors are all ultimately morally responsible individual agents, a decision to go to war made by a government is very different from a decision to use force by an individual person or a voluntary association of individuals. It is a non sequitur to observe, for instance, that because a physically capable person reasonably can and perhaps should intervene to stop a bully, a state should go to war against a perceived bully. State-made wars involve

15 *See* Gilbert Meilaender, Faith and Faithfulness: Basic Themes in Christian Ethics 94–113 (1991).

16 This analysis builds on one I offered some years ago. *See* Gary Chartier, *Violence, Wars, and States*, Bleeding Heart Libertarians, Sep. 3, 2011, http://bleedingheartlibertarians.com/2011/09/violence-wars-and-states-2/ (*last visited* July 29, 2018).

risks and harms that are either absent entirely from voluntary individual undertakings or are vastly, often disproportionately, greater in the case of state-made wars than in the case of the justified use of force by individuals. The following considerations count strongly in favor of noninterventionism.

(*i*) Some varieties of war, notably those involving the use of weapons of mass destruction, characteristically involve the immoral purpose to kill or injure, either intentionally or instrumentally. (The Cold War idea of Mutually Assured Destruction was of course *premised* on the idea that it was appropriate to threaten population centers, and of course it was just such centers that were devastated by nuclear attack in the case of Hiroshima and Nagasaki and the unimaginably destructive conventional attack in the case of Dresden.) Modern thermonuclear war is thus in principle unacceptable morally.

(*ii*) Whether injuries are actually *intended* or not (recall that one can use force defensively without intending injury), the ways in which states conduct wars make such injuries very likely. A state apparatus's decision to go to war will very probably result in large-scale noncombatant injuries. This is particularly true in the contemporary era in which great powers treat aerial bombing, including the use of drones,[17] as a central element of warfare, since such bombing so frequently involves unfairly caused—entirely foreseeable, even if unintended—noncombatant casualties. It is also true because of the great risk of escalation—it is difficult to contain military violence—and the dangers that may result from the escalation of hostilities, in particular, by forces deploying weapons of mass destruction.[18]

(*iii*) Overseas military interventions, and even defensive military actions undertaken abroad, especially if conducted in ways that result in noncombatant casualties or that serve to prop up or otherwise promote the interests of despotic governments, predictably prompt resentment. And this resentment can lead to ongoing threats of terrorist violence and asymmetric warfare that can themselves both result in noncombatant deaths and perpetuate the spiral of violence.

(*iv*) The perceived need to mobilize resources for war and to keep morale high, along with the fear of conventional and asymmetric responses to military interventions, can lead to domestic repression—to a growth in wide-ranging surveillance, a diminution in respect for due process, the use of torture, censorship, and other abuses—and to military colonization of civilian life.[19]

17 *See* Andrew Cockburn, Kill Chain: Drones and the Rise of High-Tech Assassins (2015); *cf.* Nick Turse, The Changing Face of Empire: Special Ops, Drones, Spies, Proxy Fighters, Secret Bases, and Cyberwarfare (2012).

18 *See* Daniel Ellsberg, The Doomsday Machine: Confessions of a Nuclear War Planner (2018).

19 *Cf.* Nick Turse, The Complex: How the Military Invades Our Everyday Lives (2009).

(*v*) Dynamics similar or identical to those that prompt these state-driven abuses can lead to cultural shifts involving religious, cultural, and ethnic bigotry and resulting discrimination and violence.

(*vi*) Wars are often fought by conscripts. And since slavery is morally indefensible,[20] and since conscription is materially indistinguishable from slavery, wars fought in this way are in principle unjust.

(*vii*) Very frequently, states undertake wars for national glory, for politicians' own personal glory, for the economic benefit of politicians and their cronies,[21] to demonstrate a willingness to use force in the future ("credibility"), or to acquire others' territory or resources. The substantial risk that, whatever the public rationale offered for a war, it is in fact being undertaken for and will prove to serve these sorts of dubious and in some cases unjust ends makes a general prohibition of military intervention—of nondefense conflicts, of conflicts waged outside national borders—seem particularly wise.

(*viii*) Whatever their motives, wars do, in fact, frequently result in the imposition of imperial power and the establishment or maintenance of exploitative arrangements.

(*ix*) Predictably, those planning and promoting wars demonstrate very limited capacities to anticipate the actual consequences of the military conflicts they encourage. And, given both the costs (including, but not limited to, noncombatant injuries) of military action and the ability of violence to change on-the-ground dynamics in quite substantial ways, the unpredictability of the consequences of military intervention and occupation should make caution especially appealing.[22]

(*x*) Every time a war is undertaken, politicians' cronies receive disproportionate benefits as providers of government contracts. And the military-industrial complex (and associated complexes in areas like domestic security) grows. This is problematic because this means that money that could be spent on things consumers actually want will be coercively channeled to the politically well connected. But, even more insidiously, it is problematic because participants in the military-industrial complex can use their ill-gotten gains to lobby and otherwise influence politicians to increase the likelihood of future warfare and of increased military (and related) spending.

(*xi*) A war engaged in by a state can be expected to worsen the economic conditions of its people for more than one reason. It may do so because the war is funded directly through taxation, which deprives people of their resources and which, by sending the wrong kinds of market signals, redirects production away from the goods and services people actually want. It may do so because

20 *See* Gary Chartier, Anarchy and Legal Order 89–93 (2013).

21 *Cf.* Smedley D. Butler, War Is a Racket (1935).

22 *See* Peter van Buren, We Meant Well: How I Helped Lose the Battle for the Hearts and Minds of the Iraqi People (2011).

the war is funded through debt, which can result in inflation (if the supply of money increases) or lead to subsequent tax burdens. And it may also do so because the war is funded through the creation of fiat money, which can, again, result in inflation.

(*xii*) Because politicians can fund a war through the use of taxation, debt, or fiat money creation, they need to bear little of the war's costs themselves (and they may even profit through relationships with the military-industrial complex, among other things). That they need not internalize these costs, but can externalize them on unwilling others, means that they can hardly be expected to make rational decisions about initiating, maintaining, or funding wars.

(*xiii*) The scale of war funded through taxation, debt, or fiat money creation can lead to immense, unmanageable destruction.

(*xiv*) Because it destroys human and physical resources and redirects assets away from consumer-preferred uses, war prompts poverty in societies, often already poor, that are targets of military intervention.

These considerations do not show that *all* state-made wars, taken individually, are in principle morally unacceptable. But they provide good reasons to resist the temptation to go to war. In addition, given the temptations politicians confront to pursue wars, a clear limit, easily applied and adopted in advance of any particular potential conflict, seems particularly wise. Such a limit, I suggest, should rule out a state's engagement in a war unless the war is defensive and unless personnel (equipment of various kinds might be appropriately employed beyond these limits, provided it is used for purely defensive purposes) are deployed only within the state's territorial perimeter.[23] Even if particular wars inconsistent with these constraints might seem morally attractive, there will likely be very few such conflicts. And the *ex ante* adoption of these limits could be expected dramatically to reduce the hell that is war.

C. *The Failings of Empire*

War for the sake of empire would obviously transgress these limits. But the pursuit and maintenance of empire in other ways—through manipulation, deception, or covert operations of various sorts—is also unreasonable. The means themselves are unreasonable—as most violence and deception will be. And the maintenance of explicitly imperial or effectively neocolonial institutions will be unfair. This will be so because they will almost always be operated more for the primary benefit of (elites in) the imperial power, so that the legal and moral equality of the colonized is denied, and because imposing political authority on people without their consent is

[23] *Cf.* Smedley Butler, *An Amendment for Peace*, Woman's Home Companion, Sep. 1936, at 4, *available at* https://justwarriors.blogspot.com/2009/11/smedley-butler-amendment-for-peace.html.

itself unfair,[24] quite apart from the ways in which the authority is exercised. In addition, imperial power will frequently be imposed precisely in order to extract resources from subject territories. This motive will be itself unreasonable (since it inherently involves unreasonable harms to others) and the extraction of subject territories' resources will characteristically involve theft (and so violate the Principle of Fairness) and often also violence against persons (and so violate the Principle of Respect). Unjustified violence against persons and property will also frequently be a feature of imperial rule because violence will be used to suppress dissent on the part of those who challenge this kind of rule. Imperial rule is itself unreasonable, it is undertaken for inappropriate reasons, and it is sustained using unreasonable means.

And of course this need not be a matter of how institutions are formally organized, as the distinction between colonialism and neocolonialism highlights. Other people can be formally conquered and brought under explicit rule by an imperial power—like Rome or England. Alternatively, other people can be subjected to hegemonic authority by an entity that leaves them nominally independent (and thus avoids bearing the cost of administering or systematically defending them), like the United States in its imperial phase.

War as actually carried out is almost always unreasonable, and imperial war probably always so, as is creation and maintenance of empire in whatever form. And yet governments that proclaim their moral superiority with immense self-righteousness continue to engage in war—sometimes in imperial war. It is plausible to argue that this is precisely the case with the United States in the twenty-first century. Using the excuse provided by the attacks of September 11, 2001, the United States government has launched wars in multiple locations. As I write this, it is militarily involved in seventy-six countries—most visibly in Afghanistan and Iraq but also in Syria, Yemen, Somalia, and Libya.[25]

III. MODERN LIBERAL INTERVENTIONISM

While interventionism is difficult to square with liberalism, Beinart attempts to make a self-consciously liberal case for a hopeful vision of American possibility to which an activist foreign policy is central.[26] In an engagingly written work of unapologetic advocacy, Beinart places the most emphasis not on argument but on narrative. He seeks to tell the story of modern American liberalism—refreshingly, he uses "liberal" proudly (even if his focus is on just one strand of liberal thinking, which I'd classify as the interventionist faction of modern liberalism)—from 1946 to

24 *See id.* at 160–62.

25 *See* Tom Engelhardt, *A New Map Shows the Alarming Spread of the US War on Terror*, THE NATION, Jan. 4. 2018, https://www.thenation.com/article/a-new-map-shows-the-alarming-spread-of-the-us-war-on-terror/. On Afghanistan, *see* SCOTT HORTON, FOOL'S ERRAND: TIME TO END THE WAR IN AFGHANISTAN (2017).

26 *See* BEINART, FIGHT, *supra* note 2.

the present in a way that will highlight the natural fit between his preferred sort of liberalism and a muscular foreign policy and make clear why reemphasizing this fit is essential to liberal political success. While I appreciate his insights, from the standpoint of a more radical liberalism I am inclined to dissent from a number of his analyses and conclusions.

Beinart begins his story with the founding of Americans for Democratic Action by a group of modern liberals who were skeptical enough about Stalin and confident enough about the positive potential of the American project to believe it was worth taking sides against international communism and for American values in the burgeoning Cold War.[27] He goes on to tell a now-familiar story of how the modern liberal consensus was fractured not only by conflicts within the modern liberal coalition over cultural issues but also by the emergence of a strongly anti-imperialist position on the Left.[28] Doubtful about both American motives and the unintended consequences even of benevolent imperialism, the anti-imperialists (on my view rightly) challenged the assumption, heretofore more consistently endorsed by liberals than conservatives, that American military, economic, and political power entailed a global responsibility to promote American values. The war in Vietnam, in particular, sapped the confidence of many Americans on the Left that an activist American foreign policy could be either virtuous or wise.[29]

Under Ronald Reagan, conservatives filled the void created by a liberal crisis of confidence.[30] For a time, at least, they successfully out-narrated liberals, offering a compelling tale in which, refusing to compromise with evil and driven by a clear moral purpose, America would promote the cause of freedom worldwide and, inch by inch, take back from tyranny societies that had been devoured by communism.[31] An earlier generation of conservatives had been noninterventionists; now, conservatives enthusiastically employed American power around the world.[32] But, according to Beinart, there were at least two crucial differences between liberal internationalism and the conservative internationalism that came into its own after the collapse of liberal consensus.

First, where liberals had seen social and economic reform around the world as both morally required and strategically essential, conservatives disagreed. Some did not share the liberals' concerns with these matters. Others judged that economic dynamics in other countries could not be successfully addressed using American military power or technical expertise, doubting the capacity of social engineering to effect change in alien societies. And, perhaps most importantly, they were skeptical that economic discontent prompted people in other countries to back anti-American

27 *Id.* at 4–6.
28 *Id.* at 32–87.
29 *Id.* at 40–51.
30 *Id.* at 61–62.
31 *Cf. id.* at 189.
32 *Id.* at 114.

policies. Communist deceit was the problem.[33] To suppose that there were "root causes" of support for communism would be to abandon an appealingly Manichean worldview and to acknowledge that the policies of the United States and its allies and clients might have something to do with pro-communist and anti-American attitudes.[34] The right way to confront tyranny was not to pretend, with the communists, that economic, social, and political conditions bred opposition to capitalism and to the United States; rather, it was to confront communist tyranny with all the physical force at the US government's disposal.

Second, liberal interventionism had placed significant emphasis on cooperation with allies and respect for neutrals. Liberal foreign policy-makers in the post-World War II period emphasized that it was better to leave allies free to pursue policies at variance with American preferences and ideals than to foster toadyism and to impose American political and economic models on others.[35] Allies whose freedom and dignity were respected would be more, rather than less, likely to support America when the chips were down. By contrast, conservatives celebrated American unilateralism. They rejected the notion that the United States should be accountable to the international institutions it had itself created in the wake of World War II. A great power could be beholden neither to the fractious and irresponsible nations of the developing world—too often the puppets of the Soviets, in any case—nor to the timid and tired former colonial powers of Europe. America was the leader of the free world, and it would lead whether or not others followed.[36]

The conservative internationalism represented by Reagan won the day, on Beinart's view, because modern liberals simply lacked a counter-narrative. With their resolve sapped by Vietnam, they could not confidently defend a positive vision of American possibility; Reagan could. To be sure, Reagan himself did not always hew to the orthodox conservative line.[37] He acknowledged that the promotion of democracy could be a good thing—good not just in moral terms but also as a source of benefits to the United States—even when it led to the ejection from office of a friendly autocrat like Ferdinand Marcos.[38] And he horrified many conservatives by agreeing with Mikhail Gorbachev at Reykjavik to place the reduction—indeed, the elimination—of offensive nuclear weapons on the bargaining table. But the story Reagan had helped to construct and which he told so effectively continued to dominate the public imagination even when his practice reflected much more sensitivity to shades of gray than did his often black-and-white rhetoric. Certainly it was the conservative narrative that shaped the stances of subsequent conservatives. Thus, once the Soviet Union had vanished from the world stage, once there was no

33 *Cf. id.* at 17.
34 *Id.* at 121.
35 *Id.* at 16.
36 *Cf. id.* at 17.
37 *Cf. id.* at 146.
38 *See id.* at 114.

"evil empire" for America to confront and American imperium seemed relatively unchallenged, conservatives abandoned talk of proactive global leadership by the United States. In what must be one of the greatest ironies of recent American politics, George W. Bush emphasized the need for humility in United States foreign policy during the 2000 presidential campaign. It was not America's business to intervene in the affairs of other countries—certainly not to engage in "nation building."

In Beinart's narrative, all this changed with the September 11, 2001, attacks. Bush breathed new life into conservative internationalism. In effect resurrecting the Cold War, this time with radical Muslims rather than Stalinists as the enemy, Bush declared a War on Terror(ism). He mobilized domestic support by appealing to American patriotism and bullied and cajoled other countries, generally without regard for international opinion, into supporting invasions of Afghanistan and Iraq. Beinart argues that liberals were unprepared to respond with an alternative to Bush's account of America's place in the world. As a result, they largely acquiesced in his foreign policy decisions. They offered voters enhanced competence, but the same policies. Or (on Beinart's view) they consigned themselves to irrelevance by rejecting an activist foreign policy with an ineliminable military component as inescapably imperialist.

Beinart's preferred brand of liberalism challenges both responses to the Bush foreign policy line. It differs from conservatism in its stress on the interconnectedness of the world and on the practical as well as moral significance of cooperation. It endorses the rhetoric—if not always the practice—of neoconservatives in encouraging the spread of democracy and civil liberties. But it also emphasizes the importance of economic development and social equality as legitimate—indeed, crucial—concerns of American foreign policy. Beinart is particularly clear about the importance of development and democratization in the Muslim world, but there is no reason to think he supposes that efforts designed to promote liberalization should stop there. But efforts designed to promote democracy, increase liberty, and eliminate poverty must be undertaken in a spirit of humility, dialogue, and cooperation—building on the work of people on the ground rather than imposing an American vision through the use of political, economic, and military coercion.[39] He maintains, for instance, that the Arab Human Development Reports, for instance, embody the convictions and analyses of Arab policy-makers and intellectuals, people with an organic connection to the region they seek to serve. These convictions and analyses, and the participation of those like the thinkers and political actors who have offered them, must shape any American effort to foster social change in the Arab world.[40]

[39] *Id.* at 195.
[40] *Id.* at 195–96, 271.

However, while development and democratization are crucial, they are not panaceas. By contrast with those whom, after Arthur Schlesinger, Jr., he calls "doughface" liberals,[41] who refuse—as he sees it—to use American military power in defense of American values, Beinart argues that the use of force will sometimes be necessary—to restrain disorder, to support democratic governments, to resist terrorist violence, to protect human rights. Thus, he favors "intervention in cases of genocide or humanitarian emergency."[42] He seems also to support military action in "the stateless zones where jihadists take sanctuary."[43] "America could not have built schools for Afghan girls had it not bombed the Taliban first."[44] And this means, in turn, support for a strong military.

> When elite college campuses ban the military from recruiting because it discriminates against gays, or when Michael Moore urges rallies against the CIA because of its flawed human rights record, or when liberals casually urge cutting the defense budget, although military spending made possible American interventions in the Balkans and Afghanistan, they are succumbing to the old siren song of purity and abdicating their responsibility to do what [Reinhold] Niebuhr urged: make the tragic choices that defending freedom requires.[45]

To be sure, "the more America wants to intervene militarily in other countries' affairs, the more it needs the legitimacy, and the capability, bestowed by strong international institutions."[46] "It was America's willingness to persuade rather than simply coerce that distinguished it from the Soviet Union. America's recognition that it was neither all-powerful nor all-knowing was not a source of weakness; it was a deep source of strength."[47] However, a commitment to internationalism and cooperation need not mean acting through the United Nations. Because the United Nations cannot be counted on to support liberal values, NATO, "an alliance of twenty-six democracies [!]," should take the lead when international military action is required, perhaps "partner[ing] with ... regional organization[s], such as the African Union ..., the Association of Southeast Asian Nations, or ... the G-20, a newly created body that brings industrial countries together with third-world heavyweights like India, Indonesia, and Brazil."[48]

Further, an activist liberal foreign policy will not only be multilateralist; it will also treat American actions as subject to the same kind of moral assessment as the actions of others. While the American civil rights struggle can continue to inspire Arab activists for democracy and social justice, lack of respect for law and justice—

41 *Id.* at 7, 30, 172.
42 *Id.* at 199.
43 *Id.*
44 *Id.* at 197.
45 *Id.*
46 *Id.* at 198.
47 *Id.* at 199.
48 *Id.*

Beinart instances torture[49] and murder in American detention centers[50] and the untrammeled confinement of American citizens as "enemy combatants"[51]—can dramatically undermine American credibility.

> It is the gap between the moral stringency we demand of others and the moral complacency we exhibit ourselves that has bred ... bitterness among the very people who once took heart from America's example.... Both conservatives and liberals yearn for a return to the days when students carried a statue of liberty as they marched for democracy in the streets of Beijing. What liberals understand is that to bring about that day we must begin carrying our own statues of liberty in the streets of Washington and New York.[52]

Thus, the fact that he criticizes some liberals as too unwilling to employ force in good causes hardly means that Beinart believes military action is always appropriate. He is far too sanguine about US military activity in the Balkans and Afghanistan. But he is scathing in his criticism of the Iraq war.

He underscores unequivocally the wrongness of his own support for the invasion of Iraq. He was, he says, "wrong on the facts," "too quick to give up on containment, too quick to think time was on Saddam's side," insensitive to "the critical link between the invasion's credibility in the world and its credibility in Iraq," and unaware "that the morality of American power relies on the limits to American power."[53] He notes the unwillingness of the Bush administration to face facts about the reality that there was no reason to posit Iraqi involvement in the September 11 attacks.[54] And he is clear that assertions regarding Iraq's nuclear capability by American intelligence agencies were "so vague they permitted virtually any possibility."[55] He acknowledges the "terribly weak" character of argued links between Iraq and anti-American terrorist activity.[56]

Further, he is sensitive to the factors that could have impaired American leaders' moral and strategic judgment: he acknowledges that Iraq's oil wealth made the establishment of "a friendly government there" appealing, especially given that this could mean "reduced reliance on Saudi Arabia."[57] And he is also aware that the desire to demonstrate American military superiority could have provided a further, doubtful rationale for the invasion: "[f]or an administration yearning to make America's enemies fear it again after the supposedly feckless Clinton years, invading Iraq seemed to offer an easy, effective way."[58] In a blunt summary, he maintains:

49 *Id.* at 109–10, 136.
50 *Id.* at 201.
51 *Id.* at 109.
52 *Id.* at 201.
53 *Id.* at xiii.
54 *Id.* at 143.
55 *Id.* at 151.
56 *Id.* at 149.
57 *Id.* at 148.
58 *Id.*

> [I]n the debate over Iraq ... the Bush administration successfully prevented an "intelligent popular opinion" from being formed. It so relentlessly conflated 9/11 and Iraq that by the time the United States invaded, more than half of Americans believed Saddam was personally involved in the attacks and almost 90 percent believed he supported terrorist groups planning to strike the United States. Paul Wolfowitz declared that post-Saddam Iraq could "finance its own reconstruction, and relatively soon," even as the Bush administration kept secret a study showing that Iraq's oil sector was in extreme disrepair. And a subservient Republican-led Congress put little pressure on the Bush administration to justify its claims about Iraq's weapons of mass destruction, its terrorist ties, or America's postwar plans.[59]

IV. A MODERN LIBERAL NARRATIVE

The Good Fight is in large part a story about stories. And Beinart's own story is, of course, intended as the groundwork for the story he hopes liberals will choose to tell about America's past, present, and future. The "Cold War liberalism" created and defended by Niebuhr, Schlesinger, and others provides him with a model to which he hopes today's liberals will pay careful attention. Before Vietnam and the *Kulturkampf* of the 1960s, modern liberalism was confident, Beinart suggests. Modern liberals were quite aware of America's potential for evil. But, in Beinart's narrative, they did not allow this awareness to cripple them: they believed that it made sense to use American power to promote equality, democracy, and freedom abroad, even if they knew that these lofty goals could be and often had been used to justify less than noble imperial ventures. They saw the destructiveness of Soviet tyranny, and they believed that fighting it was both a moral and a strategic imperative. They recognized that fighting it required not only military muscle but also the active promotion of social and political change and the elimination of poverty. They saw that, morally and pragmatically, the global fight against communism in which they believed it was vital that the United States engage be undertaken in respectful cooperation with other nations, rather than from a position of arrogant imperial dominance. And they powerfully and plausibly linked the global fight against tyranny with demands for justice and equality at home. Even those Americans who might not be convinced that fighting poverty and racism mattered morally in the way the liberals did could see that America's international credibility depended on its willingness to put its own house in order.

Beinart is very much aware of the risks attendant on the use of military power. But he is not willing to say "no" to interventionism despite his sensitivity to the dangers of American overconfidence.[60] While rejecting "the hubris of dominance," the delusion that America can effectively rule the world, he wants to encourage policy-makers to walk a tightrope between noninterventionism and imperialism, between

59 *Id.* at 206.
60 *See* Peter Beinart, The Icarus Syndrome: A History of American Hubris (2010).

collective self-doubt and collective arrogance. Modern liberals should remain willing, he believes, to engage militarily with the wider world. Bill Clinton's intervention in the Balkans worked, he supposes.[61] The same was true, he seems to have thought at the time he wrote *The Good Fight*, of George Bush's in Afghanistan.[62] Contemporary adherents of modern liberalism, Beinart maintains, must recapture their predecessors' chastened confidence in American possibility. They must believe, and let the American people know they believe, that America has something meaningful, significant, good to offer the world. And they must make clear their willingness to use cultural, economic, and, when necessary, military means to defend American values in the new Cold War—a global contest with radical Islam. Liberals too frequently, he believes, understand the rise of violent Muslim fundamentalism as an unexpected consequence of American bullying and insensitivity. It's important, he believes, to see it as—also?—the outgrowth of a compelling ideological position that needs to be confronted just as communism was.[63] Fighting jihadist terrorism can reinvigorate American liberals, integrate their concerns, allow them to recover their past, provide a new rationale for domestic and foreign policies promoting social justice, and enable them to win elections.

Beinart's prose calls to mind nothing so much as the liberalism of John F. Kennedy.[64] Beinart is quite aware that Kennedy's actual performance was mixed in a way that Kennedy's record as imagined and remembered by modern liberals was not. But it is the combination of optimism, commitment to military strength, seriousness about active internationalism, identification with the interests of American allies, concern for international economic development, and the promotion of civil rights—a combination perennially linked with Kennedy in the modern liberal imagination—that Beinart seeks to encourage liberals to recapture.

It is a Kennedyesque *spirit*, more than anything else, which Beinart seems to want to call forth in his readers. For, while Beinart offers a charter for "a new liberalism," he has done rather more to revive the ethos of Kennedy and to retell the story of Cold War liberalism than to offer a detailed policy program for today's liberals.

Beinart offers his narrative of combating terrorism and promoting democracy as an inspiration for a renewal of national solidarity. In the era of Cold War liberalism, inequality was reduced and corporate leaders honored a compact with American workers that shared the benefits of burgeoning national prosperity. Today, however,

61 *See, e.g.*, *id.* at 2, 285–86.

62 *See id.* at 349.

63 I think it is, at minimum, worth taking seriously the possibility that (*i*) Soviet expansionism was driven by Russian nationalism, (*ii*) success in the Cold War was to a significant degree a function of factors independent of ideology, (*iii*) ideology was not a major driver of Cold War maneuvers on either side, and (*iv*) Soviet action was to a meaningful extent a response to American threats and exercises in empire-building. Obviously, ideology could be important in a conflict with violent Islamic fundamentalisms even had it not been significant during the Cold War, but, because Beinart stresses the analogy, I think it is at least worth asking about the independent impact of ideology on Soviet and American policy during the Cold War.

64 *Cf.* Beinart, Fight, *supra* note 2, at 23–31.

risks have been shifted dramatically onto the shoulders of middle-class, working-class, and poor Americans. Private actors have abandoned their commitments to solidarity, and the state has, Beinart argues, done little to cushion people against risk and loss. Corporations have benefited handsomely from state largesse even as ordinary people have watched their standards of living decline. "The result is inequality unseen since the 1920s. And excessive inequality threatens democracy at home, just as it does abroad."[65] In the wake of the September 11 attacks, America seemed to be experiencing what Beinart labels "a cultural revival based on citizenship."[66] But the Bush administration's cynical manipulation of patriotism and national solidarity and its failure to stem the tide of inequality that deepened national divisions meant that it lost the opportunity to renew a spirit of civic engagement in America.

A cooperative foreign policy oriented toward promoting justice, freedom, democracy, and development; a domestic policy that embodies a commitment to democracy and civil liberties, but also to generosity and protection against loss and unfair risk—these must be the backbones of a revived muscular liberalism. Beinart calls Americans to a sense of national purpose oriented on the active but humble pursuit of justice and community at home and abroad. Interventionism is itself ultimately unreasonable, for reasons I suggested earlier. But a tamed and chastened modern liberal interventionism of the sort Beinart seeks to defend here would certainly be better than a liberal interventionism indistinguishable from neoconservatism.

V. QUESTIONING INTERVENTIONISM

It will be clear from my observations in Part II that I believe a liberal foreign policy should look significantly different from Beinart's Cold War liberalism redivivus. But I want to call particular attention to some difficulties with his stances regarding several issues, including the appropriateness of the metaphor of "war" to describe the struggle with jihadist terrorism; civil liberties; the limits on the use of force; "blowback" and the sources of terrorism; and the nature of economic development.

A. *The Merits of "War"*

Beinart says that whether liberals opt to use the phrase "war on terror" is not itself especially important.[67] What matters, he says, is whether they understand that the United States is engaged in a global conflict with jihadist terrorism, that the safety of the American people and of legitimate American interests is threatened by terrorists, and that a decisive American response, a response making full use of all the varieties of American power, is crucial. But though he says that the language of "war" is not

65 *Id.* at 204.
66 *Id.* at 206.
67 *See id.* at xii, 187.

essential, he uses it repeatedly.[68] Liberals should, it seems to me, be concerned about this use.

A president of almost any political ideology, Beinart maintains, would have treated the September 11 attacks as military in nature and would have opted for a military response.[69] But he provides no extended justification for this claim. Obviously, these attacks were horrifically violent. But they were carried out by criminals. And they could have been dealt with as criminal acts rather than as ones meriting any sort of military response.[70] To be sure, this would doubtless have involved considerable work by domestic police agencies and intelligence agencies. And, like responses to other large-scale criminal operations, it might at various points have made use of the United States military. But the employment of the military where appropriate in dealing with a large criminal gang does not entail the use of the language or the practice of "war." The use of this language has had more than one troubling consequence.

(*i*) By repeatedly speaking of the nation as at war, the officials of the Bush administration disposed the public to act as if the nation were really involved in a war in a more conventional sense. And this, in turn, made it easier for the administration to justify coercive intrusions into personal privacy and odious restraints on personal liberty (as those detained without trial can testify) and dignity (as is evident in everything from officially sanctioned torture to the increasing abuse of airline passengers by the odious restrictions imposed by the Transportation Security Administration). War-talk is apocalyptic, and it underwrites efforts to give the government enormous powers to crush dissent and corral people's ordinary lives.

(*ii*) War-talk made it easier for the administration to engage in foreign military adventures, first in Afghanistan, then in Iraq, and more recently in Syria, Somalia, and elsewhere. Even if the attack on Afghanistan yielded some good consequences, it does not follow that the occurrence of those consequences justified the attack. Responding to the September 11 attacks did not warrant the use of military force against Afghanistan even if one regards the extraterritorial deployment of military personnel as appropriate and necessary—the Taliban were prepared to surrender Osama bin Laden for trial in a neutral country provided his responsibility for the September 11 attacks was demonstrated.[71] And

68 See *id.* at 186, 196.

69 "It took President Bush less than a day to declare the country at war [after the September 11 attacks]. The implied contrast was law enforcement: American wouldn't send police to apprehend the terrorists; it would send soldiers to kill them." *Id.* at 112.

70 *Cf. id.* at 181 (examining John Kerry's approach to transnational violence from a law enforcement perspective).

71 *See, e.g., Bush Rejects Taliban Offer to Hand Bin Laden Over,* The Guardian, Oct. 14, 2001, *available at* https://www.theguardian.com/world/2001/oct/14/afghanistan.terrorism5. *Cf.* David B. Ottaway & Joe Stephens, *Diplomats Met With Taliban on Bin Laden: Some Contend U.S. Missed Its Chance,* Washington Post, Oct. 29, 2001, at A01 (suggesting that the Taliban were looking for a way of saving face while de-escalating their conflict with the Bush administration). It is possible that one reason the Bush administration declined to offer the requested justification was simple lack of hard evidence:

even if the invasion had been undertaken on humanitarian grounds, as it obviously was not, humanitarian goals don't, for reasons I noted at the beginning of this Chapter, justify military action; and, whatever the goals of the war in Afghanistan, it has predictably been conducted in an inappropriate manner.

In the case of the invasion of Iraq, it is clear, as Beinart documents in excruciating detail, that the right effectively framed the September 11 attacks as, in effect, an act of war against the United States sponsored by Saddam Hussein, despite his complete lack of involvement. Inclined to see terrorism as an agency of state power, conservatives rapidly attached themselves to the view that Saddam was ultimately responsible for the bombing of the World Trade Center—a conviction that made it easy to view Iraq as a focus of military action. War-talk prepared the country for engagement in an imprudent and unjust war.

Of course, a law enforcement approach to the September 11 attacks and other terrorist activities would not have involved the United States in the ideological conflict with Islamic fundamentalism Beinart wants to encourage.

Given the negative domestic and international consequences of speaking about a "war on terrorism," the choice whether to use this language is not neutral. Americans can and should oppose injustice and violence around the world. But pundits and politicians need to use the language of "war" sparingly—in cases of actual, declared, military conflict. Otherwise, they run the risk of encouraging domestic tyranny and international adventurism.

B. Constraints on Force

As I noted in the Introduction and at the start of this Chapter, the Principle of Respect precludes purposeful (including instrumental) killing, while the Principle of Fairness precludes the unfair imposition of risks of harm. These principles are fundamental norms of justice in war. They are not simply matters of pragmatic convenience. They are moral requirements. As it stands, Beinart's vision of a muscular foreign policy fails to take them seriously. Beinart's unapologetically moral version of liberalism is characterized by an awareness of the Principle of Fairness—that the same standards that apply to one side in a conflict should apply to the other.[72] Both this principle and the Principle of Respect should be used to assess the legitimacy of proposals involving the use of force in warfare.

"On September 23rd, Secretary of State Colin Powell told a television interviewer that 'we will put before the world, the American people, a persuasive case' showing that bin Laden was responsible for the attacks. But the widely anticipated white paper could not be published, the Justice Department official said, for lack of hard facts. 'There was not enough to make a sale.'" Seymour M. Hersh, *What Went Wrong: The C.I.A. and the Failure of American Intelligence*, THE NEW YORKER, Oct. 8, 2001, *available at* https://www.newyorker.com/magazine/2001/10/08/what-went-wrong.

72 "Conservatives rail against moral relativism. But, in fact, by denying there is a moral standard above and apart from American actions, it is they who have made morality situational." *Id.*at 200. "In its

These principles, I have stressed, have practical consequences for the kind of military policies a responsible liberalism will support. Beinart implicitly, gently, but clearly criticizes the nuclear freeze movement and opponents of a US nuclear presence in Europe as abdicating America's responsibilities to the world.[73] But this assumes that the use of strategic nuclear weapons could ever be morally appropriate in the first place. However, using such weapons to attack population centers would clearly be unjust.[74] If undertaken to terrorize, it would violate the norm precluding purposeful killing or injuring. And if undertaken to disable a military installation, it would—at least in essentially all realistically conceivable circumstances—represent a grossly unfair imposition of the risk of suffering collateral damage. But the logic of deterrence as ordinarily understood requires precisely the willingness to attack population centers directly. And the strategy of maintaining strategic nuclear weapons while intending never to use them—to use them to bluff—is untenable. Were it widely known that an entity possessing these weapons did not intend to use them, they would not exert any retardant effect on the behavior of those against whom they might be used; in this case, their possession would be pointless. And were this not widely known, then many persons would likely be involved in the immoral project of preparing to use them intentionally, with all the corrupting influence this would unavoidably exert, and the risk of accidental use—which would, again, unfairly cause collateral injury—would be great.

Beinart castigates American liberals for imposing what he supposes are unreasonable constraints on the use of American military power against terrorists in Afghanistan and their state sponsors. Liberals were unreasonable, he argues, when they maintained that force could be used, but only if there were no harm whatsoever to noncombatants.[75] The only alternatives Beinart presents are this kind of—as he clearly views it—excessive scrupulosity and a willingness to use force as needed to disable opponents in Afghanistan. But why are these the only options? The Principle of Fairness is certainly consistent with some decisions to use force that impose some risks of collateral injury. It does not follow, however, that all such risks are fair. Again, a risk will be fair to the extent that it is one the person imposing the risk would treat as acceptable if she or her loved ones were potential victims of comparable force in a comparable situation. This constraint will certainly sometimes permit the use of force in ways that pose serious risks to noncombatants or friendly troops, but it will certainly limit the use of force in many others.

treatment of terror suspects, the Bush administration informed the world, America would be bound by no international rules, only by its own, unfailing, moral sense." BEINART, FIGHT, *supra* note 2, at 136.

73 *Id.* at 58-59, 64-66. Beinart writes: "When Western European governments asked America to deploy nuclear missiles on their soil what they were really seeking was a tangible guarantee that the United States would go to war against the Soviet Union to protect London and West Berlin, even at the price of Chicago and New York." *Id.* at 65. But the United States need not have attacked Soviet noncombatants in order to defend London and West Berlin.

74 *See* FINNIS ET AL., DETERRENCE, *supra* note 3. *Cf.* OLIVER M. T. O'DONOVAN, PEACE AND CERTAINTY: A THEOLOGICAL ESSAY ON DETERRENCE (1989).

75 BEINART, FIGHT, *supra* note 2, at 171.

Adhering to the demands of justice in war does not require pacifism or other varieties of what Niebuhr and Beinart would both characterize as irresponsibility. But these norms—the requirement that we not identify with attacks on basic human goods and that we exhibit an unfailing commitment to fairness—do limit what we may justly do in war. A moral foreign policy must recognize that even the best causes do not turn unjust means into just ones.

C. *The Growth of the National Security State*

Beinart sometimes seems frustrated with liberals who object to invasions of privacy and other restrictions on civil liberties proposed—and often, doubtless, carried out—by the Bush administration.[76] He is unequivocal in his condemnation of due process violations and torture by US authorities[77] and the potential for wide-ranging abuse created by the Patriot Act and so-called national security letters.[78] But I would be happier if he didn't sometimes seem to be castigating liberals for opposition to the expansion of a national security state he, too, clearly sees as potentially dangerous.

This is true, of course, simply because personal freedoms matter, and they matter more, not less, when American security is under threat—especially if, as Beinart maintains, it is under threat by terrorists who sharply dispute the aptness of liberal values. As Benjamin Franklin famously quipped, "They who would give up an essential liberty for safety, deserve neither liberty nor safety." But limitations on state power are especially vital when the rhetoric of war is used to enhance that power and to make decisions behind closed doors. When it is almost impossible to monitor what state actors are doing, it is particularly vital not to give them license to do too much.

Beinart argues that "[t]he central question dividing liberals today is whether they believe liberal values are as imperiled by the new totalitarianism rising from the Islamic world as they are by the American right."[79] Of course Islamic fundamentalism—and not only the violent sort which is obviously, and appropriately, Beinart's primary concern—is in principle much more at odds with liberal values than is the American right (even if resurgent ethnonationalism makes this a closer call than it seemed to be when Beinart wrote *The Good Fight*). Those in the tradition of Niebuhr can surely agree that liberals would do well to "rouse as much passion for fighting a movement that flings acid at unveiled women as they do for taking back the Senate in 2006."[80]

76 *Id.* at 136, 172 (noting liberal objections to increased surveillance efforts or funding for the Central Intelligence Agency).
77 *Id.* at 109 ("the consequences of America's shadow prison system have become hideously clear").
78 *Id.*
79 *Id.* at 197.
80 *Id.* at xii.

It is, frankly, puzzling when Beinart writes that if liberals "believe it is only George W. Bush who threatens America's freedoms, they should ponder what will happen if the United States is hit with a nuclear or contagious biological attack." He argues: "No matter who is president, Republican or Democrat, the reaction will make John Ashcroft look like the head of the ACLU."[81] But what Beinart seems to be saying is that, should such an attack occur, a national political leader would be likely to violate Americans' basic freedoms even more than the Bush administration has already done. This may, in fact, be the case. And there is certainly good reason for liberals, like all other Americans, to work to prevent an attack of the kind Beinart envisions. But what Beinart is himself describing is a reactive assault on Americans' freedoms by their own government. The kind of terrorist attack he describes would obviously be a horrible and unjust assault on Americans' lives, health, and property. But if restraints on Americans' freedom followed such an attack, in reaction to it, the political leaders who imposed these restrictions would be the ones responsible for them, not those to whose villainy the restrictions were a reaction. Anticipating the possibility of further attacks, liberals need to be prepared now to stand firm in support of personal privacy and civil liberties, rather than treating state intrusion as a necessary, unavoidable—and therefore legitimate and justifiable—response to terrorist outrages.

D. Acknowledging Blowback

Beinart implies that anti-imperialist liberals border on monomania in their attempts to explain threats to the United States using the notion of "blowback."[82] Identifying the September 11 attacks, among other things, as unexpected fallout from American misadventures abroad serves as an excuse for paralyzing moral hand wringing, he supposes.

It would indeed be arrogant and monomaniacal for Americans to assume that everything others do in relation to their country is best explained primarily as a response to America's own behavior. Other actors have their own motives and their own agendas. Harm to Americans and American interests can surely result from others' strategic maneuvering, ideology, or confused blunders, and not merely from the American government's own wrongs. It does not follow, however, that the concept of blowback has no application.[83]

81 *Id.* at xii; *cf. id.* at 110.

82 *See id.* at 171. Indeed, he refers to the September 11, 2001 hijackers as "willing to kill to prevent the mongrelization of races and religions." BEINART, SYNDROME, *supra* note 60, at 348. But this is probably best read as Beinart's summary of the views of many younger New York liberals rather than an expression of his own understanding of the terrorists' states of mind.

83 *Cf.* CHALMERS JOHNSON, BLOWBACK: THE COSTS AND CONSEQUENCES OF AMERICAN EMPIRE (2d ed., 2004); CHALMERS JOHNSON, THE SORROWS OF EMPIRE: MILITARISM, SECRECY, AND THE END OF THE REPUBLIC (2004).

Beinart is rightly quick to emphasize that Americans must be aware of their capacity to misuse their great power. Sometimes, the misuse of American power may result from a Manichean dualism that issues in a self-righteous willingness to manipulate and coerce others. On other occasions, it may reflect the American government's participation in cynical games of power—perhaps not infrequently engaged in for the purpose of benefiting politicians' cronies. In any case, military and intelligence operations and diplomatic and economic gambits may, and surely often do, have unintended consequences. Attentiveness to the possibility that these consequences may obtain and may significantly affect America's global position need not be an exercise in guilty liberal breast-beating; it can, instead, emerge from a sensitive awareness of temptations and liabilities associated with the possession of great power.[84]

Take the example of Iran. By supporting the coup that overthrew Mohammed Mossadeq in 1953,[85] the United States understandably earned the enmity of nationalist Iranians. Ongoing American support for Shah Mohammed Reza Pahlavi's authoritarianism similarly alienated liberals and other dissenters. Given the track record of the United States, then, the 1979 embassy takeover should hardly have come as a surprise. Certainly by failing to support Mohammed Khatami and his reformists during Khatami's eight years at the helm of Iran—and, indeed, continuing to treat Iran, even on the reformist Khatami's watch, as part of an "Axis of Evil"—American policy-makers played into the hands of hardliners convinced that dialogue with the United States was not only wrong but pointless, and paved the way for the rise of the reactionary and bellicose Mahmoud Ahmadinejad.[86] More recently, the Trump administration's withdrawal from the Iran nuclear deal has obviously not led to improved relations with Tehran. American bullying and intervention yield predictable—and avoidable—outcomes.

Beinart is certainly not unaware that American policies have consequences. But I believe that at least two issues deserve greater attention: the global American military presence and the worldwide American pursuit of resources.

The use of American military force abroad to extend the reach of empire, protect corporate interests, and prop up authoritarian regimes does little to endear Americans to others. The American military presence in countries like Saudi

[84] This is a point to which Beinart is certainly sensitive. *See* BEINART, SYNDROME, *supra* note 60. But he seems to view his justified criticisms of overconfidence on the part of American policy-makers as compatible with his support for a revival of Cold War liberalism. He acknowledges the foolishness of American participation in World War I, the Vietnam war, and the second Gulf War, while evidently viewing the Korean War and the first Gulf War, among others, as justified.

[85] *See* STEPHEN KINZER, ALL THE SHAH'S MEN: AN AMERICAN COUP AND THE ROOTS OF MIDDLE EAST TERROR (2003).

[86] *Cf.* ALI ANSARI, CONFRONTING IRAN: THE FAILURE OF AMERICAN FOREIGN POLICY AND THE NEXT GREAT CRISIS IN THE MIDDLE EAST (2006); BEINART, FIGHT, *supra* note 2, at 97-98 (noting the morally mixed character of the current regime in Iran).

Arabia, for instance, does not self-evidently promote justice and democracy;[87] it does, however, promote resentment (it was, famously, among the key reasons for Osama bin Laden's hostility toward the United States government). And if bases can breed discontent, military action by the United States or other countries acting with its encouragement can breed much more intensely negative reactions. A commitment to nonintervention, together with the abandonment of weapons systems that are not only costly but also deeply troubling morally, would reduce the federal budget and Americans' tax burdens even as it blunted hostility to the United States and increased the difficulty of recruiting terrorists and selling anti-American policies.

Similarly, the American quest for global economic dominance can birth anti-American attitudes. International trade rules made under the influence of the world's most powerful economic player can certainly be sources of annoyance. Flawed institutional design, American bullying, and American support for oppressive elites can create and perpetuate poverty.[88] And it would be naive to suppose that pressures to secure dwindling fuel supplies have not informed a variety of international American adventures, including but hardly limited to the invasion of Iraq[89] and ongoing support for authoritarians like those at the helm in Saudi Arabia.[90]

Beinart clearly recognizes the role of American bullying and overreaching in prompting anti-Americanism;[91] but he seems to me to give them insufficient attention. But ideologies, which Beinart blames for much anti-Americanism, are not free floating, and both their contents and their attractiveness to those who endorse them reflect the material conditions of the environments in which they are developed and propagated. A full-orbed liberal analysis of American foreign policy will rightly emphasize the ways in which American policy choices create unnecessary risks for American prosperity and security.

E. Promoting Development

Beinart is an interventionist. And this means not only that he favors the non-defensive use of American military power but also that he seems to suppose that the state should not only intervene in the economy at home but also

87 The point is not to argue for "a withdrawal from the Muslim world," BEINART, FIGHT, *supra* note 2, at 102, but rather to defend a noninterventionist account of engagement there and elsewhere. Trade and cultural exchange are valuable—and powerful. Military involvement is problematic for all the reasons I have noted.

88 Compare Beinart's discussion of the role of "economic despair" in breeding terrorism; *see id.* at 118–20.

89 "Iraq has huge reserves of oil, and establishing a friendly government there offered the prospect of reduced reliance on Saudi Arabia, whose instability 9/11 had laid bear [sic]." *Id.* at 148. "[D]uring the looting that followed Saddam's fall, American troops guarded only the oil ministry." *Id.* at 161.

90 Thanks to Jeffrey Cassidy for discussion on this point.

91 BEINART, FIGHT, *supra* note 2, at 138.

actively promote economic development abroad.[92] We should certainly care about global poverty on moral grounds and in light of its destabilizing consequences. But this doesn't mean that we should propose, endorse, or support efforts to foster economic development *through large-scale state-driven schemes*. Indeed, *consistent nonintervention* (including non-interference with trade and migration) is itself precisely a means of fostering global economic development.

Military intervention is itself a prime driver of economic ill-being in multiple societies. Simply avoiding intervention will reduce the risk of dire impoverishment. So will the elimination of efforts to meddle in the elections and manipulate the governments of other countries. The unilateral elimination of all trade barriers imposed by the United States would dramatically enhance the welfare of many poorer societies. And the establishment of open borders would also exert a significant effect on poverty in multiple ways. Individual immigrants will improve their economic circumstances, and the economic circumstances of societies to which they emigrate. Remittances they send to their countries of origin will improve the well-being of their friends and family members and of the countries' economies more generally. And the fact that they are free to leave will incentivize their countries of origin to seek to retain them, and thus to adopt better policies.[93]

None of these policy changes is a panacea. But each could be expected to contribute significantly to an improvement in the well-being of the global poor. These measures will be most effective when poor countries' governments *also* adopt institutional changes likely to foster economic development. But, even without those changes, an end to military intervention and political meddling along with the embrace of free trade and open immigration will substantially improve the life chances of people around the world. What's needed is not a program of intervention but rather an end to unjust interference with people's voluntary cooperative activities.

[92] On Beinart's view of the state and global economic development, *see, e.g., id.* at xi, 15–18, 84, 117, 121–23, 194, 198, 221, 249.

[93] On global economic development and the role of wealthy nations in promoting such development, *see, e.g.*, Jay R. Mandle, Globalization and the Poor (2003); William Easterly, The Tyranny of Experts: Economists, Dictators, and the Forgotten Rights of the Poor (2015); William Easterly, The Economics of International Development: Foreign Aid versus Freedom for the World's Poor (2016); Jagdish Bhagwati & Arvind Panagariya, Why Growth Matters: How Economic Growth in India Reduced Poverty and the Lessons for Other Developing Countries (2014); Charles Kenny, Getting Better: Why Global Development Is Succeeding—and How We Can Improve the World Even More (2011). *Cf.* Deirdre N. McCloskey, Bourgeois Dignity: Why Economics Can't Explain the Modern World (2010); Deirdre N. McCloskey, Bourgeois Equality: How Ideas, Not Capital Or Institutions, Enriched the World (2016); Bas van der Vossen & Jason Brennan, In Defense of Openness: Why Global Freedom is the Humane Solution to Global Poverty (2018).

VI. LIBERALISM AND FOREIGN POLICY AFTER BUSH

Beinart's attempt to outline a foreign policy for modern liberals appeared designed to offer an (electorally appealing) alternative to neoconservative and nationalist accounts of American foreign policy. What has become apparent during the intervening years is that, while rhetorical framing may change, little of substance has changed along with it.

Thus, Barack Obama campaigned as a peace candidate, questioning the first use of nuclear weapons and vowing to talk with hostile foreign leaders. But Obama in effect served George W. Bush's third and fourth terms. While Obama did seek to normalize relations with Iran, the seemingly endless wars in Afghanistan and Iraq continued. The United States government's involvement in warfare around the world expanded. And assassination by drone—even of adolescents—was persistently employed as a tool of American foreign policy. Obama employed the sort of rhetoric of which Beinart might be expected to approve. And he arguably embraced multilateralism much more enthusiastically than had Bush. But there was little change in substance.

In 2016, Democrats nominated a presidential candidate who had shown repeated enthusiasm for violence—for hostile relationships with Russia and Iran, among other countries, and for fomenting the kind of brutality that led to the lynching of Muammar Qadhafi in Libya. "We came, we saw, he died!," she famously chortled. Despite occasionally saying things that sounded vaguely noninterventionist, Donald Trump opted for immensely bellicose rhetoric, threatening to murder the families of putative terrorists and to use destructive force against perceived US enemies like Iran (against which he also reinstituted draconian sanctions), even as he signaled hostility to Muslim countries by seeking to ban passport-holders from many of them from entering the United States. Rhetorically, he was as far from Beinart as possible. And he assembled a foreign policy team that seemed ill-disposed toward peace and reconciliation.[94] Trump rejected international economic cooperation through exchange and mouthed absurd platitudes about trade, even as he used force—in the form of tariffs and sanctions—to interfere with Americans' abilities to trade with their preferred partners.

It was striking how little politicians and pundits who might have been supposed to be (modern) liberals pushed back against many of Trump's abuses. To their credit, they challenged his stance on trade. But his actual and threatened use of military violence seemed to meet with general approval—as when his approval ratings bounced after his first air attack on Syria, an attack that led Fareed Zakaria to declare after the bombing, "I think Donald Trump became president of the United

[94] *See, e.g.*, Caitlin Johnstone, *Anti-War Trump Voters Just Officially Ran Out of Reasons to Support This President*, MEDIUM, May 22, 2018, https://medium.com/@caityjohnstone/anti-war-trump-voters-just-officially-ran-out-of-reasons-to-support-this-president-8318f6456ad4.

States."[95] Indeed, some of the strongest pushback against Trump appeared to come in the rare cases in which he might have been understood as actually pursuing reduced tensions with North Korea and Russia.[96] Whether modern liberals can be said to have pursued the kind of course recommended by Beinart is doubtless open to question. But there should be no question at all that modern liberals in the Obama and Trump years showed little interest in embracing the opposition to war and empire that had been the province of the American Left for a few years beginning in the mid-1960s.

VII. A LIBERAL FOREIGN POLICY?

Beinart has no desire to carry water for Washington's hawks. Criticizing many modern liberals' willingness to embrace militarism, he recently observed: "on foreign and defense policy, the [Democratic P]arty barely exists."[97] But he's also not willing to embrace anti-interventionism.

His message in *The Good Fight* might be summarized as the claim that support for interventionism at home and abroad, in both the military and the economic spheres, should be understood both as correct on its own terms and as a recipe for political success for modern liberals in the United States. I believe that liberals should indeed be concerned with political and economic issues beyond the borders of their own countries. But liberals should express that concern by adopting noninterventionist policies. They should decline the temptation to engage in military intervention and political manipulation. They should promote economic well-being not only by avoiding war but also by opening their borders to free trade in goods, services, and labor. And their rhetoric and their examples should embrace the global adoption of economically and socially open policies.

I recall repeated debates, conducted with considerable vigor during my teenage years, with my father, a veteran of World War II with broadly noninterventionist views, in which I defended the use of American military power to promote various good causes. It strikes me now that he was much closer to the truth than I was.

Beinart recognizes that the muscular foreign policy he seeks to promote need not be wedded to American self-righteousness. "[I]n the liberal vision," he argues,

95 Joan Walsh, *Too Many of Trump's Liberal Critics Are Praising His Strike on Syria*, The Nation, April 20, 2017, https://www.thenation.com/article/too-many-of-trumps-liberal-critics-are-praising-his-strike-on-syria/.

96 *See, e.g.*, Caitlin Johnstone, *Centrists Are Very Concerned That Donald Fucking Trump Isn't Hawkish Enough*, June 13, 2018, Caitlin Johnstone, https://caitlinjohnstone.com/2018/06/13/centrists-are-very-concerned-that-donald-fucking-trump-isnt-hawkish-enough/. Trump's withdrawal of the United States from the Intermediate-Range Nuclear Forces Treaty certainly suggests that he lacks much interest in reducing tension between the United States and Russia.

97 Peter Beinart, *The Democrats Keep Capitulating on Defense Spending*, The Atlantic, Feb. 18, 2018, https://www.theatlantic.com/international/archive/2018/02/democrats-defense-spending/553670/.

> there is no contradiction between recognizing that our enemies are not intrinsically evil, and recognizing that they must be fought, just as there is no contradiction between recognizing that although we are not intrinsically good, we must still fight them. America's challenge lies not in [putatively] *recognizing* . . . [its] moral superiority, but in *demonstrating* it.[98]

But whether there is a need for the United States government to fight at all is itself one of the key questions on the table—given both that the Islamic militants on whom Beinart focuses pose no threat to the United States and that fighting them seems likely to promote more resentment, and more putative occasions for fighting. The United States and other liberal societies can achieve and demonstrate moral superiority precisely by avoiding the temptation to engage in war.

Liberal rhetoric provides effective cover for warfare and empire-building. But it is difficult to justify either in liberal terms. In the years since Beinart first sought to defend an interventionist liberal foreign policy for the United States, we have gained no new insights warranting abandonment of the earlier liberals' rejection of war and empire.

To be sure, Beinart is well aware of the temptations of empire, and he seeks repeatedly to emphasize the appropriateness of liberals' sensitivity to their existence. Nevertheless, he seems to me to devote insufficient attention to errors of omission and commission that unnecessarily complicate America's international position. Despite a clear and laudable moral concern, he seems too quick to tolerate unjust uses of military force in the name of security. Similarly, he sometimes seems to me to give more credit than may be appropriate to the notion that the United States is engaged in a conflict meaningfully analogous to a war. And this, in turn, may make him more sanguine than I wish he were about governmental encroachment on personal privacy, dignity, and freedom.

Beinart seems genuinely frustrated that American liberals do not share conservatives' belief that a global conflict with terrorism is the major challenge facing the United States,[99] though many have proved to be fully paid-up members of the War Party in the years since *The Good Fight* first appeared. While Beinart presupposes the centrality of this conflict,[100] he does not *argue* for it extensively. There is every reason to promote liberal values when they are under threat from fundamentalisms at home and abroad, but Beinart has simply not made out a persuasive case that violent Islamic fundamentalism really ought to claim the bulk of America's energy and attention, that the threat of this kind of fundamentalism would exist in the absence of American militarism and imperialism, that interventionism of the kind he favors can be used effectively to challenge illiberal actors elsewhere in the world, or that using state violence against such actors is appropriate.

98 Beinart, Fight, *supra* note 2, at 194 (my italics).

99 Beinart, Fight, *supra* note 2, at 187.

100 "No one expects the jihadist threat to disappear by the time George W. Bush starts drawing Social Security." *Id.* at 126.

Beinart makes a rhetorically attractive case for the view that a combination of domestic and international intervention can be an appropriate expression of liberal values as well as a source of greater security for the United States. But the variety of liberalism I wish to defend is ultimately different from his. On my view, Americans need to be far more sensitive to the limits that justice and prudence impose on the use of force—in both the military and economic spheres—and far more aware of the temptations to misuse it. In his desire to tell a positive story about American possibility, I wonder whether Beinart underplays the moral and prudential reasons to say "no" to war and empire and overestimates people's capacities to answer the call of "the better angels of their nature." Hume was surely right that institutions are better designed with knaves than with angels in mind,[101] not because most people are knaves (as Hume himself argued they were not) but because those who seek power likely are and because reducing the power available to knaves enhances the freedom and well-being of everyone.

"Citizenship," Beinart maintains, "can be as powerful a force for moral revival as religion."[102] But this will be so, I fear, only if our country assumes a kind of religious importance in our lives. In Chapter 7, I tried to suggest some reasons why this sort of religion of America is likely to be dangerous. An overly sanguine attitude toward war and empire fails to diminish the evident sense of danger attendant on interventionist rhetoric.

Beinart repeatedly urges us not to opt for moral purity. I think he is right if he means to emphasize that we can rarely if ever be certain that our moral judgments are correct, especially in times of crisis when opportunities for reflection and deliberation are limited, and that the consequences of our actions will often include unintended even though foreseen harms to people who do not deserve them. But while we need to acknowledge these limits on our moral purity, we must also recognize, I believe, that there are limits on our pursuit of good consequences.

If we are not careful, we can allow calls to avoid impossible quests for moral purity to serve as excuses for militarism and imperialism. Beinart is a passionate opponent of American bullying, unilateralism, and torture—he is anything but morally insensitive. But it is entirely possible to embrace a foreign policy unwedded to such quests while maintaining a clear commitment to moral principles that limit violence, war, and the pursuit of empire.

There are multiple reasons to opt for nonintervention. These reasons certainly leave room for moral suasion: the bully pulpit can be powerful. But in some ways the most powerful means of affecting the actions of other actors on the international stage may be our continued, active dedication to the creation and recreation of a polity that can exhibit liberal ideals to the world (a point, again, to which Beinart is not insensitive). We should express our activism in foreign policy through

101 *See* 1 David Hume, *Of the Independency of Parliament*, *in* ESSAYS MORAL AND POLITICAL 117, 118 (T. H. Green & T. H. Grose eds., 1882).

102 BEINART, FIGHT, *supra* note 2, at 207.

a commitment to leading by example. Doing so will help to constrain and shape our use of other means of affecting our global environment as we seek to fight a genuinely good fight for liberal values.

We have every reason to be deeply troubled by war and other exercises of actually or potentially violent interventionism, which are persistently and predictably inimical to flourishing. As long as there are states, foreign policy ought to be the primary political focus of radical liberals. That's because foreign policy is the context in which the greatest amount of violence and manipulation is undertaken and encouraged abroad and in which authoritarianism and fiscal oppressiveness and irresponsibility at home are most effectively promoted and enthusiastically accepted. But this very level of violence, manipulation, authoritarianism, theft, and waste should highlight for liberals why they should be *radical* liberals—opponents of the state, which makes these things possible in distinctive, and distinctively awful, ways. Thus, radical liberals are anarchists.

Radical liberals can offer powerful arguments for anarchism, showing that states are illegitimate, unnecessary, and dangerous, and recognizing that bad behavior is just what should be expected from state actors, whether putative dictators or putative democrats.[103] But they must also confront complex and sometimes insightful challenges. One set of such challenges is the focus of Chapter 9.

[103] *Cf.* Bruce Bueno de Mesquita & Alastair Smith, The Dictator's Handbook: Why Bad Behavior is Almost Always Good Politics (2012).

9

Anarchists

I. DEFENDING FOLK-STATISM AGAINST RADICAL LIBERALISM

Embracing radical liberalism means opting for a consensual society—one in which diversity can flourish; in which peaceful, voluntary cooperation through exchange can generate and share wealth; and in which institutions can be organized and sustained from the bottom up rather than the top down. Taken to its logical conclusion, then, radical liberalism entails anarchy, not in the sense of chaotic violence but in the sense of society without the state, an institution that is illegitimate, unnecessary, and dangerous.[1]

While many people suppose that the state is legitimate, the fact that they do so does not mean that it really is; and, even if ungrounded, folk-belief in state authority can be undermined by anarchist arguments in ways that render it unreasonable. At least some people are unreasonable in accepting state authority in the absence of positive arguments, and most others are unreasonable in doing so, in any case, because of the effectiveness of arguments for anarchism.

In an attempt to insulate folk-statism from attacks focused on the unsustainability of arguments for state authority, Mark Murphy defends a *moral* argument designed to show that most people in reasonably just political communities are obligated to obey state-made law.[2] And he advances *epistemological* arguments calculated to support two key claims: (*i*) people who believe they are obligated to obey this kind of law are entitled to retain their belief in the face of anarchist criticism; and (*ii*) a credible account of political obligation can accommodate the concerns that drive anarchist arguments in such a way that no anarchist argument against political obligation could, in principle, be successful.

Both of the premises of Murphy's moral argument face difficulty, even if reconstructed in various ways. And even if the moral argument survives challenges focused on its validity and the truth of its premises, it offers the statist very little comfort (Part II). Murphy's epistemological claim—that anarchist refutations of arguments for political obligation, even if successful, do not undermine the reasonableness of folk

[1] *See* Gary Chartier, Anarchy and Legal Order: Law and Politics for a Stateless Society 157–241 (2013).

[2] Mark C. Murphy, *Philosophical Anarchisms, Moral and Epistemological*, 20 Can. J.L. & Juris. 95 (2007).

belief in the authority of state-made law—fails finally to persuade. There are multiple ways in which it should be possible rationally to undermine belief in a duty to obey state-made law (Part III). Murphy's moral argument is not especially strong, and his epistemological arguments do not succeed in absolving many statists of unreasonableness. There is no need for the critic of the state to find Murphy's arguments especially troubling (Part IV).

II. THE MORAL ARGUMENT FROM CONSCIENCE

A. *Lack of Obligation*

Murphy does not succeed in demonstrating that ordinary people have any obligation to obey state-made law. He evidently takes a "philosophical anarchist" to be someone who denies that there is a prima facie duty of obedience to state-made law.[3] He believes the philosophical anarchist should acknowledge a widespread duty of obedience to this kind of law.[4] He argues for this position as follows:

1. In reasonably just political communities, most citizens believe that they are morally bound to obey the law.
2. If one believes that one is morally bound to Φ, then one is morally bound to Φ.
3. Therefore, in reasonably just political communities, most citizens are morally bound to obey the law.

Murphy rightly observes that this argument is "transparently valid." He maintains that, having acknowledged this, we must grant that "the only question is whether both premises ought to be affirmed." Even if Murphy is right, however, his argument carries very little weight. In the interests of charity—in order to strengthen and clarify it—the argument should be revised in at least three ways: (*i*) its assumption that states are reasonably just communities should be altered, (*ii*) its focus on *state-made* law should be made explicit, and (*iii*) the transition Murphy seems to make from focusing on objective obligation to focusing on subjective obligation should be clarified. But the argument, even as reconstructed, is problematic both because its first premise is empirically doubtful and because its second premise may be overly demanding. Even if the argument survives challenges on these fronts, it amounts to very little as a response to anarchist criticisms of the state. The argument thus poses no threat to plausible varieties of anarchism.

3 As examples of the kind of position to which he seeks to respond, Murphy notes LESLIE GREEN, THE AUTHORITY OF THE STATE (1990); JOSEPH RAZ, THE AUTHORITY OF LAW: ESSAYS ON LAW AND MORALITY (1979); A. JOHN SIMMONS, MORAL PRINCIPLES AND POLITICAL OBLIGATIONS (1981); M. B. E. Smith, *Is There a Prima Facie Obligation to Obey the Law?*, 82 YALE L.J. 950 (1973).

4 Nothing prevents the philosophical anarchist, thus understood, from acknowledging that, while state-made law has no inherent authority, there might be some moral reason for following state-made law other than the fact that it has been made by the state. But of course Murphy wants the philosophical anarchist to acknowledge that the *origin* of state-made law is one source of its authority.

B. Reconstructing Murphy's Argument

1. Refining Murphy

Murphy's argument is problematic as he states it. States are not "reasonably just," and the argument should not be framed as if they were.[5] Murphy's argument is perhaps better thought of as focusing on political rather than on legal obligation, and it will be persuasive only if it distinguishes between subjective and objective moral obligation. These alterations seem likely to clarify, if not to rescue, Murphy's argument.

2. Justice and the State

The state is massively unjust.[6] While interpersonal justice may be served even in societies dominated by states, this can be seen as occurring in spite of, rather than because of, the monopolistic, aggressive, and exploitative characteristics of the legal systems and political orders in those societies. Thus, the argument provides no grounding for the authority of state-made law in any real-world setting (or, indeed, given that states are monopolies and monopolies are unjust, in any possible setting).

It would thus be possible to dismiss Murphy's argument as relevant to the circumstances of people in state-governed political communities. But we might instead, in the interest of laying the groundwork for an assessment of other aspects of the argument, opt to bracket the injustices inherent in the existence and operation of the state, as well as those that occur predictably when the state obtains. Perhaps a state that maintains justice apart from these inequities can be described as *just**. If so, we can ignore the issue of the state's justice and proceed by revising Murphy's argument as follows:

4. In reasonably just* political communities, most citizens believe that they are morally bound to obey the law.
5. If one believes that one is morally bound to Φ, then one is morally bound to Φ.
6. Therefore, in reasonably just* political communities, most citizens are morally bound to obey the law.

3. Equating Legal and Political Obligation

Murphy's argument should refer to "state-made law" rather than to "the law" in general.

There is good reason to believe that we can and should do without the state. By contrast, there is no particular reason to think that we can and should do without *law*; it

[5] Thanks to an anonymous reader for emphasizing the need to make this point.

[6] *See* Chartier, Anarchy, *supra* note 1, at 157–241.

is certainly not the case that the anarchist must "believe in . . . no laws."[7] Rather, peaceful, voluntary cooperation can be fostered effectively without aggression. And law can still be defined and enforced in the absence of the state: *law* is not identical with *state-made law*.[8] Legal regimes in a stateless society could, for instance, feature various analogues of common-law courts, developing legal rules on a case-by-case basis.

The anarchist can thus maintain without contradiction that members of a political community are morally bound to obey at least some (consensual) laws without maintaining that they are obligated to obey any state-made laws (at least, not under that description). A successful argument that there is an obligation to obey the law will not necessarily show, therefore, that state-made law as a whole or any state-made law in particular has any legitimacy. It might make sense to recast Murphy's argument with this in mind:

7. In reasonably just* political communities, most citizens believe that they are morally bound to obey state-made law.
8. If one believes that one is morally bound to Φ, then one is morally bound to Φ.
9. Therefore, in reasonably just* political communities, most citizens are morally bound to obey state-made law.

Absent the amendment, there would be no particular reason for the anarchist to disagree with Murphy's argument. The amendment makes it clearer that the argument *could* provide support for a position inconsistent with anarchism, one that might therefore seem genuinely troubling.

4. Objective and Subjective Obligation

Murphy's argument would be clearer if it distinguished between two senses in which one might be morally bound.[9]

Murphy's argument establishes—and is clearly intended to establish—that people are morally bound to obey state-made law whether or not their belief that they are so bound is false. That they are is an acknowledged implication of the notion that, if one *believes that* one is morally bound to Φ, then one *is* morally bound to Φ. But the recognition that this is the case highlights an ambiguity in the way Murphy has stated the argument. To see why, consider an amended version.

10. In reasonably just* political communities, most citizens mistakenly believe that they are morally bound to obey state-made law.

7 Alan Ebenstein, Friedrich Hayek: A Biography 224 (2001).

8 *See, e.g.*, Chartier, Anarchy, *supra* note 1; Law and Anarchism (Thom Holterman & Henc van Maarseveen eds., 1982); Anarchy and the Law: The Political Economy of Choice (Edward P. Stringham ed., 2007).

9 I do not believe that anything turns on usage here, but for stylistic reasons I will generally refer in what follows to someone's "having a moral obligation" rather than to someone's "being morally bound."

11. If one believes that one is morally bound to Φ, then one is morally bound to Φ.
12. Therefore, in reasonably just* political communities, most citizens are morally bound to obey state-made law.

This argument, like Murphy's original argument, seems to be "transparently valid." After all, (11), like Murphy's original (2), makes no reference to the correctness or incorrectness of anyone's beliefs; (12) follows whether or not "believes" in (10) is qualified by "mistakenly." But to say that someone mistakenly believes that *P* implies that *P* is false. However, if it is false that most citizens are morally bound to obey state-made law, then it must be true that most citizens are not morally bound to obey state-made law. And the proposition that most citizens are not morally bound to obey state-made law, which follows from (10), clearly contradicts (12).

The conflict disappears, however, if we amend the argument to make explicit a distinction between subjective and objective obligation.

One has a subjective obligation to Φ if the relevant (moral or empirical or rational) considerations of which one is aware, as one understands them, count decisively in favor of doing Φ or decisively against not doing Φ. One may, of course, be mistaken. But one acts unreasonably if one ignores the applicable reasons as one understands them—one acts without warrant, in a way that misshapes one's character and disconnects one from reality. Put more simply, when confronted with a given configuration of reasons, one has no warrant for doing other than what seems, all things considered, to follow from the reasons one judges to be available and relevant. To deny this is to opt out of the sphere of reason. If one is convinced that the array of relevant reasons is such that one has a moral duty to obey state-made law then one has, in a quite straightforward sense, a subjective obligation to obey state-made law. This is analytically true; it follows from what it means to have a subjective obligation.

One has an *objective* obligation to Φ if the relevant considerations actually *do* count decisively for doing Φ or decisively against not doing Φ. One may not be aware of these considerations; or one may misunderstand them. An objective obligation obtains whether one is aware of it or not. Presuming one is not omniscient and infallible, there will be no necessity that one's beliefs are accurate: there will be a gap between, on the one hand, the relevant considerations and their salience, and, on the other, one's beliefs about those considerations and their salience. This is an unavoidable implication of belief in the objectivity of morality. Someone may have had, say, a subjective obligation to conform her conduct to the requirements of the Fugitive Slave Law of 1850. But no one had any objective duty to do so, since facilitating anyone's enslavement is, in fact, a grievous wrong.[10]

10 Murphy, *supra* note 2, at 104, grants that "those who believe in political obligation do not believe, or do not believe merely, that the obligation to obey the law is bootstrapped into existence by their moral beliefs plus the conscience principle; they believe obedience to law to be morally required independently of their particular beliefs about the matter."

With this distinction in mind, we can reformulate Murphy's argument as follows:

13. In reasonably just* political communities, most citizens believe that they are objectively morally bound to obey state-made law.
14. If one believes that one is objectively morally bound to Φ, then one is subjectively morally bound to Φ.
15. Therefore, in reasonably just* political communities, most citizens are subjectively morally bound to obey state-made law.

When the argument appears in this form, the contradiction that could be introduced by adding "mistakenly" before "believe" in the major premise disappears. Whether or not the belief in legal obligation is mistaken, those citizens who believe they are objectively morally bound to obey state-made law are, at minimum, subjectively morally bound to do so. The only obligation any of them has in virtue of *this* argument, however, is not the obligation she thinks she has. That is, it is objectively true that one acts unreasonably if one ignores what one takes to be a genuine moral obligation, even if one is mistaken in supposing that one does. But the only *source* of the obligation in this case is *not* whatever one might take to render the obligation real, but only the *belief* that one has the obligation, whether or not one otherwise does. If successful, the argument shows that someone with the right beliefs does have a genuine obligation to obey state-made law, given that it is wrong to violate a subjective obligation, but *only* in virtue of her belief that she does.[11] It's quite compatible with her being shown to be mistaken and with her altering her belief in light of whatever considerations establish that she is mistaken.

Making clear that Murphy's argument need not be question-begging, that its concern is with state-made law, rather than with law in general, and that its focus is on subjective rather than objective obligation, eliminates obvious sources of confusion and objection. Thus, doing so enables Murphy's argument to be evaluated without distraction.

C. *Questionable Premises*

The first premise of Murphy's argument seems questionable on empirical grounds. And its second may depend on an overly strong version of the conscience principle.

1. Empirical Doubts

Murphy has not shown persuasively that most people (even in a limited range of political communities) actually believe that they are morally bound to obey state-

[11] Because the obligation is genuine and *preference*-independent (albeit not *belief*-independent), one could characterize it as *objective*. But to put the matter this way might run the risk of obscuring the distinction between objective and subjective obligations as I have sought to define them; the objectivity in question is of a rather peculiar sort. Thanks to Jonathan Crowe for pushing me to think further about this matter.

made law in the way the argument requires, even on a prima facie basis. And the available evidence does not make it plausible that he can show that they do.

According to Murphy, Tom Tyler's research "concludes that most of the folk believe that they ought to adhere to the law's dictates, and that this belief correlates most strongly not with the view that adherence to the law is personally beneficial but with the view that the law is fair and evenhanded." But this need not suggest that people have any particular commitment to the authority of state-made law. To call state-made law "fair and evenhanded" is to make a substantive judgment about its content, and perhaps its application by the courts, not to acknowledge the authority of state-made law *as such*.

Murphy concedes, at least arguendo, that "there may well not be widespread belief" that state-made law "provides a content-independent, protected reason for all of those to whom the dictate applies to comply with it." But he supposes the anarchist to deny that the fact "that the law requires some action is, for most (as opposed to all) . . . persons, even a strong *prima facie* . . . moral reason to perform that action." But there is no need to say this at all about the law in general, but only about *state-made* law. And the anarchist can grant that even a state-made law's requiring some action could afford someone with a strong prima facie reason for performing that action, as long as the warrant for her doing so did not depend on the law's having been enacted by the state (it might, for instance, deserve deference because it helped to create a social convention, like one governing traffic patterns, that itself had action-guiding significance).

As I have already suggested, I am inclined to think that Murphy is too quick to identify "the law's authority" and "political obligation." No doubt, most of the ordinary people to whom Murphy refers have thought of the two together. But it does not follow that, if confronted with the live possibility of law without the state, they would be so ready to give credence to political as to legal obligation.

Most people frequently ignore laws about driving speed without regarding themselves as having violated any moral obligation simply in virtue of so doing. Or consider another example: many people flout laws precluding the copying of songs and movies for personal use without understanding themselves as disregarding any such obligation. A third instance: it is notoriously the case that many people in some democracies I suspect Murphy would assume were "reasonably just" regard the nonpayment of at least some taxes as morally acceptable. At the same time, such people are much more likely to believe that they are bound to obey laws prohibiting murder.

We would need to determine how many people fit this description or how they would be inclined to justify their views to establish that some people—a significant number—do take this kind of selective approach to ascertaining their political obligations. Does a person who believes she is morally free to ignore some state-made laws but not others believe that she is "morally bound to obey . . . [state-made] law"? It seems as if she takes a more selective view of state-made law than Murphy's argument supposes.

If it is to be plausible, therefore, Murphy's first premise must be qualified in at least two ways.

(*i*) Many people's judgments that they ought to obey state-made law are selective. The duty to obey (state-made) law for which Murphy argues is a prima facie duty. But, while the attitude toward state authority adopted by those who break speed laws, download movies without paying for them, or avoid paying taxes might be seen as consistent with belief in such a prima facie duty, it certainly seems to involve quite limited respect for the authority of state-made law as a general matter.[12] Personal interests that might ordinarily be thought to have limited moral weight are seen as providing acceptable warrants for disregarding state-made law.

This is not, I think, best understood as a matter of arbitrarily allowing personal well-being to trump the reasonable claims of others (as, say, in a case of fraud). People perform the actions I have used as examples very frequently. And they generally fail to characterize their performance of these actions as morally troubling. Taken together with the fact that most people are morally decent, these observations lead me to suspect that those who engage in the kinds of actions I have instanced believe that it's morally reasonable to do so *even though* doing so means disregarding state-made law. These cases are especially telling. For it is precisely with respect to cases in which a norm would not exist without state action that obedience to state-made law qua obedience to state-made law is clearly relevant. When people disobey state-made law in these cases, it seems apparent that they do not regard the independent claim of state-made law to their obedience as particularly strong.

(*ii*) Only if the *source* of a state command is on its own sufficient to give her what she regards as good reason to obey it *even* when the content is not such that she would otherwise judge it to be a moral imperative does someone *really* acknowledge the authority of state-made law. Tyler's research suggests that *legitimacy* does play an important role in validating the authority of state-made law in people's minds. It is not simply the moral *contents* of state-made laws but the *procedures* from which these laws emerge in virtue of which many people believe they should be obeyed. But I think the empirical evidence leaves open the question: *just what role does legitimacy play in grounding people's belief in an obligation to obey state-made law?* Clearly, someone might treat legitimacy as a *necessary* condition for conformity to state-made law, so that its absence would render obedience as such gratuitous. But she might not regard a putatively legitimate state-made law as providing her with *sufficient* reason to do something for which she thought there was otherwise no good moral reason. I think the actual behavior of many people with regard to things like speed laws and copyright laws suggests that they often believe *either* that they are not bound by these laws at all *or else* that they are bound very weakly.

[12] Violating copyright norms can, of course, be described as violating private rights. But these rights are creatures of positive legislation in a way that the kinds of property rights I believe we should defend are not. We should, indeed, regard them as unreasonable grants of monopolistic privilege; *see, e.g.*, CHARTIER, ANARCHY, *supra* note 1, at 108–30.

None of this shows that some people do not regard state-made law as affording them at least sometimes with independent reasons for action. But it is, at any rate, not obvious that as many people as Murphy evidently supposes regard themselves as morally bound to obey state-made law on a consistent basis or that those who do clearly endorse the view that they are obeying the state's commands qua the state's commands. It might be more accurate to say that, at best, "many" rather than "most" citizens regard themselves as bound in some way and to some degree to obey state-made law. So perhaps Murphy's argument should read this way (I seek to make explicit a qualifier which Murphy clearly sees as applicable):

16. In reasonably just* political communities, many citizens believe that they are objectively morally bound, prima facie, to obey state-made law.
17. If one believes that one is objectively morally bound to Φ, then one is subjectively morally bound to Φ absent relevant defeaters.
18. Therefore, in reasonably just* political communities, many citizens are subjectively morally bound to obey state-made law absent relevant defeaters.

2. Revising the Conscience Principle

According to the conscience principle, whenever a person believes she has an obligation, of whatever sort, to Φ, she has a subjective obligation to Φ. A strong version of this principle is not especially plausible. And a weak version leaves open the possibility that many people who in some sense believe in political obligation are not, all things considered, morally bound to obey state-made law.

The conscience principle as stated would seem to have dramatic and unappealing implications. For instance: it seems clear that it would be fairly easy to formulate an argument paralleling Murphy's but designed to show that enslaved people in a slave society who mistakenly regarded themselves as obligated to accept their enslavement *were* so obligated. Murphy would need, I take it, to accept this as an implication of his preferred version of the conscience principle,[13] and perhaps this ought to be a source of discomfort with it.

In any case, one way of rendering the principle as stated in (17) plausible will flow from the view that moral judgment involves responsiveness to reasons. One might say that someone would be harming her own capacity to engage in practical reasoning if she deliberately ignored reasons she took to count decisively in favor of Φing or suppressed her own awareness of these reasons. To see what appears to be a decisive reason for something and to act contrary to that reason is to deny the authority of reason and to give priority to desire or impulse.[14] If one deliberately acts contrary to

[13] Thanks to an anonymous reader for emphasizing the need to make this point.

[14] It is a separate question, of course, to which reasons one gives decisive weight. *Cf.* Gary Chartier, The Analogy of Love 126–63 (2d ed., 2017) (critiquing notions of God as arbitrary will and examining the case of Huckleberry Finn's mistaken beliefs about slavery).

reason, one makes of oneself, at least to some extent, a person disconnected from reality; one refuses to acknowledge what one understands to be the case and undermines one's own responsiveness to objective norms. And clearly there is nothing that could justify one's proceeding in this way. (This is so both because, if there were, one would not be acting contrary to reason, and because, by choosing to act contrary to reason, one is estopped from invoking any sort of normative justification for one's choice at all.)

But not all moral responses reflect judgments about the merits of available reasons. Ignoring a putative principle that seems to be absurd, to lack rational support, need not undermine one's responsiveness to reasons. Doing so does not necessarily involve disregard for reality. It need not represent an attack on one's capacity to engage in practical reasoning and so is not obviously worth condemning. Someone immersed in a morality of taboo may perform an act prohibited by that morality and *feel* terribly guilty. But her choice to perform the act need not involve her in flouting the reality principle or harming her capacity to engage in practical reasoning. She has, *ex hypothesi*, violated a free-standing, otherwise unintelligible prohibition, and it is hard to see that doing so necessarily involves her in undermining her contact with reality or her own capacity for practical reason.

Huckleberry Finn provides a particularly good example of why it might make sense to interpret the conscience principle in something like the way I've suggested.

To be a good person is to be appropriately responsive to particular, substantive reasons: *that would be unfair*; *I am your friend*; *that is beautiful*; *I am committed to doing this*; *this option is more efficient than that one*. When Huck chooses to save Jim, who has escaped from enslavement, rather than returning him to his putative owner, he acts against his conscience in the sense that he believes he ignores a divinely established duty to the owner. But in so believing he makes an inaccurate judgment about the nature and salience of the relevant reasons. At the same time, in acting to save Jim, he responds rightly to what *are*, in fact, the relevant reasons. His character is commendable precisely because of his responsiveness to *those* reasons.[15]

When Huck acts against his conscience, he believes, not that he has done wrong in the sense that he has ignored the decisive import of the relevant reasons, but that he has violated a divine command backed up by the threat of hell. *We* might reasonably reject this putative command for a range of reasons; for Huck, in any case, the moral considerations to which he *is* responsive count against its credibility. Violating it is thus not a matter of doing wrong in the sense of acting unreasonably; it is, rather, deciding to act courageously to ignore what Huck believes to be a threat of vengeance on the part of a cosmic thug, of Blake's Nobodaddy.

Good reasons for affirming the conscience principle do not seem to apply in Huck's case. His conscience is primarily a source of guilt-feelings prompted by his violation of a taboo, by his imagined offense against a supposed divine law

[15] Thanks to Fritz Guy for helping me to see this point.

safeguarding the institution of slavery. Violating this sort of conscience is not obviously self-mutilating.

> . . . I may wrongly think I have an obligation that I do not have. In the past it was widely held that my believing, even misguidedly, that I have an obligation morally obliges me to fulfill it. To many of us today, however, it seems that if a person who takes too narrow a view of her own rights rebels against a falsely assumed burden of obligations, the moral gain in throwing off some of the shackles of servility may be more important than the damage to her conscientiousness.[16]

If the conscience principle follows from the need to respect one's own capacity for practical reason, the principle will apply only when there clearly is decisive reason to opt one way or another. A person who is morally uncertain may be tugged in multiple directions. She may reflexively experience distress, guilt, or shame for choosing in one way or another, even if she does not discern decisive reasons for choosing some option other than the one she's actually selected. But experiencing distress, guilt, or shame will not be the same as discerning that, all things considered, the reasons available to her point in a direction other than the direction she has chosen—at most, it will only suggest, defeasibly, that *perhaps* they do.

So the conscience principle is most plausible, I think, when it is limited to those cases in which a conscientious judgment is intelligible, explicable in terms of a network of interlocking, supportive reasons, and when such a judgment is clear and unequivocal. If this is correct, it might make sense to state (17) more precisely to render it more persuasive. Perhaps it could be recast in something like the following form:

17a. If one believes that the reasons available to one count decisively in favor of Φ, absent relevant defeaters, then one is subjectively morally bound to Φ, absent relevant defeaters.

If the premise of the argument referring to the conscience principle is reformulated, the conclusion will follow only if Murphy's initial, empirical assumption is recast as well. So the argument will look something like this:

19. In reasonably just* political communities, some citizens believe that the considerations available to them give them decisive prima facie reason to obey state-made law.
20. If one believes that the reasons available to one count decisively in favor of Φ, absent relevant defeaters, then one is subjectively morally bound to Φ, absent relevant defeaters.
21. Therefore, in reasonably just* political communities, some citizens are subjectively morally bound to obey state-made law, absent relevant defeaters.

Narrowing the conscience principle in this way will limit the empirical applicability of (21) to some extent. Many of those who *feel* obligated to obey state-made

[16] Robert Merrihew Adams, Finite and Infinite Goods: A Framework for Ethics 247 (1999).

law have not come to feel as they do because they acknowledge what they take to be decisive reasons to do what state-made law commands. They may feel this way, instead, simply out of habit or because in virtue of arbitrary pronouncements by putative authority figures. If the argument is recast as I have suggested it should be, these folk-statists need not be regarded as having any obligation, even a subjective one, to obey state-made law. Some of those who believe they are obligated to obey state-made law do so in virtue of what they take to be decisive reasons, to be sure. But *their* positions, grounded in reasons, can be undermined by arguments. They will be subjectively obligated to obey state-made law only as long as their view of the import of the applicable reasons remains unchanged in relevant ways.

3. Constrained Effects

The empirical premise of the argument is doubtful. At any rate, it is less than obvious that most people regard themselves as obligated in the ways in which the argument supposes they are. And the version of the conscience principle employed in the argument may be overly stringent. A reconstructed version of the argument renders it less efficacious: at best, it should be seen as applicable to a smaller number of people, and the beliefs held by those people should be understood as capable of being challenged by argument.

D. *Limited Results*

Murphy's argument does not provide strong support for statism. It does nothing to show that anyone ought to reject anarchism in favor of statism. It gives state actors no objective warrant for exercising any authority they would not otherwise be morally justified in exercising. And, even to the extent that it *is* persuasive, it applies only to citizens. Thus, its value seems to be limited, at best.

1. No New Obligations

One possible function of arguments against anarchism might be to convince people that they have good, objective reasons to obey state-made law. But, *ex hypothesi*, Murphy's argument only applies to people who already believe they are obligated to obey state-made law. If one already believes that one is morally bound to obey state-made law, one does not, as it were, need Murphy's argument. And if one does not believe that one is morally bound to obey state-made law, Murphy's argument will not give one any additional reason to do so.

Murphy seems to suggest that his argument might suffice to "*generate* an obligation to obey . . . [state-made] law."[17] But it is not clear that the argument does any

[17] Murphy, *supra* note 2, at 102.

such thing. That is, it provides no reason for someone who does not already believe she has any obligation to obey state-made law to do so. The concern with practical reasonableness it highlights might well give someone who already believed that she had an obligation to obey state-made law an *extra* reason to do so. But this reason would be dependent on her other reasons for obeying state-made law. It would not give anyone who lacked what she took to be a decisive reason to obey state-made law a *further* reason to do so.[18]

2. No Grounds for State Action

Perhaps one might think that arguments like Murphy's might serve to justify the actions of institutions or communities in upholding particular norms. State actors might be reassured by Murphy's argument that their actions were legitimate: they might suppose that people really did have some obligation to obey them, whatever the arguments advanced by anarchist critics, and they might thus view their putative authority more confidently.

But it seems that Murphy's argument will not really do any work here. Suppose I am a state actor—say, an employee of a police agency—preparing to use force to compel obedience to a given state-made law. And suppose that I want to know whether this law deserves to be obeyed. Either I believe that, all things considered, it does; or I believe that, all things considered, it does not. Will the fact that those subject to this law—presuming they are like "most citizens" as Murphy describes them—have a subjective obligation to obey it help me to determine whether I should enforce it?

No, it will not. For, even if Murphy is right, they have an obligation only in the sense that they act against their own capacity for practical reasonableness if they ignore state-made law. Murphy's argument certainly *cannot* be reconstructed in this way:

22. In reasonably just* political communities, most citizens believe that they have obligations *to their fellow citizens* to obey state-made law.
23. If one believes that one is objectively morally bound to Φ, then one is subjectively morally bound to Φ.
24. Therefore, in reasonably just* political communities, most citizens have obligations *to their fellow citizens* to obey state-made law.

[18] David Gordon raises an interesting question related to someone who does not believe that she is required to obey state-made law but who experiences some inclination in this direction. Could Murphy's argument strengthen her belief? Surely, it might strengthen the belief emotionally. Would it provide further warrant for the belief? It seems as if a person in this position would not find that the argument did so, since the argument depends on her believing that she is obligated, not merely on her feeling inclined to suppose that she *might* be. Rather more would be needed to show that, if one is inclined toward accepting that one is obligated, one is in fact obligated.

This cannot be right; (24) may or may not be correct, but it cannot be deduced from (22) and (23). While there may be exceptions related to people's reasonable expectations, my belief that I have an obligation to you does not give you the right to insist that I fulfill this obligation if you are aware that my belief is (or is likely) false. If I hold the mistaken belief that I owe you $100, I may injure *myself* if I decide not to pay you the $100. But this alone does not confer on you any objective right to claim the $100 or to retain it if I give it to you in the mistaken belief that I owe it to you. If you do not believe that I am obligated to pay you $100, it is, indeed, unreasonable of you to insist that I pay you. And, similarly, you have no good reasons to insist that I pay the $100 to a third party just because I mistakenly believe I owe the money to her (presuming you are aware, again, of the certain or likely falsity of my belief).

So whether, as a state actor, I should enforce a given state-made law with respect to relevant citizens will depend, at least in part, on whether I believe they are *objectively correct* to regard the law in question as legitimate. Their belief that it is legitimate might weigh in favor of the judgment that it would be *expedient* for me to enforce this law even if I reasonably suppose that belief to be false, but it does not go very far toward showing that it is any more *just* or *reasonable* for me to proceed as if their obligation were objective.[19]

And there is a further problem. There will certainly be people whose circumstances the actions of a police agency employee might affect who do not accept the legitimacy of some or all state-made laws.[20] Does this matter? Either way, it seems as if there is a problem for Murphy. If a state-made law may be enforced with respect to someone who does not acknowledge its authority, then it seems as if her putative culpability for ignoring this law is irrelevant to state actors who must decide whether to enforce it. In this case, Murphy's argument gives these state actors nothing new with which to work. But if *only* someone who acknowledges the authority of state-made laws is subject to those laws, then the effectiveness of the state is called seriously into question. State actors could not enforce state-made laws against many people. They would need, presumably, to determine which of those they encountered actually was obligated to accept state authority. And they could not enforce state-made laws, as such, against any sociopath who denied that any moral norms obtained at all. (To be sure, the sociopath could be restrained on moral

19 As regards expediency: if relevant private citizens not only believe they have an obligation but also act as if they have this obligation, I will have good reason to take into account their propensity to do so—in resolving coordination problems, for instance. As regards justice: their belief in the legitimacy of state power may affect their reasonable expectations of other private citizens and of state actors; to the extent that honoring reasonable expectations is morally important, this will affect the rightness of a state actor's behavior with respect to the relevant obligation.

20 *Cf.* Lester Hunt, *Why the State Needs a Justification, in* Anarchism/Minarchism: Is a Government Part of a Free Country 3, 7–8 (Roderick T. Long & Tibor Machan eds., 2008) (noting that state actors characteristically claim the right to impose their wills on the nonconsenting, something people would ordinarily regard as morally objectionable).

grounds; but moral norms would, *ex hypothesi*, obtain in the absence of the state. So this possibility does nothing to support any argument for the authority of state-made laws as such.)

3. Citizens Alone

Murphy's argument is framed with reference only to citizens. And it is not clear that it could be amended so that it did *not* refer just to citizens. This is because the first, empirical, premise would surely be considerably less plausible if it referred to everyone within, say, a state's internationally recognized territory as regarding herself as morally bound to obey state-made law. Thus, Murphy's argument does nothing to show that members of large groups—like undocumented migrants who deny the validity of (say) laws restricting their movements—that do not acknowledge the prima facie authority of some or all state-made laws have even a subjective obligation, much less an objective one, to obey those laws.

4. Limited Results

The argument has surprisingly limited import, even if its premises—as reasonably reconstructed—are accepted as correct. It offers no reason to someone who is an anarchist to accept the authority of state-made law and no reason to someone who is a statist not to accept an otherwise persuasive argument against the authority of state-made law. It provides no justification for state actors to enforce state-made law apart from whatever justification they might otherwise have. And it applies, in any case, only to citizens. Thus, it does not show that noncitizens violate any obligation when they ignore state-made laws.

E. Minimal Effects

Even if Murphy's argument is fully successful on its own terms, it is nonetheless applicable only in "reasonably just" political communities. And since states are not such communities, the argument as Murphy frames it does not seem to apply to them. In any case, it does not establish any claimable obligation on the part of citizens to each other. It shows, at most, only that some citizens (not as many, I think, as Murphy supposes) would act against their own capacities for practical reasonableness if they declined to give state-made law some weight in their deliberations. It gives no one who does not believe that there is an obligation to follow state-made law any reason to accept the existence of such an obligation. It does not insulate anyone against positive arguments for anarchism or against state authority. And it gives no one any additional justification for treating others as if they were bound to obey state-made law.

III. EPISTEMOLOGICAL ARGUMENTS

A. *No Need for Positive Arguments?*

Murphy advances a general anti-evidentialist thesis about justification: to show that state-made law has no authority, one must offer persuasive *positive* arguments to that effect; it will not be sufficient to refute particular arguments for the authority of state-made law or against anarchism. He claims that existing arguments for anarchism need not be taken to undermine the reasonableness of anyone's ungrounded belief that she has an obligation to obey state-made law. He also claims that no anarchist argument *could* do so.

According to Murphy, a successful argument for the nonexistence of political obligation would necessarily be a demonstration that acknowledging a duty of obedience to state-made laws would require one to do something wrong or to forego doing something licit. But, he argues, a reasonable understanding of obedience to such laws would always excuse people otherwise obligated from obeying unreasonable commands. So it would not be possible to adduce an example of a state-made law such that a duty of obedience would require one to obey it—*despite the fact* that the claim that one had a duty to follow it was wildly implausible.

Murphy identifies two varieties of arguments for anarchism that might be thought to count against the reasonableness of someone's continuing belief in an obligation to obey state-made law. *Basis* arguments maintain that positive arguments for an obligation to obey state-made law are unsuccessful. *Consequence* arguments seek to show that anarchism leads to results that are consistent with common moral convictions. Neither sort of argument, Murphy suggests, even if successful, need be seen as undermining reasonable belief in political obligation.

Murphy defends this conclusion by taking an anti-evidentialist position in epistemology: the validity of my belief that a given proposition is true does not depend on my ability to argue persuasively for that proposition; rather, I am entitled to retain the beliefs I happen to have unless I can see good reason to reject them. Since many people simply believe that they ought to obey state-made law on the basis of say-so, having been taught they ought to do so, say, by their parents, showing that particular arguments for political obligation are unsuccessful is irrelevant to the validity of their beliefs. And showing that anarchism does not conflict with ordinary moral convictions does nothing to show that there is anything wrong with believing that there is an obligation to obey state-made law. What the anarchist needs, and has not—says Murphy—provided, are positive arguments against political obligation.

In fact, however, it *is* possible, contra Murphy, to convict the statist of unreasonableness, and that arguments that take the form Murphy envisions would do so, at least in the case of some statists. Murphy's defense of the reasonableness of statism relies on the rejection of evidentialism in epistemology. Whatever the merits of evidentialism, it is clear that, if evidentialism *is* correct, the statist is guilty of unreasonableness if she accepts statism without adequate argumentative warrant. And even if Murphy correctly rejects evidentialism, he does not succeed in shifting the burden of justification from the statist to the anarchist or in showing the anarchist cannot, in principle, meet this burden. Murphy's epistemological arguments do not succeed.

B. *Anti-Evidentialism and Ungrounded Statism*

Murphy maintains that people violate no epistemic duties by continuing, in the face of anarchist arguments, to believe that they are obligated to obey state-made law. For his argument to succeed, he needs to show that ordinary statists do not hold their belief in political obligation on the basis of reasons. He also needs to assume or demonstrate the validity of a controversial epistemological thesis: that sound judgments do not require evidential warrants. The first claim is implausible and the second, though reasonable, is certainly controversial—with the result that Murphy's argument is, at any rate, weakened.

1. Assuming Ungrounded Statism

What Murphy says is plausible only when someone's belief in state authority is ungrounded and only in this case if adhering to ungrounded—say, inherited—beliefs is rational.

Someone might, of course, accept the authority of the state without grounds. But if someone's belief in state authority depends on particular arguments—arguments, say, from fairness or from consent—anarchist refutations of those arguments will render that person's continued belief in state authority unreasonable.[21] Similarly, if someone believes the proposition that she is obligated to obey state-made law on the basis of some other proposition—whether the foundational proposition is itself warranted argumentatively—then undermining that proposition or the link between it and belief in political obligation will tend to show that the statist is unreasonable.

Murphy maintains that few people believe in state authority on the basis of arguments or of grounded reasons of the sort I have envisioned. But I do not think it obvious that he is right about this. Certainly, someone whose political convictions have been shaped by the political tradition of the United States—rooted in the Declaration of Independence, with its claim that the authority of rulers derives from "the consent of the governed"—might well treat as unproblematic the view that consent lies at the root of political obligation. Such a person might not ordinarily

21 To be sure, someone might initially acquire a belief for particular reasons while going on to accept it as valid apart from these reasons. My concern here, though, is with someone who does, in fact, continue to embrace belief in state authority for particular reasons. Thanks to David Gordon for underscoring the need to make this point.

think reflectively about the nature of political duty, but might recognize on the basis of anarchist arguments that the requisite consent was lacking.

2. Assuming Anti-Evidentialism

More broadly, Murphy's view will seem unpersuasive to anyone who endorses some variety of evidentialism. If no belief should be accepted without evidence, and if the strength of our beliefs should be proportioned to the evidence available to support them, then it seems as if folk-belief in political obligation is in more trouble than Murphy is inclined to grant.

It is not obvious that parental say-so counts as evidence at all. Parents do not, on Murphy's hypothesis, *create* political obligation. And it seems unlikely that they have access to any arcane sources of knowledge about obligations that are unavailable to their adult children: it is not obvious that parents' endorsement of a view should be taken as indirect evidence that there is—because parents are aware of and testify to it—direct evidence of whatever sort is needed to support belief in political obligation.

But suppose that parental say-so *is* regarded as evidence. Still, the evidentialist will say, it is very weak evidence. We know that people teach all sorts of incorrect beliefs to their children. So parents' testimony on behalf of a position should not lead anyone to believe in political obligation with great confidence. Further, if parental testimony is indirect evidence for the existence of good, objective reasons for belief in political obligation, why should those objective reasons not be apparent to adults who must decide what to teach their own children? The seeming absence of such reasons seems to count in favor of the view that they do not, in fact, obtain at all. A similar process of reasoning will tend to undermine evidentiary appeals to the say-so of teachers and other authority figures.

The evidentialist who does not accept the say-so of parents, teachers, or other authority figures as even indirect evidence for the truth of the claim that people are obligated to obey state-made law and who lacks other positive arguments for state authority, perhaps because arguments of this sort she formerly endorsed have been undermined for her by anarchist criticisms, will have even less reason to accept the claims of state-made law. Of course, the sheer fact that a given argument for political obligation has been successfully undermined does not show that some other, better argument is not available. But, in the absence of such an argument, the evidentialist will say, belief in political obligation appears to be on very shaky ground.

For evidentialists persuaded by anarchist arguments against standard defenses of political obligation, it will not be rational to acknowledge duties of obedience to state-made law. Evidentialism is a plausible view, even if not one I am finally inclined to affirm. But suppose the evidentialist turns out to be mistaken. Murphy's confidence that belief in political obligation could not be undermined still seems misplaced.

No plausible view will suppose that we know infallibly that beliefs we have been taught to hold are true. Nor is it plausible to suppose that, if we are entitled to affirm such beliefs absent appropriate defeaters, it will be possible to specify with particular precision just what an appropriate defeater will be. No doubt a frontal assault on an inherited belief—one that shows that it is incoherent or has wildly implausible implications—will serve effectively to undermine it. But there is little reason to suppose this is the only possible way of establishing that such a belief is unwarranted.

3. Questionable Assumptions

Murphy may well be wrong that many ordinary statists' beliefs are argumentatively or evidentially ungrounded, and, if these beliefs are, in fact, argumentatively or evidentially grounded then undermining the beliefs' grounds will have the potential to undermine the beliefs. And the argument seems to *presuppose* that evidentialism as an epistemological strategy is incorrect. Murphy's view will thus be unpersuasive if evidentialism is correct, and arguments for evidentialism will count against Murphy's position.

C. *Undermining Belief In Political Obligation*

Murphy maintains that the *kind* of argument needed to undermine folk-belief in political obligation would need to be one that demonstrated the existence of "some sort of incoherence or deeply implausible implication to the common belief in political obligation." But what would count as a "deeply implausible implication"? Murphy suggests that it would need to be the case that the duty to obey state-made law entailed a duty to engage in morally wrongful behavior or to accept an unjust restriction on morally acceptable behavior. But, he maintains, the duty to obey state-made law is a prima facie duty, limited by reasonableness, and need not be understood to require either immorality or servility in response to the law's command. Thus, a reasonable duty to obey a given state enactment could not have the kind of "deeply implausible implication" it would be necessary to show that it had in order to undermine folk-belief in political obligation.

One way of understanding Murphy's own non-foundationalist epistemological position is as broadly coherentist.[22] On a plausible understanding of coherentism, it's

[22] For more on the sort of coherentism I have in mind, *see, e.g.*, CHARTIER, ANALOGY, *supra* note 14, at 20–31. I do not mean that Murphy embraces a coherentist account of *truth*, but rather that his account of *justification* might be described as coherentist because it does not seem to treat particular beliefs as unshakeable epistemic foundations. David Gordon challenges my characterization of Murphy, suggesting that he appears to leave it open what would count as a defeater for a belief held without evidence, and thus doesn't commit himself to the kind of epistemological coherentism I have attributed to him. Nicholas Wolterstorff advances an alternative anti-foundationalism that isn't worked out in coherentist terms and that leaves open the option of criticizing ungrounded beliefs in various ways: *see, e.g.*, Nicholas P. Wolterstorff, *Can Belief in God Be Rational If It Has No*

unnecessary to meet the high burden of justification Murphy suggests the philosophical anarchist needs to meet. If coherentism of some sort is correct, it would be perfectly possible to undermine the statist's beliefs by appealing to specific moral principles the statist might endorse. Murphy's burden-shifting strategy clearly would not count against consequentialist arguments for anarchism, in particular. A general burden-shifting argument designed to undermine the statist's position, one that relies on what we might call "the presumption of anarchism," might also be possible. There is no reason to think that accepting something like Murphy's own epistemological posture would render statism invulnerable to argumentative undermining.

1. Justification without Foundations

Murphy does not spell out a comprehensive epistemological view. But, by demanding that a critic of an inherited belief show that the belief is unreasonable before it is rejected, he effectively rejects evidentialism, as I have already noted. By accepting at least one moral belief as defensible absent justification with reference to empirical or logical foundational truths, he signals his rejection of classical foundationalism. At the same time, by allowing that an inherited belief can be rejected in virtue of its *implications*, he seems to deny that inherited beliefs are foundational; so his position is not best understood as some kind of nonstandard foundationalism that treats inherited beliefs as unchallengeable. One way to think of it is as coherentist.

2. An Overly High Threshold for Belief Rejection

Once we have accepted the anti-foundationalist posture Murphy has implicitly commended, inherited beliefs need not enjoy any special status in relation to one's other beliefs. Instead of proceeding from necessary foundations at the root of the pyramid of knowledge, one will simply need, when asking whether a given inherited belief is correct, to ask how it fits with the rest of the convictions that make up one's web of belief. One will seek to achieve reflective equilibrium among one's various beliefs—normative and empirical, general and particular. Confronted by an inconsistency between two beliefs, one will need to modify or reject one or both (or else find a way of denying that the apparent consistency actually obtains). From this general procedure, nothing follows about the strength with which one ought to retain any particular belief, inherited or otherwise.

Perhaps an inconsistency between belief in a putative obligation to obey the state and some other belief will be most effectively resolved—perhaps one's web of belief will be rendered most satisfyingly coherent—by giving up belief in

Foundations?, *in* Faith and Rationality: Reason and Belief in God 135 (Alvin Plantinga & Nicholas Wolterstorff eds., 1985). On an approach like Wolterstorff's, it would remain open to the critic to note that the state was both dangerous and unnecessary. I suspect the critic could also treat the state's nonconsensual character as a positive objection to its desirability.

political obligation. Whether this is so or not will depend, among other things, on how deeply embedded belief in political obligation actually is in one's web of belief. It may not be at all difficult to show in some cases that someone who believes in political obligation is unreasonable. And even if doing so proves more difficult, it may not be necessary to meet the very high standards Murphy proposes.

3. Principles and the Unreasonableness of Statism

Adopting a coherentist moral epistemology is consistent with opting for a stable, finite set of specifiable moral principles. A statist who endorses such principles may rightly be convicted of unreasonableness if belief in political obligation does not follow from her principles.

On a plausible view of moral reasoning, we often inherit both specific moral judgments ("Women should wear veils in public," "Stealing is wrong") and more general moral principles ("Do not discriminate arbitrarily among the people affected by your actions," "Bring about the greatest good for the greatest number"). For many reasonable people, the process of achieving reflective equilibrium will involve the conclusion that moral reasonableness is a matter of acting in accordance with a finite set of such general principles. This will not be true of everyone, of course, but it is true of a great many people.

Perhaps they endorse some single principle—the principle of utility, however stated, or Kant's categorical imperative, or (less probably) Alan Gewirth's Principle of Generic Consistency.[23] Perhaps they endorse a set of complementary, nonconflicting principles like the norms of practical reasonableness I have endorsed in this book.[24] Or perhaps, with W. D. Ross, they affirm a set of prima facie principles with the potential to generate conflicts that can only be resolved through the use of non-algorithmic practical reason.[25]

In any event, it is not uncommon for a person to endorse a finite set of specifiable moral principles. And treating these principles with great confidence is surely defensible on coherentist grounds. The coherentist need not be committed only to particular moral judgments. Indeed, it is unclear what it would mean to render utterly particular moral judgments coherent with each other. Absent the ability to elaborate relevant features of such judgments, capable of being compared and contrasted, any and all judgments would seemingly be consistent with each other. And generic moral principles could surely be deeply embedded in the coherentist's web of belief. Certainly, such judgments could be at least as deeply embedded as any specific normative judgment, like "It's wrong to disobey state-made law," seems to be

23 *See* Alan Gewirth, Reason and Morality (1978).
24 *See* Introduction, Parts II–III, *supra*.
25 See W. D. Ross, The Right and the Good (2d ed., 2003).

for the person Murphy envisions who is reasonable in maintaining this belief absent a showing of incoherence or wild implausibility.

Suppose, then, that moral reasonableness involves adherence to a finite set of specifiable moral principles. A moral judgment will be justified insofar as it is consistent with these principles. And this must include, of course, the judgment that one has an obligation, and so, in particular, the judgment that one has an obligation to obey state-made law. Someone's believing that she is obligated to obey state-made law will thus be unreasonable if it does not flow from one or more of the moral principles it is reasonable for her to endorse. Obedience to state-made law is not a basic, underived moral principle for consequentialists, for Ross, for Gewirth, or for NATURAL LAW theorists. Suppose one endorses their moral theories, or other theories that do not treat political obligation as basic. Suppose, too, that disobeying state-made law is otherwise consistent with the moral principles one endorses. In this case, disobeying state-made law will be reasonable if one's act of disobedience is not ruled out by whatever moral principles one reasonably holds.

Thus, it is possible to show that belief in political obligation is unreasonable for a citizen to hold if it can be demonstrated that disobeying state-made law is not, as a general matter, ruled out by the principles it is reasonable for the citizen to affirm —or, indeed, the actual principles the citizen *does* affirm. The anarchist can ask, simply, whether each of the relevant principles rules out disobedience to state-made law, on its own or in conjunction with one or more of the others. This is likely to be a rather easier task than showing that belief in political obligation is incoherent or leads to manifest implausibility. It will be a matter of showing that one can adhere to the relevant principle or principles without acknowledging a duty of obedience to state-made law—say, that one can affirm the Principle of Fairness while rejecting fairness-based arguments for political obligation. Someone who accepts a given set of moral principles which do not appear to rule out disobedience to state-made laws but who regards herself, nonetheless, as obligated to obey such laws might be shown in this way to be making an unwarranted judgment.

4. Burden-Shifting and Consequentialism

Murphy attempts to shift the burden of justification from the statist to the anarchist. He argues that it is impossible to show that the statist is unreasonable simply by undermining particular positive arguments for political obligation. But the peculiar nature of consequentialist justification means that, if the statist is a consequentialist, she must acknowledge that a positive argument for anarchism will necessarily undermine her belief in political obligation.

Murphy discusses "consequence" arguments for anarchism, which are essentially designed to show that accepting anarchism need not have wildly counter-intuitive implications; he regards these arguments, rightly, as establishing on their own only parity of some sort between anarchism and statism. But it would clearly be possible to opt for a more proactive strategy, seeking to show that the believer in political obligation was unreasonable by demonstrating that anarchy was preferable on consequentialist grounds to adherence to state authority.[26] If the believer in political obligation was already a consequentialist, the argument would simply take the form of a demonstration that the net benefits of anarchy would exceed those of rule by the state. (If the believer in political obligation did not accept the appropriateness of global consequentialist reasoning, it would obviously be necessary to demonstrate that she ought to do so for this sort of argument to work.) So the anarchist could make a positive case for anarchy on consequentialist grounds.

Such a defense might or might not be credible. I do not believe that consequentialism is viable as a general approach to moral theory or practice,[27] and I am certainly not arguing here, therefore, that the consequentialist would be correct. I am simply suggesting that the distinctive structure of consequentialist argument means that it would be possible for the consequentialist anarchist to mount a straightforward, positive case for anarchism with the potential to show that the statist was unreasonable. Deontological arguments for anarchism might often take the form of dismantling the positive claims made on behalf of state authority; and deontological theorists of a pluralist stripe might have some difficulty in rejecting the ungrounded belief in political obligation that Murphy attributes to his imagined statist. But the consequentialist would be able, in principle, to give minimal weight to ungrounded moral beliefs. And *if* a consequentialist argument were successful in demonstrating the superior merits of anarchy, it would have gone a long way toward showing that anarchy was to be preferred to obedience to the state.[28]

26 *See, e.g.*, David D. Friedman, The Machinery of Freedom (3d ed., 2015).

27 *See, e.g.*, Alasdair C. MacIntyre, After Virtue: A Study in Moral Theory 61–63, 67–68, 185 (2d ed., 1984); John Finnis, Natural Law and Natural Rights 111–19 (1980); John M. Finnis, Fundamentals of Ethics 80–108 (1983); John M. Finnis, Joseph M. Boyle, Jr., Germain G. Grisez, Nuclear Deterrence, Morality, and Realism 177–296 (1987); Germain G. Grisez & Russell Shaw, Beyond the New Morality: The Responsibilities of Freedom 111–14, 131–33 (3d ed., 1988); David S. Oderberg, Moral Theory: A Non-Consequentialist Approach 65–76, 97–101, 132–33 (2000); Paul Hurley, Beyond Consequentialism (2011); Nel Noddings, Caring: A Feminine Approach to Ethics and Moral Education 86–87, 151–54 (1984); Bernard Williams, Morality: An Introduction to Ethics (2d ed., 1993); Bernard Williams, *A Critique of Utilitarianism*, *in* J. J. C. Smart & Bernard Williams, Utilitarianism: For and Against 77 (1973); Stephen R. L. Clark, *Natural Integrity and Biotechnology*, *in* Human Lives 58–76 (Jacqueline A. Laing & David S. Oderberg eds., 1997); Germain Grisez, *Against Consequentialism*, 23 Am. J. Juris 21 (1978); Adams, *supra* note 16, at 298–300.

28 Obviously, the question whether anarchy is to be preferred to rule by the state is a different question from whether, in any given case, the consequentialist ought to do as state-made law demands. But, given the nature of act-consequentialist reasoning, the act-consequentialist's deliberation regarding the question whether she ought to obey state-made law in any given case can give little or no independent weight to the authority of the state as such. And other sorts of consequentialism, I believe, ultimately reduce to act-consequentialism.

5. The Presumption of Anarchism

Murphy seeks to shift the burden of demonstrating that political obligation does not obtain onto the anarchist. But it may be argued that there is a presumption of anarchism that rules out this move.

Someone who believes in political obligation but who does not treat her belief as ungrounded confronts what might be referred to as the *presumption of anarchism*. This plausible principle begins with a dilemma. When a state actor demands obedience from a citizen, either the behavior the state actor seeks to compel would be morally required absent her action or it would not. If it would not, then the question of state authority does not, per se, arise. If it would, then some justification of her claimed authority is required. Absent this sort of justification, her claim to obedience seems indefensible.[29]

Suppose one believes, for instance, that the state has the right to kill the members of a certain class of criminals in the course of maintaining justice but that, as a non-state actor, one does not have this right oneself. How will one understand the relevant circumstances? Presumably, one will judge that there are reasons for the public executioner to heed state-made law and so to kill, reasons that would not obtain in the absence of that command. But the reason cannot simply be that state-made law deserves obedience. The very fact that the state has ordered the executioner to do something that, apart from its command, would clearly be wrong compels the executioner, and anyone who scrutinizes the executioner's activity, to ask about whether the state is justified in making the particular law at issue.[30] The executioner in particular, and the citizen more generally, acts unreasonably if she does not ask, *What is it about the relevant state-made law that renders reasonable a distinction between killing in obedience to that command and killing in the absence of that command?* An intelligible answer to this question for someone who accepts general moral principles will involve situating the relevant state-made law in relation to these principles. And it will involve showing what special reasons, flowing from these principles, make it reasonable for someone to obey state-made law when it asks her to do something it would ordinarily seem unreasonable for her to do. Departure from the moral baseline—which obedience-to-the-state *qua* obedience-to-the-state necessarily involves—requires *some* sort of justification. Failure to provide this justification will render it unreasonable to accept the authority of state-made law.[31]

[29] *Cf.* Hunt, *supra* note 20.

[30] *Cf.* Michael Huemer, The Problem of Political Authority: An Examination of the Right to Coerce and the Duty to Obey (2013); Carole Pateman, The Problem of Political Obligation: A Critique of Liberal Theory (2d. ed., 1985).

[31] Of course, the issue of state authority arises not only with respect to state actions that would be generally regarded as immoral if performed by non-state actors but also with respect to commands issued by state actors that purport either to require an action someone would not otherwise regard herself as obligated to perform or to prohibit an action someone would otherwise regard herself as at liberty to perform. Here, it seems as if someone confronted with such a command will need *some* reason to conform her behavior to it. The reason need not be explicit, though, if it's not, she will

The person who believes in political obligation could, of course, maintain that, while she was unable to see how political obligation flowed from the moral principles she endorsed, and could not see any reasonable basis for revising those principles so that they entailed political obligation, she still intended to acknowledge a duty of obedience to state-made law. And perhaps, if such a person's belief in political obligation were deeply embedded in her web of belief, such a stance might be reasonable. My goal is not to show that no one could reasonably affirm the authority of state-made law, but only that it would be easier to show that many people were unreasonable in so doing than Murphy seems inclined to grant.[32]

6. Unpersuasive Burden-Shifting

Murphy appears to operate with a broadly coherentist position that does not require that beliefs be demonstrably grounded in good evidence in order to be acceptable. There is nothing wrong with coherentism. But in general, there is no reason for someone who adopts this kind of position to endorse the very high standard for belief rejection Murphy embraces; adopting a less demanding position might well make the task of convicting the statist of unreasonableness rather less difficult. Certainly, if the statist's own moral principles render the state illegitimate or make the statist's imposition of the state's authority on others unacceptable, this can reasonably be emphasized in a way that can be seen as undermining the statist's justification for retaining her statism. This may be particularly true if the statist is some sort of consequentialist. And since there is arguably a presumption in favor of anarchism, the statist might well be seen as responsible for making a positive case in favor of statism, and as rationally challengeable if she failed to do so.

presumably need to suppose that it *could* be made explicit. Thanks to David Gordon for pressing me on this point.

[32] The argument in the text focuses especially on positions that affirm general principles. Similar kinds of points can be made in relation to positions that take particular moral judgments to flow from morally relevant considerations, even if in less straightforward fashion. Thus, because the deontological particularist believes that moral judgments must be made case by case, she is unlikely to maintain that there is a general duty of obedience to state-made law any more than that there is a general duty to do or refrain from doing anything else. If the virtue theorist, like John McDowell, *see* JOHN MCDOWELL, MIND, VALUE, AND REALITY (1998), maintains that virtue is a matter of sensitivity to reasons, a sensitivity that cannot be captured in general principles or rules, the virtue theorist, too, will not endorse a general principle of obedience to state-made law, though her character might incorporate the disposition to accept the authority of state-made law. In neither case would it be necessary to argue, as Murphy suggests, that the general principle requiring obedience to state-made law was incoherent or yielded implausible conclusions, for the principle would serve, at best, as a summary of a range of particular judgments. It would be possible to show that the particularist or the virtue theorist who was a statist was unreasonable simply by amassing reasons relevant to particular cases or kinds of cases and showing their salience vis-à-vis the choice to disobey state-made law.

D. Folk-Statism and Rational Critique

Murphy's defense of the rationality of folk-statism will be persuasive only to someone who does not accept evidentialism as a general approach to epistemology, and even then only as a defense of the rationality of someone who does not accept political obligation for some substantive reason that can itself be argumentatively undermined. So, for instance, "basis" arguments of the kind Murphy judges unsuccessful will undermine the reasonableness of anyone who accepts political obligation in light of the reasons the basis arguments attack. Murphy grants this, while maintaining that most people do not believe in political obligation in virtue of such reasons. I am not sure he is right about this.

Even if his anti-evidentialism is correct, so that it's necessary to offer defeaters for belief in political obligation, the anarchist can still convict the believer in political obligation of unreasonableness more readily than Murphy supposes. Murphy's anti-foundationalism might be read as a kind of coherentism in which one searches for reflective equilibrium among one's various beliefs and in which justification is a matter of showing that such equilibrium can be satisfactorily achieved. And on this sort of epistemological view, there can be no a priori specification of just what must be shown to undermine a given belief.

It is possible to show that belief in political obligation is inconsistent with other beliefs held by the believer in political obligation. Just how much inconsistency the anarchist will need to demonstrate will depend on how deeply embedded belief in political obligation is in the believer's web of belief. But it might well be possible to do so by demonstrating far less than the wild implausibility Murphy supposes is necessary. The anarchist might well note the degree to which states are dangerous—including, especially, dangerous to the interests that are often valued for protecting. The anarchist might also seek to highlight the ways in which most of the goods people hope states will realize or safeguard can be had in the absence of predatory territorial monopolists. And the anarchist can note the difficulties associated with the state's nonconsensual character, something that might strike reflective people as both abusive and risky. The anarchist might also seek to show that belief in political obligation is not consistent with moral principles to which the believer in political obligation is more deeply committed than she is to belief in political obligation. Whether the focus is on particular beliefs or on more general moral principles, it is possible, in principle, to show that a web of belief marked by reflective equilibrium will not include belief in political obligation even absent a showing of wild implausibility.[33]

[33] Or, if one opts for some sort of anti-foundationalism that isn't coherentist, that there are good positive reasons to reject state authority.

IV. THE CONTINUED APPEAL OF ANARCHISM

Murphy argues that most citizens of reasonably just political communities are morally bound to obey laws made by their own governments, and that anarchist attempts to undermine the reasonableness of ordinary people's beliefs that they are thus bound both do not and cannot succeed. But radical liberalism seems to me to survive Murphy's arguments.

States are not reasonably just political communities. Even if they were, however, it would still be the case that the moral argument failed to show that there was any objective obligation to obey state-made law—only that some citizens would undermine their own practical reasonableness if they failed to act as if there were such an obligation. We have reason to wonder whether "most" people really are bound even in this way, even if the conscience principle takes the form Murphy suggests it does. A plausible account of this principle gives us reason to doubt that it does take this form. And, even if the argument were completely successful, it would not do anything to show someone who did not believe she was morally bound to obey state-made law to suppose that she was, to demonstrate the objective unreasonableness of such a person, or to offer anyone a justification for exercising state authority when she otherwise had no such justification.

Murphy's epistemological arguments are designed to defend the reasonableness of ordinary people's putative belief in political obligation. But these arguments do not serve to insulate the believer in political obligation against the charge of unreasonableness. The evidentialist anarchist can maintain that Murphy has not shown that evidentialism is incorrect and that basis arguments deprive statists of their entitlement to belief in political obligation because they show that this belief lacks appropriate evidentiary support. The coherentist anarchist need not show that statism is wildly implausible or incoherent, as Murphy claims she must. Instead, she can demonstrate inconsistencies within the statist's web of belief; note that belief in statism does not follow from the statist's moral principles; highlight positive reasons for finding anarchism attractive; emphasize that the state is dangerous and unnecessary; or show that the statist has not defeated the presumption of anarchism.

Anarchist arguments against the authority of state-made law and for the benefits of a stateless society are very attractive. But it is not my purpose here to show that they are correct. I simply want to suggest that Murphy's arguments do not show that most people are morally bound to obey state-made law in any very interesting sense, that anarchist arguments have not seriously weakened the case for political obligation, or that they could not do so. Murphy's critique of anarchism is unsuccessful. Radical liberalism remains an appealing and viable approach to safeguarding our capacities for flourishing and fulfillment.

Conclusion

Radicals

A version of radical liberalism articulated and defended using natural law theory can foster flourishing and fulfillment.

The liberal tradition prizes diversity, equality, creativity, reason, criticism, and individuality. In turn, therefore, it values institutions and practices that enhance the extent of personal flourishing, opportunities for critical reflection and engagement,[1] and the range of personal choice: the capacity for choice and critical reflection is, after all, an aspect of flourishing (linked with practical reasonableness), and choice and critical reflection, in turn, make flourishing possible. At the same time, liberalism challenges those institutions and practices that subordinate, exclude, and deprive, because such instances and practices undermine flourishing and (given that they so often treat people as members of undifferentiated collectives) exhibit disregard for individuality.

The growing liberal tradition has divided many times in recent centuries. Today, classical liberals and modern liberals embrace the same inclusive and egalitarian social and cultural values while differing in their views of state and market: classical liberals characteristically favor small government and cheer for markets, while modern liberals believe that liberal social values can be effectively implemented only by a strong state that can correct market imperfections. Some people identified as both classical and modern liberals have opposed war and empire, even if others have, unfortunately, embraced both.

Liberalism began as a *political* tradition, securing markets, promoting free trade, and resisting royal and aristocratic power. But the liberal spirit has implications that extend beyond the political sphere, the sphere in which force is employed. Liberals value not only freedom from violence but also autonomy in institutional and societal settings. They treasure not only legal protections for diverse ideas and diverse market participants but also social norms that nourish individuality and, indeed, eccentricity. They oppose not only the legal prohibition of disfavored ideas but also norms and policies that foster monocultures in workplaces, affinity groups, and religious

[1] *See* Sheldon Richman, *For the Love of Reason*, The Libertarian Institute, Aug. 17, 2018, https://libertarianinstitute.org/articles/tgif-for-the-love-of-reason/.

communities. They challenge not only legal rules that inhibit the development of varied lifestyles but also social attitudes that discourage experiments in living.

Radical liberals are convinced that a thoroughgoing abandonment of state-secured privilege and, where possible, a thoroughgoing rectification of state-sanctioned and state-perpetrated injustice can effectively foster liberal political and social values, and the diverse aspects of flourishing, without state action. Radical liberals are, in a word, anarchists. They maintain that even small governments are so readily subject to capture by elites that they will tend to promote the interests of the wealthy and well connected at the expense of others. Modern liberals are right to be concerned about concentrated wealth and power, but perhaps, modern liberals suggest, it is precisely the state apparatus modern liberals often see as playing an empowering role in society that helps to *keep* wealth and power concentrated. The elimination of those often-cartelizing privileges that Benjamin Tucker labeled "monopolies,"[2] radical liberals maintain, can liberate people for prosperity and community.

Radical liberals celebrate genuinely liberated—freed—markets as sources of prosperity and sites for experimentation and reject monopolies and cartels as privileged funnels of resources away from consumers and into the pockets of the wealthy and well connected. They value rights to justly acquired possessions as safeguards for autonomy and opportunities for productivity, while objecting to property acquired through state-secured special privileges. They cherish freedom of association, while working to undermine patterns of association that stifle self-expression and critical judgment and that exclude dissenters and aliens. They cheer for genuine merit, even as they decry *apparent* achievement that turns out to be mediocrity protected by unfairness. They welcome due process (as a commitment of both legal institutions and associations entirely distinct from the legal system) and the rule of law, even as they deny the legitimacy of monopolistic state institutions that seek to provide these goods in arbitrary, exclusive, prejudiced, and inefficient ways.

Radical liberals have drawn on a variety of philosophical resources as they have sought to explain and defend their positions. In this book, I have chosen to frame a version of radical liberalism rooted in NATURAL LAW theory, a humane and flexible approach to critical reflection ethics, society, law, and politics. Aristotelian in character, it puts flourishing—fulfillment, welfare, well-being—on center stage. It is concerned with moral requirements, to be sure, but it understands these requirements as safeguards for fulfillment, and it sees choosing in accordance with

[2] *See* Benjamin R. Tucker, *State Socialism and Anarchism: How Far They Agree, and Wherein They Differ, in* MARKETS NOT CAPITALISM: INDIVIDUALIST ANARCHISM AGAINST BOSSES, INEQUALITY, CORPORATE POWER, AND STRUCTURAL POVERTY 21 (Gary Chartier & Charles W. Johnson eds., 2011), *available at* http://radgeek.com/gt/2011/10/Markets-Not-Capitalism-2011-Chartier-and-Johnson.pdf. *Cf.* Charles W. Johnson, *Markets Freed from Capitalism, in* MARKETS NOT CAPITALISM, *supra*, at 59, 66–74.

them as itself one of the ways in which we flourish. It acknowledges an immense diversity of ways in which freely chosen lives can go well. And it rejects arbitrary rules and narrow concerns with limited aspects of humanness in favor of an understanding of personal lives as individually created adventures.

I take NATURAL LAW theory to be first of all a *moral* theory, concerned with what makes particular choices by particular persons reasonable. But it is precisely for that reason also a social, legal, and political theory. For it grounds constraints on the use of force and social pressure even to promote good ends. The kind of NATURAL LAW theory I employ here rejects the use of force (except in the serve of defense or restitution) and unnecessarily intrusive and conformist social pressure. It thus affirms autonomy. And it provides guidance to individuals not only as their actions bear on themselves, not only as they engage in interpersonal relationships, but also as they shape norms, rules, and institutions governing the use of force and the application of social pressure.

Institutions are best understood and assessed with reference to their microfoundations in the particular choices of particular people. Rules maintained by social institutions can and should be different in important cases from the principles and commitments to which particular persons adhere. But the maintenance of rules by social institutions is itself a matter of the individual choices of individual persons, and must thus itself be subject to the same underlying moral principles that govern all other individual actions. As an institutional actor, one may appropriately act in any particular case only in ways that are consistent with the requirements of practical reasonableness. An institutional role does not exempt one from the need to choose in these ways. Thus, for instance, manipulative lies and aggressive acts of violence are unreasonable for particular agents, so they are also wrong for those agents acting in institutional capacities.

Of course, institutions sometimes foster broad patterns of social interaction—as, say, by articulating and defending particular possessory rules. When they do, institutional actors, precisely as individuals, choosing *in particular cases* in accordance with the requirements of practical reasonableness, will need to take this into account. In light of the systemic effects of their individual actions, respecting the same principles that should govern their private actions, rather than any sort of putatively collective rationality, these actors will have reasons to treat the institutional rules they sustain with a consistency they would not need to exhibit in their individual capacities.

Morality is about self-constitution, not godlike universal responsibility. So moral choices can be made, in most cases, in view of a narrow range of factors, immediately evident and immediately within the control of the agent. That isn't true, of course, of decisions about whether to join in boycotts of enormous industries. Liberals affirm agency and responsibility, refusing to view people as passive in the face of social pressure. But liberals also recognize that agency and responsibility aren't universal: people aren't morally liable for just any state of affairs with which they might be connected. I seek to respond to this concern by showing how NATURAL LAW theory provides a crisp, clear approach to thinking about the kinds of responsibilities involved in calls for industry boycotts. I attempt to illuminate this approach by focusing on calls to boycott the meat industry in particular—calls that reflect liberalism's inclusiveness and concern for the flourishing even of the vulnerable and marginal.

Any agent chooses unreasonably if she endorses injury to nonhuman animals. In addition, some agents' choices will have tangible market effects; and these agents choose unreasonably if they do not participate in the meat industry boycott. And some agents will confront alternatives to consuming the flesh of dead animals that they themselves take in relevant respects to be adequate substitutes; they, too, should join the boycott. In other cases, agents willing to accept rules permitting the imposition on themselves and their loved ones of the kinds of risks they impose on animals are under no obligation to join the boycott. They may, however, rightly do so, not as a matter of moral duty but rather as an exercise in expressive protest.

Our lives go well, as do those of the agents with whom we interact, when we don't tell lies. Liberals, who value freedom and reason, recognize that a culture of truth-telling enables all of us to be autonomous decision-makers who can trust each other to avoid manipulation. Casual lies, even if justified as means of oiling the social machine, treat others as our inferiors, seek to subordinate them to our wills, and deprive those to whom they are told of opportunities to make up their own minds. At the same time, some lies tend to strike (most of) us as appropriate. The Principle of Fairness and the Principle of Respect, I believe, provide reasonable constraints on lying, constraints supportive of core liberal concerns, without yielding unpalatable and counter-intuitive conclusions.

Truth matters in multiple contexts. Liberals want to see people judged on their own merits. They want to see people assessed truthfully and they want information about how people are assessed to be *communicated* truthfully. *Radical* liberals are, of course, aware of the ways in which injustices can stack the deck in some people's favor: merit can be hidden or distorted in various ways. But, allowing for that possibility, as also for the value of cognitive economy, liberals want to see particular persons evaluated accurately and as individuals—at home, at work, in the context of interpersonal relationships and voluntary associations, and in educational settings.

One kind of evaluation, the assignment of grades by school or university instructors, can understandably seem like a relatively trivial matter. But choices about grading implicate significant moral concerns related to fairness, desert, and truth. A genuinely liberal approach to grades will, I suggest, avoid consequentialist and retributivist detours and opt instead for truthful communication regarding, and individualized assessment of, each student's COMPETENCE.

The Principle of Fairness offers all of us, including those occupying some institutional roles, reasons to participate in and support adversarial practices—practices that, whatever the immediate concerns of the participants, contribute to well-being in various ways. In the marketplace, in the courtroom, in the world of ideas, and elsewhere, liberals believe, the cause of truth, in particular, can be served by conflict. Each of us has reason to understand conflict in the context of adversarial practices as entirely appropriate, as a source of important benefits, if it can be appropriately constrained and channeled. This doesn't mean, however, that the value of adversarial practices is such that attacks on truth and other instances of what would clearly qualify as moral wrongdoing outside the contexts of those practices are permissible for adversaries occupying institutional roles. The Principle of Fairness itself, along with the Principle of Respect, should be understood as precluding attacks on truth even in support of valuable adversarial practices. Liberals rightly emphasize that an adversarial ecosystem can facilitate the quest for truth even if advocates are thoroughly partial. The *radical* insight, however, informed by natural law theory, is that this does not mean that they can or should purposefully undermine the quest for truth.

Adversaries in the courtroom are not, of course, *just* adversaries in the courtroom. Adversaries have lives. And these lives, the value of which is temporally and logically prior to peoples' occupancy of adversarial and other professional roles, should not be fettered by responsibilities to clients in ways that interfere with key aspects of their nonprofessional identities. The tension between *informational privacy* and privacy in the sense of what's needed to secure the autonomous space required for an inherently valuable *life* requires further attention. Liberals, after all, value fair legal processes, and have no reason to want to see these processes compromised; but they also have no reason to ask lawyers to sacrifice their own personal lives in order to be effective professionals (even if, of course, some lawyers, perhaps unreasonably, *do* sacrifice their lives in service to their professions).

Liberals care about the performance of lawyers primarily because they care about the flourishing of clients. (They also doubtless value the opportunities for good work, self-creation, and the flourishing facilitated by prosperity which are predictably offered by legal practice to those who engage in it.) And this means that they want all those subject to the force the legal system deploys treated fairly and respectfully, in ways conducive to their flourishing. They will thus note with dismay that there is no robust justification for the practice of taking victim impact testimony into account in parole hearings from any credible school of thought regarding criminal law. And this means that, even as they question the entire enterprise of state-driven criminal law, radical liberals can reasonably appeal to proponents of diverse approaches to share their rejection of a place for this kind of testimony in the parole process that plays a significant role in the existing criminal justice system.

Calls for harsh sentences often seem to reflect a religious vision, a vision of a judgmental God of whom human participants in the legal system should be seen as representatives. This sort of vision is horrific. But liberals have sometimes supposed that alternative religious visions might be profoundly helpful politically. A kind of civic religion emphasizing American possibility can be seen as inspiring, one that liberals of multiple varieties (along with others seeking positive social change) might be tempted happily to endorse. But this kind of civic religion can arguably come too easily to serve as a source of legitimation for American nationalism, and so for both militarism and for nationalistic economic policies. If any sort of religious or spiritual tradition is to prove politically useful, it must be one that, even as it affirms positive features of a society's public life, facilitates the adoption of a *critical* perspective on that public life and that declines to endorse or presuppose tribal or other nationalistic fantasies.

Nationalism is an inherently destructive idea, both because of the inherent opposition to those *outside* the nation it embodies and because of the suppression of dissent and individuality *within* the nation it encourages. Putatively liberal versions of nationalism and similar kinds of stances are inherently unstable: if they become fully liberal, they will cease to be nationalistic, and, if they become fully nationalistic, they will cease to be liberal. Liberals may grant pragmatic value to local institutions (which are sometimes more responsive and flexible than regional or national ones), and more than pragmatic value to particular noncoercive associations. They may also acknowledge the inherent, identity-constitutive value of individuals' relationships with local communities (sharply differentiated from local or other political institutions). But liberals, especially radical liberals, will first of all opt for concern at the *most* local of levels, the level of the individual. And they will embrace a (cultural, social, economic—not political or military) cosmopolitanism that presupposes the freedom of all individuals to love, befriend, trade with, and learn from each other, whatever their geographic locations.

Thus, the liberal spirit fits nicely with the opposition to war and empire long voiced by many prominent liberals and strongly reinforced by NATURAL LAW restraints on violence and requirements of fairness. A credible defense of militarism is unavailable on radical liberalism's terms, but also on classical or modern liberalism's. Such a defense runs the risk of offering moral cover for destructive violence, domestic repression, burdensome debt, and campaigns for global hegemony.

This sort of criticism is perfectly reasonable when voiced in light of classical and modern liberal concerns about state power. (Even though modern liberals favor state superintendence of many aspects of social and economic life, they certainly retain an awareness of the importance of freedom and individuality.) But it is surely even more at home in the context of radical liberalism's *rejection* of the state, its conviction that states are illegitimate, unnecessary, and dangerous. There are multiple *positive* arguments to be offered for the anarchist opposition to state power, but of course radical liberalism must also respond to *challenges* to specific anarchist arguments and to anarchism more broadly. And radical liberalism *can* respond effectively to a cluster of anti-anarchist arguments: people aren't required to accept state authority because they unreflectively assume they must, the radical liberal can reasonably maintain, and anarchist arguments against state authority can't be ruled out without being considered.

I believe NATURAL LAW theory matters in various ways in relation to the topics I've explored here. The Principle of Fairness and the Principle of Respect are especially salient. The other requirements of practical reasonableness, especially the Principle of Commitment, would surely be germane in actual cases viewed less generically. (For instance, someone committed to publicly representing an animal advocacy organization might have substantially stronger reasons to express support for animals by boycotting the meat industry than those significant for someone in a different role.) So, for instance, the Principle of Respect serves as a bulwark against attacks on people's bodily well-being, while the Principle of Fairness grounds robust rights in fairly acquired possessions: both help to create the space needed for personal flourishing. The Principle of Respect rules out telling lies as a matter of (for instance) hostility, while the Principle of Fairness precludes telling lies one would not be willing to have told to oneself or one's loved ones. The Principle of Respect is inconsistent with *purposefully* attacking anyone (combatants or noncombatants—one can seek reasonably to stop a combatant without *intending* injury to her), while the Principle of Fairness limits the imposition of collateral damage. The Principle of Fairness underlies the concerns with respect for individual persons, regard for merit, and due process that prove relevant in reflections on grading, adversarial legal proceedings, and parole hearings, while the Principle of Respect is inconsistent with ignoring these concerns as a means of imposing or facilitating injury to some aspect of someone's flourishing.

I've sought throughout this book to take an approach that not only embodies NATURAL LAW reasoning but also exemplifies the liberal spirit. Lying, for instance, needs to be understood in relation to liberal concerns with both autonomy and privacy. Grading practices need to be framed with due regard for fairness, merit, and individual difference. Adversarial legal proceedings effectively reflect the liberal understanding of the value of embedding conflict in an overarching ecosystem that yields general benefits from the (constrained, fair, respectful) pursuit of individual goals. Liberal commitments to minimizing harshness and affirming reason means that even liberals who see the current criminal justice system as legitimate should doubt the value of incorporating victim impact testimony in parole decisions. A liberal understanding of the relationships between lawyers and clients will value the privacy of each. A liberal willingness to recognize the possibility of expanding the moral community, without falling victim to a puritanical moralism, must inform our thinking about potential boycotts of the meat industry. The rejection of war, empire, and nationalism should be seen as embodying liberalism's individualism and cosmopolitanism. (Because raw conquest has been deprived of moral legitimacy, modern imperialism and neocolonialism can of course wear the cosmopolitan mask while denying the equality of the subjugated and the subjugating.) And anarchic institutions should matter to liberals because such institutions respect autonomy and because they leave space for creativity and experimentation.

In relation to some of the issues I consider here, liberalism appears relatively moderate. The exclusion of victim impact testimony from parole hearings, for instance, embodies and promotes liberal values; it is consistent with, but it isn't an expression of, any sort of radical rejection of retribution and deterrence or of the contemporary criminal justice system more generally. There's a sense in which, while they appeal to familiar liberal values, arguments for grading in ways that focus on COMPETENCE are, perhaps ironically, more radical, in their dependence on general principles, in their self-conscious individualism, and in the challenge they pose to many familiar practices.

A reassertion of traditional just-war norms should not itself seem radical; but, given the degree to which such norms have been increasingly ignored since the rise of modern warfare, it is bound to *seem* radical. The same is true of anti-imperialism, especially when it is extended to include the denial of legitimacy not only to traditional empires but also to various neocolonial arrangements that remain disturbingly popular. And the position I take regarding war and empire is no doubt especially the case when just-war and anti-empire norms are linked, as they consistently should have been, with explicit anti-interventionism, which has never, to my knowledge, been anything like a prevailing view on the part of major powers at any point in history (perhaps unsurprisingly, since major powers are often *defined* precisely as those willing and able to deploy military force at will and effectively outside their borders).

The conviction that the meat industry acts unjustly and that boycotts of the industry are required of those closest to it and admirable when engaged in by others is an outgrowth of a radical extension of liberalism's commitment to giving serious consideration to calls for the expansion of the moral community and NATURAL LAW theory's rejection of purposeful injury. The rejection of Richard Rorty's approach to social justice in the name, not of conservatism and hierarchy, but rather from a perspective that sees state power at the root of subordination, deprivation, and exclusion poses a radical liberal alternative to modern liberalism, conservatism, and even varieties of classical liberalism. And the defense of anarchism against moral and epistemological challenges is intended to ensure that a radical option in social and political theory remains on the table.

Radicalism is only explicit, then, in some aspects of what I say here. But the underlying approach I take here, the variety of liberalism I seek to illustrate here, is deliberately radical, even if its radicalism is sometimes more evident in other contexts. (*i*) A radical willingness to ask about the foundational justification of moral choices and of social, legal, and political practices lies behind this project. (*ii*) So does a persistent attempt to keep in view the recognition that state power is itself illegitimate, unnecessary, and dangerous and is used to prop up the privileged positions of the wealthy and well connected. (*iii*) A concern with fairness and a rejection of domination, manipulation, and hierarchy—implicit in the Principle of Fairness as I understand it, and alluded to, even if not intensively explored, here—may seem relatively saccharine. But such a concern can, if taken seriously, yield *both* the rejection of state-secured privileges that support hierarchies *and* of voluntary but unreasonable patterns of behavior in various associational contexts.[3] (*iv*) The idea of robust property rights is often perceived as a bulwark of inequitable privilege. However, when it is used to challenge unjust acquisition or to resist legal interference with autonomy, it can certainly have radical implications.[4] (*v*) The view I take here is also radical in that it focuses on the roots of social phenomena. It embraces not only normative but also explanatory individualism (even as it enthusiastically affirms the value of—consensual—communities, relationships, and social cooperation).

Liberalism is of course not the only approach to society and politics that can be articulated using NATURAL LAW theory. Many varieties of liberalism are anything but radical. And liberalism can be defended in light of Kantian, utilitarian, and other theories quite different from the broadly Aristotelian-Thomist approach I employ here. But I believe a radical liberalism framed in light of NATURAL LAW theory has the potential to contribute fruitfully to flourishing, fulfillment, welfare, well-being. Commitments to substantive views of the good sometimes go hand in hand with paternalistic stances that encourage violations of autonomy with impunity. But I've tried to suggest that NATURAL LAW liberalism can exemplify the possibility of generating constraints on the use of force (and on the restrictive deployment of moralistic or paternalistic social norms) from within a theoretical approach dedicated to a substantive view of flourishing. Moral, legal, and political theory *matter* to the extent that they facilitate the leading and enjoyment of good lives. Liberalism—moral, social, political—is an account, hardly exhaustive, of important features of good lives: experimentation, creativity, discovery, interchange, rational criticism, extended social cooperation, individuality. And, I believe, NATURAL LAW theory enriches liberalism by making clear the broad range of ways in which flourishing is possible, and the even broader range of ways in which people might *seek* to flourish without interference by agents deploying force or social pressure. Radical liberalism, expressed in NATURAL LAW terms, highlights the kinds of social changes that could be expected to allow liberalism to flower even more than it already has. Radically liberal norms, practices, and institutions, shaped in accordance with NATURAL LAW theory, can play a vital role in enabling and encouraging flourishing lives.

[3] *See, e.g.*, GARY CHARTIER, ECONOMIC JUSTICE AND NATURAL LAW 89–107 (2009).

[4] *Cf.* Karl Hess, *Where Are the Specifics?*, *in* MARKETS NOT CAPITALISM, *supra* note 2, at 289.

Index

About the Author

Gary Chartier is Distinguished Professor of Law and Business Ethics and Associate Dean of the Tom and Vi Zapara School of Business at La Sierra University in Riverside, California. He is the author, co-author, editor, or co-editor of seventeen current or forthcoming books, including *Public Practice, Private Law* (Cambridge, 2016), *Anarchy and Legal Order* (Cambridge, 2013), *The Logic of Commitment* (Routledge, 2018), and *An Ecological Theory of Free Expression* (Palgrave, 2018). His byline has appeared over forty times in journals including the *Oxford Journal of Legal Studies*, *Legal Theory*, and *Law and Philosophy*. He is a member of the American Philosophical Association and the Alliance of the Libertarian Left and a senior fellow of the Center for a Stateless Society.

After qualifying for a BA in history and political science from La Sierra (1987, *magna cum laude*), he explored ethics, the philosophy of religion, theology, Christian origins, and political philosophy at the University of Cambridge, earning a PhD (1991) with a dissertation on the idea of friendship. He graduated with a JD (2001, Order of the Coif) from UCLA, where he studied legal philosophy and public law and received the Judge Jerry Pacht Memorial Award in Constitutional Law. The University of Cambridge presented him with an earned LLD in 2015 for his work in legal philosophy. A proud southern California native who wishes he had attended UC Sunnydale, he shares a slowly improving 1920 home in Riverside with Willow Rosenberg the Kitty and Rupert Giles Feline. His hobbies include film, long-arc television, fiction (genre and otherwise), biography, spicy vegetarian food, politics, writing, adventures in unfamiliar haunts, human psychic and social dynamics, interminable conversation, and the esoteric, the quirky, and the arcane. His motto is E. M. Forster's "Only connect." Visit him online at http://www.garychartier.com.

About the Author

[illegible]